S0-BBU-243

10-24
STRAND PRICE
FOR 5 .00

The great law of culture is:
Let each become all that he
was created capable of being.

—CARLYLE

The Story of
Spelman College

The Story of
Spelman College

BY FLORENCE MATILDA READ

ATLANTA, GEORGIA · 1961

Copyright © 1961 by Florence M. Read
22 East 54th Street, New York 22, N.Y.
Care of United Negro College Fund, Inc.

ALL RIGHTS RESERVED

Library of Congress catalog card number: 61-18158

❖

Printed in the United States of America
by Princeton University Press
Princeton, New Jersey

Miss Packard and Miss Giles

*This poem was written by Owen Dodson of the
Spelman College Faculty and was first read at the
Founders Day Exercises, April 11, 1940
by a verse-speaking choir of students*

*Two Women, here in April, prayed alone
And saw again their vision of an altar
Built for mind and spirit, flesh and bone.
They never turned away; they never said:
"This dream is air, let us go back to our New
   England spring
And cultivate an earth that is not dead;*

*Let dark mothers weep, dark children bleed,
This land is barren land
Incapable of seed."
They made their crucifix far more
Than ornament; they wrestled with Denial
And pinned him to the floor.*

*They made defeat an exile:
And year by year their vision shed its mist:
And still they smiled their Noah smile,*

*Knowing that they had no death to fear,
Knowing that their future would be now
And all the Aprils we assemble here.*

FOREWORD

THE story of Spelman College goes back into early American history to the old town of New Salem, Massachusetts, where lived the forbears of Sophia B. Packard and Harriet E. Giles and where they themselves were born. It involves the temper of the New England, Middle Atlantic, and North Central States during the 1850's, '60's, '70's and '80's, in those decades when consciences were probed and decisions forged as to slavery and the freedmen; as to the right of women to be educated; and as to the patriotic duty of Christian people to promote and maintain the ideal of Christian home life for all America. It involves also the conditions of life in the South for white people and for colored people in the years following the Emancipation Proclamation of President Abraham Lincoln in 1863 and the Peace at Appomattox in 1865. It will inevitably reflect to some degree the state of race relations as the story of the educational advancement of Negro women unfolds.

Although the book is specifically about Spelman College, the general picture drawn will apply to all the private colleges for Negroes, just as it will suggest the progress of Negro education in the United States. Had it not been for the Home Mission Schools and the Northern teachers who taught in them, most of them from New England, the advancement of Negroes could not yet have reached its present level. "Thanks to the Negro college," said Ira DeA. Reid, professor of sociology at Haverford College, "we have in the United States the most highly literate mass of colored people in the world."

The course is not finished; but the women of the Negro race who have received education and training in Spelman College have kept the faith placed in them by the Founders of that College.

ACKNOWLEDGMENTS

MY thanks to the Board of Trustees of Spelman College for their request that I prepare a history of the College, and for an initial grant of funds which enabled me to begin the work of research and the writing, are here gratefully recorded. I am indebted especially to Trevor Arnett, chairman of the Spelman College Board for nearly thirty years, and to John D. Rockefeller, Jr., two men without whose personal encouragement and confidence, the venture would not have been undertaken; to the alumnae members of the Board for their steadfast backing; and to Lawrence J. MacGregor, present chairman of the Board, for reading the manuscript in its first draft. The offices of Mr. Rockefeller, Junior and of the Rockefeller Brothers were most helpful.

Cooperation from President Manley, other officers of the College and members of the staff was indispensable. Especially valued is the help received from John L. Coe, Ernestine Erskine Brazeal, Elizabeth Jackson Macomson, Vaughncziel Burch, Mexico Hembree Mickelbury; and from Dorothy K. Clark, who, in an earlier day in my office, had transcribed on 3 x 5 cards much early historical data.

The officers of the American Baptist Home Mission Society and of the Woman's American Baptist Home Mission Society provided for me easy access to their archives. The citizens of New Salem, Massachusetts, through their records and their reminiscences were a rich source of information. Their friendliness and knowledge of early New Salem provided many a useful lead. This was particularly true of Miss Eunice R. Goddard; and also of Ralph Eaton Stowell, Town Clerk for forty-one years, succeeding his father who had held the office for the previous twenty-six years; Arthur B. Haley; Mr. and Mrs. Edward L. Eaton; and Malcolm Freeman. I received important data from Rev. Jesse F. Smith, Alumni Secretary of Suffield Academy.

A record of this sort obviously could not have been written without the aid of libraries. Not to be taken for granted was the interest shown by the librarians of the American Antiquarian Society in Worcester, Princeton University and Princeton Theological Seminary; they gave me free access not only to books but to a place to work. I am especially indebted to Miss Flora Belle Ludington, Librarian at Mount Holyoke College, for a haven to work in through several summers.

Encouragement came from retired members of the Mount Holyoke College faculty and staff whose interest in reading the manuscript by instalments held up my hands. I mention particularly Professors Ellen Deborah Ellis and Dorothy Foster; Miss Florence Clement, Publication Editor; and the Mount Holyoke College graduate, Mrs. Constance Italia Bagg, who typed two revisions of the manuscript without, so she alleges, losing her liking for it.

I had unbelievable good fortune in having two critics who gave me professional advice: Miss Mary Ellen Chase whose interest in the cause was her incentive to read and criticize the manuscript, and who applied both spur and reins with consummate skill; and Walter Phelps Hall, professor emeritus of History in Princeton University, whose experience, insight, and occasional argument were a constant stimulus.

I am grateful to a score of friends who helped me find the pictures pertaining to the early years. For most of those relating to the later period, I am indebted to Walton Reeves of Reeves Studios, who had taken hundreds of photographs from which selections were made and who cheerfully went back through his files for twenty-five years to find films and make new prints.

There are scores of other persons I have met along the way who have been helpful to me—and to Spelman. Although they may not be included here by name, I pay tribute to them in my heart.

My own spirit has been lifted and my faith strengthened by my association with the characters in this *Story*. I am constantly thankful for them all.

CONTENTS

CONTENTS

x

ILLUSTRATIONS

xiii

ABBREVIATIONS USED

ABHMS	American Baptist Home Mission Society
CLI	Connecticut Literary Institution
GEB	General Education Board
JDR, Jr.	John D. Rockefeller, Junior
NAACP	National Association for the Advancement of Colored People
TPC	Teachers Professional Course
UNCF	United Negro College Fund, Inc.
WABHMS	Woman's American Baptist Home Mission Society
WAC	Women's Army Corps

CHAPTER I

THE FOUNDERS OF SPELMAN

TWO New England women, Sophia B. Packard and
Harriet E. Giles, were the founders of the school in
Atlanta, Georgia, which is now Spelman College.
Miss Packard was 57 years old and Miss Giles was 48, when
the start was made. Who were they? What was their background? What moved them to embark upon such an undertaking? What supported them through their trials and discouragements? What enabled them to create, out of nothing but faith
and love, a living, ever-growing ministry to minds and souls?
What were their roots? What were their dreams? And what is
the result of their faith and their determination—

"To strive, to seek, to find, and not to yield?"

Let us begin at their beginnings and look first at the family
life from which they sprang and the community life which en-
compassed their early years.

Sophia B. Packard

Hanging on the wall of a charming New England house in
Northfield, Massachusetts, now the home of the widow of a man
whose father married a niece of Miss Packard, is a sampler
"Wrought by Rachel M. Packard, Aged 10 Years, in 1831."
Rachel had worked in cross-stitch the names and dates of birth
of her father, Winslow, her mother, Rachel (Freeman), two
older brothers, Joseph and Hubbard Vaughn, one older sister,
Mary J. (who was born in 1815 and died in 1838), her own,
and lastly *"Betsey S. Packard, Born January 3, 1824."* Miss
Betsey S. was Sophia B. Packard, born in New Salem, Massachusetts, on January 3, 1824, and known as Betsey for at least
seven years of her life.

Winslow Packard, her father, lived in the town of New
Salem, at the foot of Packard Mountain, on a sizable farm for
that community comprising about 100 acres, 30 acres of tillage,
30 acres of pasture and 40 acres of woodland running over the

top of Mount Packard. The family homestead, a white painted house, included a long string of buildings, all connected,—the main two-story building with an ell; then a woodshed with a cheese-room overhead, next a horse stable with a pig-pen underneath; finally at the far east end, a carriage house. The advantage is obvious of being able to go under cover to horses and carriages in the deep snows of winter. The barn was situated about 100 yards west of the house. Both house and barn were on the south side of the road, and faced Packard Mountain, which the *History of New Salem* states to be the highest point of land in a direct line, between Albany and Boston. The foundations of house and barn may still be seen.

When Rachel Maria made the sampler, Sophia B., or Betsey, was seven years old. She probably attended the district school at North Prescott, and went to church with the family in North Prescott where at that time there was a Baptist Church.

On the farm were cows, sheep and horses. With two sisters and two brothers, Betsey as a child no doubt had a lively time. Joseph J., the eldest, was more than 12 years older, and we surmise that he took a chivalrous interest in his youngest sister, as there is evidence that such a relationship continued to the end of his life. In summer and fall, there were raspberries and blueberries to be picked, apples to be sliced and strung on strings for drying, chestnuts and butternuts to be gathered, and many, many farm duties. Besides there was Packard Mountain to be explored. In winter, there were sleighing, and coasting, and skating. Snowbound that homestead must often have been in winter. What Whittier pictures in his poem must frequently have applied to the winter scene on the Packard farm in New Salem, where

> Shut in from all the world without,
> We sat the clean-winged hearth about
> Content to let the north-wind roar
> In baffled rage at pane and door,
> While the red logs before us beat
> The frost-line back with tropic heat: . . .

The apples sputtered in a row
And close at hand the basket stood
With nuts from brown October's wood.

We sped the time with stories old
Wrought puzzles out, and riddles told
Or stammered from our school-book lore
The chief of Gambia's golden shore.

The mother meanwhile "turned her wheel or run the new knit stocking heel," and the talk doubtless ranged from classic legends to Yankee pedlars.

When Sophia or Betsey was 10 years old, she became an aunt. Her oldest brother, Joseph, then 22, had married the year before and his daughter, Susan, was the first grandchild of Winslow and Rachel Packard. But with a family of six—Mary J., 19; brother Hubbard Vaughn, 17; Rachel Maria, 12; and Sophia B. herself, there was work even for a 10-year-old girl. There were dishes to be washed, lamps to be cleaned, beds to be made, stockings to be knitted and darned, gardens to be weeded, chickens to be fed, and other farm chores to be shared. Years later, one of the gifted early graduates of Spelman Seminary (Emma B. DeLany, '94) wrote that the quickness with which Miss Packard "caught the droll side of a subject would make her laugh and cause others to laugh," and also that Miss Packard believed this trait to be "her besetting sin and guarded against carrying it too far." If such a characteristic was observed when Sophia Packard was 60, it seems an inescapable conclusion that she was fun-loving in her youth, and probably mischievous as well. She always was a "doing" person, affectionate yet independent, impulsive, yet studious and conscientious.

Winslow Packard believed in education for his children. He believed also in religion. The Bible and its teachings were a constant source of strength and gave direction to daily living.

When Sophia reached her middle teens, her social life expanded with community "sociables," which must have included parlor games such as blind-man's-buff, going to Jerusalem, and "spin-the-platter"; and surely they included "sings," for

3

"sings" were popular in New Salem. In 1846 even a brass-band was organized and functioned for 11 years, but before that time, Betsey, now called Sophia B., had begun to teach. She attended New Salem Academy for at least a term in 1845. She would teach a while, then study a while. She was a student, then an assistant teacher, in Charlestown (Mass.) Female Academy when Catherine Badger was head of it. It was then "justly esteemed among the best," ranked with Ipswich and South Hadley. Her diploma from Charlestown dated 1850 hangs on the wall in Rockefeller Hall on the Spelman College campus.

After leaving Charlestown Academy, she taught in schools on Cape Cod, including Marston Mills and Osterville, but the seacoast climate was hard on her throat. In 1854 she served as Preceptress and Teacher in New Salem Academy. This was one of the earliest Massachusetts academies and boarding schools; and almost unique in admitting from the beginning both girls and boys.

Sophia was 30 years of age when she became Preceptress of New Salem Academy. It was there that she met Harriet E. Giles, a senior student who was also an "assistant pupil," and who was destined to share with Sophia those dreams and visions of their later life.

Harriet E. Giles

Harriet E. Giles also was born in New Salem, Massachusetts, on June 23, 1833, the youngest of the 10 children of Hon. Samuel Giles. She was baptized by the Rev. W. H. Hayward in the Central Congregational Church September 3, 1853. Her father had been born in New Salem in 1791. The United States Census of 1790 names her grandfather, John Giles, as a citizen of New Salem and "head of family." On May 9, 1813, Samuel Giles married Hannah Foster and to them were born five boys and five girls. The eldest was a son, William Trask, born in 1814, and the tenth was Harriet.

From conversations with Mrs. Linnie May Belden Van der Meulen, grand-niece of Harriet and a great granddaughter of

Samuel Giles, a rough sketch of his farm house in New Salem has come to life for us. Linnie May was born on the Samuel Giles place in 1882, and lived there until she was six years old. She remembers the organ in the corner of the living room, the sofa against one of the walls opposite, the front yard, a "charity garden" which was separated from the vegetable garden and the flower garden. She recalls particularly the "huge sing" held when folks were stranded in the blizzard of 1888.

The foundations of the house can still be seen in an un-submerged section of the Quabbin reservoir. They indicate, by size and arrangement, a better-than-average farm house, located several yards from the present road which is lined with rock maple and oak trees. The old stone posts with their holes for wire or rope, outline enclosures for flower and vegetable gardens, and perhaps for chickens. A fine old desk which belonged to Samuel Giles, and two sand-shakers for blotting are still in existence, one of the latter at Spelman College.

Trees growing around the site of the house include chestnut, hickory nut, hazelnut, butternut, black cherry, white birch, black birch, oak, ash, white maple, sugar maple, pine and hemlock. There were also many ferns, large and small; especially noteworthy are lovely clumps of maiden hair ferns.

Harriet's second oldest brother, with whom she was always closely associated, was born in 1820. He went West in 1837 as far as Chautauqua County, New York, where relatives of their mother were living. He joined a brother who was lecturing on electricity and travelled in Ohio, Kentucky and Tennessee. For a time he attended Fredonia (N.Y.) Academy. In 1844 he went to Wisconsin Territory.

An editorial in the Wisconsin State Journal at the time of his death on May 10, 1895, is revealing of his character and activities:

Our old friend Hiram Giles is dead. For seventy-five years as boy and man he carried about an honest, simple heart, which never failed him or any other of God's creatures that crossed his path. . . .

Hiram Giles was a pioneer, one of a generation of whom few are left

in Wisconsin—remembered Madison when it was a forest clearing.
. . . He spoke slowly and nothing ruffled him. He could never shake
off his downeast accent; he loved plain things; he drank only cold
water; he was happy all alone following up a trout brook. . . . He had
taught school and lectured into the 'new west' in those dawning years
when country people rode miles to see experiments in electricity, and he
knew his fellows all through and loved men and women for their very
simplicity.

And he was a shrewd man, this dead friend of ours. A Republican
from the beginning he had been in the midst of struggles and was powerful when giants wrestled for the supremacy. He knew all the notables
of Wisconsin. . . . He was a prophet of warning to the railroad manage-
ments when they insisted on imposing still higher wheat rates on the
farmers of the northwest.

Mr. Giles was honored by his state. He sat in both branches of the
legislature, and was presiding officer of the senate just before the war.
He was in the internal revenue service under Governor Atwood, but it
was in connection with 'Charities and Correction' that Mr. Giles will
long be remembered. For twelve years to speak of the old 'Board of
Charities and Reform' was to think of Hiram Giles traveling from one
institution to another. The 'County System' of the care of the insane
is his monument. . . .

In the 1860's, Hiram Giles was on the Board of Visitors of
the Oread Institute. In the early '80's, Miss Giles and Miss
Packard visited him in Wisconsin, and found him helpful regarding plans for Spelman. He and his daughter Ella visited
Spelman Seminary more than once.

The home farm could not have been a lively place for Harriet when she was growing up. Half of her brothers and sisters
were away from home. Her oldest brother was married when
Harriet was six. Her favorite brother Hiram, as we have seen,
left New Salem for the west when she was five; her very
youngest brother was eight years older than she, and her sisters
were too much older to have been her playmates. Harriet was
quiet, perhaps even solemn, good at her lessons, thoughtful,
conscientious and serious-minded. She may have been lonely
but perhaps was not aware of it. She liked the trees and out-
door life; she loved music and early learned to play the organ.

She was intelligent, and even-tempered, somewhat diffident, but steady.

At 16 she received a certificate to teach. It was signed by the School Committee of New Salem, May 19, 1849, and stated: "Miss Harriet E. Giles appears qualified to instruct a common school and is authorized to teach in this town the present school term." The certificate was renewed in 1850 and again in 1852. After three years of teaching, Harriet resumed her studies in Salem Academy; completed the classical course; and a friend-ship began which developed into a life-long working partner-ship with the then Preceptress, Sophia Packard.

New Salem thus occupies a unique place in the pre-history of Spelman Seminary, and New Salem Academy may be said to have been one of the ancestors of the school in the South.

What manner of place, then, was New Salem and what kind of school was New Salem Academy?

New Salem

New Salem, Massachusetts was like many another New England town founded in the eighteenth century. Although it was not incorporated until 1753, a grant for the township had been made as early as 1729, 60 home lots had been laid out about 1735, "one for a minister, one lot for the support of the minister, one for the benefit of schools." In August 1736 the proprietors voted to build a meeting house. The house was built, although not finished, in 1739. The town was settled in 1737 by a band of hardy, energetic, and intelligent men and women from Salem, Danvers and other towns in the eastern part of the State. Among the first half dozen settlers was Amos Foster, great-grandfather of Harriet E. Giles, on her mother's side, who made the journey from Salem in Eastern Massachusetts, with an ox-team through a mostly unbroken wilderness, and settled in the west part of the township.

New Salem Common stands on a long, narrow ridge, 1,100 feet above sea level. From this ridge can be seen almost a complete circle of the horizon, with small lakes (now in the Quabbin Reservoir) and rolling green forests broken here and there by the white spires of New England churches and the patchwork of green and brown fields. Fifteen miles to the north rises Mount Grace, surrounded by long ranges of lower hills; to the east is Mount Wachusett; and 40 miles to the northeast rises Mount Monadnock "in its solitary grandeur about 4,000 feet above sea level." New Salem Center is eight miles south of Orange and 40 miles north of Springfield. The population in 1790 was 1,543; it had increased to over 2,000 by 1820; then gradually diminished. To the Revolution, it gave 142 soldiers supported by taxes on the inhabitants who remained behind. In the Civil War, it furnished 113 men, although by that time the total population was less than 1,000.

In the more prosperous period of the town when it could boast of farmers, merchants, lumbermen, tanners, saw- and grist-millers, and, at one time, a flourishing home industry in braiding Panama hats, the need of better schools for the children became of paramount interest, and the question of the organization of an academy was discussed by the citizens over several years. In 1794, a committee was chosen to present a petition for such an academy to the General Court; and at a town meeting duly called it was voted to move the old meeting house to another site and to make it suitable for use as an academy and town house.

New Salem Academy

The Act of Incorporation dated February 25, 1795, and approved by Samuel Adams, the Governor, provided

that there be and hereby is established . . . an academy by the name of New Salem Academy for the purpose of promoting Piety, Religion and Morality, and for the instruction of youth in such languages and in such of the liberal arts and sciences as the Trustees shall direct. . . .

It named 15 Trustees who formed a self-perpetuating Board, with power to conduct the school and make rules for its government.

At the first meeting of the Trustees held August 5, 1795, officers were elected and laws and regulations were adopted. These included the following articles:

1. The school . . . shall be ever under the instruction and government of a Preceptor of good and liberal education, and of unblemished reputation and morals.

2. The students who are admitted to the school shall be able to read without spelling and advance the tuition money for the terms for which they propose to enter. . . .

5. The studies to be pursued in said school shall be English, Reading, Grammar, Writing, Arithmetic, Geography, Philosophy, and the exercises of speaking, according to the intention of the student, and the description of the Preceptor, together with the Latin and Greek classics when desired.

Article 7 required that every student must attend punctually the classes and public prayers.

Article 9 called for "strict attention" to the government and morals of the students and forbade "all gaming and every unlawful diversion"; and in addition stated that the students are "required to be at their respective boarding houses before nine of the clock in the evening."

Article 10 required attendance at "public worship on Lord's Day."

Article 11 is here quoted in full: "The students will be required to observe the strictest decorum in their conduct toward the Preceptor, and the males to keep their heads uncovered when in communication with him, unless bidden to cover them, and shall observe the same rule with regard to any of the Trustees, at the times of their meeting. It shall also be enjoined upon the students to treat all people and one another with true civility and politeness."

Corporal punishment was not allowed but provision was made for discipline by "admonitions," to be administered in private or public; for fines not exceeding 50 cents or less than five cents; and for expulsion.

The inhabitants of New Salem subscribed for the benefit of the Academy the sum of $5,800, giving their notes and paying annual interest, but the receipts from tuition and from interest on money due proved insufficient. In 1797, a petition was sent to the legislature of the Commonwealth for some public grant. The legislature granted the petition and by resolutions adopted in June, 1797, made a grant of "one half of a township of land six miles square" to be located in unappropriated lands of the District of Maine. From the sale of the land, the Academy received about $5,000. New Salem Academy flourished for many years. In October 1837 the original building was burned, but in 1838 was rebuilt. Hon. Samuel Giles, father of Harriet, was elected a trustee in 1834, and annually thereafter until his death in 1875. He served as Secretary of the Board, as a member of the Standing Committee, and as Auditor from 1838-1874 except for two or three years. Every one of his 10 children attended New Salem Academy.

Eugene Bullard, a student of this Academy, 1852-1856, and later a trustee, compiled a *History of New Salem Academy* (1913) in which are included, in addition to valuable data about trustees, teachers and students, short biographical sketches of many of the preceptors together with their pictures. These early preceptors (later called principals) were through 1867, with one exception, graduates of Dartmouth, Yale, Brown, Harvard or Williams. Later the spread was wider, but up through 1912, all were from New England colleges save one from Ohio.

The first term of the Academy opened September 3, 1795, with Fowler Dickinson of Amherst, a graduate of Dartmouth College, as Preceptor. Fowler Dickinson, grandfather of Emily Dickinson, the poet, and one of the founders of Amherst College, was a man of vision, energy, and ideas who might be classified as "one of Christ's fools" since he sacrificed his time, his property, even perhaps his family, for the cause of Christian education.

The broadside, called *Catalogue of the Trustees and Students of New Salem Academy*, dated October 1819 (the first one issued so far as the records show) gives the names, residence and New Salem location of 66 Masters and 37 Misses. Two 'Masters' from Athol and one 'Miss' give their New Salem boarding place as with 'Captain Giles.'

The academic year was divided into four terms of 11 weeks, each succeeded by two weeks' vacation. The 103 pupils listed in 1819 represent 22 different towns including Gardner and Holden in Massachusetts, and New York City. Needless to say, none of the early catalogues of New Salem Academy refers to the pupils as 'boys' and 'girls.' In 1819, they were 'Masters' and 'Misses.' By 1829 they had become 'Males' and 'Females,' and by 1844 'Gentlemen' and 'Ladies,' remaining the latter until some time in the '80's.

Memories of academy days written by the students of the early years and published from time to time in the *Reunion Banner* (printed annually since 1888) show that these early students thoroughly enjoyed their life together. Their pleasures were simple, but they had fun at work and play. They mention 'social events, such as botanical exercises, chestnut walks, and reunions.' They enjoyed croquet in summer; huskings in the fall. They celebrated the first of May by eating breakfast at sunrise on Saxton's Hill. It was cold and frosty, but they were all on hand when the bell rang at four o'clock in the morning and 'it was fun.' One writes of the 'old double-ripper coasting on the West Hill,' of skating, baseball, and again of the 'chestnut walks.' The chestnut walks were continued and made an occasion for a school holiday until the chestnut trees were ruined by blight a few decades ago.

Sophia B. Packard attended New Salem Academy in 1845, but most of her schooling was elsewhere. Harriet Giles was registered from the time she was 10 years old, with terms out for teaching.

The catalogue for the year ending November 15, 1855, lists Hon. Samuel Giles as a member, and as Secretary, of the corporation; Miss Sophia B. Packard as Preceptress for the Spring term, and Harriet E. Giles as a student in the Classical Department and in the Ornamentals Department. There were 175 students that year. Harriet Giles was one of 'fourteen females' in the Classical Department and one of six in Ornamentals.

Expenses were as follows, with three terms per year: Tuition per term: for the languages, $5.00; higher English branches and Mathematics, $4.00; common English branches, $3.00;

music, with use of instrument, $7.00; penmanship, extra charge. Board including room-rent, washing, and wood was obtainable at $2.25 per week.

The catalogue further stated:

The institution is furnished with valuable apparatus, so that experiments illustrative of the Sciences are daily performed before the classes as they recite.

There is belonging to the institution a Library of about 500 volumes. . . .

There are two Literary Societies, one conducted by the Ladies, the other conducted by the Gentlemen. They occasionally hold united meetings.

A program is preserved of the "Exhibition at New Salem Academy" held on November 10, 1854. The morning program started at 10 o'clock and contained 20 numbers; that of the afternoon at 1:15 and contained 24 numbers. The following six orations delivered on this occasion sounded an international note: Lord Byron to the Greeks; Spartacus to the Roman Envoys; Kossuth to the Hungarians; Cataline Denounced; the Yankee in France; and The Partition of Poland. Immediately after the last-named is this item, "Discussion H[arriet] E. Giles, New Salem, C[ornelia] E. Alden, Hardwick."

Our own country was not ignored in this Academy program. One oration was entitled "Predictions of Disunion," and a discussion took place on the subject "Have the United States arisen to the zenith of their glory?"

The range of interest and ideas to which these boys and girls were exposed is noteworthy. So also is the stature of the men with whom Sophia Packard and Harriet Giles were early associated at New Salem Academy. Certain of these preceptors deserve brief record:

John Stacy, Yale '37, was Preceptor for 10 years from 1840-1850, the period when, according to Historian Bullard, 'our Academy enjoyed its greatest degree of prosperity,' and when Harriet Giles was a young student.

Virgil M. Howard, Yale '51, was Principal during the year

when Miss Packard was Preceptress and Harriet Giles was senior and assistant. Mr. Howard resigned after four years; taught elsewhere one year and then became principal of Deerfield Academy, where he remained 15 years.

Ozi W. Whitaker, who with Harriet Giles was an assistant teacher, 1853-1855, became an Episcopal rector in 1863, bishop of Nevada in 1869, and bishop of Pennsylvania from 1886 to 1911.

Another principal of this period was Joseph Alden Shaw, graduate of Harvard, who later served more than 40 years as principal of Highland Military Academy in Worcester, Massachusetts.

Their Life as Teachers

Sophia B. Packard, as has been said, became acquainted at New Salem Academy with 20-year-old Harriet Giles. Their families both lived in the town of New Salem, five miles apart, but in those horse and buggy days, with the interruptions caused by teaching and studying alternately, it is not strange that they had not previously met. They had similar ambitions. One of their former students states that "before the end of the school year, they had made a compact to enter jointly upon the profession of teaching, and as soon as practicable establish a school of their own."

The two young women were engaged to teach the following year in the village school of Petersham, with the privilege of receiving tuition-paying students from nearby towns. The plan worked, but the location, 10 miles from a railroad, was not promising. They then made a similar arrangement in the thriving village of Orange. Here they had all the students they could make room for, and employed two assistants. Miss Alta Carpenter, a graduate of New Salem Academy and a teacher for 50 years, was present at the 1957 Reunion in New Salem. She recalls that two aunts of hers, students at the Orange school, frequently related anecdote and story about Miss Packard and Miss Giles, and said that their impact on their students was enduring.

13

After three years in Orange they felt able to establish a school of their own. They opened this in Fitchburg, Massachusetts, a town of 8,000 people, 50 miles northwest of Boston, in March, 1859. Good teachers apparently were scarce then, as they have ever been. Records show that some students followed these two teachers from New Salem to Petersham and to Orange, and that some of their Orange scholars followed them to Fitchburg, and later to Suffield.

Among these were James Hills, an incorrigible youth, and Lucian Drury, whose sister, Jane Drury, had been their pupil at New Salem Academy. To Lucian Drury's typed manuscript of personal reminiscences written for the benefit of his children and grandchildren the writer is indebted for most of the details of these years.

Lucian attended the school in Orange in the fall of 1857. He writes:

I read Virgil with Miss Giles, who was a good Latin Scholar. With Miss Packard, I had Arithmetic, Algebra, and Grammar. I was fond of language. Grammar was a delight. There were about fifty in our Grammar and Parsing class. We chose sides, arranged on opposite sides of the room. One for each side was appointed to choose members for his side. Four of us held about equal rank, James Hills, William Howe, Lizzie Simmons, not to mention myself. . . . We had many lively discussions in our analysis and parsing exercises.

Some of their Orange scholars, including James Hills, William Howe, and myself, followed them to Fitchburg the next spring.

But the "well-established reputation" of Miss Packard and Miss Giles as teachers did not let them remain in Fitchburg. As Lucian Drury says:

One afternoon in the early June days, a tall man came to the door desiring to speak with Miss Packard. He was conducted to her desk. She offered him a chair. He turned it so as to sit with his back to the scholars. With low tones upon what seemed an important subject, they talked a full half hour. Miss Giles was called from her room and they talked another half hour. Then he left. An hour later school was dismissed. Miss Packard then told the scholars what had been done. The caller was Mr. H. A. Pratt, Principal of the Connecticut Literary Institution in Suffield, Connecticut. He had persuaded Miss Packard to become Preceptress of that Institution, with Miss Giles teacher of painting, drawing and music.

Connecticut Literary Institution
1859-1864

"In the year 1833, in the providence of God, the Connecticut Literary Institution was located in Suffield. In those days, High Schools had not been established in the towns and villages throughout the state. This was a Christian school under Baptist control, founded for the purpose of giving academic education to young men and young women." Thus wrote alumnus Reverend George Olcott King in 1905, 23 years after he had introduced Miss Packard and Miss Giles to John D. Rockefeller in Cleveland, Ohio.

The CLI, which later became known as Suffield Academy, was like Harvard two centuries earlier, established to educate young men for the ministry. But townspeople who had contributed $5,000 toward its establishment, desired a "female department." The Trustees deemed this "inexpedient," but after continued agitation, they opened the school to females in 1846, and built a three-story brick building to accommodate them. The first year there were only 41 young women registered, 15 of whom were in the classical department; but 10 years later there were about three times as many, and 75 of the 117 listed in the catalogue were non-resident.

Miss Packard and Miss Giles began their work in Suffield in the fall of 1859. According to Lucian Drury, "Nearly all their old Orange pupils who had come to Fitchburg, went with them to Suffield." Lucian himself had to go to work because of lack of funds, but September, 1860, found him enrolled in the Suffield school with James Hills for roommate, and giving his time to Latin and Greek. He adds, "I enjoyed every day of the term."

This was the fall of the exciting Lincoln campaign, and the sentiment of the school was strongly pro-Lincoln. About a dozen of the men students got permission to attend a great mass meeting in Springfield and walked the whole 10 miles to get there and three miles of the way back, reaching their rooms about midnight. They heard speeches by U.S. Senator Henry Wilson and Congressman Anson Burlingame, both of Massachusetts. The second day after the election, when they were sure of the outcome, every front window in the three large four-story brick buildings was brilliantly illuminated in Lincoln's honor. And the Academy bell (cast in 1834, and still on the campus) rang in rejoicing just as it rang victory peals at the close of the Civil War and of four other wars. It tolled all night in April 1865 to lament the death of President Lincoln.

The experience of Miss Packard and Miss Giles at the Connecticut Literary Institution is important from many angles to their later work at Spelman.

A loose leaf from Miss Packard's diary dated January 1, 1862, reads:

A New Year. A Happy New Year!!!
Last night very unexpectedly received a most beautiful present from the members of Conn. Lit. Institution. Nothing less than the Cottage Bible, in two volumes, most beautifully bound — & my darling Hattie a splendid work-box from the same source . . .
O my Saviour, lay me out for usefulness!

The Institution was an established academy, with excellent buildings in an attractive setting, with a strong Board of Trustees made up of men from Hartford, New Haven, New London, Bridgeport, as well as from Suffield. It was organized as a result of efforts by the Connecticut Baptist Education Society, but, in accordance with Baptist liberal principles, "Baptist" was not part of its name. The course of study was "designed to prepare young gentlemen and ladies in the most thorough manner, for any of the American Colleges." Consequently, its academic standards were high. Christian living was emphasized not only as of supreme importance to the school but to all a person's activities.

PLATE I

Sophia B. Packard

Harriet E. Giles

New Salem, Massachusetts

PLATE II

Charlestown Female Seminary

New Salem Academy

Connecticut Literary Institution

The Oread Institute

Tuition in the Classical Department and in the Higher English Studies was at the rate of $21.00 per annum. The charge for Ornamentals was extra. Room rent in the Ladies' Building where all the rooms were furnished was $12.00 per annum. Board at the Boarding Hall, provided at cost, ranged from $1.75 to $2.00 per week.

Probably their positions at CLI were the first which provided Miss Packard and Miss Giles what would have been called "a good salary for a woman." Miss Packard's salary with board was $500 a year, $100 more than had previously been paid to any Preceptress at CLI. Miss Giles' salary as "assistant" was $300 with board.

A warning to parents which appeared in the catalogue for 1870-71 reminds one of Spelman Seminary regulations which still prevailed in the nineteen twenties:

Boxes of confectionery, cake, etc., sent to students, so far from being the kindness intended, are a positive source of evil. Their contents, eaten, as is generally the case, irregularly and late at night, produce sickness and impair scholarship, perhaps more than any other single cause. Unless parents and friends heed this remark, we shall be obliged to make the reception of such boxes and parcels by the pupils ground for animadversion.

That Suffield's standing remained high is attested at the Centennial celebration by the presence on its campus in one academic procession of Presidents Cutten of Colgate, Angell of Yale, Barbour of Brown, Woolley of Mount Holyoke; of Dr. George E. Vincent, President of the Rockefeller Foundation, Professor Charles R. Brown of Yale, and Governor Wilbur L. Cross of Connecticut.

Among the students of CLI and a pupil of Miss Packard was *E. Benjamin Andrews*; he enlisted in 1861; served in the Civil War 1861-64 and lost his left eye; was Principal of CLI 1870-72. He served as President of Brown University 1889-98, and there was chiefly responsible for the establishment of its women's branch, Pembroke College. He was one of the men who inspired John D. Rockefeller, Jr., and John Hope, to name two of his Brown University students.[1]

George Olcott King, the man who in 1882 introduced Miss Packard and Miss Giles to John D. Rockefeller, entered the Connecticut Literary Institution in 1859, the same year that Miss Packard and Miss Giles became teachers in that academy, and Miss Packard its Preceptress. He was graduated in 1862; in 1867 he married Eliza Adams, a CLI graduate of 1864. The average number of students ran roughly from 110 to 160 during the tenure of Misses Packard and Giles. They were two of seven teachers their first year. Mr. King was graduated from Brown University in 1866; and from Rochester Theological Seminary in 1869. He held pastorates in Jamestown and Fredonia, New York, and in Cincinnati and Cleveland.

S. Dryden Phelps, father of the late Professor William Lyon Phelps of Yale University, was a trustee during the Packard-Giles years on the administrative and teaching staff.

Orrin P. Gifford, CLI, 1870, became an eloquent Baptist preacher whose sermons in the Delaware Avenue Baptist Church of Buffalo, New York, the writer has recalled with profit for over 50 years. His name appears in the Packard and Giles diaries during their Boston years.

Undoubtedly, the exposure of Miss Packard and Miss Giles to "first-rate" persons had much to do with their own measure of excellence, both as to standards of achievement, and procedures. Their association with such men and women throughout their lives is notable.

[1] In his *John D. Rockefeller, Jr.; A Portrait,* Raymond B. Fosdick quotes a letter from Dr. William Rainey Harper, President of the University of Chicago, to JDR, Jr., advising him to enroll at Brown if President Andrews remained there. Dr. Harper wrote: "Mr. Andrews is a man, who more than any other man in my acquaintance has it in him to stimulate the men with whom he comes into relationship." Raymond B. Fosdick writes further of President Andrews: "He was a powerful personality, utterly fearless, strong of body, intellect and will."

The Oread Collegiate Institute
1864-1867

In the summer of 1864, after five years at CLI, Miss Packard and Miss Giles resigned their respective positions in Suffield to accept work at the Oread Collegiate Institute in Worcester, Massachusetts. This was a promotion in responsibility, especially for Miss Packard.

The Institute founded in 1849, was one of the first to furnish a college education for women. In those days no college except Oberlin opened its doors to women. Mount Holyoke was a Seminary. There was yet no Vassar or Wellesley or Smith or Bryn Mawr to furnish higher education for women.

Oread existed only one generation, from 1849 to 1881, but the record of the 127 graduates of the Institute and of the scores of other women who attended for a shorter time than required for graduation gives tribute to the value of the Oread training. The women, many of them, continued their studies after leaving school and took positions of prominence in educational and literary work. Some went to home mission fields and foreign mission fields. Others married men who were ministers, college professors and deans, and through their homes promoted social, educational and religious work. The record of the students is impressive. They came from other states than Massachusetts, and from other sections than New England. Harvey Buel Spelman in Ohio sent his two daughters, Laura, who later became Mrs. John D. Rockefeller, and Lucy, who never married and lived in the family of Mr. Rockefeller until her death in 1920.

The founder, Eli Thayer, was one of the remarkable men of his generation, or of any generation in this country. He was born in 1819, seventh in direct descent from John Alden and Priscilla through Ruth, daughter of Rev. Noah Alden of Bellingham, who married Eli's grandfather. Eli Thayer prepared for college at Amherst Academy and Worcester Academy, and was graduated from Brown University in 1845, the salutatorian of his class. He taught in Worcester Academy and was its Principal. He gave up the position in 1849 in order to assume the management of the new school which he desired to create, the Oread, situated on the opposite hill in Worcester, then known as "Goats Hill."

Mr. Thayer held the startling conviction that young women should have the same opportunity for study and intellectual development as young men. The establishment of the Oread was his original conception, and he carried out his plan without asking advice or assistance from anyone. He was his own architect and drew the plans for a remarkable building modeled after a feudal castle of the Middle Ages. He personally supervised the work of construction. His intention to erect a young ladies' school on the summit of the hill was not known until a part of the structure was nearly completed. Circular towers, 50 feet in diameter and four stories high were to be placed at the four corners. These were to be connected by four halls, each three stories high and 40 feet long, the whole to be used for dormitories, recitation and lecture rooms, dining-rooms, reception rooms, and other apartments which such an institution would require. The building thus planned was designed to accommodate about 600 students, more than were then found in any American college. Only two towers were completed, together with the east hall connecting these two towers. The frontage was 250 feet. The stone used in the construction of the building was quarried from the hill on which it was erected.

The name, The Oread Collegiate Institute, was suggested by Virgil's lines on the mountain nymphs who followed Diana. The building was called Oread Castle by the pupils; the hill Mr. Thayer renamed Mount Oread.

Mr. Thayer had the approval and moral support of eminent persons, among them two presidents of Brown University, Francis Wayland and Barnas Sears; Rev. George Bushnell, the first pastor of Salem Street Congregational Church and the first Superintendent of Schools in Worcester; Edward Everett

Hale, then at the Church of the Unity in Worcester; and Lydia Maria Childs, the distinguished author and anti-slavery champion.

Printed in one of the early catalogues is this statement: "Individual effort originated and has thus far sustained this institution. It has received no endowment from private municipants or public bounty, except good wishes and liberal patronage. This is all the endowment it will receive in the future. Whatever may be the result, it must stand on its own merits, and the will of the people. . . . We sell education at cost. If our merchandise is not worth our price, or if we have brought wares to the market for which there is no demand, we ask no one to share our loss.

"Oread Castle was founded in good faith under the honest conviction that it might serve the country, and the world, by advancing, in some degree, the able cause to which it is devoted. Such we hope may be its destiny."

Eli Thayer believed not only in the education of women, not then a popular idea, but also in abolition of slavery, and he did something about that too. He originated and organized the New England Emigrant Aid Society, which resulted in Kansas becoming a "free" state. He was a member of Congress, 1856-61. But we are here concerned with his educational venture.

In the Collegiate Course the pupils were required to take Virgil, Cicero, Horace and Tacitus or Livy, Mathematics as far as calculus, French and German, Natural Philosophy, Universal History, Chemistry, Theology, Astronomy, Mental Philosophy, Ethics, Evidences of Christianity, Rhetoric and English Literature. Greek was optional, as were also Italian and Spanish. Oread students had unusual opportunities. In a lecture course in Worcester which they attended in 1855-56, the speakers included: William M. Thackeray, Ralph Waldo Emerson, Bayard Taylor, George W. Curtis, Starr King, Theodore Parker.

The 1854 catalogue states, moreover, that students are required to exercise daily in the open air . . . take excursions ac companied by teachers. "Buildings designed for a Riding Academy for the pupils are now in process of erection on the ample grounds of the Institute. Equestrian skill and grace are a useful and appropriate branch of Female Education."

During the first two or three years of the school's existence, Mr. Thayer took an active part in the classroom, teaching Latin and mathematics in the higher classes. When his outside interests came to interfere with his teaching, he still conducted morning devotions and was often present at the Friday evening social gatherings. His name remained in the catalogue as Principal of the school until 1857. After a term's interim Miss Dodge, who had for four years been preceptress, became acting principal and held this position until 1859. In 1859 Rev. Dr. Robert E. Pattison became principal. Dr. Pattison was an old-time scholar; classic literature and poetic quotation came to him readily. As one student of that day later remarked, "We journeyed not so much to get over the ground as to understand and enjoy the world we passed through, and the cultivated and literary tastes of Dr. Pattison and his family made them guides to be highly prized. The Bible was a valued text-book and Sunday was a welcome day."

After Dr. Pattison, Miss Packard was chosen to serve as the executive head of the Institute, in what was called "The Shepardson-Packard Administration." Associated with her was the Rev. John Shepardson, pastor of the Baptist Church of Petersham, Massachusetts. In the catalogue, their names were bracketed as Principals. Mr. Shepardson did not give up his pastorate and spent only a part of the week in Worcester, leaving to Miss Packard "the chief responsibility for its instruction and discipline."

"This charge," states the *History of the Oread Collegiate Institute*, "Miss Packard was most competent to assume. She was a woman of powerful intellect and strong will, aggressive and energetic, with almost a masculine genius for business and capacity for leadership, and in addition was a thoroughly consecrated and devoted Christian. In spite of a dignity and authoritative manner that in some persons would have been almost forbidding, Miss Packard's strong and positive qualities of mind and heart made her a woman to inspire deeply-felt admiration and devotion, and many of *her pupils were roused through her influence to an eager ambition for intellectual achievement or to a lifelong consecration to Christian service*."

Dr. Shepardson, a big, hearty, genial man, was so cordial and kindly that the affectionate nickname of Father Shepardson, given him by the girls, seemed most appropriate. He was, like Miss Packard, deeply interested in their moral and spiritual welfare.

The *History* continues:

Miss Packard was ably assisted in her duties of instruction and discipline by Miss Hattie E. Giles, her devoted friend, with whom she had been constantly associated in all that she had done for ten years. . . . It would have been impossible for a school girl of those days to speak or think of one without the other. They dressed alike and in leisure hours were nearly always together. Miss Giles was in character quite unlike Miss Packard, being most gentle, mild, and self-effacing, but constantly watchful and quietly observant that everything went well. . . . Under this administration an excellent corps of teachers was gathered together.

The Oread Collegiate Institute afforded excellent opportunity for Miss Packard to develop her considerable capacity for administration and for teaching. She was not only co-ordinate *Principal*, but her name stands first under *Instructors*, as teacher of Metaphysics and Literature; Miss Giles' name came second for Ornamentals and Music; and that of Rev. Joseph Banvard third as Professor of Elocution, Natural Sciences and Moral Philosophy. Thirteen other teachers were then listed. The curriculum of the Oread was of collegiate rank. The ratio of students to teachers is noteworthy.

Dr. Banvard was a well-known citizen of Worcester; his wife became in 1877 the first president of the Woman's American Baptist Home Mission Society. He wrote to Miss Packard as follows in May 1881: "How time has fled since you and I first became acquainted. What pleasant times I used to have at the Oread. I don't believe you were aware how I enjoyed myself then. Those were halcyon days to me. . . ."

The students listed, all young women, numbered exactly 100, and they gave addresses from: Maine, New Hampshire, Vermont, Massachusetts, Rhode Island, Connecticut, Wisconsin, Illinois, Colorado, Indiana, Delaware, New York.

The charge for tuition in English Branches, Latin, Board, Lights and Fuel was $275 per year, with an extra charge for Greek and Hebrew, Modern Languages (French, Italian, German). Laundry was extra, and one dollar was the "charge for a seat at Church." The Ornamental and Music Department had a separate list of charges; for Drawing and Painting in classes, $5, $7, and $10 per quarter; and for private lessons in Piano, Organ, and Vocal Music - $12.50 to $15 per quarter.

"The Ornamental and Music Department under the tuition of Miss Hattie E. Giles is in a *very flourishing* condition," the catalogue states. "Those who aspire to symmetrical education cannot wisely dispense with the cultivation of taste and the love of the beautiful which this department affords. . . ."

The 1865 catalogue lists the brother of Harriet Giles, the Honorable H. H. Giles of Wisconsin, as a member of "Examiners and Board of Reference."

The Shepardson-Packard administration continued for two years. At the end of June 1866, Rev. Mr. Shepardson resigned; and the next year he founded Highland Institute in Petersham. Harris R. Greene, principal of the Worcester High School, succeeded him at the Oread. According to the *History of the Oread Institute*, Miss Packard was associated as Principal with Mr. Greene in 1866-67.

One item has come to light showing his friendliness at the beginning of that academic year. A book by Mrs. Jameson entitled, *Sketches of Art, Literature and Character*, published in Boston in 1865, is at hand bearing on the first blank page an inscription: Miss Packard – From Mr. & Mrs. H. R. Greene, December 25, 1866. This book, with its gold-leafed edges, is

the greatly prized property of a Spelman graduate, Mrs. Sallie
E. Walker Wilder, and carries a book-plate:

Private Library

S. B. Packard and H. E. Giles

No. 267

A matter of more consequence, however, developed in the
spring for which no explanation is available. Four seniors, including Ella Cole of Stockbridge, were listed as prospective
graduates in the catalogue published that spring; none was
graduated.

Usually the majority of the students who attended the New
England or other academies and colleges of this period did not
pursue the course to graduation, but were in attendance for
only one or more years. Thus it was at Oread Institute. The
number of graduates in the four classes from 1861 through
1864 was 22. In 1865 the graduates numbered five; in 1866,
four; in 1867, none, although four had been listed that spring
in the catalogue as "prospective graduates." Why no graduates
in 1867?

Miss Packard retired at the end of that year. In 1867-68,
Mr. Greene assumed entire control of the school. What is the
explanation?

Careful study of the catalogues, the *History of the Oread
Collegiate Institute*, and a search of the issues of the *Massachusetts Spy* covering the period does not answer that question,
but yields some evidence as to the character of Mr. Greene, or
at least as to his administrative ability, a certain lack of judgment, and refusal to state the facts.

The catalogue for the four terms ending June 30, 1867, does
not include the names of either Miss Packard or Miss Giles.
The "complete list of faculty and staff," in Mr. Greene's administration printed in the Oread History, includes a statement: "This does not include the teachers of 1866-1867." The
catalogue for that year names Mr. Greene as teaching subjects

25

previously assigned to Miss Packard. The instructors listed were all new, with two exceptions.

Under Mr. Greene's administration, covering the years 1866-1879, there were nine different women in the position of Preceptress (eight different ones in 11 years, the ninth one being Mrs. Greene, his wife). There were eight different Matrons in 11 years, only one of whom stayed longer than one year.

A broadside printed by the Oread for distribution at the International Exhibition of 1876 mentions its founding in 1848 by Eli Thayer; states that the Institute was under the charge of the founder for several years; that it was presided over successively thereafter by Miss H. P. Dodge, Rev. R. E. Pattison, Rev. John Shepardson, and Harris R. Greene, A.M., the present incumbent. No mention of Sophia B. Packard.

The failure to list Miss Packard's name in any catalogue connected with Mr. Greene's administration; the omission of her name from the flyer giving as historical facts the names of the Principals; the substitution of Mr. Greene himself for Miss Packard as teacher of metaphysics and literature; the omission of both Miss Packard and Miss Giles from the 1867 list of teachers, the question about the graduates for 1867 – why were there none – all of these things add up to more than ordinary coincidence. At the close of the year 1867, under date of July 5, there is an item in the *Massachusetts Spy* about the closing exercises of the Oread, but no mention of Miss Packard or the fact that she was leaving. Yet New England men and women at that time, and all the rest of her life credit Miss Packard with success as Principal of the Oread Institute.

Mr. and Mrs. Robert H. Cole of Southbridge were longtime friends of Miss Packard and Miss Giles. Mr. Cole who organized the American Optical Company and served as its president for 21 years, was one of the early benefactors of Spelman Seminary. He was one of the men who signed the application for its Charter; and was a trustee from 1888 until his death. Their daughter, Ella M., was a student at the Oread for two years, entering in 1865. In fact, she was one of the 1867 seniors who were not graduated. She wrote an article for the *Spelman Messenger* of May, 1895, in which she states that Miss Packard and Miss Giles, at the end of three years "closed their connection with the school under trying circumstances." They rested at Southbridge for several months and "then found employment in Boston that would furnish means for their support, in surroundings not uncongenial."

In view of the opposition to women's education and to women's rights in the professions, there is ground for believing that Miss Packard left the Oread because her very competence was not tolerable to her associate, Mr. Greene. One recalls that it was considered unseemly for women even to speak from a public platform with men. Catherine Beecher used to get her brother to deliver her speeches for her; and Lucy Stone refused at Oberlin a few years earlier to write a graduation essay and turn it over to be read by a man, which was the college policy. To share administrative responsibility with a woman was apparently a giant step for Mr. Greene that he was not prepared to take.
of his Brown University students.

Only a few lines in a Worcester clipping record Mr. *the Oread Institute* published in the '90's gives a full page to the accomplishments of Miss Packard and Miss Giles.

CHAPTER II
THE YEARS IN BOSTON
1868-1880

Their Work and Interests

AFTER a few months of recuperation, Miss Packard accepted a position with the Empire Life Insurance Company in Boston. The manager was a retired minister and her friend. Phineas Camp Headley, author of several books with titles which vary from *Kossuth* to *Massachusetts in the Rebellion, 1861-63,* was an official of this company and a member of the Board of Reference of the Oread Institute. He wrote of Miss Packard as being "so capable, accurate, and faithful." And later he wrote of "our business relations when she so faithfully and intelligently served the company whose complicated affairs required a clear and accurate mind and also a sound judgment and unbending integrity." He added, "She never failed to meet any responsibility which attended her position, and won the perfect confidence of those to whom she sustained business relations."

Miss Giles kept house during this Boston interim, and gave music lessons. Both were active in church work. Lucian Drury mentions that he "was honored" by their attendance at his graduation from Newton Theological Seminary in 1869. Miss Packard encouraged him to make a trip to Europe before taking a pastorate, and "with some help from Miss Packard," he sailed for Glasgow. His passage "intermediate between saloon and steerage" cost $35; his four months' trip abroad was not an exorbitant expense. Miss Packard and Miss Giles were his steadfast friends. In an article he wrote for the *Suffield Alumni Quarterly,* he states that at the age of 16 when he entered their school in Orange, Massachusetts, he "became at once their admiring and devoted knight." They were, he said, like older sisters to him, as long as they lived.

A niece, Phoebe Williams, daughter of the Maria Rachel

Packard who had made the sampler, spent the month of September, 1874, with her Aunt Sophia in Boston in preparation for her wedding. Phoebe was a successful teacher in Swampscott, where Rev. Lucian Drury was minister and also member of the school committee. After a year's acquaintance, during which Phoebe's mother died, Lucian and Phoebe became engaged. They were married in the Baptist Church in Swampscott by the Rev. George C. Lorimer on September 29, 1874. They had two sons, Lucian Lorimer and Harold Williams.[1]

The Boston years came at a time for both women when family interests and inevitable inroads of change and death therein made demands on their time and strength. Although Miss Giles was the one who kept house, we know that she taught a Sunday School class of young men at Tremont Temple. Records show, too, that she frequently, but not always, accompanied Sophia on her visits to churches and women's societies in New England. There is a fascinating reference in her diary — an item dated September 22, 1880, about going down town for Sophia to see about the tickets for the "Lecture Course." She "called on Professor Longfellow in the morning to consult him about the giving of *The Golden Legend.*"

In Boston both women became members of the Shawmut Avenue Baptist Church of which Dr. George C. Lorimer[2] was pastor. He recognized Miss Packard's ability, and persuaded his church in 1870 to appoint her as pastor's assistant, — a position

---

[1] Lorimer Drury was for more than 25 years editor of the *Mount Hermon Alumni Quarterly*. He died in 1930. Mrs. Lorimer Drury still lives in Northfield, and to her the writer is indebted for access to the personal-reminiscences-manuscript of her late husband's father. Harold W. Drury, the younger son, has helpfully supplied data and a few pictures. He was twelve years old when Miss Packard died in 1891, and it has been a satisfaction to communicate with a relative of Sophia B. Packard who knew during his boyhood both of the founders of Spelman College. Harold and his mother, Mrs. Phoebe Williams Drury, were at Spelman for the last six months of Miss Packard's life.

[2] George C. Lorimer: b. Scotland 1838; came to U.S. as a professional actor; abandoned stage for ministry; pastor, Shawmut Avenue Baptist Church two years; Tremont Temple 1873-79, 1891-01; First Baptist Church and Immanuel Baptist Church, Chicago, 1879-1891; Madison Ave. Baptist Church, N.Y. City, 1901-04. Man of magnetic personality, popular preacher whose discourses were carefully prepared and full of literary allusions; delivered Lowell Lectures, Boston, in 1900 (DNB).

more in line with her ideas of usefulness, and most unusual in that era. Miss Giles wrote of Miss Packard's acceptance of the church position as meaning a great financial sacrifice, as she received as pastor's assistant only one quarter as much salary as she had earned with the insurance company.

When Dr. Lorimer became pastor at Tremont Temple in 1873, he invited the two women to transfer their church membership to Tremont Temple, and Miss Packard to serve there as pastor's assistant. That title was, in fact, printed on her calling cards. She was family visitor, conducted the women's prayer meeting, taught a large Bible class in the Sunday School, and was active, sympathetic and helpful in visiting the sick.

Tremont Temple was one of the leading Baptist churches in the country, and Dr. Lorimer, one of its leading clergymen. The work as pastor's assistant provided an outlet for Miss Packard's interest in people, her practical good sense and teaching skills. We may think of her work with Dr. Lorimer as adult education or as training in family life, with a Christian outlook, conducted on an individual, not a classroom, basis.

Here, however, were two women in the prime of life, who had been pre-eminently successful as teachers, who wanted "a school of their own," deprived by fate, or misfortune, of the opportunity to serve in the ways best suited to their training and experience. Miss Packard, to be sure, became a pioneer in two areas – in a business office and in a church position of a kind then altogether uncommon. But remember that at the Oread she had roused students to *an eager ambition for intellectual achievement*, a trait sometimes overlooked because of her outstanding qualities as a completely consecrated Christian.

Miss Packard worked with Dr. Lorimer for eight years. Yet a wider field called.

Growing Interest in the Freed People

Catherine Beecher's tract, "The Duty of American Women to Their Country," published by Harper's in 1845, was indeed a clarion call to women. The slavery issue had stirred the consciences of church people. The historic Woman's Rights Convention held in Seneca Falls, N.Y. in 1848 had grown out of the refusal to accept women, notably Elizabeth Cady Stanton and Lucretia Mott, as delegates to the World Anti-Slavery Convention convened in London in 1840. The abolition societies not only forced women to face their responsibilities as citizens, but also provided scope for their energies and activities and a measure of experience. The important place held by religion, and the patriotic fervor that linked Christianity and education, giving rise to scores of church related academies and colleges across the land, worked together to compel action.

Women, particularly in the New England and the Central States, were roused to the urgent need to educate and to convert to the Christian way of life the freed people and the Indians, as well as the immigrants then pouring into the United States by the thousands and tens of thousands.

The Woman's American Baptist Home Mission Society

In consequence, a group of New England women met in Boston in 1877 and organized the Woman's American Baptist Home Mission Society, as an auxiliary to the American Baptist Home Mission Society which had been supporting missions and building mission schools since 1832. Hereafter, for the sake of brevity, these two organizations will be usually referred to as the ABHMS and the WABHMS.

Miss Packard was the catalyzing agent of the women's organization. She presided at the meeting in Tremont Temple of over 200 women when the Society was formed. She wrote the legal document applying for incorporation and called the first meeting thereafter. She was at once elected treasurer. Some of the meetings were held "in Miss Packard's room" at Tremont Temple. Bylaws were adopted; appeals to the churches were made; methods of procedure were discussed. The women were in 'dead earnest,' although the Society had no money. The

Minutes month after month show that Miss Packard was by motion included on virtually every committee.

The additional responsibilities added to the regular duties of her position at Tremont Temple were a heavy drain on her strength. A leave of two months granted in the summer of 1878 enabled her to make a trip to Europe in company with Col. Russell H. Conwell,[1] then a lawyer in Boston, and Mrs. Conwell. They landed in Liverpool, and visited Wales before going to Paris. Miss Packard had the background to enjoy the visits to museums, cathedrals and other places of historic interest. At first she thought she could not afford to make the trip to Italy with the Conwell party, but when she found that it would cost her almost as much to remain in Paris, she ended by going. Switzerland, Holland, England, and Scotland followed.

Under date of August 14, 1878, Dr. Conwell wrote from London to Miss Giles as follows:

Miss Packard has stood the long journey remarkably well, and is so anxious to see and to learn, and enjoys these scenes so much that I am happy as a clam seeing her enjoying herself. She is such a good woman and so pleasant a traveling companion that it is a rich treat to have her with us. . . .

Before sailing homeward, Miss Packard wrote to Miss Giles: "Have some baked beans, will you, and I shall delight myself for a while and then go to church with you. – I want some ice-cream – quarts of it!"

In September, Miss Packard was back at work, and again was named to numerous committees of the WABHMS. Many appeals for aid from women were coming in. Among the 5,000,-000 freed people, there were 3,000,000 women; one third of the latter were girls under 21. There were thousands of freed

---

[1] Russell H. Conwell's father was an abolitionist, his home a station of the Underground Railroad. Russell H. raised a company of volunteers in the Civil War; became a lieutenant colonel on the staff of General McPherson; was wounded severely at Kennesaw Mountain. Was foreign correspondent for *New York Tribune* 1868-70; practiced law in Boston 1870-79. Was ordained to Baptist ministry in 1879; pastor of Grace Baptist Church and Baptist Temple, Philadelphia, 1881-1925. Founded Temple University, and was its president, 1888-1925. Was author and lecturer. The total amount earned by his popular lecture "Acres of Diamonds" was given to educate needy students.

slaves among the Indians, a fact not generally known. The need for women missionaries was urgent. Many of the former slaves had no homes, work or wages. None had schools for their children. The task to be done was tremendous.

Miss Packard had at first emphatically declined to serve the Society as corresponding secretary, but, in spite of her refusal, she was, in October, 1878, unanimously elected to that position. She thereupon took over its full duties. She had even previously spent much time and energy in the effort to persuade the women (and the men) of the urgency of all-out support for home mission work, and in visits to churches to organize the women's groups. Her talks at many such meetings were described as "eloquent."

The brief diary notes of journeys to Maine, New Hampshire and Vermont; to Connecticut and Rhode Island, and to scores of towns and cities in Massachusetts include mention of a rough night on the boat to Portland and Bangor; "snow and blow" in northwestern Massachusetts; sitting up all night on coaches between Boston and New York; between Bangor and Boston; excessively cold and stormy weather; and in July 1879 a fearful tornado. She traveled by boat, by train, by bus; and at the end of every journey stayed not at hotels but in the homes of church people. Whenever her journeys took her through or near mountains, she found refreshment of mind and spirit. In New Hampshire views of Webster, Willy, Willard, and Washington were enjoyed from the platform of the train; in Vermont she had a "beautiful ride through the Notch"; in Maine a trip up Newjoy Mount provided a view of islands that "dotted the Bay at our feet" and "the lofty ranges of the White Mountains" she had just passed through.

In addition to the travel, the speaking, the conferences, and the organizing of women in the churches, there was arduous office work whenever she returned to Boston. Many letters had to be answered, and this before the day of typewriters and secretaries; accounts had to be figured; various administrative matters had to be discussed; interviews held. The persistent pursuit of the objective went on without let-up through 1879 and, at the same pace, into 1880. Nevertheless, Miss Packard sometimes had her doubts. Was she really "in the path of duty"? Were the needy people being reached? What actually were the end results of the efforts? She decided that she ought to know at first hand just what the conditions were and what work was underway to meet them. A trip South for the purpose was authorized by the WABHMS.

CHAPTER III

THE FIRST JOURNEY SOUTH AND
ITS RESULTS—1880

MISS PACKARD left Boston at six p.m. on February 24, 1880, and was in Philadelphia the next morning. She attended church in Richmond on Sunday, February 29; visited the Normal School on Monday; left for Nashville on Tuesday. The fare from Richmond to Nashville is set down as $24.25; the diary items deal with the beauty of the ride over the Blue Ridge and Allegheny Mountains. "An Italian cloudless sky. . . . Have passed over the most lovely scenery. Mountainous . . . the peaks of Otter . . . the noble Blue Ridges and lofty Alleghenies."

She visited Fisk University in Nashville; a Methodist school; several colored elementary schools. She went into the classes, talked with the teachers. She saw a baptism at a Negro Baptist church which caused her to exclaim in her diary. "Never shall I forget it. Never." On the way to New Orleans, she traveled along the Mississippi River; enjoyed the cypress trees covered with moss, and other sights of the palmetto.

In New Orleans, she met Miss Joanna P. Moore, that hardy pioneer missionary to colored people, who started her work during the Civil War on an island in the Mississippi and later originated in Tennessee the plan of "Fireside schools." She visited New Orleans University (Methodist) and Straight Institute (Congregational); made calls in Negro homes; attended classes; talked with teachers. Then she became sick, and Miss Giles was sent for. She started on March 25, but with stops and waits and changes, the journey took four days. She found Miss Packard "very weak and sick" but by April 11 she began to gain steadily. Her improvement gave Miss Giles a chance to visit homes and schools. On one Sunday she taught a Sunday School class, on another attended a funeral, both in colored churches. In her diary she wrote: "Am so much interested in these colored people." After 10 more days, Miss Packard was able to travel. They left by boat to Cincinnati on April 22; from there by train to Boston. They reached home at midnight on May first, "very tired indeed" but thankful to be home and happy from the warm welcome given them by their friends.

Miss Packard and Miss Giles returned from the trip filled with the desire to start a school in the South for Negro women and girls. They were fired by the desperate need they had encountered; they were fitted by training and experience for such a task. But the women of the WABHMS – including a few of the officers – were by no means ready to endorse their proposal.

Miss Packard was present at eight meetings of the WABHMS from June 4 to November 11, 1880, inclusive; and at six regular and special meetings held in January, February, and March, 1881. The minutes of these meetings give ample ground for discouragement.

There was, to be sure, some basis for hesitation on the part of the Society. The treasury was empty. The responsibility of supporting a school for Negro women seemed to some too overwhelming to be considered. Moreover, some of the women were outspoken in their opinion that Miss Packard and Miss Giles were too old to undertake such a work. Some counselled delay. For months the Society temporized.

The opposition was depressing. Miss Packard and Miss Giles pointed out, that, while the Baptist denomination had a school for Negroes in every Southern state, there was no provision in Georgia for the education of women and girls. Yet Georgia had the largest colored population and the large proportion of them were Baptists. Still, favorable action was not taken by the Society.

Meanwhile, Miss Packard had to earn her living. She was not on salary after June 4. There was rent to pay, and food to buy. She conferred with Col. Conwell, and was given a job of sorts. Three weeks of Miss Packard's work plus one day's work of Miss Giles brought them $30 on September 13, and the diary comment "God bless Col. Conwell. . . ."

Col. Conwell, who had given up the law for the ministry, had been ordained in 1879; he became pastor of a run-down church in Lexington the next year and revitalized it. Miss Packard helped him, but she was troubled in mind, and prayed that God would make her duty plain to her. Miss Giles apparently had not found a satisfactory position. A longing to undertake the work among Negro women remained. Miss Giles' diary on December 31, 1880, reflects their perplexed state of mind. "What a year of trial this has been. Sickness, disappointment. . . . May it all prove for good to us."

Miss Packard greeted the New Year hopefully, but her doubts as to her duty remained. Her diary reads on January 2, 1881: ". . . Dear Master, do Thou lead me to know fully what Thy will to me is and what Thou would have me to do & *where* to labor." Many, many names and addresses appear on the next pages; then a note that the WABHM Society Board met on January 13; on January 16 (Sunday) Miss Packard writes: "Am disheartened. . . . Guide me, O Thou Great Jehovah, Pilgrim through this barren land. May I know Thy will and do it. . . ."

Then apparently they decided to raise the money to send themselves South. Miss Packard noted on February 7: "At Executive meeting tonight, Col. Conwell presented my resignation." The entry for Miss Giles on February 7 was, "O, these dark, dark days. When will they come to an end. When will our dear Father bring us out of these trials. – Sophia resigned her position. . . ."

The February diary entries reveal the grievous concern of both women as to their future work. They coveted the endorsement of the WABHMS. The conviction as to their duty remained – and disturbed them. Miss Packard's diary on February 16 reads:

Burdens of great responsibility are still to be carried. Work there is to be done of which eternity alone will make report. Sorrows there have been & sorrows there may be again to endure – But he 'who has never broken his bread in tears knows little of the Heavenly powers.'

37

Miss Giles writes on February 18: "One of the darkest days of my life. The question is what shall we do. . . .?"

Speaking of herself and Miss Packard in the third person, Miss Giles wrote in retrospect in 1895 — "their eyes were opened [by the Southern trip] to the appalling need of help for the colored women and girls. The conviction was profoundly impressed upon them that their lives should be given to the education and Christianization of these downtrodden people. On their return to the North, this conviction deepened. . . . Even in the still night watches a voice seemed to say: "Go South and help these women and girls who have never had a chance."

The anguish they suffered over the uncertainty and the delay in gaining approval for the enterprise seems to have been caused by a very few women in the WABHMS who were actively opposed. At long last, however, Miss Packard was called upon on February 24, 1881 — ten months had passed since the Southern trip — to express her views formally at a special meeting of the Board of the WABHMS. She is recorded in the official minutes as saying that "She had long wished to be more directly engaged in the interests of the Freed people, especially so since she had met them in their homes and seen their great need. She desires our Society to establish a school, in a good locality, and she is ready to spend her best efforts to make it a success and a blessing to the Freed women of the South."

She continued in her effort to raise enough money to make a start; and she still earnestly desired to have the WABHMS sponsor the work. One February day she called on several persons including Mrs. C. A. Ogden to solicit their help in raising money. The following Wednesday she wrote in her diary: "Mrs. Ogden called this AM, quite discouraged about the money to send *teacher*. I accompanied her to call on Mrs. Roberts." On March 3, she received from the Ladies' Society of Everett, 15 dollars. On March 3 she wrote to Charlestown, her old academy.

Finally Miss Packard said to one of her most interested

Home Mission friends, "I am going to see Mr. Abbott in Medford. If he discourages the undertaking, we must abandon it for the present." She and Harriet Giles went to Medford on March 5 and told the Rev. J. P. Abbott of the burden on their hearts. He said: "Come to my church tomorrow night."

Miss Packard presented her plea with earnestness to the people in the First Baptist Church of Medford. They were stirred, and pledges totaling $100.00 were made. Miss Packard's diary on Sunday, March 6: "Medford raised fifty dollars and pledged fifty more. May the dear Master bless them. Now we have $150. pledged." This was their first encouragement, the first considerable sum they had received, and they had gone to Medford resolved to accept for the time-being the answer of the Medford friends, whether favorable or not. They believed the Medford Church gift indicated that it was God's will for them to proceed with their plan.

The next morning, March 9, after return from Boston, Miss Packard wrote "Mrs. Gannett called and left ten dollars. . . . Thanksgiving & praise are due to Thy name." On March 9, Miss Giles went to see Deacon Chipman. He gave 50 dollars and pledged 50 more in the autumn. Each one worked to raise money for her own travel expenses and her own salary.

At the March 10 meeting of the WABHMS, Miss Packard was asked again to speak of the plans for a school in the South. After a free discussion, it was voted "to establish a school in the South for women and girls, Dr. Mason of the ABHMS fully concurring in such action." Another motion was made and seconded that Miss Packard and Miss Giles be appointed to commence the school in Atlanta, Georgia; but after remarks by Miss Packard and others, it was thought best, as so few members were present "to wait further action for an early meeting of the full Board."

Miss Giles the next day wrote: "Sold my Piano — a hard thing for me to do, but thought it best."

Obstacles still remained. The members of the Board of the WABHMS who thought the project premature controlled the vote at a special meeting on March 12. In consequence, the Board reversed its action of March 10, and voted to postpone matters until there had been further deliberation and correspondence.

Miss Giles that day wrote: "Proceedings of Thursday's meeting all upset. Dark days these. . . ." Miss Packard wrote on Sunday, March 12: "This the darkest for a sunshiny day I ever witnessed." Disconcerted as they felt, they did not give up. On March 17, Miss Packard wrote to Mrs. Thomas Nickerson, president of the WABHMS, offering a compromise suggestion. She wrote:

. . . As the idea of establishing a school seems so great an undertaking, could we not be appointed as missionaries and teachers, or simply as missionaries, for mission work must first be done under whatever name we are sent. Miss Giles thinks in the Autumn she would prefer to give herself to the educational work. The foregoing measure obviates all fear of any draft on the friends of the Society.

We can put into the Treasurer's hand the money for our expenses as soon as appointed.

The step the colored people themselves in Georgia have just taken shows the *necessity* of the work we had in view there for the women and girls. Can not a meeting of the Board be called immediately to decide this question? . . .

Thus matters progressed, or did not progress. A number of additional meetings had to be held, and there was much discussion pro and con before Miss Packard and Miss Giles were again commissioned to open a school for colored women and girls wherever in the South Providence seemed to direct.

A meeting on March 24, called by Mrs. Durant, considered the plan of work presented by Miss Packard. "An hour was spent in free conversation about it." Each member of the Board present expressed approval of the work and of sending Miss Packard and Miss Giles. They then unanimously passed a resolution "That we appoint Miss S. B. Packard and Miss H. E. Giles as teachers to Atlanta, Georgia." An earnest desire was expressed also that they go with the assurance of united cooperation from the Society. Mrs. Sturtevant closed the business of the session by a gift to the treasury of $25.00.

Miss Packard's Diary:

March 25. This has been the happiest day for months. . . . God bless those dear good women who came so lovingly yesterday after giving us our appointments as workers in the *South*.

CHAPTER IV

BEGINNINGS IN ATLANTA—1881

LESS than a month – only 23 days, in fact – after the meeting in the Medford Church, they were on the way to Georgia – and their destined field of work – a work to which they gave every ounce of their skill and devotion as long as they lived. They traveled by train to Stonington, Connecticut; by boat to New York and ferry to Jersey City; changed trains at Washington, D.C., and at Cincinnati, after a delay in Chattanooga caused by snow storms. They reached Atlanta on Friday, April Fool's Day, in the evening. They had been on the road three nights and three days. Dr. Shaver, a teacher at the Atlanta Baptist Seminary, an ABHMS school to train Negro ministers, met them at the depot and took them to the National Hotel. The next day Dr. Shaver called and took them to a house at 132 So. Forsyth Street to board. The landlady, Mrs. Cheshire, agreed to take them for $40 per month, or $45 "if she finds fuel." A drayman delivered their trunks to the boarding-house that afternoon, and they went soon after and were there for tea. At last, their time had come.

The Reverend Frank Quarles

The most important person in Atlanta for Miss Packard and Miss Giles to see, Dr. Shaver informed them, was the Rev. Frank Quarles. Affectionately called Father Quarles, he was regarded as the most influential colored preacher in the state. He was pastor of Friendship Baptist Church, a church which he had organized three years after Emancipation. The first members were former slaves of Atlanta families, who with him had previously worshipped in the First Baptist Church (white) and with him had been removed from the church rolls.

In 1881, Friendship Church had 1,500 members. Father Quarles had become influential in the educational and civic life as well as in the religious life of Georgia. He had been a leading spirit in having the Augusta Institute moved to Atlanta in 1879 and then incorporated as Atlanta Baptist Seminary.

As soon, therefore, as Miss Packard and Miss Giles had found a place to live, Dr. Shaver took them to see Father Quarles. Since he was not at home, they went to the church. The door was locked, but it was believed that the pastor was in his study. The visitors stooped over, picked up a few small pebbles and tossed them at the window. This fact has been authenticated by Mrs. Claudia White Harreld '01, who told the author that, when Miss Giles used to tell of the incident, she would bend over and sweep her arm downward and up to illustrate. It was further attested by an elderly Negro who in recent years told the author that he was a small boy with his father outside the church that day and he saw the pebbles picked up and tossed against the window pane.

Father Quarles appeared. Miss Packard and Miss Giles, introduced by Dr. Shaver, explained their mission. Whereupon, the pastor exclaimed: "When I was praying, the Lord heard and answered. I was on my knees pleading with God to send teachers for the Baptist women and girls of Georgia. We fully believe the Lord has sent you." As they talked, he said: "I do not know where you could hold such a school. You could use my church if it wasn't for the funerals. But there is the basement."

Father Quarles proposed to call a meeting of the colored preachers for Monday morning; Miss Packard and Miss Giles were to meet with them. As Miss Packard wrote that Saturday to Mrs. Pollard in Boston, "Mr. Quarles is deeply interested in the education of the colored girls who he said had been sadly neglected throughout the entire state, and he had been praying for help for years."

The notice sent to the Negro ministers was written on the letter-head of Atlanta Baptist Seminary with "Rev. J. T. Robert, President and Rev. D. Shaver, Professor" printed at the top. It ran as follows:

April 2, 1881

Rev. & Dear Sir,

We respectfully and earnestly request your attendance at the study of the Pastor of the Friendship Baptist Church at 10 o'clock Monday morning, to consider what steps may and should be taken to promote the education of the young ladies connected with your congregation.

Yours in the faith of the Gospel

S. B. Packard

H. E. Giles

Sunday morning, April 3, Mrs. Cheshire took them to the First Baptist Church of which the Rev. Mr. Gwinn was pastor. In the evening, they went to the Methodist Church. "Enjoyed the day very much," wrote Miss Giles. They truly had reason to feel contentment of mind, now that, only 10 days after their appointment by the WABHMS in Boston, they were actually in the field where they longed to work, with practical arrangements under way for beginning that work. They felt also humility of spirit and great need of God's help.

Miss Packard writes, under date of

April 4   A cold morning this. Lord, prepare me for this day's business for Thee. O to know Thy will — Teach Thou me & Hattie dear that we mistake not Thy mind.

Met the Colored Pastors this morning at the Pastor's study of the Friendship Church, Dr. Quarles. There were seven ministers & five pastors present. They seemed very glad to welcome us & Dr. Quarles' church offered us the use of their vestry. . . .

With the encouragement of all the Negro pastors present at the conference, Miss Packard and Miss Giles decided to open the school on the following Monday, April 11. They attended the early Sunday School at Friendship Church on April 10 and both of them were called upon by Father Quarles to tell of their plans.

Eleven pupils of varying ages and attainments reported at the basement of Friendship Church the next morning, and teaching began that day. The second day they had "25 scholars"; and the number steadily increased week after week. When

44

they closed the school on July 15, the enrollment was 80. The biggest difficulty of the first nine months rose out of a misunderstanding with some of the women in the WABHMS over a circular regarding the school, which led to a request that Miss Packard and Miss Giles report to the Board in Boston on August first. The latter felt that it was essential for them to remain during the summer to work with the people in their homes and churches.

Father Quarles gave Miss Packard and Miss Giles stalwart help in this emergency. From the very first day he had shown deep interest in the progress of the school, and anxiety lest the teachers should become discouraged. He frequently walked quietly into the school and after greeting them would say "I hope the Lord will not let you get discouraged. You ought to have a better place." He constantly sought to enlist the support, financial and other, of the colored people in behalf of the school. News reached colored people best, then as now, through their ministers. So a circular or leaflet was prepared which gave general information about the school on the first page; and included on the second page a course of study,* plan of work and the date the school would open in the fall. The leaflets were for distribution at the state convention of the colored Baptist ministers of Georgia, in order to enlist their support in providing funds and in sending students. As a further line of promotion, additional copies of the first page were printed for distribution to the white Baptist ministers whose state convention came first. The latter were circulated at the white convention by Rev. Mr. Daniel, pastor of the Central Baptist Church which Miss Packard and Miss Giles had joined, and by Professor Shaver of Atlanta Baptist Seminary. A copy of this Circular reached Boston and caused consternation, particularly to the Corresponding Secretary, who felt that Miss Packard and Miss Giles had overstepped their authorized work.

Father Quarles was so distressed that the ladies of the Board had requested Misses Packard and Giles to return North that

* See Appendix.

he wrote a long letter, dated July 25, completely exonerating the latter from any responsibility for the "Circular." He even made a trip to Boston in August, but the persons he tried to see in behalf of Miss Packard and Miss Giles were not available. He returned to Atlanta, where Miss Packard had a long conversation with him on September 5.

Father Quarles left on a second trip North on November 15 to plead for the School and its teachers and to raise money for the needed school building. He made visits in and around Boston, first to Mr. Mason of the ABHMS; then to Mrs. Pollard who, after he had "preached a sermon" on the subject of Miss Packard, agreed to call the Board together. He called on three other ladies of the Board and won them over. Then he went to the Ogdens. They invited him to dinner Wednesday and to Thanksgiving dinner the next day. "Mrs. Ogden," as Father Quarles wrote Miss Packard under date of November 23, "is a fine Christian lady and is fully in favor of you and Miss Giles. . . ." He remarked that the people in Boston were all thinking of nothing but Thanksgiving, so but little else could be done until that was over, and added that besides there were a thousand and one persons there after money for different objects and the people were getting tired of so much begging.

But he was hopeful. He was also homesick for home and his wife and family, but wrote, "For the sake of the Cause I will try to bare (sic) it a few days longer – And do what I can – though it is very cold here for me today. . . . I cannot write well . . . will tell you all when I come home. See my wife and tell her what I say and give her and the children my best respects and all the rest of the People. I hope to leave here Monday next, and stop in New York a day or two and then leave for home. Pray for me. Yours truly, Frank Quarles."

Even in Atlanta it was cold. Miss Packard wrote in her diary for the day after Thanksgiving: "O, it is so cold today in our School – am very much afraid we will be obliged to abandon our work," and prayed for help in their great extremity. But for

Father Quarles, the cold led to pneumonia. He went to New York, and died at the home of his son on December 3, 1881.

A letter sent to Miss Packard and Miss Giles from Mrs. C. A. Ogden well describes the days he spent in Boston and is quoted below:

"I have just received your postal with its sad, sad news. How grieved I feel for you & for his church, for the colored people at large. All have lost a friend and helper in the good man who has gone home. . . . The Rev. Mr. Quarles called forth esteem and confidence from all who conversed with him and we did feel that such a mission of unselfish love for the colored people would be crowned with abundant success. And it was a success in many respects. Wonderfully so. But alas! I fear it cost him his life. Once in speaking of his journey and his exposure to the change of climate he remarked, 'I do not know but it will be my death coming North at this time of year, but I felt it an imperative duty and if it should be, it will be all right. The Lord knows best.'

"The afternoon before Mr. Quarles was to start for home, he called here, and said Mr. Ogden wanted him to call before he left, and asked me if I thought he had better try and find Mrs. Leander Beal, to whom he had a letter of introduction. I told him 'yes, by all means' – and directed him how to find her. I then told him that he had better come back here, and take tea, and afterward he could call again upon Mrs. Loud, who said she would do something, and also upon Deacon Converse. He concluded to do so. He found Mrs. Beal – had a very interesting interview with her. She gave him 25 dollars for the Institution, I think it was, and wished him to call again and see her husband between nine and 10 o'clock that night. Her husband had gone to a party and would not be back before then. He came back to the house, and took tea with us, and seemed very much pleased with his calls."

He told Mrs. Ogden all about the way the Society had treated Miss Packard and Miss Giles. She said that she thought the Society ought not to be in existence, that they did not know

47

how to manage properly. Whereupon he showed her the paper containing the resolutions made by the Board the Saturday previous, and handed to him, *unsigned*; literally without beginning or ending – Commencing We (no names) have resolved that all moneys designated, shall be paid to Miss Packard and Miss Giles toward their support and that we will rescind the former votes taken etc. Those are not exactly the words, but to that effect. 'Now,' said Mr. Quarles, 'this involves my going again to Beacon Street and applying to Mrs. Pollard to sign it. It may be simply a copy, but still if it is, the names should be copied also I think.' Mrs. Ogden continues: "Well, after tea, the good man hurried away in order to be sure and find Deacon Converse in his home, and also Mrs. Loud. When I shook hands with him in parting that evening I said 'I did hope he would succeed in raising the two thousand needed,' and he replied 'I have not a doubt about it the way things are going – It will be a success.' Since that time we have not heard a word from him until your sad Postal came. How sudden his decease must have been. We are anxious to learn particulars. *Will you not write immediately on receiving this, all you know about it.* Rev. Mr. Ellis of the Tremont Temple, was very much interested in him."

"I feel so sorry for you, dear friends. How keen, how bitter have been the disappointments that have assailed you since you commenced your noble work. 'These are they that have come out of great tribulations.' Mr. Ogden says another way will open for you, he feels sure.

"Mr. Quarles said when here once, that he had no idea he had so many rough places to go over, in regard to prejudices concerning your work, but that they had all become smooth, and any animosity that formerly existed was all laid down. This he felt was his work, And he was happy in the thought. . . ."

As Dr. Quarles requested, Miss Packard had called to comfort Mrs. Quarles about not hearing from her husband. Then almost immediately the telegram came announcing his death. He was truly a shepherd of his people, and they mourned his

PLATE III

The Basement School

Mrs. Lucinda Hayes

Mrs. Emma S. DeLamotta
(with her husband)

PLATE IV

The Reverend Frank Quarles

His Great-Granddaughter
decorates bronze tablet
honoring Miss Packard
Founders Day, 1952

PLATE V

Miss Packard

The
Four
Who Taught
in the
Basement
School

Miss Giles

Miss Champney

Miss Grover

Ella Barksdale Brown
of the first Seminary Class, 1887

PLATE VI

Victoria Maddox Simmons, '88

Selena Sloan Butler, '88

Miss Packard and Miss Giles in the buggy behind "Billy Gray"

The Faculty of Spelman Seminary in 1890

passing. At his funeral, more than 2,000 persons assembled to pay their tribute; and there were 116 carriages in the procession to the cemetery.

His works followed him; his influence did not die. Like an ancient patriarch pleading for help for the women and girls of Georgia, using the words of Miss Packard, he had stood before the Board of the Woman's Society, and dying he left to them the school in Atlanta as a legacy.

The Basement School — 1881 and 1882

Miss Packard and Miss Giles literally allowed no grass to grow under their feet in their first days in Atlanta. The day after their arrival, the notices were sent to the colored pastors; two days later the meeting with them was held. The following five days were mostly occupied in calling on Negro families in the interest of the school-to-be. Their first professional act, however, was to visit the Atlanta Baptist Seminary, not only the offices but the classes of President Robert and Dr. Shaver. They visited the Storrs School, related to Atlanta University, and called on Mr. Sidney Root, a trustee of the Atlanta Baptist Seminary, who later gave them stalwart support. They received calls from three interested Negro women, Mrs. DeLamotta, Mrs. Sallie Shell and Mrs. Mary Williams. Mrs. DeLamotta became an enthusiastic supporter of the school, and also a student determined to learn in spite of the ridicule she received for the effort. She was encouraged to study by her husband, a minister, and later became what would now be called a field agent. She knew how to talk to her people, had both earnestness and a sense of humor, was direct and dynamic, and became a very effective promoter of the school.

Miss Packard and Miss Giles received a call also from Mr. Palmer of Stonington, Conn.; one from Rev. F. M. Daniel, pastor of the Central Baptist Church, who invited them to attend his church; and one from Dr. and Mrs. Shaver. These they "enjoyed very much indeed." They wrote a letter to Dr. Henry L. Morehouse of the ABHMS.

Twenty-one calls was the Saturday record, "canvassing several streets on which we had not been." In almost every house they found those who could not read. It was a first week more than full of activity and planning. Sunday, April 10, they "attended Rev. F. Quarles SS" and "were both of us called upon to make some remarks." They went across town later to hear Rev. F. M. Daniel preach; went to a meeting of the Cold Water Templars; and in the evening listened to Miss Frances Willard at the Methodist Church.

Monday, April 11, 1881, was the opening day of the basement school. They had 11 pupils "of all ages and attainments," and Miss Packard notes that they had a good time with them. Her diary further records on that day: "Rev. F. M. Daniel called and introduced us to Mr. Morris on Peters Street. Engaged two rooms there at ten dollars per month – $3 per month at vacation. Called on two families and secured scholars. Also on other girls who promised. May God help us."

They wrote that very day for their furniture to be sent.

On April 12, Miss Packard's diary item was: "Had 25 scholars today. We feel strange in this room – floor broken away and perfectly uneven – benches high and straight – glass broken from the windows. . . ." Miss Packard described the place as "dark and very damp, the floor laid right upon the bare earth . . . hard seats and no desks, in fact everything unfavorable for a school room."

Further quoting Miss Packard's diary:

April 13. Had one new scholar today. Received a call from Mrs. Ware.[1]

Rev. W. J. White[2] of Augusta called in our school today. He seriously objects to our having pupils less than 15 years of age. Don't know what arrangement we can make for those already commenced.

April 14. This is a very stormy cold day. We need a fire but

---

[1] Whose husband was Edmund Asa Ware, President of Atlanta University.

[2] William Jefferson White, leader of Negroes in Georgia, in education, religion & politics; publisher and editor of *The Georgia Baptist*, founder of Atlanta Baptist Seminary.

have no coal. The sexton said he would see to it but none was brought. 'Tis very slow indeed getting ready to do our work. Wish we could have a good room for teaching.

April 15. Have been obliged to send out for coal. We took cold yesterday staying in this cold room. Two of our young ladies are quite sick. Paid two dollars for 5 bushels of coal.

Long to go to a good lively prayer meeting tonight.

April 16. . . . Called on 15 today. Some were my scholars – others promised to come to school.

Wrote to Mrs. Cole today. Received a good long letter from dear Phoebe & Lucian. Also Rev. W. J. White wrote a note & sent his Atlanta, Ga.

April 17. Went to Rev. F. M. Daniel's S.S. Central Church this morning. Also remained to the sermon which was very good.

April 21. First Steps in English Literature. A. S. Barnes & Co., Chicago.

They sent away all the children under 15 years of age on the following Friday, by the advice of the committee of Negro ministers. They also attended a prayer meeting at a Negro church. On April 25 Miss Giles wrote "We are very happy in our work." On April 30, their furniture came and they spent the day unpacking.

On Sunday, May first, they went to church and also "called on the sick." The next day Miss Packard speaks of having "a good many students" and adds "We find them anxious to learn – very ready to do as we want them to." May fifth, they were both "very tired" by night. The next day, they went to Rev. Mr. Tilman's church and "had a good meeting." By May tenth the number of pupils was 51. They went every Friday to hold a meeting at Mt. Pleasant, on Mondays to Macedonia, and on Saturdays, they had a meeting for children at Friendship Church. One week in May Miss Packard wrote: "Held our regular meeting at Mt. Pleasant. O it was so hot that we did feel as though we could hardly get there but we did and had a good time. . . ."

On the last day of May, the Commencement exercises of

the Atlanta Baptist Seminary were held in Friendship Church, and on June 16, Atlanta University exercises were held in the same place; so the school was closed on those days. Money was scarce; when $20.00 came from Everett, it was paid at once to Mrs. Cheshire for board. They moved to 231 Mitchell Street on June 18, "and Mr. Price pays for doorbell & putting it on." The cottage was shared with Miss Kimball, a Methodist home missionary from Illinois. Miss Giles' comment the day they moved – "So glad to have a home of our own."

Sunday, June 19, was "very warm indeed, even oppressive" but it did not deter them from going to Macedonia to S.S.; then to downtown church.

On June 20, the warmest day of the season, an Educational Society was organized to raise money for a building for the girls and women. Rev. William Jefferson White, Corresponding Secretary of the Negro State Baptist Convention, with two other ministers, had come into the school about three weeks before its close, and proposed this Society, each member to pay 5¢ a month toward a building. All the pupils were appointed a committee of the whole to solicit members. By September 7, they had raised $25.00 which was paid to Rev. Mr. White as Convention Treasurer. This marks the first money-raising by the students for the school.

The two women were "received into the Central Baptist Church on Sunday, June 26, and had 'a cordial reception.' " On the following Sunday, Miss Packard walked to the Macedonia church to teach a class but she "took cars to return home."

School was closed on July 15. It had lasted three months. The enrollment had steadily increased from *11* the first day to *80*. A number of students had in this period decided to accept Jesus as the guide of their lives; this made their teachers feel that God had indeed given the work His seal of approval.

After the school closed, Miss Packard and Miss Giles paused not at all in the pursuit of their ends. They went to the Macedonia church on Sunday, July 17; they promised to go to

Antioch church the following Sabbath. "So our work is growing on our hands."

On Monday, they met 53 women from various churches to organize a Mission Band; every one of them "signed the temperance pledge and gave their names for Missionary work," though to sign the pledge cost many of them a great struggle. One said: "It does not seem as though I could give up tobacco but the Lord helping me I *will*." The number of Mission Board members soon increased to over 100.

Tuesday morning they met with ten colored pastors at church. One said: "I have no Sabbath School; won't you come over and help me organize one." Another said: "You have been beyond us and this side of us, and we are poorer than all; Won't you come and help us?"

The following Monday, they met with the women again, who reported over 60 new scholars brought into the various Sunday Schools – the result of only one week's work. Miss Packard and Miss Giles met the women weekly and gave them instruction. During the summer, the attendance in Sunday Schools increased by over 450.

More appointments were requested than they could fill. Weekly sewing classes for the children were continued through the summer. These had been started when the younger children had to be turned away from the school, and they were kept up until October.

Miss Packard and Miss Giles kept the members of the Board of the WABHMS well informed of the condition and progress of the school, amazingly so in those days before typewriters and carbon copies were in use, for they kept copies of their letters to the two Societies and many others. For example, Mrs. Pollard, the treasurer, acknowledged an early report from Miss Packard; said the ministers' meeting was just the right thing; and quoted Mrs. Nickerson, the president of the WABHMS, as saying: "By all means, let us call them 'Teachers,' as their work is teaching in homes or a schoolroom. We are believing more and more in teaching." Yet in spite of their numerous letters and reports, the Circular announcing the school brought a summons from Mrs. Hesseltine, the Corresponding Secretary, that they return North and explain matters at a meeting of the Board on August first at 11:00 a.m. Apparently, a "school" with a "course of study" was too much.

Miss Packard had in June and again in July, outlined in her letters to the Society, the work they planned to do in the summer, and the request that they return North was most disturbing. Another long letter was written and sent to the Board to be read at their meeting. "So afraid" said Miss Packard's diary, "it would not reach them that we took it to the car at 6:30 o'clock." It was then that Father Quarles also wrote a letter to the Boston office.

The two women had been in Atlanta only four short months, not long enough to become fully acquainted with the field or to have the lessons they taught become a habit with those they strove to serve. They felt they *had* to remain and they believed that if the women in Boston could see for themselves the response of the people, they would wish them to stay. The trouble seems to have been indeed "a tempest in a teapot." Yet it caused much anxiety to the women and their sponsors in Atlanta. As Miss Packard saw it, "the work of the summer was like seed sowing for the School in the autumn. The teachers became better acquainted with the people and the people with the school." They decided that it would be desertion of duty to leave, even if staying called for their resignations as commissioned teachers of the WABHMS. "In view of all these things," they wrote, "we feel it would be best to sunder our connection with you as your appointed teachers. . . ."

Miss Packard and Miss Giles sent their resignations on August sixth; they were received by Mrs. Hesseltine but did not reach the other Board members; at a Board meeting on Martha's Vineyard it was voted that if the ABHMS would appoint them, the WABHMS would pay their salaries; Miss Packard and Miss Giles accepted the proposals gladly. The Woman's Board meanwhile backtracked and voted to accept the resignations, after Miss Packard and Miss Giles had recalled them. The Board even rescinded the Martha's Vineyard actions, and declared void the offer to pay their salaries. Dr. Morehouse tried to help; but the ABHMS had a $40,000 debt and could not be responsible for the salaries.

The annual report of the WABHMS had ignored Miss Packard and Miss Giles entirely; their names, the school, the work done, had no mention; nothing from their letters had been published to create interest and bring in money for their support. Some of the Boston women, however, were strongly on their side. Mrs. C. A. Ogden wrote encouraging words; hoped they might work under the jurisdiction of the general Home Mission Society; added, "It is what I have longed for, that you should not be under the *control of any woman's Board.* . . ."

In spite of all the added anxiety and the extra labor involved, Miss Packard and Miss Giles carried on through the summer. Ella Cole of Southbridge sent $20, a great help, since their salaries had been suspended. Their conviction never wavered. They wrote: "We do not feel this is *our* work; it is *God's work.*" One recalls Mary Lyon at Mount Holyoke, who said, "You must not call this Miss Lyon's School. . . . I would have you ever remember that you are studying in an institution built by the hand of the Lord"; and President Finley at Oberlin, who told the graduating students that they were being "educated in God's college."

The two women in Atlanta opened the school in October 1881 as scheduled, again in the dark damp basement. In spite of ups and downs concerning support from the North, financial and otherwise, the work itself prospered. On October 3, opening day, 65 pupils had reported; by October 17, the number had grown to 92. On that day a gifted German teacher of music, Professor E. H. Kruger, began to give vocal lessons. He must have helped relieve the constant burden in more ways than one. A lift of spirit obviously was needed.

One day the preceding week Miss Packard's diary recorded only, "Tired tired tired tired tired tired." On October 17 a letter from Dr. Morehouse brought sore disappointment, stating that the New York Board could not undertake their support. Still the work of the days went on. Miss Giles played the organ at the Central Baptist Church for the first time on Sunday. Miss Packard had earlier joined the Sunday School, and taken a class of "lads – good scholars." Both actions were taken in the hope of cultivating more interest among white church people in the schools for Negroes.

It called for superhuman qualities to keep the school going in the basement. As Miss Packard described it: "The boards of the floor were laid upon the bare earth, and were loose, decaying, in many places broken away and entirely wanting. When the windows were open to let in the air, being on the level with the street, clouds of sandy dust of which the streets seem composed, poured in. In winter during the severe rains, the water dripping down the walls would cause the earth under the floor to become muddy. The health and lives of teachers and pupils were daily endangered, but wonderfully preserved."

A student of the earliest days and a graduate in 1888, Rosella B. Humphreys, waxed more eloquent:

When it rained, we had water about on the floor, in which our teachers must stand in order to help our hungry, starving souls; then it would turn so dark, at times, that we had much trouble in our endeavors to see. We were very sorry to have those to whom our hearts were so closely tied stand on such, not damp, but wet floors; so some of the wise heads brought pieces of carpets, and others took corn sacks and made rugs for them to stand on. Then the stove would lose a part of its pipe, and the smoke would pour forth, and our next job would be to mend that good old companion. . . .

How the teachers divided the space can be understood better from the remarks made by Miss Grover at the tenth anniversary: "At the desk was Miss Packard with her advanced classes of Fourth Reader, Fractions, and Green's Grammar." The pupils recited to be heard and often in concert.

"At her right, near the window, Miss Giles' class was seated on three sides of a hollow square formed of the movable benches. The water from the muddy street oozing through the wall glistened in the uncertain light. . . .

"In the opposite corner was another class arranged in the same form, a hollow square [Miss Grover's class]. Here the words – 'loud! LOUDER!!' were spoken, since the only hope at times of hearing a recitation was by excelling in tone the other classes." Having enforced silence by surprise and drowning out the other groups, recitations were quietly resumed until again the stratagem had to be repeated.

"In the coal-room, Miss Champney held gentle sway with open door to let in light and heat" – until the noise of the other classes led to closing it.

The women who had been students in the Basement School always recalled their time there with pride and affection. Those who continued their studies to complete the Seminary course valued their earliest acquaintance with the Founders. Those who had not been able to continue their studies until they could become "graduates" were equally loyal; some of the latter organized a Packard-Giles Club which continued to have meetings as late as 1928. At anniversaries, they liked to tell new generations of students how "Miss Giles would break up a lot of little sticks and lay them across the seams of the planks, where there were planks, and make us count them, and take up one, and so we learned to add and subtract."

Miss Packard and Miss Giles each taught 10 or 11 classes daily, for five and a half days each week. In addition, each one conducted four prayer meetings; four Bible readings; taught two Bible classes a week; made 35 to 45 religious visits; and distributed in October about 200 Bibles and tracts. A typical monthly report. How would today's accrediting agencies evaluate a load like that!

Nor were their calls on students monotonous routine. For example, consider this day in November, 1882:

The two women went out immediately after school to make

calls. First they visited one of the older "scholars" who was sick – a widow who took in washing. On the street, they met two women who asked, "Are you looking for a corpse?" and pointing to a house, said, "It is in there." They went in. There was but one room – in the center of it lay the body of a young man. The coffin was pine, just stained a little on the outside, unpainted on the inside, with no lining. Four or five women were sitting in one corner around the smoking embers of a fire. Two beds were in the opposite corner; on one of them lay a little girl, Janie, who had sometimes done errands for the teachers from the North and who was now sick with consumption. "It was a sad sight."

What courage and sense of mission were required, girded by "faith, hope, and love" in fullest measure, to sustain these women. Reared in comfortable though modest homes, they had studied in New England academies like New Salem and Charlestown, had lived and taught in impressive buildings like those of Suffield and Oread, and were now committed to work in the Negro section of Atlanta, Georgia, in the '80's, visiting homes most of which had no comforts or conveniences, and were crowded, ill-kept, disorderly, located on unpaved streets where deep ruts in the red clay of Georgia, slippery or dry according to the season, made the going slow, disagreeable, and dangerous for man or beast. As late as 1930 there were many houses, really just shacks across the street from the Spelman campus, which had neither running water nor electric lights and no sanitary conveniences (they used pit privies) – and this within five minutes of the Union Station and 10 minutes of the City Hall!

Not every school day was inspiring, although no discouraged note was ever sounded. This entry in October came the closest to one: "Hard, hard day, this – no lessons. May it be otherwise hereafter. A great deal of patience it needs to teach these dear girls and women." But by another month, the diary ran: "This has been a good day. Classes have gone off well. O teach me how to teach, dear Lord."

Thanksgiving Day came while Dr. Quarles was in Boston. It passed quietly in Atlanta with Miss Packard and Miss Giles. A call from Mrs. DeLamotta gave them pleasure; as did that of two others, Mrs. Hayes and Mrs. Palmer, each bringing a jar of peaches.

December came and brought the death of Father Quarles. Dark then were the days for the school. Miss Packard called them the darkest in its history – without the leadership of the "wise counselor and firm friend." Yet his influence did not die. After his funeral, 10 of the colored ministers came to the school in person and pledged their cooperation. The students, too, responded with diligence, and the teachers were cheered by their faithful attendance even on stormy days.

In addition to the work in the classroom, the principals visited sick students; entertained visitors, some from the North, including Col. and Mrs. Banes[1] of Philadelphia; with the pupils they attended the Cotton States Exposition. They received a "barrel filled with good things" from their friends, the Coles, in Southbridge three days before Christmas. School was closed at noon on December 23. The departing year had been filled with trials and sorrows and difficulties; it had also seen beginnings of great promise.

[1] *Charles H. Banes* of Philadelphia, a lieutenant-colonel of the Civil War. He became a manufacturer after the war; and President of the Market Street National Bank. He served in the Select Council of Philadelphia when manual training was introduced as part of the public school course. He was a trustee of Drexel Institute; and President of the Franklin Institute; also director-general of the International Electrical Exhibition held in Philadelphia.

CHAPTER V

A YEAR OF MIRACLES
1882

A YEAR when miracles came to pass!

Right at the beginning, Col. Banes proved to be a strong friend. It must have cheered the heart when Miss Packard received a letter from him which ran: ". . . I did not intend the check to be a portion of the amount pledged but as a contribution toward the expenses of you and Miss Giles and not to be reported. The subscription I pledged to the Boston ladies I have paid to Mrs. Pollard. . . . I have no doubt about the New York Board making the appointment. Dr. Morehouse promised it. Let me know if you do not hear soon and I will 'agitate' the matter."

On January 9, Miss Packard listed five causes for thankfulness: "My lameness better; note from Ella [Cole] containing two dollars; letter . . . bearing the good news of reappointments; letter from Mrs. Durant repeating the same facts regarding the action of the WABHMS Board; dear Mrs. Palmer brought in her offering of nice preserves." A few days later, Mrs. Pollard, Treasurer of the WABHMS, sent us "a delightful letter stating a unanimous vote by a full Board was taken, reinstating us in their support. . . ."

Their Reappointment by
the WABHMS

A glad greeting from Dr. Morehouse came also, about their reappointment by the Woman's Board in Boston, and giving assurance of their appointment and commissions from the ABHMS Board of New York. In the same mail was a postal from Ella Cole and a letter enclosing a P.O. money order for $45. from Ella's brother Alfred who had recently visited the school and its principals. "One of my happiest days. Surely my cup runneth over," wrote Miss Packard.

Regarding their reinstatement, there was more involved than meets the eye through the diaries. Even parts of the official Minutes of the WABHMS have been expunged.

A special Board meeting was held on November 26, 1881, to hear a statement by the Rev. Mr. Quarles. Dr. Mason of the ABHMS also was present. Mr. Quarles "spoke with much feeling of the importance of the girls' school" . . . and "begged the Board to send help by re-appointing the teachers." Dr. Mason expressed his full approval of these views. The Board passed a resolution offered by Mrs. G. S. Harwood of Newton and voted to adjourn. The regular meeting was held on December 5. After other business, it was voted "to take up the resolution passed at the last session of the Board at the next meeting" which was January 5.

At the January regular meeting, Mrs. Nickerson was welcomed back in the chair after a long journey and absence. She read the resolution which waited the action of the Board relating to the Misses Packard and Giles and asked Dr. Mason (present by invitation) for his counsel. He spoke . . . and decidedly and fully approved the re-appointment. After due consultation it was voted to reconsider the resolution. Remarks followed, and a letter from Miss Packard and Miss Giles was read, after which it was unanimously

Voted, that Miss Packard and Miss Giles be re-appointed teachers in the school for women and girls in Atlanta, Georgia with salary of 500 dollars each, to commence December 1, 1881.

Thereafter, be it said, the full and cordial and hard-working support of the Society was given to Miss Packard and Miss Giles and to the growing school. In fact, the school was for years the recipient of about one-third of all the funds the Society raised.

The number of students continued to grow. Barrels of clothing came from various churches in the North. The efforts to raise money for a building continued. Mrs. Cole sent $50. "for the girls' building." More and more visitors came to see the school. On the whole, the classes went well, yet there were trials. "An unusually hard day – L. Crawford was very naughty but must be conquered" was immediately followed by "Had a good time all day – scholars did well," and the day after "a smoky house prevented our teaching today – too bad – when shall we have things better for our dear, dear pupils." They had devotions every morning. When, as the day wore on, the smoke from leaks in the stovepipe became too thick, it was their custom to have Bible verses, prayer, singing. An Estey organ was rented for $2.50 per month.

New Teachers

In February a letter was sent to the WABHMS stating that, with 150 pupils enrolled and only two teachers, the doors must be closed to further admissions. The Board in Boston responded by transferring Miss Sarah H. Champney[1] from a mission in Nashville. She had previously worked with the freedmen of the Indian Territory; then in Mississippi, Texas, and Tennessee. She arrived in Atlanta on April 6, 1882, and the coal room became her classroom.

Fortunately, a fourth teacher arrived in December, 1882, Miss Caroline M. Grover. Miss Packard had talked with her during the summer and wrote in September to ask her to come. She hesitated to accept, but did arrive on December tenth. And she remained 37 years. She and her pupils for the first weeks had to use space in one corner of Friendship basement.

Even before Miss Champney came, Miss Packard and Miss Giles extended their program by opening a Sunday afternoon Sabbath School for those who could not attend on Sunday morning. Seventy-two were present at the first meeting; over 200 on March 5. The meetings held each Friday evening for Bible study, especially for Sabbath School teachers, continued to prosper. On February 17, 100 or more came; on March 17,

[1] She died on November 22, 1886. Her varied experience, good sense, and devotion to the work made her a valued counselor. "Died in her duty" was graven on her casket. She left to Spelman Seminary a legacy of $500.

was the largest meeting to date – "300 present or more – God help us!"

Meantime Pastor Daniel of the white Baptist Church continued to be friendly. He brought seven deacons and laymen to call on February 6. Miss Packard wrote: "We had a very delightful time. All were really more interested in our work than we had any idea of."

Through the kind offices of Sidney Root, both women attended a Sunday School State Convention in Savannah late in May; Miss Packard "addressed the Sunday meeting on our work"; and as a result received a donation toward the girls' building of $250.00. Mr. Root had by this time been entirely won over. A letter from him published in the *Home Mission Monthly* (July 1895) tells the story:

"It was late in the spring of 1881 that I was sitting in my office, busy with plans to promote the success of our great International Cotton Exposition – the first of those famous displays which have done so much for the South – when two very polite ladies walked in and handed me some most unexceptionable introductory letters, saying they were about to establish a school of high order for colored girls and women in Atlanta! Now the schools already had by no means given satisfaction to our somewhat excited people, and I fear I told these noble women (who were no other than Miss Packard and Miss Giles) rather roughly that I could not help them, that I was opposed to the kind of education they were giving colored girls, which appeared to be chiefly classical.

"Well, the school began with eleven students in a low, dark basement of Friendship Church, which was only half-floored. . . . I carefully questioned the students as to their studies and method of teaching, and soon became satisfied with the school, and pledged it my hearty support. . . ."

The 'scholars' in day school were "wide awake and very energetic." At their public oral examinations in May, outsiders were present, and Miss Packard was "delighted that my dear girls and women do so well." On May 31, a grand good concert in

Friendship Church was given by both schools, the men's and the women's. The students gave $11.25 to the new building.

Miss Packard outlines in her diary courses of study; incentives to learn; to create the love for reading history; advises "examinations by topics – not many dates – Framework of facts." Altogether the school year ended with spirits high, but the most momentous event of 1882 was still to come.

George Olcott King, whom we met with his wife, Eliza Adams King, at the CLI of Suffield, was pastor of the Wilson Avenue Baptist Church of Cleveland in the '80's. He and his wife from their schooldays were lifelong friends of their former teachers.

Mr. John D. Rockefeller

Now Rev. Mr. King knew Mr. John D. Rockefeller through association with him in church and in Sunday School activities. Mr. King invited Miss Packard and Miss Giles to make their trip North after school closed by way of Cleveland. He promised them that if they would speak about their school in his church he would invite Mr. Rockefeller to hear them. This plan was carried out.

In her 1895 report, Miss Giles modestly and briefly writes that at the invitation of Rev. and Mrs. G. O. King, she and Miss Packard "providentially went to Cleveland, Ohio, and were asked to speak. . . . It was at that meeting that Mr. John D. Rockefeller first became interested in the school. After having emptied his pockets when the box was passed, he asked them the characteristic question, 'Are you going to stick?' and added, 'If so, I will do more for you.' The history of Spelman proves how faithfully he has kept his promise." The collection that day was $90.72. In addition, Mr. Rockefeller pledged $250.00 for the building fund.

Mr. Rockefeller's gift that eventful day in Cleveland was his first gift to Negro education.

Gifts made by him personally, gifts made through the General Education Board, and later gifts made by his son, John D. Rockefeller, Jr., have totaled many millions of dollars for the development of schools, colleges, and universities for Negro students.

The significance to Spelman College of these five days Miss Packard and Miss Giles spent in Cleveland compels our interest in their diary comments.

June 16. (SBP) Arrived at our dear Mrs. King's about 4:30. . . . Met with a warm reception – Mr. & Mrs. Adams, Mr. & Mrs. King.

(HEG) Arrived in Cleveland about four o'clock – two tired children. Dear Lizzie's pleasant home seemed beautiful and restful to us, very.

June 17. (SBP) Mrs. Allen and Mrs. A. Elgersperger came and dined with Mrs. King today. Hattie went to one Mission and I to another.

(HEG) Met several friends, among them Mrs. Adams, President of the Women's Home Miss. Association. Met Missionary Board of Cheerful Gleaners and talked to them of our work. Faithful workers are Mr. and Mrs King.

June 18. (Sunday)
(SBP) Mr. King's hour for sermon was suspended and my humble self invited to speak of our Atlanta work. Held audience until 9:30 o'clock. Collection $90.72. Building Fund $250 by John D. Rockefeller.

(HEG) . . . Attended S. School and took a class of little girls. S. spoke in the (evening).

June 19. (SBP) This morning Mr. King took us out to view the beauties of the Grand Old Convention City. Visited Euclid Avenue. . . . at 4:45 Mr. Rockefeller and family came with three carriages and took us all to his beautiful Forest Hills residence. . . .

Miss Packard and Miss Giles left Cleveland early on June 21 for Boston. They went to New York June 24 for a conference with Dr. Morehouse at the Mission Society rooms, and then to the Coles in Southbridge. Just imagine their enjoyment of a few quiet days in a home, with old friends, after their 15 months' sojourn in rented rooms bordering a slum area in southwest Atlanta – facing every day the never-ceasing urgent needs of their work.

After a Board meeting in Boston on July 6, they took a Fall River boat to New York, then another boat up the Hudson River, and spent a few days in the Catskills. Miss Packard especially loved the mountains, and writes enthusiastically of a mountain climb where they lost the trail but reached the top "after four hours jumping over rocks and springs." Another day they took a trail over the West Mountain, past waterfalls, around a lake and home again.

With only a fortnight to catch their breath, they were back at the speaking and money-raising job in churches around Boston. In fact, wherever they went, they told of the work under way, its promise, and the money required to go ahead with it.

At Martha's Vineyard, they attended lectures on history and visited classes in zoology and botany. Hither and yon, they spoke of the imperative need for a better place to teach than the damp basement room. They made individual calls. They were glad to tell of their work – spoke of "very pleasant" meetings. They enjoyed "such delightful air and sunshine" when a friend took them to ride even if the objective was to solicit funds. The collections were not large; yet every dollar counted.

They visited Medford, of course, and had good fellowship with the group that had given them funds and courage to go ahead. Then on September 12, 1882, a rainy morning, they left Boston by the Stonington line on the first lap of their return to Atlanta. Wednesday morning in New York they saw Col. and Mrs. Banes, Dr. Morehouse and Dr. Gregory; bought a *Universal Encyclopedia*; and had a good visit from James E. Hills, one of those early students who followed them from Orange to Fitchburg to Suffield, and now was at work in New York. He came to the Pennsylvania Station and remained with them until their train left that evening.

A cyclone had injured the corn all the way from Greensboro to near Atlanta, and three weeks of rain in August had ruined the cotton crop. Yet at the opening day, even again in the dark, damp basement, there were causes for thanksgiving – in fact, 102 of them – the 'scholars.' The second day nine more, and the third three more. "Marvelous" – "Wonderful," they wrote.

They spoke at Friendship Church the first Sunday after their return; met the Mission Band the next day – some had met every week during the summer and had prepared seven quilts for "the new building"; held a Bible reading in the Basement the second Sunday. At the morning service in Friendship Church, President Robert of the Atlanta Baptist Seminary had preached, and a collection was taken for the 'girls' building.' Miss Champney returned. Teachers' meeting was held.

The number of students at the Atlanta Baptist Seminary by October 6 was 20, whereas at the girls' school the first week closed with 120. By the end of the year the number in the Basement School was 201; at the men's Seminary, 122. The Female Seminary throughout its early years had many more students than the Atlanta Baptist Seminary for men, which then was mainly to train ministers. The Atlanta Baptist Seminary catalogue of April, 1883, gave the total number of students in both schools as 425, of which number 303 were at Spelman.

The classes became so large that the teachers found it impossible "to do justice to them." Miss Giles had a grammar class of 45; and classes in Geography and Arithmetic nearly as large. The enrollment in December, 1882, was 220.

The poverty of the people was distressing. Clothes sent by Northern church people were a big help. *Exempli gratia*: the organist at Mr. Jones' church in Summer Hill, who wore on cold winter days a very thin pair of linen pants mended with coarse white thread in long stitches and a coat "all tatters," was supplied with coat and trousers. One pupil, not atypical, a half-orphan, the daughter of a widow, had no underclothes, only a coarse black skirt and a calico waist for outside garments. Miss Giles wrote on December 16: "Have spent most of the afternoon distributing clothes, as I have most of the afternoons recently."

On Sundays, Miss Packard and Miss Giles gave help to the Negro churches, especially the Sunday Schools in the poorer churches. Most Negro churches which requested help in Bible classes and Sunday Schools were primitive. The church at Summer Hill, for example, met in an unfinished building which had been made larger by raising the ceiling four feet and building on at one end – a dark place with laths and boards scattered around, some piled up at the back. Yet these teachers promised the pastor that one of them would go over (across town) every Sabbath for a while to help him. It was at this Sunday School that one of the men asked Miss Packard, who was talking about faith, "Did the Bible say you must not pin your faith on the coat-tail of any man?"

The noisy baptisms, with people shouting at the top of their voices, and throwing their arms about, distressed the New England women. Such services might start more reverently. At one such, "they marched two by two to the water singing all the way from the church. The minister had on a white robe, the candidates dressed in white." But the minister talked a long time and the people became overdemonstrative.

A few weeks later, Nora Gordon (of whom we shall hear later), was baptized at Friendship Church. She "was very quiet in the water and did not shout, for which we were very thankful."

Yet there was depth of sincerity too. One pupil said "I am almost willing God's will should be done, but I want my own will a little."

All these months, the struggle to get a new building for the school was a nagging ever-present concern. Dr. J. M. Gregory, superintendent of the Southern schools of the ABHMS, came late in November to look into the problem. One lot considered was too far away, and was given up. The old barracks property, used by the United States army before facilities were installed at the present Fort McPherson, came to be thought of as *the* place; negotiations for its purchase were begun by the ABHMS.

The colored ministers' convention promised to give $5,000. It required "sacrificial giving" for the ministers and churches to raise that amount. One minister, who was made happy to the point of tears by the gift of a suit for himself from the barrel, a dress with a scarf for his wife, and some papers to read, told Miss Packard that his receipts from church collections had been: December \$1.15; January \$1.35; February \$2.00.

Good news arrived at the turn of the year. A penny postal card, addressed "Miss S. B. Packard, Atlanta, Ga." came from the American Baptist Home Mission Rooms, Temple Court, New York, dated December 30, 1882. The New Year was to provide the better place to teach that Miss Packard had longed for.

CHAPTER VI

THE SCHOOL MOVES TO THE
ARMY BARRACKS

"Dear Madam,

The property is purchased, and preparations will at once be begun to put the buildings in order for occupancy. Now, you can ask friends & S. Schools to help furnish rooms, &c &c –

Happy New Year to you all –

Yours,

H. L. Morehouse"

SO read the postcard. "The property" consisted of nine acres of land and five frame buildings, – four barracks or "quarters" of the Federal occupation troops and the camp hospital; purchase price $17,500. The down payment had been made by the ABHMS from the proceeds of the sale of part of the Atlanta Baptist Seminary property near the railroad; a mortgage was given for the balance.

The Woman's American Baptist Home Mission Society had from its beginning been an arm of the American Baptist Home Mission Society. The general Society was vitally concerned in the development of Miss Packard's and Miss Giles' work. Dr. Henry L. Morehouse, the Field Secretary of the Society, held the view, however, that the education of the girls should be carried on as one part of the Atlanta Baptist Seminary.

When the nine acres of land and five frame buildings formerly used as the barracks, or more correctly "quarters" for officers of the Union Army, were purchased by the ABHMS, it was in his mind that the two institutions would use and develop the same physical plant. He recognized, however, that the need of the women was desperate. The arrival of the new teacher, Miss Grover, was a boon; but it meant that three teachers held recitations in the main room of the original basement; and that

70

Miss Champney's class still met in the coal room. The exigence of the students, 200 of them, could not be shoved aside; and the well-being of the four teachers claimed his concern.

Rejoicing from the scholars greeted the word from Dr. Morehouse the day after New Year's, 1883, that the school might move to the barracks. The teachers redoubled their energies, as they gave attention not only to the students, but also to the matter of stoves, carpets, beds and mattresses, furniture, kitchen equipment, classrooms. Hard rains had made the new site very muddy, but to them "the place looked cheerful notwithstanding the rain."

The school in the basement was closed from Wednesday, January 31, 1883, to the following Monday. The pupils aided Miss Packard and Miss Giles to pack up their personal belongings and few pieces of furniture, and made up committees to clean the new buildings. On February 2 everything was moved "from the little cottage where we have spent so many happy hours as well as sad and anxious ones. The carpets were placed in our new home, and we found a resting place. 'Tis homesick work moving, especially when we are obliged to go into homes more uncleanly than those we left." So wrote Miss Giles on February 2. And on February 11: "Have been all the week to school. We have found it a long-long walk with all our other work. Have been obliged to open the boarding department without anything to commence with. One box of sheets and pillow cases came from Vermont, one box of comforters from Akron, Ohio, when we were in greatest need."

They had their opening exercises on February 16 in the chapel – a room in the building that had been the hospital of the army post. Mr. Sidney Root presided. Remarks were made by Dr. Gustavus J. Orr, Georgia State School Commissioner, Reverend Messrs. Gwinn and McDonald, and President Robert of Atlanta Baptist Seminary. An occasion of thankfulness it was. "Our school never appeared better or sang more sweetly."

The last day of February found them with thirty boarders. Two barrels containing comforters and sheets miraculously arrived after the last comforter had been put on the bed of a new-comer and provided, in the nick of time, for the next arrival. The month was physically exhausting, as they had to provide meals as well as beds for the boarding students and themselves, in addition to teaching all day and holding evening Bible classes. Fortunately for them all, Mrs. C. P. Griswold arrived from Bangor, Maine, early in March to be their Matron. Her arrival enabled them to find time to write their thank-you letters to the churches and individuals whose help had met their direst needs.

The barracks buildings required repairs: partitions removed; floors tightened; closets for dishes and pantry provided; a central study hall in each dormitory which could be heated by one stove and so save expense; also a wardrobe for each teacher's room. Stationary or portable vestibules over the front and rear entrances were recommended. A pit in the backyard for storing buttermilk was authorized. Some of these changes were made in 1883; others had to wait.

A "Model School" to train student-teachers was started at once under the supervision of Miss Grover. Within a month 24 children under 15 years of age were enrolled; a school room was fitted with intermediate desks; other equipment, including blackboards, was improvised. Miss Packard wrote: "We thought our hands were full when we were teaching in the basement, but the work there was light compared to this." They now had time for no outside work except in Sunday Schools; with 250-odd pupils, "all our strength should be given to school duties." Then there was the care of the girls out of class-time. The housework was divided among them, but it had to be supervised. Miss Packard did all the marketing and purchasing, and in addition had care of the accounting and of the reports to be sent to New York. She and Miss Giles realized that the success of the school or at least of the boarding department depended on the management the first spring. "We do care what reputation we get and the first few weeks always determine it," she wrote Mrs. Pollard; and to Dr. Morehouse: "Every week lectures are given to the entire school in Physiology and Hygiene."

When groceries such as flour, sugar, and other supplies were ordered from the Atlanta merchants in those early years, white deliverymen refused to deliver them to the buildings and threw them over the fence whence teachers or students had to lug them to the kitchen.[1] Nevertheless, by April 11, 1883, the year's enrollment was 293, with over 30 students boarding on campus – if the muddy ground could be so-called; an Industrial Department had been started; and the student-teachers were teaching under supervision of a teacher in the Model School.

School work went forward in spite of obstacles. There were touching experiences, as of the student who walked through the mud six miles to and from school; and amusing incidents as when Miss Giles in her Geography class asked what the word "aqueduct" meant and the answer came: "the lively actions of the ducks in the water." Mrs. Nickerson wrote Miss Packard how gratified she and Mrs. Pollard were with their first visit, expressed concern over the unpainted barrack in which the Founders lived, and closed with "But those interesting girls, that was the crowning thing."

The school year ended, after examinations, on May 28. A concert given at Friendship Church on May 29 yielded over $100.00. The first day of June Miss Packard, Miss Giles, Miss Grover, and Mrs. Griswold started North. Miss Champney remained in Atlanta "to hold the bag." But even vacation was not to be a relaxation from work for Miss Packard and Miss Giles, nor for the women in the WABHMS, as the mortgage on the Barracks property was due in December.

Only those who have struggled to meet a deadline in raising funds for schools or social agencies can properly sympathize with the money-raising agonies of these months. Besides the mortgage, money was needed to furnish the rooms at the barracks; classrooms; bedrooms for boarding students; kitchen, – Miss Packard wrote, "*Everything* had to be purchased at the

[1] From Mrs. Cora Hardy Adams, a member of the Spelman staff, 1905-1915, 1919-1920, 1944-1948.

commencement for we had not a stone *dish* or anything." Money had to be raised also to pay the teachers. The Boston women strove valiantly, and so did Miss Packard and Miss Giles.

The teachers returned from New England in mid-September. School opened October first. Apparently nothing was in readiness except the pupils. The repairs were not finished; the buildings were in confusion. Over 300 pupils had reported in the first 10 days; by Christmas there were over 400, with over 90 boarders.

The reports from older pupils who had gone to country places to teach were heartening. One went to a place 250 miles from Atlanta where she had never been before. She found that the children did not know how to count five. She gathered up stones and taught them to count 100. She made a blackboard from a "goods box" and soot from the chimney, which she set with vinegar. That did not work well, and she tried shoe blacking. She taught the children to make the letters of the alphabet as she had seen Miss Grover teach the children in the Model School. They rang a tin pan for a bell. "I tried to be a light to them, and prayed the Lord would [help me]."

Other students related their summer experiences. These, and the zeal of the pupils in class, gave renewed life to the school.

The WABHMS voted to raise the salaries of Miss Packard and Miss Giles to $600; the other teachers to $400. The Slater Fund, through its General Agent, Dr. Atticus G. Haygood, promised to give $2,000 toward the salaries of Miss Packard, Miss Giles, and the other teachers, but the Slater money could not be used to pay for the property.

There was $11,500 to be raised to finish payment of the mortgage. Gifts from two women – one of $250, the other of $100 – were encouraging, as was $100 from Deacon Converse of Boston. Most gifts from churches were of smaller sums. Some money came to furnish rooms. Mr. Milner, a manufacturer of painted chamber furniture of Boston, wrote that following a suggestion in his Sunday School which resulted in a collection of $30 to furnish one room, the school voted to name the room for him; that "the furnishing has cost a little more but as they were so kind to name it after me, thought I would have a good room." The students through their Educational Society contributed $75. A Massachusetts friend gave $100 toward a bell, but only if the school was to be a girls' school. Chester W. Kingsley, a Boston banker, who had visited the school during the summer, and who wrote Miss Packard and Miss Giles, "I became interested in your work, and particularly with the zeal and devotion with which you advanced your views," subscribed $500 toward the property purchase, "upon the same terms of your friend in Cleveland."

The school itself prospered. There were 450 students registered in January 1884, and over 100 boarders; by April the number of boarders was 120. Miss Giles wrote in her diary on March 25:

These pupils are as clay in the hands of the potter. They strive to live as they see us live. Our responsibility is tremendous. Nothing but the best teachers with the best methods can do justice to the work. The hope of the race lies in their getting not knowledge alone, but with it a true appreciation of the value of labor and its necessity together with right ideas of Christian living.

New friends were made, especially among the visitors from the North. Notable among them were:

Dr. Robert H. Cole, founder of the American Optical Company, and his family, whose home in Southbridge, Massachusetts, became a home to Miss Packard and Miss Giles on their trips North until they came to have one of their own.

Deacon Mial Davis, a lumber merchant, and his wife, from Fitchburg, Massachusetts, who first visited the school in February, 1884. They gave valiant help for the rest of their lives.

General Thomas J. Morgan, principal of the Providence (R.I.) Normal School, who with Mrs. Morgan visited the Atlanta school in January 1884; and thereafter both took an active interest. They wrote stirring articles and made frequent addresses in support of the school. General Morgan had been a commander of Negro troops in the Civil War. Mrs. Morgan felt Spelman Seminary was "on a rising tide"; and lent her enthusiasm in pushing it.

Miss Packard and Miss Giles possessed in high degree the art of making friends of the people whom they met in public or private as they traveled about, both friends of themselves and of their cause. When a Portland (Maine) church group sent $25 toward the girls' building, and 10 months later $30 for furnishing a room, a letter came to Miss Packard that the gifts were inspired by her visit to Portland a few years before. Early in 1883, Mrs. J. W. Cook in Greenwich Park, Massachusetts, with the help of one friend, collected the money to purchase an organ which was duly received. She was "so glad they liked it." Atticus G. Haygood of Oxford, Georgia, agent for the John F. Slater Fund, testified that "in a five minutes talk in the fall of 1883, Miss Packard won my confidence." Miss Joanna P. Moore, founder of the "Fireside Schools," whom Miss Packard first met in New Orleans, was a frequent visitor and devoted friend.

But in no instance was this power to make friends more noteworthy than in their relationship to the Rockefeller-Spelman family. From their first meeting with Mr. John D. Rockefeller on June 18, 1882, they commanded his interest and his respect. The next day, when the ladies of the family entertained them at the Forest Hills residence, marked the beginning of a congenial relationship, in which personal friendship flourished between Miss Packard and Miss Giles on the one side, and Mrs. Harvey Buel Spelman and her two daughters, Mrs. Laura Spelman Rockefeller and Miss Lucy Spelman on the other – friendship which lasted as long as any of them lived. Mr. Rockefeller wrote Miss Packard in January, 1884, "I believe in the school and in the good women who have charge of it."

CHAPTER VII

PROBLEMS AND PROGRESS
1883-1891

The Problem of a Separate School for Girls

CREDIT is due to Mr. John D. Rockefeller for making it possible to keep the school founded by Miss Packard and Miss Giles a separate school for young women. As a result of the visit to Cleveland in June 1882, Mr. Rockefeller wrote Miss Packard on February 19, 1883, in his own handwriting, enclosing his check for $250 toward furnishing rooms; and told her he had sent $250 more to Dr. Morehouse in New York. His faith in these women and in the work they were doing was made more and more clear as time went on.

The proposal for the union of the schools made by the Home Mission Society and supported by the Atlanta Baptist Seminary was strongly opposed by the Founders and teachers, and by the Woman's Society in Boston, all of whom believed earnestly that better and more effective work in all departments could be done by women working with women. Nevertheless, as early as February 1, 1883, Dr. Morehouse had written Miss Packard that "our Board now consider the school for young women and young men, at Atlanta, *practically one*," and he suggested that Miss Packard's reports should be sent to the Society through Dr. Robert, president of the Atlanta Baptist Seminary.

Mrs. Nickerson and Mrs. Pollard, president and treasurer of the WABHMS, and good friends of Miss Packard and Miss Giles, arrived in Atlanta in late March to visit the fast-growing school. On Mrs. Pollard's return North, she talked with Dr. Morehouse. He did not favor the institution's being called the Atlanta Baptist Female Seminary, but agreed to "The Girls' Department" of the Atlanta Baptist Seminary. As to catalogues, he said, "have them as you suggested, separate for distribution in our New England churches, and a part bound with the Seminary, as Dr. Robert [president of Atlanta Baptist Seminary] suggested; and as you said you would be willing to have them." In reply, Miss Packard and Miss Giles said, "We must call our School 'Female Seminary,' not a *department* in our separate catalogue."

On April 20, 1883, Dr. Morehouse wrote Miss Packard: "The question of adjusting the work in the fall will be one that will require serious consideration. You know the arrangement is to bring both departments together as far as possible. In so doing a re-organization to some extent of the teaching force may be required. . . ." On April 26, 1883, he wrote again to Miss Packard:

I cannot at present go into a detailed statement of our understanding of the relations of the schools for girls and for boys, at Atlanta. . . . I think I wrote you recently that our understanding was, that the Institution is practically one, and that Dr. Robert is the President of the 'Atlanta Baptist Seminary,' of which we have taken it for granted the 'Girls Department' would be a part. Certainly it is the understanding of the Board that the present purchase, which is now occupied by you for the girls' school, is intended as much for young men as for young women. It was not purchased for a girls' or for a boys' school, but for the Atlanta Baptist Seminary, which should embrace instruction to both sexes. . . .

Miss Packard continued to advocate a separate school for girls; wrote Dr. Morehouse that the members of the Woman's Board were enthusiastic about having a separate school; wanted it to be women's work for women; and were determined to make it the *best school* possible. She felt the urgency of teaching the women that morality is a vital part of religion, and noted that the kind of daily instruction needed the teachers "could not impart in the presence of gentlemen." She saw improvement in the students day by day in character as well as knowledge, and her faith was strong in "their ability for culture."

In July 1883, Dr. Morehouse wrote Miss Packard two letters on this subject. He told her on July 12 while she was in Southbridge, Massachusetts, "The Board has planned for three years or more to have one school in Atlanta for the education of both men and women, and the Society cannot afford to pay for two separate properties. . . ." Try hard to raise the money for "the matter is urgent, the time is short, and arrangements for next year must be matured soon."

On July 27, after a reference to the support of teachers by the WABHMS, he wrote:

I think all engagements should be conditioned upon the possibility of a consolidation of the schools. In case that is done, six ladies may not be needed, as there are three or four male teachers. If the schools remain separate, however, you will probably need the six teachers mentioned. We hope that a decision on this subject may be speedily arrived at by the gift of a sufficient amount to keep the girls' school separate.

In August, Dr. Morehouse told Mrs. Pollard that it was unlikely that any material change in the schools would be made before January, and he thought it would be best to arrange for the opening of the schools as they were conducted last year; that is, for the girls to occupy the buildings at the barracks, the young men the building in town till January; future arrangements to be determined by future developments.

Pressure to keep the property for an exclusively girls' school was hitting the Home Mission Board from many directions. Sidney Root, an influential man in Atlanta as well as a trustee of both schools, had strong views on the subject, and he assured Miss Packard she was "on the right track." By late August, the opinion of Dr. Morehouse had changed. He then informed the Woman's Society and the Founders that if they would take over the mortgage, the new site should be devoted to the girls' school. He graciously added, "I am heartily desirous of seeing the girls' school established as an independent school."

Both their educational policies, and the successful conduct of the school by Miss Packard and Miss Giles which in turn gained for it friends and financial support, worked together to bring about this outcome.

79

Money raising efforts redoubled. Mr. Rockefeller wrote in mid-October that he would make a small donation if the subscription list were sent him and if they were sure of the whole. In November he pledged $2,500 if the total was raised.

Dr. Morehouse wrote on November 12, asking if the women realized that only 45 days remained before the Atlanta property must be paid for. Then on December 5, he wrote Miss Packard as follows:

You know that Mr. James of Atlanta holds the mortgage. I have written him this day asking for an extension of 90 days for $5,000 of the amount. I think your persuasive arguments with Mr. James will be a valuable reinforcement to my letter, and I wish you would see him personally at once and secure this extension if possible. . . . Do and defer not.

The prospect was bleak. As the Woman's Board in Boston wrote Miss Packard on December 26, "Dr. Morehouse . . . expects our check for $6,500 this week, and no one will pay till all is pledged. I do not despair but it looks dark."

In the meantime, in December, Miss Packard and Miss Giles wrote a persuasive letter to Mr. Rockefeller, telling of the work and of its prospects. They painted a vivid picture of the school, the eagerness of the students to learn, and the great need. They told him of the grant from the Slater Fund to help carry on the Industrial Department. They invited Mr. and Mrs. Rockefeller to come South, visit them, and give help in the dilemma facing the school, since "if the schools are united, the whole plan of Christianizing the people is thwarted." They earnestly appealed for "a donation that will bring us on sure footing and so exercise a comforting and heartfelt interest in this that it so much needs. They suggested that Mr. Rockefeller "give it a name — let it be called 'Rockefeller College,' or if you choose not to give it that name, perhaps your wife's maiden name," or "some other which best suits you." They referred to the desirability of incorporation after the money was raised to pay for the property, with a Board of Trustees made up of men from both the North and the South. They

PLATE VII

Union Hall and Army Barracks

Class of 1887

Class of 1888

PLATE VIII

Rockefeller Hall Then . . .

. . . and Now

thanked him for his previous help and begged him now to "be the special Benefactor or patron and feel that this is *yours specially*." They said they had hesitated to write him, but now "we write because we could not help it. We are sure we gained our inspiration from Him who moves the heart to action."

An extension of time to April first, 1884, was granted by the holder of the mortgage. Likewise, Mr. John D. Rockefeller extended the time for meeting the conditions of his pledge. By a process of attrition, the necessary amount due on the mortgage was whittled down – to $6,800 in January; to $2,500 in February; to $2,200; to $1,800; to $1,600 by the end of March. So much of the money now sent in was designated for buildings that money for salaries suffered, and the recall of one teacher was ordered. Happily, the hard work, accompanied by faith and prayer, finally achieved the goal. An additional gift from Mr. Rockefeller brought the victory.

The Name of Spelman

Friday, April 11, 1884

Picture a crowded chapel in Union Hall. Visitors in Atlanta to attend a Convention had been many throughout the week. Visitors were no rarity to these students.

Earlier in the week there had been an evening of entertainment, with recitations, duet, double quartet, in addition to an anthem by the 19 young ladies in the Educational Society, "Who Are These in Bright Array?" This program was followed by an exhibition of the Industrial Department in the "Labor Song." One of the visitors was Mrs. Mary A. Foster from Mount Holyoke Seminary, "to which the schools bears resemblance in its organization."

But Friday was *the* day.

Miss Packard, Miss Giles, Miss Champney, and Miss Grover were seated on the platform; probably also four other teachers, besides Professor Kruger and Miss Hunter, teachers of music. The students, numbering now over 100 boarding students plus 350 or more day pupils, were crowded into the room.

After an opening hymn, Miss Packard began to speak out of a thankful heart. This was the third birthday of the school. Above all the discouragements, good results had crowned their efforts and answered their prayers. "I bless the Lord that I have lived to see this day" was the sentiment echoed with full hearts.

"Into the midst of the solemn joy," quoting words of Miss Grover, came "a party such as one rarely meets in one day on such an errand," made up of

> Mr. John D. Rockefeller
> Mrs. John D. Rockefeller (Laura Spelman)
> Mrs. Harvey Buel Spelman
> Miss Lucy Spelman, her elder daughter
> Dr. Edward Judson, pastor of the Berean Church
>   in New York and son of Rev. Adoniram Judson,
>   the first missionary to Burma
> Dr. H. F. Biggar of Cleveland

They were escorted by Mr. Sidney Root, the Atlanta trustee who had given help and encouragement through dark days. Mr. Root presented the guests to Miss Packard. Each one was invited to speak. (Two of the Rockefeller children, John Jr. and one sister, also were present.)

Mr. Rockefeller was introduced as the man "whose generous gift has finally established the school as a school for women." "Confidence is a plant of slow growth," Mr. Rockefeller told the students. "It is in your hearts to make the school one that people will believe in. God will take these small beginnings to do a great work. I am thankful to be here."

Mr. Root, in behalf of the trustees, took this occasion first to ask of the students the name of their school; they responded in unison, "The Atlanta Baptist Female Seminary." "Not so," he replied. Then he proceeded to announce that the Board had voted to change the name of the institution to Spelman Seminary. It was so named, he said, "in honor of a lady of the company and in memory of her honored husband."

Miss Packard thereupon called upon the students to manifest their acceptance of the name by pledging upon its adoption
never to bring reproach upon the new name. The students responded by standing up, every one, to give their enthusiastic
assent and indicate their allegiance.

Dr. Judson, apparently the first of the visitors to speak,
urged the importance of walking in the footsteps of the Lord,
tying his remarks in with the age of the school – three years,
the most interesting age of a child when he begins to walk, to
talk, and to love his mother.

In her remarks, Mrs. Spelman spoke of the power of song;
Mrs. Rockefeller recalled the days of effort of the Founders
and their friends; Miss Spelman said she would always look
with interest upon an institution that bore her name, and spoke
briefly of her father.

This was many years before the Rockefeller agencies for the
welfare of mankind were organized. The first one, The Rockefeller Institute for Medical Research, was incorporated in 1901;
the General Education Board began in 1902; The Rockefeller
Foundation in 1913. But Mr. Rockefeller's personal philanthropies had begun with his first earnings. He was already
prominent in the religious life of Cleveland. He was superintendent of the Sunday School, and his wife supervised the
infant department.

His principles for sharing his wealth were in process of being
developed. He wanted his gifts to stimulate others to give;
and he chose to assist organizations that had vitality, not to
bolster dying causes. So his statement in Union Hall that April
day in 1884 carries special weight. He said that if a person
gains money, he must look about for the best places to invest
it; and among the many calls for help, the desire follows to
seek the best places to bestow it, the places where it will do
the most good. He was convinced that "those who have in-
vested here have made the best investment of their money that
could be made."

Gifts varying from $1.00 to $1,000 had been received,

mainly from New England men and women; but Mr. Rockefeller of Cleveland, Ohio, gave more than half of the $11,500.

The next catalogue stated that Spelman Seminary "receives
its new name from the large donation made by Hon. J. D.
Rockefeller toward the payment for this property, which in-
sures this Institution ever to be kept as a school for girls and
women."

The official name was simply *Spelman Seminary*. The Boards
of both the American Baptist Home Mission Society and the
Woman's American Baptist Home Mission Society so designated the school in April, 1884. Both Boards agreed also that
the institution was to be kept as a school for girls and women.
The Founders, in view of all the struggle to get that fact established, may have been inclined to say "Spelman Female Seminary," a common term in those days for the academies for
women. ("Female" was not officially dropped from Mount
Holyoke Female Seminary until 1888.)

In his April 17 letter to Miss Packard reporting the resolution passed by the Board of the ABHMS, Dr. Morehouse
wrote: "There were very decided objections to the use of the
word 'female.' Would it not be better therefore to put it Spelman Seminary, and on the title-page add the words 'for girls'
or 'for young women' as you choose?" A month later, he wrote
Miss Packard again: ". . . I would not favor the retention of
the word 'Baptist' in the name of the institution. In some in-
stances it will have a tendency to repel desirable students. They
may think that if we hang our banner on the outer wall, a good
deal of proselyting may be done inside."

It is worth noting here that Mr. Rockefeller's gifts were not
conditioned on the naming of the school. Miss Giles made that
clear in a letter in which she wrote: "The money given by Mr.
Rockefeller toward the purchase of the property . . . was not
given with any condition, but the suggestion that the seminary
should bear his wife's maiden name *we* made to him, and he
complied with our request."

Mr. Rockefeller's acceptance of the name reflected his desire to honor his wife and also her parents, Mr. and Mrs. Harvey Buel Spelman. Mr. Spelman, who had died in 1881, had been an influential friend of colored people and their cause. He also was recognized as a leader in promoting public schools in Ohio where he had had a part in developing what was known as "the Akron plan." Mrs. Spelman was a woman of strength who shared her husband's interests. She and her daughter, Lucy, lived with Mr. and Mrs. Rockefeller after Mr. Spelman's death. The closeness of the family feeling between the Spelmans and Mr. John D. Rockefeller's family reflects credit on them all. It is therefore relevant that sometimes speakers and sometimes the written page in reports or in the *Spelman Messenger* have stated that the school was named in honor of *the father*, or after Mrs. Spelman's death, in honor of *the father and mother* of Mrs. Rockefeller. Mrs. Rockefeller's maiden name was *Spelman*; the name and much else came to her from her parents.

Obviously in answer to a request for more information about Mr. Spelman, Miss Lucy Spelman wrote a letter to Miss Packard from New Orleans dated April 13, 1884, enclosing a "simple sketch" of her father.

The "sketch" reads as follows: "The man whose name this Seminary now bears was for more than forty years the steadfast friend of the colored people. At a time in their history when it cost much to befriend the enslaved he gave liberally of time, strength, active sympathy and intelligent service in their behalf. Clear in his convictions as to the wrong of human slavery; believing that all men were created free and equal; profoundly impressed with the need of enlightened public sentiment on this question, he read and thought unceasingly upon it and presented the subject with logical clearness and forceful utterance in both private and public life.

"A native of Ohio, where he spent the greater part of his life, he died at the age of seventy years in the year 1881 in New York City.

"Through the Emancipation Proclamation he had realized

the truth of his convictions that, freed from physical and mental bondage, the colored race would make for itself a place and an influence. . . ."

After the return home of the Rockefeller family party from California, Miss Spelman wrote again to Miss Packard and Miss Giles, acknowledging the receipt of the two photographic pictures of the school-buildings and pupils of Spelman Seminary, together with the annual catalogue for the year 1883-4.

"We are thus reminded," she wrote, "of the morning we recently spent with you in Atlanta and recall with vivid interest those scenes indelibly impressed upon our memories. We can never forget the bright faces so full of eager thirst for knowledge and of appreciation of the earnest efforts made in their behalf by their kind teachers and friends.

"Will you kindly tell us what amount will cover the yearly expense of one boarding pupil, including tuition, clothing and necessary incidental expenses? . . . .

"With the kindest regards of Mr. & Mrs. Rockefeller and my dear Mother, I remain,

Very cordially yr's

Lucy M. Spelman"

New Courses and New Teachers

The move to the Barracks buildings and grounds made possible an expansion of courses. A "Model School" opened in February, 1883, under the direction of Miss Grover, with four classes, provided opportunity for observation and practice teaching; and in consequence, an elementary normal course was instituted. Even in the basement-school days, the older students had taught in the summers in rural schools – often held in churches – and sought to teach others as they had been taught.

A school infirmary, in charge of Dr. Sophia Jones, a young colored woman from Canada who was graduated from the University of Michigan Medical College, not only took care of sick Spelman students, but made possible courses in Nurse

Training. Regular lectures in physiology and hygiene were given to all students by an Atlanta physician, Dr. Hicks.

The academic courses in mathematics, English grammar and literature, geography, and natural philosophy increased in scope as the students increased in ability to take them. Spelman students even beat the Atlanta Baptist Seminary boys in a spelling match!

The industrial department received special attention. The students were taught cooking, sewing in all its branches, general housework and laundry work. The Spelman exhibit at the Piedmont Exposition (attended by President and Mrs. Grover Cleveland) showing nurse training techniques, needlework, printing, drawing, and penmanship, drew favorable comments.

A printing office was furnished by the gift of a printing press from the Slater Fund. The *Spelman Messenger* began publication; first issue, March, 1885; terms, 25¢ per year in advance. Students were given training in type-setting and composition – and accuracy! The experience opened up another avenue for employment.

As an aid to orderly procedure, mention must be made of the arrival from New England of a new bell. It was an important piece of equipment made available by a gift of $100 which could be used only if the institution remained a girls' school. To quote a note of Dr. Morehouse to Miss Packard: "That new bell must be 'a thing of beauty' and I hope may be 'a joy forever.' " It is impossible for the present generation to realize the necessity of having a big bell. Clocks and watches were scarce – non-existent so far as homes and schoolrooms were concerned. The bell indicated the time to get up in the morning and the time to go to bed; the time for chapel, for classes, for meals – and even served the surrounding community as a signal for their time to go to work.

The faculty in the second year of the Barracks era had increased to 16, nine of whom were supported entirely by the WABHMS. All except four were from Massachusetts or New York. There were then over 600 students, about one third of whom were boarders. An addition to the faculty that deserves special mention was the arrival in February, 1885, of Miss Packard's half-sister, Miss Mary J. Packard, who rendered effective service for the next 25 years.

Hon. Gustavus J. Orr, Georgia's State Commissioner of Education, was present at the 1885 Commencement Exercises, held jointly with Atlanta Baptist Seminary in Friendship Church, and heard the essays and orations given by the students. The main address was by Rev. Atticus G. Haygood of the Slater Fund. Certificates testifying to the completion of a normal course were presented by Miss Packard to 13 students.

The curriculum of study, reads the first *Spelman Messenger* (1885), "is that given in all the higher normal and academic schools of the North, and the progress of the students is something wonderful." The charge for board and tuition was $7.00 per month; instrument music was extra and cost $2.00 per month. The school year was from early October to the end of May.

Mr. Morris K. Jesup of New York, Treasurer of the Slater Fund, and Mrs. Jesup, visited Spelman Seminary in March. Mr. Jesup said that Spelman "was the brightest thing he had seen in the South and gave him hope for the future of both races."

Mr. Haygood, General Agent of the Slater Fund, had written to the WABHMS a year before: "My judgment is, no school in proportion to the investment of money in it is doing so much good work. Few do so much, viewed in any light, measured by any test. Miss Packard seems to me to be a providential woman in Atlanta."

The closing exercises of the year 1886-87 covered 10 days including the annual examinations. The Nurse Training School received impressive notice in the *Atlanta Constitution*, as did the exhibitions and yearly examinations. At the joint commencement on May 18, certificates for completion of the Elementary Normal Course, which entitled the holders to teach, were granted to six students.

Diplomas were given to six young women, the first class that had completed the Higher Normal and Scientific Course. They were *the first graduates of Spelman Seminary*. Their names were Ella N. Barksdale, Clara A. Howard, Lou E. Mitchell, Adeline J. Smith, Sallie B. Waugh, and Ella L. Williams. All of these young women were engaged in teaching after graduation. All of them but Clara Howard were married after a few years; and all continued to be branches that bore the fruit of community helpfulness.

Final exercises the following year were all held in the new Rockefeller Hall except for the Commencement program which was given in Friendship Church. The exhibition of the nurse training school; the oral examinations; the music recital by the students; the joint baccalaureate service on Sunday afternoon, all attracted large crowds from Atlanta and surrounding towns. The students in nurse training rated a special item of commendation in the *Atlanta Constitution*. That, and another item from the *Atlanta Constitution* describing the joint commencement exercises of Spelman Seminary and Atlanta Baptist Seminary on May 24, 1888, have significance. Here are excerpts from the latter:

The commencement exercises of these institutions occurred at Friendship Baptist church, where there was some difficulty in getting all seated, because of the crowd. . . .

On the platform were seated the representatives of the two seminaries, Mrs. Nickerson, of Boston, president of the Women's American Baptist Home Mission Society of New England, Mrs. Reynolds, of Wallingford, Connecticut, secretary of the Society, Judge Hook, Dr. Kendrick and others, while in the audience were seen many deserving of notice. . . .

The orations were well composed and well delivered, evincing a great degree of proficiency and careful, close reading on the part of all. They must have been a revelation to those who consider the colored race incapable of thinking deeply and accurately. . . .

Judge Hook gave an eloquent and stirring 'five minutes talk' which was frequently interrupted by applause. He expressed himself as highly pleased with the exercises, and assured the principals of his lively sympathy with their work, and of the pleasure he should take in being present on similar future occasions. [Judge Hook was Mayor of Atlanta.]

Dr. Howe of Cambridge, Mass., in a most happy manner addressed the graduates of the industrial department, thirteen in number, and presented each with her certificate. His words were received with marked attention. It was evident each pupil recognized in him a true friend. . . .

Then Miss Packard, with words of loving advice, gave the diplomas to the nine graduates of the Higher Normal Department of Spelman. . . .

Mrs. Harvey Buel Spelman sent a small package of books, one for each Spelman graduate, as a token of her interest. She wrote on the flyleaf the name of the student and "a helpful verse of Scripture." A question was recently put to Mrs. Selena Sloan Butler of this class, who shows her treasured book on occasion, as to whether the same verse of Scripture was written in each book. Mrs. Butler replied, "No. We girls compared them with each other. The verses were different." Each name and each verse was in Mrs. Spelman's handwriting. A message to the group was included in the covering letter to Miss Packard and Miss Giles, written by Miss Lucy Spelman in behalf of her mother.

When one considers the life work before them and the rare opportunities for usefulness, one might be tempted to exclaim 'I envy you, my sister.' With intelligence, courage, tact, and a *high sense of self-respect,* they will teach humanity at many points and learn that for them as for every one 'power is the measure of responsibility.' . . .

New Buildings

Even the additional facilities provided by the Army Barracks did not meet the needs of the growing school. It grew like magic as one report stated. Deacon Mial Davis and his wife entertained Miss Packard and Miss Giles in Fitchburg in the summer of 1884. Their visit had far-reaching consequences for Spelman. In their chats with the Davises about the school, their distress was marked that unless they had larger facilities, they must refuse applications. Their anxiety and their question, "What shall we do?" pricked Mr. Davis as he came home from his office one evening. After they had talked it over, they retired "to rest and pray God to open the way." The next morning, Mr. Davis suggested that effort be made to raise funds "for an extensive building." Miss Packard and Miss Giles gave hearty approval. So did Dr. Morehouse. Subscriptions began immediately. Mr. and Mrs. Davis themselves gave the first $1,000. A pledge blank set forth the need of a substantial brick building to include a chapel, rooms for teachers' use, for recitation, library, apparatus; the pledges were to be binding only when $10,000 should have been subscribed; the amount needed was raised from $15,000 to $20,000; and later, with changes in plans, a cost of $25,000 was approved.

Robert N. Cole of Southbridge, Massachusetts, subscribed $500. Mrs. Mial Davis visited churches in New Hampshire, Vermont, Connecticut, speaking about Spelman. By October 23, she had spoken 20 times. She wrote Miss Packard and Miss Giles, "People seemed to be pleased to hear about the work, but what hard work it is to get people to *give*. How they do hang to money! . . ."

Days of working and waiting there were.

Miss Packard, Miss Giles, and Miss Champney each gave $100. Rev. William Howe of Cambridge, Massachusetts, gave the money for the chapel, in memory of his wife. But what really made it possible to begin construction in the spring of 1885, or perhaps to begin at all, was a pledge of $10,000 from Mr. Rockefeller.

The design for the building submitted to Mr. Rockefeller and approved by him would cost $25,000 — more rather than less. The chapel was to contain no pillars, and would seat, with a gallery on each side, 800 persons.

A New York friend, John J. Jones, was asked "to furnish the library." He said that he would; and would send his check after learning the estimated cost . . . ; then added, "I do not understand that furnishing includes books." Probably a wise precaution, considering how fast the needs of Spelman increased and had to be met!

Dr. Morehouse wrote at length from Atlanta to Miss Packard in New England on July 31 that he had that day concluded the contract for the erection of the new building; that the chapel space had been extended to make a beautiful room 45 x 75; that the chapel was to be completed by February 1, and the entire building by April 1, if the funds could be procured.

This detailed account is here included lest anyone should conclude that the Founders had only to lift a voice or write a letter to get the money to provide needed facilities. On the contrary, they were always under heavy pressure to raise money.

Miss Packard and Miss Giles abhorred the idea of having work on the building suspended although $5,000 had still to be raised, and more if steam heat was included. Nevertheless, they felt it would be impossible to heat the new building without steam. They wrote Dr. Morehouse: "We now have 40 fires built daily during the school days. The building of these fires, caring for them, taking down pipes frequently for cleaning, as must be done on account of the soft coal, requires much of the time of two men besides what the girls can do. Two recitation rooms cannot be used this morning because the pipes must be cleaned. . . . A cheaper quality of coal could be used if we had steam. . . . Will it not be less expensive in the end, as well as more comfortable, to have steam?"

Dr. Morehouse, in reply, reviewed the financial status: "The Society could not advance money on promises; heating by steam would cost $2,500 to $3,000 and we don't have the money; it must be secured from some other source."

The day-by-day ups and downs need not be recorded here. The *Home Mission Echoes* (March, 1886) quotes a report from Mrs. Pollard, Treasurer of the WABHMS, that in building Rockefeller Hall, Mr. John D. Rockefeller gave largely, and others made considerable gifts but eventually the funds were exhausted. "Special hours were set apart for prayer, and soon the answer came. Mr. Rockefeller gave $3,000 more and Rev. William Howe of Cambridge gave $2,000 for the chapel, and others smaller sums, so that the work could go on. To finish and furnish the building, we must still have $3,000."

Robert H. Cole of Southbridge had paid his building pledge in full in January; then he gave daughter Ella a check for $300 to send Miss Packard 'for the inside of the new building, not to be acknowledged publicly.' In May, a woman in Lowell, Massachusetts, gave $500, half the amount required, for blinds for Rockefeller Hall.

In February, Rev. William Jefferson White of Augusta, Georgia, visited Spelman. After expressing to the students regret that funds for the completion of the building were not sufficient, even with the additional generous donation of Mr. Rockefeller, Mr. White proposed to the scholars that each should write to one or more friends asking them to give, if only a brick, toward the new building; then asked the pupils who received replies to forward the names to him, to be published in the *Georgia Baptist*. The proposition was adopted by the students unanimously. The WABHMS reported in March 1886 that $16.20 had been received from people solicited by the students. The value of this self-help attitude should not be belittled.

The date of dedication was set for May 18. The rain came down in bucketsful, but hearts were full of gladness. Sidney Root, as chairman of the Board of Trustees, presided. Dr. William Howe gave the address. There was fine singing under the direction of Professor Kruger.

This first brick building on the Spelman campus fittingly bears the name of John D. Rockefeller. The letters stand out from the curve above the center doors, with the figures, 1886. They too tell a story. There was not money in the building fund to carve the name. The May, 1886, *Messenger* described the building as nearing completion, its entire length 133 feet, three stories, the chapel, halls, recitation rooms and dormitory rooms, then added: "The entire building is finished in Georgia pine, with oak stairways, and will be lighted by gas and heated by steam. The basement is unfinished, the rooms are unfurnished, and the arrangements for heating and lighting are incomplete." Obviously, with so many essentials unprovided, there was no money for extras.

Mr. Rockefeller was not interested in paying for a bronze tablet bearing his name; he even eliminated the item from estimates submitted for repairs. Not until 1902 was the building's name installed. Then Miss Giles proposed to the students that their birthday gift of money to her be used to provide the name. So it was agreed, and so it was done.

The story of Rockefeller Hall should include a tribute to the contractor, Mr. Benjamin H. Broomhead, white citizen of Atlanta. On examining the plans for the building, it was found that an addition of 10 feet to the chapel would be a great improvement. Mr. Broomhead made the needed extension at his own expense, and he made other improvements in the foundation, amounting to hundreds of dollars in value. Two years before, Mr. Broomhead had contributed liberally toward the cost of the belfry to house the bell. He was a friendly man, interested, competent. Miss Packard said, "the building will stand as a monument to the work of an *honest* man," and so it has to this day.

The first five years, 1881-86, had been strenuous. Resources in teachers, equipment, money had been far behind the minimum needs for a school. Only faith and character – what Mr. Rockefeller called "stick" – and their habitual pattern of culture supported the Founders. They inspired the students with a zeal to learn and a longing for action.

The first meeting in the Howe Memorial Chapel was held on October 8, 1886. The students blessed the names of their benefactors, especially Mr. Rockefeller who made the building possible and the Rev. Mr. Howe who had finished and furnished the chapel on the second floor. They prayed their thankfulness to God under "a soft halo of gaslight."

Dr. Howe later told what prompted his gift of Howe Memorial Chapel. In the summer of 1896, at his home in Cambridgeport, Mass., he dictated a letter to Miss Mary J. Packard, which records a significant episode in American history.* Dr. Howe wrote:

I was born with a natural sense of justice and when born again by the energy of the Holy Spirit, that sense of justice was kindled into a flame of righteous indignation against all oppression, especially Southern slavery. God, in his great kindness, gave me a companion of like spirit, who immediately after her conversion in a colored Sunday-school sought an humble place in which to serve her Master. This for a white person of that day, especially from the higher walks of life, was deemed anything but respectable. But, identifying herself with those whom she taught, her feeling soon became intensified in interest for the poor slaves in the South. She soon sought a place and became a member of a circle of about thirty ladies from some of the first families of the city who met for prayer, for consultation, and to devise means, and work persistently for the liberation of the slaves.

In the midst of agitation raised in the matter of slavery by Wm. L. Garrison, and Geo. E. Thompson from London, the great philanthropist, both of whom, it was reported, were to meet with this Circle, to encourage them in their grand object, a mob, not of the lower order, but of so-called respectable men, merchants and their clerks, gathered around the modest quarters to break up the assembly. A rope was provided for Garrison; the aspect was threatening without, and the mayor with officials appearing in the midst of this peaceful circle informed the ladies that their meeting must be closed, and if they wished protection, they must follow him, and no harm would come, as his police was in force in the street.

There was no alternative but obedience. They followed the Mayor; when reaching the street in the midst of the crowd, Miss A. A. Amidon (who afterwards became my wife) true to her instinct, extended her arm to a colored teacher of Boston, the only one in the Circle – and with firm and undaunted step continued her march amidst the groans and hisses of the mob; passing on their way home the Courthouse where Simms, the slave who escaped from the South, was in his cell in chains guarded by a double file of soldiers, waiting the decision of the Court on the demand of the South that he be returned to them.

This spirit animated her . . . through the whole course of her life, and she was permitted to see slavery abolished and liberty proclaimed to

* A full account of the meeting of the Boston Female Anti-Slavery Society which Dr. Howe described appears in the biography of William Lloyd Garrison written by his children; Volume II, chapter one. Note especially pages 14-16, including the footnotes.

the captive. She lived to see scorn changed to praise and admiration of the stand she and her companions had taken. She lived in sorrow to see Simms returned to captivity, marched down State Street to the wharf in double ranks of old Bay State soldiers at Southern dictation. She lived to hear the tramp of those same Bay State soldiers marching down State Street to demand of all the Southern States, at the command of President Lincoln in loyalty to the righteous laws of the King of Kings, the liberation of her millions of slaves to enjoy the blessings of 'life, liberty and the pursuit of happiness.'

You will not be surprised, knowing from these few words what a wife was given me, why in memory of that noble spirit . . . I was moved to do what I have done for Spelman Chapel. . . .

The 50 additional dormitory spaces were not enough. Students would arrive with their baggage with no notice in advance; but after their weary months of effort to earn the money to come, the teachers did not have the heart to send them home. As early as April first, 1887, Miss Packard made an appeal by letter to one of their visitors, asking if he could not get friends to raise money for a new building to be named in his honor. Mr. Root wrote to a woman of wealth making a similar appeal for funds to build a new building. There was need not only for another dormitory; there was need for additional land; and an effort was begun to raise money for a hospital. In fact, in June, 1887, a New Jersey woman pledged $1,000 toward erecting a wing of the proposed hospital. Questions repeatedly arose about the lots adjoining the Seminary property. There was fear that they might be purchased for uses damaging or dangerous to the school.

In June, Miss Packard and Miss Giles visited Harriet's brother Hiram in Madison, Wisconsin. En route, they stopped in Minneapolis and obtained from their friend of New Salem days, Samuel C. Gale, a promise of $1,000, which, with a note due them at the Gate City (Atlanta) Bank, would provide two-thirds of the sum needed to purchase adjacent land.

The letters to and from Mr. Gale are revealing. Miss Packard wrote him from Madison on June 23, the day before Union Hall burned.

It gives us pleasure to inform you that arrangements have been made for purchasing the land that we told you about, and the papers are being made out, for $3,200 with an additional sum of $100 for the privilege of closing a street. . . . This brings all our land for Seminary purposes together free from all restrictions. . . .

Two weeks later, Mr. Gale wrote from Saratoga Springs to Miss Giles:

. . . I am glad that you have secured the land in question for your institution. My donation for the purpose of helping the fund for this purchase will be sent you as soon as you will write me that it is needed and that your institution has such legal corporate existence that it can and will take title itself in its own name to this land. You will remember I made a point of this in my conversation with you at Minneapolis; and I make it because my interest is in you two ladies and this your noble institution which you almost alone have created. I do not make this gift to benevolence at large.

The Founders had to raise the balance required, and they did. The source of the money is not entirely clear; it may have come to them for Spelman's needs from non-Baptist friends. In their report to the Women's Society for 1888, Miss Packard and Miss Giles mention "the gift of money for three acres of land adjacent to our former property, amounting to $3,200, every cent of which was given by personal friends, and over $2,000 by friends outside the Baptist denomination."

Nevertheless, with Rockefeller Hall available, in addition to Union Hall, the summer of 1887 bade fair to be the least harrowing summer period that Miss Packard and Miss Giles had experienced for seven years. From Wisconsin, they went to New England, but even before they reached Boston, a new blow struck.

Union Hall was burned to the ground on June 24, 1887. Gone were the organ, furniture, bell, coal, kitchen and dining-room equipment, provisions, and one teacher's wardrobe. Union Hall consisted of a two-story central building, and two ells.

The central part was used for dormitories. One wing, which had served as chapel and school room before Rockefeller Hall was built, housed the Model School. The other ell, previously divided into recitation rooms, made a pleasant and comfortable diningroom, albeit too small.

The fire was first seen about 5 p.m. on June 24, and was "probably caused by a spark from the work shops on Culver Street." Within little more than an hour, when Sidney Root arrived, the destruction was almost complete. The barracks-dormitories caught, but were saved, as he wrote Miss Packard, "by the good conduct of the occupants and the firemen." The building was insured for $3,500, and inside equipment for $400. Even before this misfortune occurred another building was needed. The fire made one imperative. Plans were discussed at once, as to its size, facilities to be provided, and location.

Mr. Root assured Miss Packard that the fire "was a great misfortune but not a disaster"; that it had "turned the sympathy of the people toward us"; and that "if we can manage to get a better building in a better location," it might well turn out to be an advantage. "It is not time for hesitation or discouragement." He wished to have the new building on line with and north of Rockefeller Hall, to make the beginning of a quadrangle.

Yet there were discouragements in the offing. The wife of a Congregational minister, Mrs. E. A. Slack, then residing in Merrimac, New Hampshire, agreed in September to give $6,000 in memory of her mother, Mrs. Howard, who was a Baptist, if the building could be named Howard Hall. This was confirmed to Miss Packard, and two payments, one year apart, were agreed on.

On the strength of this pledge, plus the insurance on Union Hall, a conditional gift from Mr. Rockefeller, and smaller gifts from other friends, the work was begun. Ground was broken *just four months* from the date Union Hall was burned. The cornerstone of *Howard Hall* was laid on November 15; a Massachusetts man named Blanchard had given a granite stone for the purpose and paid the freight on it to Atlanta. A new 679-pound bell also had been given; the crowd of 500 had assembled around the bell after the cornerstone ceremony, while the students sang "Keep the Ark a-movering."

Three days later, the letter of conveyance from Mrs. Slack was sent to the WABHMS. This document contained a new stipulation "that the School should always be under the control of the Women's ABHMS. Should the School ever pass from its hands, the money must be returned to Mrs. Slack or her heirs."

This was a body blow to the building fund. Efforts were made to have the stipulation withdrawn or modified. The Seminary had plans under way to apply for a charter which involved incorporation with a self-perpetuating Board of Trustees — ample grounds for considering the restrictive condition unnecessary. Negotiations in the next months did not succeed; Mrs. Slack finally and absolutely withdrew the gift in March, 1888, but by request public announcement of the fact was deferred. Miss Packard wrote: "Woe betide us! We do not feel as if we can go on soliciting as we have done, and we need the . . . building so much!"

In the meantime, Spelman Seminary carried on under many and varied obstacles. A structure of rough boards was erected between two buildings for a dining hall; a small building of two rooms was utilized for the kitchen. The seating capacity proved too small; there were 300 boarders and the dining hall overflowed into the hall of No. 4 barracks, then also into the hall of No. 3. In every available nook and corner, cots were placed. The saving grace was that all cheerfully submitted to the necessary crowding.

Deprived of the large initial sum, $6,000, the struggles to find new funds were heartbreaking. By March, 1888, $9,000 was in hand, including a gift from Mr. Rockefeller of $1,500. A personal friend of the Founders collected $500 in Philadelphia; the Quakers of Philadelphia gave $400; visitors to the campus gave $35.00. Other gifts came slowly.

More space was a crying need; the building, at least part of it, had to be. So plans were made to build first the center section, the south wing, and the annex for kitchen, diningroom; if absolutely necessary, the north wing would be deferred.

All sorts of economies had to be considered. There was objection to using large and unsightly brick piers; iron piers would cost $275 more; Dr. Morehouse suggested to Miss Packard that she present the matter to Mr. Rockefeller. It is doubtful if she did; but finally iron pillars were approved. At another time there was a question about an expense of $68.00 which was not counted in before the contract was signed; so it had to be cared for outside the contract. That illustrates how close the figuring had to be in order to get the building completed even in part, and paid for; the latter was an absolute requirement.

Miss Packard and Miss Giles needed vacation and rest after such a strenuous year. They could not, however, "lay down their weary load." In June, Miss Packard spent a day in New York. "Had a good time to plan for Spelman – Dr. Morehouse very genial – very. . . . Must try to raise $6,000. Must have the wing put up now."

The estimate from the contractor for building the north wing was $4,200, a figure lower than they had expected. All during July, the matter of funds for the north wing was pursued. By getting $1,000 here, $500 there (from Miss Champney's legacy, in fact), and $40 elsewhere; from this friend and from that; they reached the point where Miss Packard, recounting to Dr. Morehouse these items above-named, said, "We will trust God for the balance. We know it will come. . . ." The Board voted to name the building Packard Hall.

The contract for building the north wing was closed on July 23, 1888. The matter of heating had to be deferred until fall. Additional money had to be raised for furnishings; and necessary grading was costly but unavoidable.

The Founders wrote to Mr. Rockefeller that from $2,500 to $3,000 was needed for the heating and completion of the building. In reply, he promised an additional $1,500 on condition that the remainder could be raised, thus again coming to their aid. He realized, as they did, that it would be more economical if the whole building could be built at one time.

Yet even then the finishing of the basement was omitted, and other unfortunate economies had to be made. For example, the Annex which was to house the printing department, the sewing room, and the kitchen and diningroom, and which 40 years later housed the studios for the Music Department of Spelman College, had and still has only thin board partitions – no plaster. Noise and vibration are the result. Again, only a small wooden porch and stairway led from the main entrance. Later generations have here the answer to their wonderment why a wide stairway with varnished steps and banisters led from the main floor of Packard Hall to their trunk room, and yet the outside exits looked like temporary construction.

So it was, in 1888, after delays and tribulations, that Packard Hall became the third brick building on the growing campus of the growing Seminary.

New Friends

The years 1883-91 were noteworthy in bringing many visitors who became friends of Spelman. Among them were:

Ex-President of the United States, Rutherford B. Hayes, of Fremont, Ohio, President of the Slater Fund.

J. W. Hyatt, ex-Treasurer of the United States, and Mrs. Hyatt.

Judge Francis Wayland, Dean of the Law School Faculty of Yale University.

President J. M. Taylor of Vassar College and Mrs. Taylor

Dr. William C. Wilkinson of Tarrytown, New York, who presented greetings of Wellesley College.

Judge Hillyer, Mayor of Atlanta, who later became a Spelman trustee.

Thomas Nickerson, of Boston, president of the Atchison, Topeka and Santa Fe Railway, with Mrs. Nickerson and their grandson, Charles Rogers.

Hon. S. C. Gale of Minneapolis, with son and daughter.

General Samuel Armstrong, President of Hampton Institute.

Rev. H. Grattan Guinness, of London, who wrote in the *Home Mission Monthly*, vol. XI, no. 9: "The pupils at Spelman Seminary are well-disciplined, well-taught, happy. . . . The recitations in classes which I attended were admirable, and the instruction of a high order."

Charles Dudley Warner, who published an article in *Harper's Weekly* on "Colored Schools South" which began

One of the best schools anywhere, tried by several standards, is the Spelman Seminary at Atlanta, Georgia. . . . In the course and thoroughness of instruction and the character of its scholars, it is worthy of special mention among the most beneficent educational institutions of the country.

Dr. Russell H. Conwell, who after giving his famous "Acres of Diamonds" lecture in Trinity Church, was for two days a guest on Spelman campus. He spoke in chapel; he sang hymns; and at an impromptu entertainment given by the students, he sang for them a humorous song.

Another visitor was Mrs. J. E. York, long a teacher and one-time principal of Charlestown (Mass.) Female Seminary, where she knew Miss Packard as student and teacher. After leaving Charlestown, Mrs. York served for many years as Principal of a Young Ladies' School in Washington, D.C. Because of her long experience, the following extracts from a letter she wrote Miss Packard, dated March 4, 1888, after her month's visit at Spelman take on special significance:

Before I came I thought I knew *about* your school; I now feel as if I could say, I *know* your school. . . . I had expected to see a great number of women and girls, whose eyes you were endeavoring to open to the light of knowledge, and whose hearts you were trying to lead to Christ. But I did *not* expect to see so many eyes already so widely open, and glistening with intelligence; so many hearts so earnestly intent on leading Christian lives. . . . There is here a hungering and thirsting after knowledge, with its consequent intellectual culture, which I have seldom if ever seen surpassed in any school I have visited; while their religion, instead of being apart from their lives . . . is emphatically a part of their lives, so that a more consistent, gentle, courteous assemblage . . . it has never been my privilege to meet. . . .

The outlook for the future . . . of the entire south has never seemed to me so hopeful as since I have seen what even one school of this kind can accomplish.

Furthermore, as Miss Packard and Miss Giles traveled about, they invariably made friends. During the summer of 1888 on their journey north, they went to Anacostia, D.C., with Mrs. York, to call on the Hon. and Mrs. Frederick Douglass. They did not find him at home, but were invited by Mrs. Douglass to 'take a quiet lunch' with her, awaiting his arrival. "This we accepted," states Miss Packard's diary, "and on his arrival we really had a good time."

A remarkable tribute from C. F. Currie of Camden, New Jersey, who served for eight years on the Camden Board of Education, was published in the *Home Mission Monthly*. He had visited schools in all parts of the United States but Spelman Seminary was the first school for Negroes. He wrote Miss Packard:

> During all my experience, I have never seen a school as well managed and under such perfect discipline as yours. It is really marvellous. I cannot understand it; how you, with the few assistants you have, can manage 650 pupils, keep up the high standard of education and maintain the discipline you do.
>
> I was particularly struck . . . with the eagerness of your pupils; they seemed to want to get at the bottom of everything, and to do this, would ask questions without any reluctance. . . . You have made me a strong advocate of your school.

The Granting of the Charter: 1888

The year 1888 marked a significant step forward in Spelman's development. Plans for incorporation, long pending, got action. Application to the State of Georgia for a charter was filed on January 9. Its object was stated as "the establishment and maintenance of an Institution of learning for young colored women in which special attention is to be given to the formation of industrial habits and of Christian character." The Board of

Trustees was to consist of not less than nine nor more than 16, three-quarters of whom should be members of Baptist churches, a requirement changed in 1928.

The charter was granted, and the certified copy was received, dated March 7, 1888.

A meeting of the trustees was held on March 16, 1888. The trustees, elected in three classes as provided by the charter, were as follows:

CLASS I – 1888-89

Hon. Sidney Root, Atlanta
Judge George Hillyer, Atlanta
Professor William E. Holmes, Atlanta
Rev. Henry McDonald, Atlanta
Rev. William J. White, Augusta

CLASS II – 1888-90

Hon. John D. Rockefeller, New York City
Rev. Henry L. Morehouse, New York City
Hon. James L. Howard, Hartford, Connecticut
Hon. Chester W. Kingsley, Cambridge, Massachusetts
Deacon Mial Davis, Fitchburg, Massachusetts

CLASS III – 1888-91

Robert H. Cole, Southbridge, Massachusetts
Mrs. Sylvia Nickerson, Newton, Massachusetts
Mrs. Irene Bosworth, Wakefield, Massachusetts
Mrs. Louisa McWhinnie, Cambridge, Massachusetts
Mrs. Ellen A. Harwood, Newton, Massachusetts
General Thomas J. Morgan, Providence, Rhode Island

Officers were elected as follows:

President of the Board, Dr. Henry L. Morehouse
Vice President of the Board, Rev. William J. White
Secretary of the Board, Hon. Sidney Root
Treasurer of the Board, Miss Sophia B. Packard

The Executive Committee consisted of:

Dr. Morehouse, Judge Hillyer, Mr. Holmes, Mr. McDonald, Mr. Root

This was an independent, self-perpetuating Board of Trustees. The 16 members included two Negroes, and the Executive Committee of five included one Negro. The American Baptist Home Mission Society and the Woman's American Baptist Home Mission Society had representation on it, happily and rightly. But they did not own the institution. Title to some of the property was already in the name of the Seminary; and some of it was owned by the ABHMS and some by the Principals. At a later date the ownership of all the land and buildings was turned over to Spelman Seminary.

The charter ran for 20 years; in 1908 it was renewed for 20 years; in 1912, it was amended; in 1924, it was again amended, and the name changed from Spelman Seminary to Spelman College; in 1928, the charter was renewed and extended with amendments for 100 years; in 1955, it was again amended. By-laws also were adopted in 1888, and have been altered from time to time to meet changing circumstances.

At least two years prior to the granting of the Charter and adoption of the By-laws, the plans for incorporation were under way. A letter from Mr. John D. Rockefeller to Miss Packard and Miss Giles, dated January 20, 1886, has been preserved. It reads:

Dear friends:

Your beautiful letter of 16th duly received. I have advised Dr. Morehouse I would serve on the Board of Spelman Seminary, but he understands that I cannot surely be relied upon for very much real work — I am so busy.

Yours truly,

John D. Rockefeller

Some Outstanding Early Graduates

Mrs. Ella *Barksdale* Brown is the only graduate of the first Seminary class now living. She is today a respected citizen of

Jersey City, New Jersey, as citations from the Mayor and others bear witness. After her graduation and a period of teaching and newspaper work, Ella married a business man of Macon, Georgia, John M. Brown. They moved to Jersey City, where, in Mrs. Brown's words at the time of her 70th reunion, "I have tried to sweep before the doors of my community, to help improve conditions." She organized a Negro Migrants League. During the first World War, she served as chairman of a unit for Negro War Relief; with a military pass, she boarded incoming transports and interviewed returning soldiers. She was a member of the Women's Committee of the Federal Council of Churches. She was elected secretary-treasurer of the New Jersey Interracial Committee of Church Women at the time when Negro girls obtained admission to nurse-training courses of the Jersey City Medical Center; and she was president for 15 years of Friendly Big Sisters which was active in World War II. Two accomplishments she is proud of having brought about are 1) the continuing observance of Negro History Week in Jersey City Schools and Libraries; and 2) the annual exhibits in Jersey City of works of art by Negroes. She is still active in community affairs.

Her four children, two sons and two daughters, and their children, all college educated, are engaged in useful work. One granddaughter, Judith Fisher, was graduated from Spelman College in 1957.

Clara Howard of the same class, 1887, is known to many generations of Spelman students for her work in Africa (q.v.) and her later work as a member of the Spelman College staff.

Two graduates of the class of 1888, Mrs. Selena *Sloan* Butler and Mrs. Victoria *Maddox* Simmons, are still living.

Victoria Maddox was born in Stone Mountain, Georgia. When? In her words, "Dates in those days for Negroes were not known in figures but by events. My grandmother told me I was born 'two years after Surrender.' "

The father and mother of Victoria Maddox had been slaves on adjoining plantations in Georgia. They wanted to marry. The father-to-be was so competent that he used to be hired out to other slave-owners including Mr. Maddox, the mother's owner; and so the two slaves met. They wished to marry and be able to live together. By amicable agreement of the owners, the man was sold to Mr. Maddox. After emancipation the ex-slaves took the name of Maddox. The father had learned to read and write during slavery and he became a leader of his people. He taught the first school for Negroes in DeKalb County, Georgia; it met Sunday afternoons; the only textbook was Webster's Blue Back Speller. Both father and mother died when Victoria was very young, and she and a sister were reared by an aged grandmother. A brother older rented a small farm; the girls picked cotton. After a few years, the brother left the farm, and got a job in Atlanta as a Pullman porter. He heard of the school started in Friendship Church basement, and made plans for his sisters to attend it. Victoria entered the basement school in October, 1881, living in a rented room. When the move was made to the barracks site in February 1883, she was among the first 32 boarding students. All the work of the boarding department and of the dormitories was done by students under the supervision of New England women.

As a student, Victoria taught in the Model School; completed the industrial courses in 1886; set type for the *Spelman Messenger* in the Seminary printing office; served as president of the Congo Mission Circle and the Literary Society. Work in Sunday Schools and house-to-house visitation, reading the Bible or a tract to those who could not read made up her Sunday program. She taught a rural school in the summer of 1884 and the succeeding five years. After her graduation in 1888, she returned to Spelman to teach again in the Model School. She next taught in the Howe Institute, Memphis, Tennessee. In 1890, she returned to Spelman to take the Missionary Training course, which included some nurse training, and received her certificate from this course in 1893. Experience as a rural worker in the country around Madison, Georgia, within a radius of 20 miles or more was followed by city experience as the only worker in Columbus. Then she married Rev. F. M. Simmons, and for a number of years her teaching 'was intermittent.' She is the mother of six boys and two girls; only one son and one daughter are now living. After her husband died, she returned to the schoolroom and remained a teacher until her retirement in 1946. In 1956, one of the public elementary schools in Atlanta was named in her honor, the Victoria Maddox Simmons Elementary School.

Mrs. Simmons celebrated her 70th anniversary on the Spelman campus in 1958. She lives in Atlanta and has a habit of being present at most of Spelman's special occasions. She writes, "Spelman College, my church, and my family are the dearest things on earth."

Selena Sloan entered the basement school in the fall of 1882 when about 15 years old. She boarded in the city with three or four other students until the move to the barracks property. She too was one of the first boarding students, and helped get the barracks clean and livable when the move to the new site was made in February 1883. She was a scholarship student. Her father was a white man; her mother, part Negro, part Indian. It was her mother's Negro pastor in Thomasville who recommended her to Miss Packard. She came from one of the larger towns, as did Ella Barksdale; and her achievements later were connected more with the city than with the rural life of Negroes.

After her graduation in 1888 from the Higher Normal and Scientific course, she taught in the public schools of Atlanta for several years. She won the commendation of the city superintendent of schools, and was given the task of organizing the first night school for Negroes, and making it succeed. She taught a few years in the State Normal School, Tallahassee, Florida. She was a pioneer in developing YWCA work for Negro girls in Atlanta and helped to build the Phillis Wheatley branch. She organized a Parent-Teachers Association for Negroes in Atlanta; then helped to build a state-wide organization; and finally became the founder and first president of the National Congress of Colored Parents and Teachers. The organization grew from 100 units to 1000 units with a membership of 100,000.

In 1895 Selena Sloan married an able physician and respected citizen of Atlanta, Dr. Henry Rutherford Butler. He died in 1934. Their only son, Dr. Henry Rutherford Butler, Jr. is a graduate of Harvard Medical College; held a Rosenwald fellowship for study and work in a London hospital; after the United States entered the war, he became a captain in the U.S. Army Medical Corps, and at the end of his service, had the rank of lieutenant-colonel. He was the first Negro to serve on the staff of Good Samaritan Hospital in Los Angeles.

Mrs. Butler accompanied her son to London. Introduced to the British officers of the Parent Teachers organization, she worked in the Nursery School Association program headed by the Duke of Gloucester; assisted in the cancer campaign; and worked on a school committee of which Lady Astor was head. Back in the USA, she worked with the American Red Cross; took the necessary training and served as a Gray Lady in the hospital at Fort Huachuca, Arizona.

Her interest in community affairs remains with her and keeps her young in spirit; and her loyalty to Spelman never falters. She traveled from California to Atlanta to be present at the Commencement Exercises in 1958 and was one of the speakers at the Alumnae Dinner. She is an active member of the Spelman Club of Los Angeles.

Mrs. Simmons and Mrs. Butler are among the very few persons now living (1959) who have vivid personal memories of the Basement School and of Miss Packard.

Nora Gordon, another 1888 graduate, decided to go to Africa as a missionary. She had entered Spelman in 1882. "She was ignorant, uncultivated and superstitious with mistaken ideas of religion." How much had happened to her during her years at Spelman is revealed somewhat by the article praising Mary

Lyon which she wrote for the November 1888 *Messenger*. It shows, too, in her letters to Mrs. Harvey Buel Spelman, and to Miss Packard and Miss Giles. A farewell service for her was held at Spelman on March 6, 1889. The examiner for the Mission Society, Dr. Murdock of Boston, found her "very sensible, modest, self-possessed, cultured, and devout."

She went to Washington, D. C., where she was met by Mrs. York, the former Charlestown Academy principal who had visited Spelman the previous year. Mrs. York took her to see the Capitol. She went on to Boston, and to Wollaston, the home of the Founders. "It was such a long, lonesome journey. No one to speak a single word. How I did wish for you, Miss Packard, or Miss Giles. . . ." On her arrival at the house in Wollaston, she found a welcome. She made a perceptive comment in her letter: "I see what pleasant surroundings you had to leave, and somewhat of the sacrifice you have made. I have always appreciated my teachers, but more so now than ever."

From London, en route to Africa, Nora Gordon wrote that when she unpacked, the sight of the American flag stirred her – it had never before seemed so beautiful; "I am glad that Miss Grover put one in my box." In London, Nora attended a Missionary Training Institute conducted by the Rev. and Mrs. H. Grattan Guinness, who had founded missions in the Congo. Mr. Guinness had been a recent visitor and speaker at Spelman Seminary. She proceeded from London to the mission in Palabala, and there she demonstrated well her caliber and her Spelman training.

Carrie Walls of the class of 1888, while still a student edited a department in the *Spelman Messenger* called "The Children's Exchange." After graduation, she taught in Belton, South Carolina, a school having 100 children; 16 were boarders. She married Mark H. Gassaway, and in 1889 they were appointed principals of Greeley Institute in South Carolina.

A graduate of 1897, Mrs. Minnie *Thomas* Brown, said at her 60th reunion that in the days following the Civil War, Negroes were so anxious to learn to read and teachers so scarce that her first grade teacher had been through only the second grade; that she herself had memorized the definitions of the parts of speech but did not know when she came to Spelman what they meant. Yet such was her continued ambition even after she married and moved to San Diego that she entered San Diego College, the second Negro to be admitted. She received her A.B. degree at the age of 54, and became the first Negro to teach in the San Diego public schools. Her daughter Thelma who finished the Spelman High School in 1925, and Spelman College in 1929, carries on as a teacher in her mother's spirit.

One marvels at the growth in wisdom and grace of young women such as those just named and others in the few years they had the opportunity to learn. Nor did their zest for growth in mind and soul stop when they left the Seminary.

CHAPTER VIII

THE TENTH ANNIVERSARY YEAR
AND THE DEATH OF MISS PACKARD

DR. MOREHOUSE once compared the beginnings of Spelman Seminary to a mustard seed, with its phenomenal growth due to the faith of the Founders and their associates, faith that had removed or surmounted mountains of difficulty.

The Seminary had moved from the borrowed basement to a place of nine uncultivated acres. By gradual acquisition the size had increased to 14 acres, and grew to look like a campus, with landscaping, grass, and varieties of shrubs and trees. Only the year before, there had been added to previous plantings 15 elms, two water oaks, two magnolias, three Spanish oaks, two holly and one special cedar tree, a gift from Josiah Sherman, rooted in a tub, and shipped to be planted out-of-doors "as one of the permanent adornments of our grounds." Presumably this was the deodar cedar which continued for 60 years to give joy to all who entered the campus, and which served in its last quarter-century of life as the blue-lighted Christmas tree in front of Sisters Chapel.

Two large brick buildings, Rockefeller Hall and Packard Hall, now provided classrooms, music rooms, library and chapel in addition to dormitory rooms for students and teachers. The four barracks buildings still housed students and teachers, including Miss Packard, Miss Giles, and Miss Upton. Packard Annex, also of brick, held the kitchen and pantries, the printing office and "a light airy sewing room." The dining room was in the above-ground-level basement of Packard Hall.

Speaking of the boarding department, Miss Packard had made a contract with a grocery firm to supply as required for the year 1890-91: Beef steak, beef roast, lamb, and veal at 6¢ per pound; liver at 3¢ per pound; pork at 8¢ per pound; sausage at 8¢ per pound.

A commodious brick laundry with arrangements for 80 girls to wash at one time was built in 1890. Here again, the generosity of Mr. Rockefeller supplied what had become a pressing need.

Better equipment for academic work had been obtained, by purchase and by gifts. A library had been accumulating mainly through the gifts of friends – of not just cast-off books, but of standard authors and reference books; for example, a Webster's *Unabridged Dictionary*, early supplied by G. & C. Merriam of Springfield, Massachusetts, and the *International Cyclopedia* in 15 volumes. A gift of school apparatus came from a legacy left for the purpose by the late ex-Governor Coburn of Maine. The first lot included a chemical outfit, a telescope, a school lantern and 80 pictures, an air pump, a polariscope attachment for the microscope, and botanical apparatus; still more was to follow. A solar camera, given by Ella Cole, was used to show pictures of foreign lands to the students for the first time as part of their Christmas festivities.

A microscope, gift of Ella's father, Robert H. Cole, founder of the American Optical Company, was made an incentive to study and good conduct! Note this –

"Students who have passed properly in studies and in moral standing are allowed to see exhibitions with the microscope given in the library." So reads a *Messenger* item in February, 1889.

No boarding accommodations were possible until the move from the basement in 1883. By 1885, there were 200 boarding students; by 1891, the number had increased to 464, with the boarders outnumbering the "day-scholars." This was important, for the Seminary could make its greatest impact and have greater hope of permanent influence on students who lived on the campus. Students came from 12 different states, including Indian Territory, Texas, Louisiana, Maryland, North Carolina, Massachusetts. The total number of pupils was 830; that number includes the children in the Model School.

The number of teachers had increased by four years after the founding to 17; in seven years, to 27; in 10 years, to 34 of whom 33 lived on the campus. Of the 33 resident teachers, 11 were supported by the WABHMS; the teachers in the industrial departments were supported in part by the Slater Fund; other teachers gave their services entirely, or were content with receiving the bare cost of living. "It is remarkable," it was said, "that so many choice women of rare ability and experience have given their services to the school."

Dr. Malcolm MacVicar, who had resigned his position as Chancellor of McMaster University to become Superintendent of Education of the ABHMS, spent 10 weeks on the Spelman campus in the spring of 1891. He made a study of present work and future needs. After many conferences with Miss Packard and Miss Giles, a program of development was worked out which called for an expansion of the resources. It was his hope that the ABHMS and the WABHMS would cooperate fully in carrying it out. The organization suggested was: 1) Collegiate Department; 2) Academic Department with a thorough English course for prospective teachers or missionaries; and a College Preparatory course with foreign languages; 3) Training School Department with (a) Normal course; (b) Missionary Training course; (c) Nurse Training course; (d) Industrial course including sewing, dressmaking, and type-setting. For this program, better facilities were needed, especially a hospital, – so his report read – and for the Normal course, a new building. Scientific equipment and library books were other needs.

Religious training and Bible study were and would continue to be emphasized but no mention of them can give an adequate idea of the spirit that animated Spelman Seminary. Daily devotional exercises, weekly preaching service, Sunday School lessons, all had a part. On Sunday mornings Miss Packard taught a Bible class of over 300; even outsiders attended it. But it was from their daily living rather than from their words that the most abiding lessons were learned by Spelman students from their teachers. The Founders, and certainly most of the teachers, were genuine Christians with love in their hearts and without cant. The students "caught" Christianity from the contagion of their spirits, but it was not a quick or easy triumph. They had to learn to "endure hardness" and to accept discipline as necessary to growth.

Anniversary Exercises with many participating were held on April 11, and formal exercises, with an Anniversary Sermon, on Sunday, April 12. The Saturday session brought out touching reminiscences from the earliest students. One of "the first eleven" said, "the teachers seemed to have something like magic about them. . . . We soon understood that the school was to be for women and girls and was to be called *The Female Seminary.* [We] did not know what *Seminary* meant but we were very proud of our name. . . . Our first catalog was as large as a common sheet of paper. . . ."

But the backward glance was not its chief theme. To be sure, the record was displayed, showing the contrast between 1881 and 1891, under and above the caption, *What Hath God Wrought*! It was an impressive record, but there was no tendency to pause to relish it. Miss Packard quoted a psalm of praise, but she did not allow herself or others to rest on past accomplishment or to delay the forward look. She said on this anniversary occasion: "Great is the contrast between 1881 and 1891, but what a drop in the bucket is one school! . . . We must do a hundred times more in the next decade than in the past. . . . Every branch of Spelman Seminary is to be made more effective. This is only a beginning."

One item that was frequently mentioned with pride during the Tenth Anniversary Year was the work of Spelman graduates in Africa. Nora Gordon, '88, had been the first to go — in 1889. Her letters describing her experiences kept Africa very much alive in the minds of the students. Her letters were in serious vein, with here and there an unintentional humorous turn. For example, she had had to lay aside her bustle [they were in vogue and her Spelman teachers had worn them] be-

cause the natives were constantly referring to her as "that de-
formed missionary."

The second Spelman graduate to go to Africa from Spelman
was Clara A. Howard, who had entered the basement school
in the spring of 1881. After her graduation in 1887, she taught
school in the country, over 200 miles from Atlanta – in a log
cabin with a dirt chimney which fell down, and a roof covered
with boards, and when it rained Clara had to raise an umbrella.
She had 60 pupils in this school, of all grades. Later she taught
in the Atlanta schools and boarded at Spelman. Then she decided that the need in Africa was even greater than at home,
and that she was one who should go to the distant field. She
passed the scrutiny of the Woman's Foreign Board of Missions in Boston, and was appointed to go to Lukungu on the
Congo to take charge of a school of about 100 pupils.

A service was held on February 16, 1890, of consecration and
farewell. Clara Howard's going to Africa was not looked upon
by anyone as a gay adventure. She well knew that the trials and
disappointments of a missionary's life are many. There were
short talks by fellow students, Mamie White '90 and Selena
Sloan '88; by ministers, white and colored; by Judge Hillyer.
The most touching "charge," with both muscle in it and deep
affection, was given by Miss Packard. Not in sadness but in
almost words of poetry, she spoke to this young woman leaving
home and family "to become a stranger in a strange land, in the
midst of a strange people, speaking a strange language, where
no Sabbath bell will call to prayer. . . . Thus you go forth alone
with not even one familiar friend to journey with you by land
or by sea, or to welcome you at the journey's end; but you have
counted the cost and know Him in whose strength you trust.
Our love and our prayers will follow you. You will have much
to try you in your new home; brain, heart and soul will be
taxed to the utmost; may your patience and strength be equal
to your day! This will be a new school for you – learn well its
lessons, not forgetting those you learned here. . . . God bless
you, my dear Clara, . . . and give you courage and faith to meet

bravely all the trials. . . ." Thus she commended her "to God and to the word of His grace who is able. . . ." In reading the account of this occasion, one could fairly hear the jubilant chorus of past and present students of Spelman singing:

> His guiding radiance above her shall be
> A beacon to God, to love and loyalty.

The Death of Sophia Packard

At the end of the eighth year, Miss Giles wrote in her diary "The best year we have had in the history of the school." Yet an ominous note appeared two days later. "Miss Packard very ill with one of her old headaches." The two women went North; visited Dr. William Howe in Cambridge; went in July with the Coles to the White Mountains; and in August to Martha's Vineyard, presumably for WABHMS meetings. By mid-September, both were back at Spelman. At first, Miss Packard seemed to be improved in health, although she got tired more easily. In January, 1890, she fell a victim to what must have been an influenza epidemic, as "about eighty were sick with 'la grippe.' " Meanwhile, the demands of the Seminary did not lessen. A laundry was an imperative need. Dr. Morehouse agreed with Miss Packard regarding the need, "but," he wrote, "where is the money to come from?" Money was required also to put in a six-inch main from the city water supply. The library in the south wing of Packard Hall, which was to be named Quarles Library, needed books for which solicitation must be made. All these special appeals were in addition to increased administrative duties, as the number of students and teachers and buildings grew. As a result, her health did not improve. In March, "at the request of the Trustees," she "took a vacation," the annual report states, "and made a journey to the Holy Land. . . ." Miss Upton sailed with Miss Packard, as did Mrs. Kemp, a congenial member of the staff. Miss Giles, Miss Mary J. Packard and Miss Werden, the editor of the *Messenger*, joined Miss Packard's party in Europe in July.

The trip in the Holy Land was refreshing, even if strenuous.

We went from Jerusalem to Nazareth passing through Samaria, and it took four days to make this journey on horseback. There are no carriage roads through Palestine and we were on horseback fourteen days of from six to nine hours each, and for more than half the way, the paths were stonier and steeper than can be well imagined. . . .

We start every morning at six. . . . We wonder that we can endure it, but we are becoming accustomed to it, and are in better physical condition than we were a week ago after our visit to the Dead Sea and the Jordan.

They took delight in the flowers, in detail and by name. "We have noticed as many as eighty different kinds of wild flowers. We like to think that Jesus loved these very flowers." "The Sea of Galilee, low among high hills, with snowy Hermon looking down on it from afar, is much more beautiful than we had thought. Our party tried to catch fish in it. . . . We saw it by moonlight; we saw it at sunset and sunrise; we saw it smooth as a mirror, and we saw it ruffled by a gentle breeze; but we could not imagine it changed into a dangerous sea, so peaceful and small did it look."

Miss Packard's travel schedule indicated that she would visit the pyramids of Egypt on April 17. Accordingly, the Spelman students arranged a trip to Egypt for themselves for that evening. First, information about the country and people was presented; then stereoptican views of places of interest were shown. An impromptu song – "Let's go down to Egypt" – added to the zest of the occasion. Extracts from Miss Packard's letters from Egypt and Palestine had been shared with the students; in them she had even cited specific references for them to read from *The Pharoahs of the Bondage and the Exodus!*

Miss Packard returned from her journey with renewed vigor and improved health. She spoke to the students on the opening day. She was glad to welcome a new associate, the Rev. George B. Sale, recently elected President of Atlanta Baptist Seminary. She entered fully into the routine of administration and of planning for the years to come. From early in the second semester, however, she was often not dependably well, and she sent for her niece, Mrs. Phoebe Drury, to help her and relieve Miss Giles and others of her care. She had ups and downs of strength and vigor, until the end of the academic year. Her last formal talk to the students was on Founders Day. "A thrilling talk," it was called by one adult listener, "long to be remembered by many." Miss Packard went to Friendship Church on May 21 for the Commencement Exercises, but on account of the great heat, she did not remain to the end. Miss Giles presented the diplomas, and spoke briefly to the 16 graduates.

Miss Packard as Treasurer signed a contract for alterations of the laundry building just the day before she and Miss Giles started North. Her last act before leaving Atlanta was to order library furniture to be made during vacation.

Not long after the train left Georgia, Miss Packard became ill and soon was unconscious. She and her party, including a nurse, left the train in Washington and went to the St. James Hotel. After medical attention, Miss Packard seemed more comfortable and looked peaceful. On June 21, 1891, in the morning hours, she quietly passed away. Everything had been done that could be done for her comfort. She was buried in beautiful Silver Lake Cemetery in Athol, Massachusetts, where her oldest brother, Joseph, had been buried eight years before.

Among a dozen brief remarks "Gleaned from Letters of Condolence," printed in the Memorial issue of the Spelman *Messenger* was this one, whose author surely must have been one of Miss Packard's Spelman girls:

"I can only think of dear Miss Packard as leaping forth with overwhelming bliss into the higher work and opportunities of heaven. No restraints can affect her ambitious soul now."

Even a brief overview of Sophia B. Packard's life reveals her great qualities. Brought up in a home where education was valued, she got her own schooling by perseverance over obstacles, teaching and studying alternately for 10 years. In appearance she was tall, with blue eyes and light brown hair, of generous figure, strong expressive face, and graciousness of manner. She had ambition and determination, plenty of energy and a strong sense of humor. She stood erect and walked briskly, to the end of her days.

Abundant witness exists to her excellence as a teacher. Students followed her from school to school. The Connecticut Literary Institution provided a strong college preparatory course. The move from CLI to the Oread Collegiate Institute offered Miss Packard a chance to teach and administer on the college level. Her experience as a department head of an insurance company developed her practical side and brought praise of her 'clear and accurate mind,' her 'sound judgment and unbending integrity.'

Dr. George C. Lorimer, pastor of Tremont Temple in Boston, from his first acquaintance with her in 1869, marked her as "a woman with a great lifework before her." Incidentally, Dr. Lorimer was a person who believed that a woman should be permitted to do anything God had given her power to do. He persuaded Miss Packard to leave business life; made her 'pastor's assistant' with that title, and she so remained until within a month of the close of his first Tremont Temple pastorate. It was from her office in Tremont Temple that she took a leading part in organizing the Woman's American Baptist Home Mission Society.

She left New England where she enjoyed the comforts of home and congenial friends, where she held the confidence of men and women who themselves were persons of achievement, and truly she gambled with her life on the love of Christ.

She went to Georgia, a land torn by strife, to give herself to the education of the women of the Negro race. In spite of trials and discouragements and fatigue, her enthusiasm for the work — for the students and the people — never wavered.

"The early teachers," Dr. Mordecai Johnson recalled in a talk at Spelman's 75th anniversary, "lived in ostracism and lived in loneliness, but they had no bitterness. . . ." Then he made this significant comment: "I can remember no time in which I ever heard them say a bitter or an invidious or a hateful word about the Southern white people. Rather they labored ever joyfully because they had confidence in the capacity of their students for growth in body, mind, and spirit; and the students justified their faith."

Now, Dr. Johnson is too young to have known Miss Packard. He knew Miss Giles, Miss Upton, Miss Grover and Miss Werden, all of whom served under Miss Packard and long after. The statement he made, however, was completely true of Miss Packard; it was Miss Packard who created the climate, abetted by Miss Giles and the New England women she enlisted in the school.

There was magic in Miss Packard, in her personal relations. She had the power of 'awakening the latent energies of her pupils and of lifting their minds to noble ideas.' New England culture, reflected in the poets and prose writers, European culture reflected in literature and history, enriched by her visits to Europe and the Holy Land, she shared with her students. They got from her an awareness of world events, past and present. To quote Selena Sloan Butler '88, she placed on the students the responsibility for Spelman's standing and good name; and so they grew more quickly into responsible and earnest women.

Notwithstanding the seriousness of her aim, and her convictions, she had, said Miss Upton, an irrepressibly buoyant spirit, and an inimitable way of mingling fun and pathos, warning and entreaty.

Another Spelman teacher, Mrs. Barrett, spoke of her "coming to the diningroom after a sleepless night, and refreshing us with merry conversation spiced with ready wit." Victoria Maddox Simmons '88 recalls that she was full of fun and had an infectious laugh, and Emma DeLany stated that with her cheerful, joyous nature, her mixture of deep pathos and love of fun, it was impossible to feel dull in her company.

Dr. Samuel Graves, president of Morehouse College, 1885-90, made this perceptive comment: "There was a divine and noble contagion in her. The old basement of the Friendship

Church was full of it. It pervaded the Seminary when the school took on the larger proportions; and with its growth the enthusiasm grew. Her friends in the North and the East felt it and . . . responded to it. . . ."

A visitor in 1886, C. H. Mead, wrote in a published article: "Miss S. B. Packard is a born general, and I doubt if more than one such woman is given to each generation."

In an incredibly short time, the students of Spelman Seminary absorbed knowledge, breathed deeply of an atmosphere of industry and refinement, and experienced the helpfulness of the Christian way of life. They left filled with a desire to continue to grow and to share their benefits with others.

Tributes from Dr. Morehouse, General Morgan, Dr. Mac-Vicar, spoken and implied, run all through the history; but perhaps the man who knew her most deeply was Dr. George C. Lorimer. He understood and valued what someone called 'the contrarieties' of her make-up. A shrinking sensitiveness — and a bold aggressiveness. A rare union of culture and religion, qualities too often separated. She was eminently religious, believing in the power of religion; at the same time she was 'a devotee at the shrine of culture, and a believer in its charm and usefulness.' He saw in her also to a degree seldom met a uniting of the ideal and the practical, for "she dreamed her dream; but she made her dream a living reality." Dr. Lorimer in his address at Athol attributed to Miss Packard the quality of "knowing how to meet responsibilities independent of the world's praise or approval," and quoted Carlyle's saying that no man begins to live until he can dispense with the applause which instinctively he may covet. Measured by its ideas and ideals, and its continuing influence, Sophia Packard's work meets every qualitative test of greatness. In ability and achievement, she deserves to stand in the same echelon of workers in unpopular causes as Mary Lyon, Emma Willard, Lucretia Mott, or Catherine Beecher. Like recognition might have come to her if her field of work had been almost anywhere in the world except in our own Southern States, where the beneficiaries were American Negroes, a people who have lived and learned and worked and suffered, and had their trials and joys *and* their achievements *overlooked*, sometimes *belittled*, more often *ignored*.

Yet after all, Miss Packard never sought the applause of men. The last two lines of the Spelman song written by Samuel Francis Smith, author of *America*, apply as well to her as they apply to Spelman College.

> The wreaths for her brow are not perishing bays
> But love of her children and their grateful praise.

CHAPTER IX
HARRIET GILES AND LUCY UPTON
1891-1909

ON July first, 1891, Miss Giles had a long talk with Dr. MacVicar about Spelman, and the next day, sad in spirit, she attended the Board meeting. She was then appointed Principal of Spelman Seminary, and Miss Lucy H. Upton was appointed Associate Principal. Miss Giles shrank from the responsibility, but developed the required strength and force to handle it.

Miss Lucy Houghton Upton's name has not appeared before in this narrative, except for casual mention. She was one of the most cultured and best beloved of the early teachers. She had come to Spelman Seminary in 1888 to assist the Principals. She soon made herself virtually indispensable. Quiet and modest, she loved Nature and books; she identified the birds on the campus and taught the students to become acquainted with them; she knew the trees and shrubs, and made the students recognize them as friends. Her mind was keen and disciplined. Her range of interests was broad. Miss Giles relied on her ability, her wisdom, and her loyalty to her and to Spelman. It was Miss Upton who presented each year to the Board of Trustees the Annual Report of the Principals.

During Miss Giles' administration, teacher training received great impetus. Dr. MacVicar's plan for its development was heartily endorsed by the conference of presidents of the Home Mission Society schools; was approved by Dr. Morehouse and by Frederick T. Gates, Secretary of the Baptist Education Society and one of Mr. Rockefeller's trusted advisers; and was heartily endorsed at a National Convention of Colored Baptists in Dallas, Texas, on September 17.

The plan, if carried out, would require a new building. There was correspondence on this matter between Miss Giles and Dr. Morehouse in October. Dr. MacVicar discussed it with Dr. J. L. M. Curry, who from 1891 to 1903 served as General

Agent of the Peabody Fund and as Director of the Slater Fund; Dr. Curry was friendly to the project, and promised help from the Slater Fund toward salaries of teachers. It was hoped, even expected, that the Slater Fund would give $6,000; what the Slater Board voted was $4,000.

At the March, 1892, annual meeting of the Board of Trustees, Dr. Morehouse was able to report that, as the outcome of Mr. Rockefeller's generosity, Spelman Seminary was to have a new brick building to cost $35,000. At the same meeting, the trustees elected Miss Giles a member of the Board and Treasurer of the Seminary. Mrs. Alice B. Coleman, the new president of the WABHMS, also was elected to the Board, to succeed Mrs. Nickerson who had recently died; she added strength and wisdom to it for the next 40 years.

The new building, at the request of its donor, John D. Rockefeller, was called Giles Hall. As the plans for it developed, the estimate of cost mounted. The contract, as signed in July, was for $51,793.00. The additional cost of furnishings for 27 classrooms, laboratory, and assembly hall was in round numbers $5,000, which had to be raised.

A larger than usual grant from the Slater Fund made it possible for the Normal work and the Practice School to be enlarged at once. The trustees of the Slater Fund reduced the number of schools aided from 35 to 13, in order to concentrate on those giving most promise in training of leaders and teachers. Spelman's grant was increased and was second only to that given to Hampton Institute.

The Practice School was reorganized under the superintendence of Miss Elizabeth V. Griffin, a gifted and able graduate of the Potsdam Normal School. Arrangement was made with the Atlanta Baptist Seminary to join in the normal training program by maintaining a practice school for boys on their own campus, while both the young men and young women would receive instruction at Spelman.

Quarles Memorial Library came into being in 1891-92. The dues of five cents a month paid by members of the Educational

Society, started in the Basement School in 1881, had been accumulating with interest. It was decided to use this money toward a better library. A large room in Packard Hall, therefore, was fitted up; the books were moved and reclassified according to the Dewey system. By 1897, the Library had from 2,000 to 3,000 volumes. The library furniture ordered by Miss Packard – 'her last act before leaving Atlanta' – was installed. And, so ran the *Messenger*, "this Quarles Memorial Library is now, next to the Chapel, the most attractive room at Spelman, as it ought to be."

Nurse training was augmented, and the medical care of the students was improved by the addition of two small buildings joined together and called Everts Ward. This contained operating room, surgical ward, medical ward, classroom, closets, bathroom. The money for it, given by a Northern lady who wished her name unknown, came through Dr. Everts of Chicago, an active Spelman supporter.

The Missionary Training Course, begun in 1892, was proving its value from the field work done by the seven young women who constituted the first class. They had spent the summer months on the field and had started Bible bands, temperance bands, Christian Endeavor societies, assisted in Sunday Schools, visited homes, held mothers' and children's meetings, and ably assisted the pastors of churches which received them.

At the annual meeting of the Board of Trustees in March, 1893, the Principals' report, submitted and read by Miss Upton, the Associate Principal, was so interesting and gratifying that the trustees, by resolution, expressed the desire that it be published in *The Journal and Messenger* of Cincinnati, *The Standard* of Chicago, and the *Watchman* of Boston, in addition to the *Georgia Baptist, Christian Index*, and *Spelman Messenger* of Georgia. The financial report read by Miss Giles showed that the Seminary had been managed with wisdom and the lightest expenditure of funds consistent with efficiency. The trustees complimented the Principals on this outcome.

The second year of Miss Giles' presidency included the usual events, academic and non-academic. Life on a Negro campus is never monotonous, for hazards constantly threaten just around the corner. Yet friends help meet them. The January *Messenger* expressed gratitude to "the chief of police for sending two of his force to protect us during the Christmas season" and added "We were pleased to entertain them also at our Christmas dinner."

Miss Giles breathed a prayer of thankfulness that the year closed successfully. It was not easy for her to carry on without Miss Packard. As Claudia White, one of Spelman's first two college graduates, wrote: "Diffident to what was sometimes to her a trying degree, Miss Giles shrank from publicity. Even the duties contingent upon her office, which brought her into prominence, were not altogether pleasant to her and never grew to be perfectly easy to perform. Only a stern sense of duty nerved her retiring spirit to their performance." Miss Giles met life with humility, but she carried her growing responsibilities with growing power.

Her summer included about a month in Wisconsin, where she visited her brother, Hiram Giles. She met Dr. Morehouse in Chicago; went to the World's Fair; visited the Cook County Normal School; attended closing exercises of a kindergarten school en route to Madison. In Wisconsin she presented the cause of Spelman to the Winona Lake Assembly. On the way to her home in Massachusetts, she inspected the Potsdam Normal School organized for N. Y. State by Dr. MacVicar. The previous summer she had visited the State Normal School in Oswego, New York. She thus acquainted herself with teacher training at its best.

The dedication of Giles Hall took place in December 1893. "No dearth of speakers," the *Messenger* reports — and good speeches came from them. At the afternoon session, Mrs. Victoria Maddox Simmons, class of 1888, gave an historical account. Dr. Malcolm MacVicar and Dr. Morehouse gave the principal addresses.

Dr. MacVicar referred to his call by the Home Mission Society to become superintendent of education of the Baptist Home Mission Schools in the South; he said that Spelman Seminary was the first institution to which he was directed, and that the impression made by Spelman went far to bring him to a favorable decision. After his acceptance, he spent two weeks on the campus, conferring with Miss Packard and others. The WABHMS, the ABHMS, and the Slater Board, together with Mr. John D. Rockefeller's gift of Giles Hall, had made possible the program he proposed.

Dr. Morehouse's address dealt with the evolution of Spelman Seminary from the "germinal idea" of two Christian women of New England "to found for the colored young women of the South a Christian school somewhat on the order of Mt. Holyoke Seminary . . . to a thoroughly graded institution with nurse training, missionary training," and now "this high grade normal school for more thorough preparation of teachers than is now afforded by any other institution of either race in the south." He added:

"There has been a natural development along the lines of existing conditions; a school adapted to the needs of the day, and ready to take on other and higher work when the fulness of time shall come so to do. For we are not to regard this as the end. . . . On the part of thousands [of colored people] there is an eagerness and a spirit of self-sacrifice for education that I have never seen equalled elsewhere. . . . *And so some day look out for an institution here which,* while retaining its present excellence, *shall take on other features and provide as good an education as is provided by any other institution for any other young women in the land.* . . . The bread and butter theory of education ought to be outlawed. . . . Any theory of education that does not look to the largest possible development of the human mind and the formation of the noblest character . . . is radically wrong." Rather Christian education should aim "to make more intelligent, thoughtful, refined, and better men and women, and *in the process of evolution, Spelman Seminary will do yet a grander work along this line.*"

Dr. Morehouse paid tribute to Miss Packard and to Miss Giles, and expressed thankfulness to many friends who, inspired by Miss Packard and Miss Giles, had given support to the school from its earliest days toward the purchase of land, buildings, and equipment. "Chief among these was Mr. John D. Rockefeller. . . ." He then noted the amounts given by Mr. Rockefeller as follows:

$ 7,500 toward the purchase of the land
20,000 toward the erection of Rockefeller Hall
2,700 for heating purposes
3,000 for Packard Hall
3,000 for the laundry
50,000 for this new and noble structure which he wished to be called "Giles Hall" in honor of its Principal
6,500 for the excellent steam heating plant for the three brick buildings

The total is $92,700.

Dr. William Jefferson White of Augusta, Georgia, presented a resolution which was adopted by the colored people present, "white folks having nothing to do with it," expressing to Hon. J. D. Rockefeller and his wife "heartfelt thanks" for their "magnificent contribution for the education of our youth" and praying "that heaven's richest blessings may rest upon you through life."

At the evening session, the main address was made by General Thomas J. Morgan, D.D., of New York, Corresponding Secretary of the ABHMS, who had led Negro troops to victory in the Civil War. He emphasized the revolution that had taken place in 30 years and the opportunities now open through education and Christian culture, and ended with a ringing challenge. As the 100,000 colored men enrolled as soldiers had left a "record of credit, courage, chivalry, power of self-control, patience, industry," so now, with schools open to them, he proclaimed that "the highest attainments are possible for any aspiring, competent colored man."

M. W. Reddick of the Atlanta Baptist Seminary introduced a resolution citing General Morgan as among the dearest of the Negro's friends "who, on the battlefield, put to test the chivalry, patriotism and loyalty of the Negro soldiers," and who is now spending his life and labor for the advancement of the Negro race.

The fitting jubilee for the end of the day would surely have been

> Great Day, the Righteous Marching . . .
> God's goin' to build up Zion's walls.

The trustees at the next annual meeting of the Board approved the program for future development set forth at the dedication of Giles Hall. Dr. MacVicar, in behalf of the ABHMS, informed the trustees that the Society intended to raise the standards of its institutions and "that Atlanta Baptist Seminary and Spelman Seminary are among the schools named to do advanced work of as high order as any college in the Southern States. The trustees authorized changes in the charter if they were needed to carry out the move toward higher education.

Primary and intermediate departments formed the practice school in the normal training department, and were housed in Giles Hall. The grammar department and the academic department were in Rockefeller Hall. The "academic diploma" was to supersede the "normal and scientific diploma" granted hitherto. Twelve seniors out of 54 "academic" students received the diploma for completion of the academic course, which now included no instruction in methods and practice of teaching, but gave more time to other branches. In the normal department, four students were granted certificates for completing the Teachers Professional Course, which came to have the highly honored designation of TPC.

The graduates of the Missionary Training Course received

certificates. There had been seven in 1893; two in 1894; and thereafter never more than three. The course represented additional courses for two years, plus field work, and served a useful purpose while it lasted. It was discontinued in 1906; the total number of graduates from the course in 14 years was 27. A main cause for its discontinuance was the lack of opportunity for American Negroes in foreign mission fields, including Africa.

Certificates were given to students who completed the courses in printing and in nursing, but the students who finished only those courses were not regarded as graduates of the Seminary.

There was for all students training in household duties, serving, cooking, and laundry work; every pupil was taught to take care of herself and her room. The students, under supervision, did in shifts most of the work of the boarding department.

The Home Mission Societies, in their meetings and in their publications, began early to call attention to the approaching Fifteenth Anniversary. The *Home Mission Monthly* for October, 1895, devoted three columns editorially to Spelman, its growth and need of support. In addition, it printed a history of Spelman Seminary written by Miss Giles, which with pictures ran to 14 pages; this was followed by an "Outline of Life at Spelman" four pages long, by Miss Upton. Articles by graduates and other friends of the Seminary occupied 10 pages more. In fact, virtually the whole issue with the exception of the Society's financial statement was devoted to Spelman Seminary. The cover of the magazine bore the heading, *Spelman Seminary Number*.

The desire to develop and improve the educational program and the need of greater resources constantly compelled the attention of the Principals and the officers of the Mission Societies. Dr. MacVicar and Dr. Morehouse, with General Morgan, worked out a plan of development, a University plan, if you please, which Dr. MacVicar discussed many times with Miss Giles and Miss Upton.

Under date of March 16, 1896, the case was strongly presented to Mr. Rockefeller in a letter signed by Dr. Morehouse and General Morgan in the hope that Mr. Rockefeller might make a special gift to signalize the celebration of the Fifteenth Anniversary. The Plan included the following items:

Atlanta is strategically located for a southern educational center; now located here are the two seminaries, Spelman for women and Atlanta Baptist Seminary for men; they should provide complete *college instruction* for both groups. To do so would require more buildings, teachers, assured income. The suggestion was made that there be constituted Spelman University, planned by Dr. MacVicar, President Sale, Miss Giles and Miss Upton. For a beginning, the income at 5% on one million dollars would be needed; the sum of $200,000 in the next twelve months would give the program a good start. Such an income would enable the Baptist Mission Boards to deal constructively with other pressing needs. The hope was expressed that approval of the plan by Mr. Rockefeller might be announced at Spelman's fifteenth anniversary.

The plan was not accepted by Mr. Rockefeller. This was a great disappointment to those who knew of the proposal. Perhaps "the fulness of time" had not come for it.

The Fifteenth Anniversary—1896

Stirring addresses were made as the Seminary celebrated the Fifteenth Anniversary. Especially noteworthy were those by General Thomas J. Morgan on "Higher Education for Colored Women"; by Dr. Malcolm MacVicar on "Normal Training at Spelman Seminary"; by Miss Upton on "Needs of Spelman Seminary"; and by Dr. Henry L. Morehouse on the subject, "The Worth of Spelman Seminary to the World." There were also addresses by the State School Commissioner of Georgia, Hon. G. R. Glenn; by Mrs. Selena Sloan Butler, class of '88; and by Mrs. Mary C. Reynolds, Corresponding Secretary of the WABHMS, on "Spelman Seminary: Benefactors."

Each address was followed by a conference on the subject presented; several of the conference meetings were presided over by Spelman graduates. Miss Giles opened the first session with an Historical Sketch which fully merited the applause and congratulations it received.

The paper on "The Needs of Spelman" read by Miss Upton at the afternoon session on April 12 revealed her prophetic insight. It took into account the aims, the achievement, possibilities, the present assured resources, and financial needs for the future. Miss Upton placed no limits to her view of the possibilities. "We see in imagination, among the daughters of Spelman," she said, "college graduates, physicians, poets, editors, artists. Is it asked, 'Why cherish such aspirations?' 'Why not be satisfied with the Spelman of today.'" Her answer was that new horizons are a natural increment of growth. Just as a busy man is ready for more responsibilities, so is a school already flourishing, with fine buildings and equipment, hundreds of pupils, consecrated teachers and with a lofty ideal become a living reality, fitted to carry on other and more advanced "work that is in the line of the purpose of its existence. Spelman ought to become the Wellesley of the South."[1]

"Spelman," said Miss Upton, "holds her financial prosperity on an uncertain tenure. The receipts from the students for board and tuition barely cover a third of the running expenses; the generosity of the Slater Fund supports the normal and training and a part of the industrial work; some of the teachers assist by taking only a nominal compensation; the liberality of the WABHMS of New England and of personal friends sustains the rest. How will it be in the future? . . . the day may come when the hearts of the women of New England will turn to the East or the West rather than the South. After those who laid the foundation of Spelman have entered into rest, there may arise a king who knew not Joseph. . . ." So she made a plea for a liberal endowment, to provide for salaries of competent teachers and carry on the present program; and "for the Spelman of the future . . . a still larger endowment to enable her to carry out her aim with all its possibilities."

No doubt some of Miss Upton's hearers thought her vision-

[1] Patterned, Dr. Morehouse suggested, on Mount Holyoke; some visitors later labeled the Seminary the "Vassar of the South." Here Miss Upton names "Wellesley" as its ideal. The significance of such references is that a college of first rank was projected.

ary. But she did not omit the practical present. "This large need must not blind us to other necessities," she continued, and proceeded to enumerate them: new type for the printing office; a hospital to offer more varied experience to the student nurses; microscopes and other apparatus for biology and chemistry; new dictionaries, maps, globes, books for the library; gymnasium equipment; better space and equipment for kitchen and dining rooms; music practice rooms; electric lighting; loan funds.

Then she cited more vital needs that money can never fill: the love and prayers of all her friends; the loyalty, love, prayers of every one of her children translated into action; and a continuance of the harmony and consecration that have been a distinguishing characteristic of her teachers. The exercises of the Anniversary were reported daily with considerable detail in the *Atlanta Constitution*.

The Cotton States Exposition held in Atlanta in 1895 attracted national and to an extent, world-wide attention. The Negro building, which included a Spelman exhibit, was a revelation to many visitors of the rapid advance by the Negro in education of head and hand. The speech made by Booker T. Washington at this exhibition enlightened Southern white people and gained the support of many of them who chose to take his reference to separateness as an ultimate applicable to all areas of life. The controversy it caused among Negro educators was for many years bitter and divisive.

The Exposition brought many visitors to Spelman. One session of the annual Baptist Foreign Mission Convention was held in Spelman's chapel. Representatives of many national groups such as the National Council of Women, the Smithsonian Institution, the U. S. Bureau of Education, came to the campus. The visitors included: "Miss Lucy M. Salmon and Miss A. M. Ely, professors of Vassar College; Booker T. Washington, Principal of Tuskegee Institute; Bishop John Vincent, father of 'Chautauqua'; Rev. Dwight L. Moody and his singers." Also many men and women came whose names are not so well known but whose lives and influence in their own communities were outstanding.

In the fall of 1897, two students were for the first time registered as freshmen in the college department. They were Jane Anna Granderson and Claudia T. White.

Atlanta Baptist Seminary officially changed its name to Atlanta Baptist College in 1897. In 1898, Quarles Hall on the Morehouse campus was dedicated, situated to face Chestnut Street. As Brawley's *History of Morehouse College* states, it was "So placed as to be equally accessible to the young men of the college and the college students of Spelman Seminary. . . . Spelman Seminary bore her part of the cost of instruction by regularly contributing the services of one teacher, or, at first, the equivalent thereof. . . ." Services of several Spelman teachers were used; for example, one taught Latin, another History, and another English. Miss Giles apparently hesitated to make a change in name and in program to "college" at this time. She wrote to Dr. MacVicar: "I have come to the conclusion that it will not be wise to agitate the change of the name from Seminary to College for the present or until we get an endowment. . . ." Hind-sight raises a question whether the development into "college" might have come about more rapidly if the change in name, and correspondingly in the emphasis, had been made earlier. The name was changed by amendment to the charter in 1924.

After a decade of use, the four brick buildings and the frame buildings badly needed repairs. The old barracks buildings were badly outmoded for dormitories; the chapel in Rockefeller Hall needed an additional stairway; roofs and floors needed repairs; heating and lighting had always been a problem. Miss Packard and Miss Giles, and later Miss Giles and Miss Upton, did not fail to cast their burdens on the Lord; nor did they fail to provide their earthly friends with the opportunity to help. And in 1900 another miracle was wrought.

There were of course, negotiations, letters exchanged, estimates of costs obtained for repairs and for new buildings, discussions with Mr. Frederick T. Gates and Mr. Rockefeller, and later with Mr. Rockefeller, Junior. Both the Rockefellers planned to go to Europe early in June, and two months before, Mr. Rockefeller had brought his son into the negotiations. Then one day came letters from General Morgan to Mrs. Mary C. Reynolds, Secretary of the WABHMS, with copy to Miss Giles, reporting the decision.

The letter from Mr. John D. Rockefeller, Jr., received June 5, 1900, "giving the authority of his father" was indeed one to cause "gratification and jubilation."

The improvements authorized by Mr. Rockefeller were summarized as follows:

1. The erection of a residence for the President.
2. The erection of a hospital.
3. The erection of a dormitory for 75 persons.
4. The erection of a second dormitory for 75 persons, connected with a large dining hall and kitchen to accommodate 400.
5. The erection of a new power house, with complete steam heating and electric lighting.
6. The purchase of ground so as to complete the square embraced within the campus.
7. The grading of Dewey Street, and laying of a brick sidewalk on one side.
8. The completion of the iron fence around the entire campus.
9. Making all necessary walks and drives, and grading of the campus.
10. Improvements of the old buildings, including a new stairway to the Chapel; and toilet and bathrooms in Rockefeller and Packard Halls; repairing roofs and flooring; kalsomining walls, etc.
11. The sinking and equipping of an artesian well.

A princely gift indeed it was! And it satisfied the basic needs of Spelman for years to come.

Miss Packard just must have been aware of this from one of the mansions above. "Glory, hallelujah! Praise the Lord."

Such a list of improvements looks simple enough to accomplish, provided money to pay for them is supplied, but any reader who has been involved in building construction will realize that a tremendous amount of preliminary study, planning, counting of costs, balancing of this against that, is required. The new power plant was to provide steam-heating and electric lighting for Spelman, and steam-heating for the men's college as well. Spelman Seminary was authorized by the City to construct a tunnel across Greenferry Street to connect the Atlanta Baptist College with the steam plant. The brick chimney was imposing; the 110 horsepower engine a marvelous addition. Cables laid underground to every building could carry electricity for 1,700 lights, including an arc light of 2,000 candlepower for the chapel and four of like power for night lighting of the grounds. The power plant was ready for business by November, 1900. It was specially blessed by every student for providing steam for use in the laundry. Previously each girl had to go to the laundry in the afternoon before her scheduled wash-day and put a pail of cold water in the boiler; this entitled her to a pail of hot water next morning with which to wash her clothes.

The matter of names for the four new main buildings had careful consideration. Mr. Rockefeller was unwilling that they be called for any members of his family. As Mr. Rockefeller, Junior, wrote Miss Giles in reply to her proposal: "My Mother and Father rather agree with me that . . . they prefer not to have the names of our family used." After further consultation through Mr. Rockefeller, Junior, the following suggestions were adopted:

Reynolds Cottage for the home of the President, in honor of Mrs. Mary C. Reynolds, corresponding secretary of the WABHMS.
MacVicar Hospital, in honor of Dr. Malcolm MacVicar, Superintendent of Education of the ABHMS, who had been the architect of the curricula for nurse training and the teacher professional courses at Spelman.

Morgan Hall, dining-hall and dormitory, in honor of General Thomas J. Morgan, corresponding secretary of the ABHMS.

Morehouse Hall, in honor of Dr. Henry L. Morehouse, corresponding secretary of the ABHMS 1879-93, 1903-17; president of the Spelman College Board of Trustees.

Mrs. Reynolds was pleased to have her name bestowed on the residence; she had never been satisfied with the earlier living arrangements for the Founders. The WABHMS, incidentally, was at this period supporting 16 of the Spelman teachers.

When General Morgan heard of the proposal to name a building for him, he demurred. "My name," he wrote Miss Giles, "is already connected with one or two Indian School buildings, and at least one Negro school building, which will serve to perpetuate my memory at least fifty years, – when I shall be very generally forgotten. If I have been in any wise instrumental in promoting the welfare of Spelman Seminary, I have already been abundantly repaid for it in the good work it has done for the Negro race."

General Morgan gave wise counsel regarding the management of MacVicar Hospital, keeping in mind that its chief purpose was to afford a school of practice for students in training as nurses. The by-laws adopted by the Trustees in 1902 followed in the main his suggestions. He advised that the physicians for the medical staff should be selected for fitness and not color; also that the insane, inebriates and imbeciles, the incurable, aged, and infirm, be excluded. Too many of the last-named in the hospital's later years, made a problem, as they limited the experience to be gained by student nurses.

The white physicians and surgeons who served on the staff were from Atlanta's best. MacVicar Hospital had the first closed staff in Georgia, and admission to it was regarded as an honor. One Negro doctor, Dr. McDougald was a member of the staff for a very short time. Otherwise, until 1928, MacVicar Hospital was staffed with white doctors only.

However well-trained the Negro doctors might be, after graduation from Rush (Chicago), Harvard, Howard or Meharry Medical Schools, they were shut out from even the city hospital practice and clinics in Atlanta until 1953, and were not admitted to membership in medical societies in the South (or to many in the North, for that matter), and so had negligible opportunity to keep abreast of progress in medicine or surgery except inadequately through the printed page.

Their exclusion from the staff of MacVicar Hospital during the years when outside patients were cared for became increasingly a cause of friction. A Negro doctor could have a patient admitted to MacVicar only through a white doctor. Thirty years or so later, there were a few first-class white physicians[1] who were willing to work out a plan to expand the MacVicar Hospital service and work with Negro physicians. After nurse training was discontinued in 1928, the hospital became a college hospital only, and served both Spelman and Morehouse students. Mrs. Ludie Andrews was made Superintendent of the hospital; Negro doctors were selected as College Physicians; and a consulting staff was retained, made up of white physicians and surgeons.

Early in February, 1901, Miss Giles and Miss Upton moved into Reynolds Cottage, which, as Miss Giles wrote General Morgan, "is everything that can be desired. . . . We . . . now for the first time realize how many inconveniences and deprivations we had at No. 1. . . ."

Morgan's walls were lifted in February, and the Morehouse foundation was dug. Six months before, the question of furnishings for the new buildings was raised, and a list was prepared for submission to Mr. Rockefeller. Happily for Spelman, the money was given, not only for furnishing the President's house and the hospital, but all the new buildings.

Mr. John D. Rockefeller, Jr., made his first visit to Spelman in April, 1901. He arrived Saturday morning and left on Sunday evening. He spoke to the students in the chapel Saturday night, and they in turn sang their best for him. He looked over

---

[1] Notably Dr. Edwin S. Byrd, who was head of MacVicar's consulting staff from 1928-45.

all the buildings, old and new, and also visited Atlanta Baptist College. Another group of about a dozen visitors led by Robert C. Ogden and accompanied by Dr. Frissell, president of Hampton Institute, was due on Sunday. A joint meeting of Spelman and Atlanta Baptist College waited for them in the Spelman Chapel from 11:00 a.m. until 1:00 p.m.; by that time some other visitors, one of whom was Judge Hillyer, were persuaded to speak. Mr. Ogden and his party came at five o'clock; the students were assembled again; there were some speeches, but the guests made only a short stay.

The visit by Mr. Rockefeller, Jr., was an important milestone, as it marked the beginning of his personal interest. Before the summer was over, he authorized, in behalf of his father, an additional $5,000 for improvements at Spelman. There had already been authorized in June in connection with the repairs and renovations requested, items estimated to cost $6,850. This sum included a house for the engineer or superintendent of buildings and grounds. The list indicates to the unknowing how hungry a college or boarding school can be! "The Lord gives us all these wonderful blessings," said the Principals' annual report, "through the generous hand of Hon. John D. Rockefeller." Yet one big financial worry was always present. Additional buildings require more money for maintenance.

Because the new buildings were not finished, the Twentieth Anniversary exercises were postponed to the following November. By that time, all the frame buildings belonging to the barracks had disappeared from the campus except Number One, which was moved to the north end to be used as shop and barn. The old Leonard Street had been shifted — closed where it had been inside the campus, and moved to become its eastern boundary.

A significant step in the growth of Spelman belongs to the year 1901. Claudia Turner White and Jane Anna Granderson mainly through classes at Atlanta Baptist College, completed the college course and were awarded the Bachelor of Arts degree – the first College graduates. They would have been an honor to any college in the land. The Commencement Exercises were held jointly with Atlanta Baptist College, as was customary. The speaker for the occasion was the Hon. Judson Lyons, Register of the U. S. Treasury, husband of Jane Hope Lyons, who later was Dean of Women at Spelman College.

The Twentieth Anniversary—1901

The Twentieth Anniversary exercises were held, and the four new buildings were dedicated in November 1901; *Reynolds Cottage*, the residence of the president; *Morehouse Hall*, a dormitory for 100 girls situated on the grounds where were formerly the old barracks; *Morgan Hall*, a dining room for the community and a dormitory for 70 students; *MacVicar Hospital*, with light, airy wards and a few private rooms, where young women already were in training for nurses. The steam heating plant, built in 1893, had been so enlarged, rebuilt, and expanded to provide electric lights for the campus, that it was regarded as a new building. Extensive repairs also had been made in Rockefeller, Giles, Packard; and the grounds provided with new walks and drives, trees and shrubbery. With the additional lots purchased, Spelman could now boast of a campus of 20 acres.

The aggregate of Mr. Rockefeller's gifts was about $180,500 – as General Morgan wrote, "truly a magnificent sum."

A visit to Friendship Church and its damp, dark basement made by some visitors pointed up to them more vividly than anything else the growth of Spelman Seminary and the contrast between its beginnings and its state at the end of 20 years.

Spelman, said the *Home Mission Monthly* editorially, "has already made for itself a place among the most forceful factors in the great work of reconstructing the South along new lines. It is thoroughly appreciated by the Negroes and – a very few white people. Such representative men as Dr. J. L. M. Curry, Commissioner Glenn, Judge Hillyer, and Dr. Landrum of the First Baptist Church recognize its significance and beneficence, but the mass of the citizens of Georgia know very little of it. Few of the citizens of Atlanta[1] have ever been on the campus, and most of them know it only as a 'nigger school.' But one white pastor was present at any of the interesting exercises of dedication. . . . Nevertheless, Spelman and kindred seminaries are silently working a revolution which is to affect the South profoundly. . . ."

The anniversary paid tribute to the Woman's American Baptist Home Mission Society which steadily gave the Seminary moral and financial support; also to the essential but less obvious-to-the-public help from the American Baptist Home Mission Society. The latter had originally purchased the site on which Spelman stands, for a school of both sexes. Not only did the Society relinquish the site for the purpose of a girls' school, but some of its officials rendered efficient aid in raising money to pay for it. Nearly all the large amount which had been expended for Spelman's land and buildings passed through its treasury, while plans of buildings, contracts for their erection, supervision of construction, and attention to complicated legal questions which at times arose had its special care. In all those matters as well as in the development of the educational program, three officers of the ABHMS, Dr. Malcolm MacVicar, Dr. Henry L. Morehouse, and General Thomas J. Morgan, gave freely of their time and interest and rendered invaluable service.

An anniversary address full of import was made by General Thomas Morgan on "What Spelman Seminary Stands For." He discussed the significance of the Seminary with its aim to do as far as practicable for the Negro women precisely what is being done for white women by Smith, Vassar, Wellesley, and other institutions. "Education as carried on at Spelman," he said, "has a three-fold value: it is an instrument of livelihood; it qualifies its possessor for service; it has a culture value. Cul-

---

[1] Exceptions were Dr. E. L. Connally, member of the Home Mission Board of the Southern Baptist Convention. His wife, a daughter of Governor Joseph Brown, war governor of Georgia, was a warm friend. She provided a mile of violets and roses for the campus. Their daughter, Mrs. John Spalding, was a trustee of Spelman College, 1926 to 1933.

ture that is to fit man not simply to do but to be, is an inalienable right."

The quality of academic work at Spelman continued to be high. Nor should it be overlooked that even a short residence on the Spelman campus left its impress. One student wrote: "When a girl comes to Spelman and returns home, everybody can see great improvement in her manners, housekeeping, and in fact in every respect. . . . One special thing Miss Giles requires of her girls is quietness, which always shows the mark of a lady."

Money for operation and maintenance was insufficient, and it was becoming harder and harder to raise money. On March 6, 1902, Miss Giles wrote in her diary, "The burden of unpaid bills seems greater than I can bear." At the Trustees' meeting on March 18, the Principals' report cited the difficulty. "We are in financial embarrassment such as has never before existed in the history of the school." Expenses had multiplied with the new buildings; the income remained the same from year to year. Fortunately, succor was soon to come – through the General Education Board – although it did not yet cast its shadow where Miss Giles could see it.

Dr. Wallace Buttrick, Secretary of the General Education Board, and Mrs. Buttrick, spent Sunday, April 27, with Miss Giles. In the afternoon, Dr. Buttrick spoke to the students; as did also William H. Baldwin, Chairman of the General Education Board; George Foster Peabody, its Treasurer; and Dr. William Moody, president of Northfield Seminary. The officers of the General Education Board reported that the Board had made a "generous donation" to Spelman for current expenses; also an anonymous donor, later revealed to be Mr. Peabody, gave $1,000 for free beds at MacVicar Hospital and promised help for a department of nature study.

In June, 1902, Miss Giles went to Cleveland for a fortnight; again in the summer of 1903, Miss Giles visited the Rockefeller-Spelman family in Cleveland. President Faunce of Brown University and Mrs. Faunce were guests at the same time. Miss Giles found Mr. Rockefeller's interest in Spelman as keen as ever. The visit ministered to the needs of the flesh as well as to the spirit; she wrote in her diary the full menu for each meal!

On their part, the students more and more responded to the campus atmosphere of culture and decorum. Miss Giles made official comment of it to the trustees: "The loud laugh is less frequent; the visit to the library more often made. Growth in culture and skill are apparent on every side . . . better care of the body, consequently better health."

One student wrote an essay about the trees on the campus. They included seven varieties of oak – post, red, water, pin, scarlet, white and magnolia; elms – American and cork; paulownia; ailanthus; locust; Lombardy poplar; willow; and fruit trees–apple, peach, plum, cherry, and persimmon. Miss Upton delightfully described the birds seen on Spelman campus – 41 species in all.

A notable lecture on "The Influence of Beauty on Development" given by Professor John Hope on April 14, 1904, was a tonic in turning eyes and minds away from absorption in present and material things to an awareness of beauty in things and people. Below are two quotations, though they do not fairly represent the well-developed logical address:

"Save some space from corn and cotton and plant a rosebush. Sage and thyme are pleasant but the sweet uselessness of a violet bed adds a dignity to your life and labor."

"In the trials and struggles of life, beauty is good to turn to. Learn its comfort and its inspiration."

The controversy over the place of industrial education in schools for Negroes engendered a bitterness which later generations cannot appreciate or understand perhaps because of the stature of the chief disputants, Booker T. Washington and William E. Burkhardt Du Bois.

General Morgan discussed the subject: "Industrial and Intellectual Education" at a meeting of the WABHMS in Boston. The real question today, he stated, is not whether industrial edu-

PLATE IX

Quarles Memorial Library in Packard Hall

Miss Upton who came in 1888

Recreation in Packard Annex

PLATE X

Two Faculty Groups in 1907: Miss Giles in center above;
below, Miss Upton in center

cation is desirable, but whether industrial education is all that is desirable; the need of intellectual education for Negroes is to any thoughtful person apparent. He said: "The future destiny of the world and of our Republic especially is in the keeping of the universities. . . . If the millions of Negroes in the country are to progress . . . become a helpful factor in the development of our national life, there must be for them an open door into the universities."

Dr. Morehouse, whose views on the bread-and-butter theory of education have been cited, said also:

"The view that the Negro cannot be educated, or should be educated for his sphere, as if he were foreordained to everlasting intellectual inferiority is in the light of facts today, antiquated nonsense."

Such was the attitude of the men who in this period were most instrumental in the development of Spelman Seminary. A glimpse at their backgrounds and their experience helps us to understand their influence. Here are biographical notes about some of them who may justifiably be called educational statesmen.

Early Advisers Were Men of Stature

Henry L. Morehouse (1834-1917), descended from Scotch Covenanters, knew Miss Packard and Miss Giles from 1879 as long as they lived. He was in consultation with Mr. Rockefeller and his advisers in the plans for the University of Chicago; was a trusted adviser of Frederick T. Gates and Thomas W. Goodspeed; had had some influence in persuading William Rainey Harper to accept its presidency. He wisely gave oversight to all the Baptist Home Mission Schools. He was for 38 years connected with the ABHMS; was a member of the American Baptist Board of Education, 1902-17; and on the American Committee of the World Baptist Alliance. He was one of the promoters of the Federal Council of Churches of Christ in America.

General Thomas Jefferson Morgan (1839-1902), graduate of Franklin College, Indiana, which his father had helped to establish; student at the University of Leipzig; and graduate of Rochester Theological Seminary after over three years of military service. He was from 1874 to 1881 a member of the faculty of Chicago Theological Seminary. From 1881 to 1883 he served as principal of the Potsdam Normal School; and from 1884 to 1889 of the State Normal School in Rhode Island. In the eighties and nineties, the "methodology" of the Normal School program had not yet taken precedence of the subject matter. He also, as U. S. Commissioner of Indian Affairs from 1889-1893, worked out an admirable program for the Indians. He accepted the position of corresponding secretary of the ABHMS in 1893 and served with rare ability until his death. He was an editor, an author, and an eloquent speaker in favor of education without arbitrary limit for the Negro.

Dr. Malcolm MacVicar (1829-1904) was born in the Highlands of Scotland. After his graduation from the University of Rochester in 1859, he became a teacher and then principal of the Brockport (N.Y.) Collegiate Institute. He had a large part in organizing the normal school system of the state of New York, and was the founder and organizer of the Potsdam Normal School which he served from 1869-1880. In 1881 he was appointed to the faculty of the Toronto Baptist College. When this became part of McMaster University, he reluctantly became its first chancellor. After succeeding in its initial organization, he resigned to accept a position as Superintendent of Education for the ABHMS (1890-1900). His last post (1900-1904) was the presidency of Virginia Union University. Dr. MacVicar's success as an administrator and his ability as a teacher were equally prominent. He invented a number of mechanical contrivances as aids to classroom instruction, one being a tellurian globe.

After he took up the duties of Superintendent of Education of the ABHMS in 1890, he often spent weeks at a time on the Spelman campus. He organized on a stronger basis the teachers professional course in 1892; revised the high school course of study; and "his hand was felt in the literary courses of Spelman more than that of any other person."

Dr. George Sale (1857-1912), Canadian born, who became Superintendent of Education of the ABHMS in June 1906, and who then established his office at Spelman Seminary, belongs in the same group. A man of rare culture and scholarship, chosen by Dr. Malcolm MacVicar for the position which at first he declined, he became president of Atlanta Baptist Seminary in 1890. The purpose of his predecessors had been to prepare Negro men for the ministry. Dr. Sale broadened the curriculum; and developed the college department and promoted it. In 1909, he went to Liberia as a member of the special commission appointed by President Taft.

Dr. Sale, in an over-view of the Baptist Home Mission Schools the year before he died, said: "It should always be borne in mind that we are not engaged in the education of the Negro people, but in the education of a few who shall serve as constructive leaders of the race, and for this the higher intellectual training is essential." He pointed to the usefulness and importance of the industrial training given in these schools; then added: "Still the faith of our schools is that 'the life is more than meat,' and that the measure of the man is not the hand, however skilful, but the mind and heart, and so we put the spiritual and intellectual first."

Equally essential to the success of Spelman Seminary was the influence of the colored Baptist Education Society of Georgia; and it was good fortune that the recognized leader of Negroes in Georgia was a man with a zeal for education. He was *William Jefferson White* (1832-1913). Founder of Morehouse College (as Atlanta Baptist Seminary) in Augusta, in 1867, he was from the beginning a stalwart friend of Spelman. When Spelman Seminary was incorporated, he was made vice-president of the Board of Trustees, and held the position until his death. Two daughters, Mary White Blocker and Claudia White Harreld, are well-known Spelman alumnae. He was a wise and far-sighted leader in church, school and state. He was editor of the *Georgia Baptist*; a revered minister; and an active citizen in political life and in education. He was a friend of Alexander Stephens; strange as it may seem, he had quarters at the home of Mr. Stephens where he stayed when he was in that vicinity. A man of vision, of wisdom, and of ability.

Dr. *Jabez Lamar Monroe Curry* (1825-1903) also belongs in the category of educational statesmen. He was born in Georgia; was a graduate of the University of Georgia, and of the Harvard Law School where he was a classmate of Rutherford B. Hayes. He was a Member of Congress, and of the Confederate Congress. He became a disciple of Horace Mann, and from him caught a zeal for universal education which he promoted for his remaining 60 years. He was an eloquent advocate of public schools in the South; he once declared to a Southern audience not in agreement that it was the proudest duty of the South to train every child in its borders, black or white; when silence ensued, he exclaimed "I will make you applaud that sentiment!" With 'irresistible eloquence,' he proceeded to do so. He was elected Agent of the Peabody Fund in 1881 on the motion of General Grant; and Agent of the Slater Fund for Negro Schools in 1890 by nomination of Rutherford B. Hayes. He became virtually the supervising director of the Southern Education Board established in 1901. For more than 10 years previous to his work with the Peabody Fund, he was professor of English in the University of Richmond. He was U. S. Minister to Spain from 1885-1888.

Dr. *Wallace Buttrick* (1853-1926) first Secretary, then President, of the General Education Board, was born in Potsdam, New York; attended Potsdam Normal School 1871-72, studied under private tutors for four years, and was graduated from Rochester Theological Seminary. As the *New York Times* stated, he had an original and penetrating mind; was impatient of learned dullness, possessed sagacity mixed with kindliness. He played an important part in the upbuilding of education in the United States. He was known to every college and university president in the United States.

The Twenty-fifth Anniversary—1906

"Look out for Spelman Seminary; there is no better school in any country for any people."

Those were the words of Dr. J. L. M. Curry, educational leader of the South, to his successor as secretary of the Slater Fund, Dr. Wallace Buttrick. Dr. Buttrick quoted them in his address at the Twenty-fifth Anniversary and heartily endorsed them. He cited as his reasons:

1. The spirit and character of the founders.
2. The permanence and stability of the teaching force. Five teachers had served over 20 years; five more over 13 years; four others over 10 years – the average length of service of the faculty of 48 was seven years.
3. The ideals and aims of the school. He praised the thoroughness of the course of instruction and the standards for promotion and graduation.

Addresses by Dr. Emory W. Hunt, President of Denison University; Mrs. Mary Church Terrill, Oberlin graduate and first president of the National Association of Colored Women; Professor S. C. Mitchell of Richmond College (Virginia); and Mrs. Alice B. Coleman of Boston, president of the WABHMS, were all noteworthy. Many Negro pastors spoke in eloquent terms of the helpful influence of Spelman.

Mr. John D. Rockefeller sent the following message:

We have your message on the twenty-fifth anniversary meeting of Spelman Seminary. Mrs. Rockefeller and Miss Spelman unite with me in greetings to the faculty, trustees and friends of Spelman Seminary. We thank you all for your services on behalf of the Seminary and rejoice that we have been associated with you in this good work.

Nothing was more impressive to the visitors than the addresses by the graduates – one by Claudia T. White, A.B. '01, was especially interesting. So were the short speeches by the earliest students of the basement school; and the talks, dramatic sketches and singing of the students. One journal noted in its article "their orderly character, the neatness of their dress, the absence of loud colors, the good taste . . . and the exceeding beauty of the songs of the girls, in the precision singing of conventional songs but especially in the Negro spirituals."

The presiding officer at most of the meetings was "the great-hearted Dr. H. L. Morehouse" in the phrase used by Professor John Hope in his report of the Anniversary.

The alumnae record presented by Claudia White, '01, reveals a commendable spread of efforts to use the training received. Spelman graduates, so the report reads, are found in 21 states, in the District of Columbia, in Canada, and in Africa. Among occupations, teaching stands first. Eighty-eight were teaching, many of whom in addition held mothers' meetings, taught in Sunday Schools, and acted as pastors' aids. Four had gone to Africa; four were at the time giving full time to home missions; four graduates in Nurse Training were nursing full time, and many of those with partial training were in demand as practical nurses. The alumnae included also one pharmacist, and 13 bookkeepers. Thirteen graduates were continuing studies at Spelman, and three were studying medicine. The report concludes: In consideration of the vast army of the unreached, this story "of but a handful of women . . . [may] sound pitiful but when we remember that 'one shall choose a thousand and two shall put ten thousand to flight,' what wonderful visions arise before us. . . ."

It is pertinent to recall that in the early academies, seminaries and colleges of the North, only a small percentage continued their studies long enough to be graduated. At the Oread Institute, in its first 10 years there were only 12 graduates. The 1924 General Catalogue of Mount Holyoke College lists 1,090 students in the first 10 years, of whom 243 were graduates. The *Memorial* of the Twenty-fifth Anniversary of Mount Holyoke Female Seminary gives the "whole number of pupils, 1837-62" as 3,401; of whom 1,811 were connected with the Seminary but one year, and 950 but two years. In 1873, as James Truslow Adams recalls in *The Epic of America*, there were only

23,000 college graduates, men and women, in the whole United States.

An endowment fund for Spelman Seminary was a constant hope of Dr. Morehouse; and at intervals he made an appeal for one. In the fall of 1905, he sent the draft of a proposed letter to Mr. Rockefeller asking for an endowment of $250,000 to Miss Giles for her comment. She replied:

"If there seems danger that we shall lose the Slater Fund appropriation, we ought to have $500,000 endowment; if not, $350,000 or $400,000. If we ask for too little, we cannot soon say we have not enough; if we do not get all we ask for, and then come short, we can say we need more. . . . We are behind now on our Nurses' Home because our estimate was too small. . . ." Dr. Morehouse readily agreed with Miss Giles' suggestion. Since sending her the draft, he had foreseen that $250,000 would be barely sufficient to meet the annual deficit and would leave nothing for larger salaries and better equipment; and, as he put it, "we may as well ask for $500,000 as for $250,000." The letter was presented, after further consultation with "a representative of Mr. Rockefeller" and with Dr. Buttrick.

The reply came in a letter from Mr. Rockefeller's attorney, Starr J. Murphy, dated March 22, 1906. It declined the request "after careful consideration." Regarding the WABHMS, the Slater Fund, and the General Education Board, Mr. Murphy stated that "at present at least there is no reason to apprehend the withdrawal of their support"; that a permanent endowment for Spelman might lead to such withdrawal; that this would be an unmixed misfortune; that it was quite possible that one or more of these supporters could be induced as the needs of the Seminary increase, to increase their support correspondingly.

Mr. Rockefeller's unfavorable replies to the various requests for endowment beginning in 1895 by no means indicated a weakening of his interest. His large gift in 1900 had been ample proof of that. As a matter of fact, a big plan for his gifts to schools was in the making, a plan which resulted in the formation of the General Education Board in March, 1902. Two months later, a member of Mr. Rockefeller's staff told Miss Giles that Mr. Rockefeller said "that he had made it possible for Spelman to be well taken care of in another way."

The General Education Board was the second of Mr. Rockefeller's foundations for philanthropy. Its chartered object was stated as the promotion of education in the United States of America without distinction of sex, race, or creed; and its immediate attention was to be given "to studying and aiding to promote the educational needs of the people of our Southern States."

The appropriation of $6,000 to Spelman Seminary for current expenses made by the General Education Board (hereafter usually called the GEB) on April 11, 1902, was one of the very first appropriations made by the Board for any purpose, and antedated its incorporation. In spite of this grant, there was a deficit of over $2,000. One-half of the deficit was promised by the GEB: Miss Giles had to raise the other half.

Dr. Wallace Buttrick became Secretary of the General Education Board in 1902. Throughout the rest of his life, he held Spelman Seminary and Spelman College in his affection. He insisted from the first, however, that he must not be leaned upon to guarantee any financial support; that requests for aid must be made annually to the Board and justified by the work accomplished.

In a résumé of the work of the ABHMS, called *A Century of Faith*, Dr. Charles L. White states that Dr. Buttrick "while on a visit to Spelman Seminary with Dr. Morehouse . . . received his first impression of the importance and value of Negro education, and in a moment of deep emotion, spoke words that registered a resolution that influenced his later life and led to a life-long service for the improvement of the Negro race. Out of that eventful visit at Spelman came results that never can be tabulated."

Dr. Buttrick's first visit to Spelman was on Sunday, April 27, 1902. At that time, he advised Miss Giles to make formal application to the GEB for aid toward the budget of the coming year, stating the specific needs. In 1903 the GEB renewed its grant of $6,000 for current operations. In the years following, the amount was increased first to $8,000, later to $10,000, then to $12,000. The GEB required that Miss Giles submit with her annual request, a statement of receipts and expenditures for the preceding year; and if an increase was asked for, a definite explanation of the occasion for it. The institution was then expected to live within its budget.

The expanded program of nurse training made possible by MacVicar Hospital had called for housing for student nurses. Mr. Rockefeller made a gift of $25,000 to build a new nurses' home, but the estimate of cost was too low, and a deficit resulted. This was a worry to Miss Giles. Fortunately, in the case of this deficit, Dr. Buttrick came to her rescue. He acknowledged her letter about it and assured her, "At what I deem to be the psychological moment, I will bring this to the attention of the Board." Within less than a week, he wrote her again that within a few days he would be able to send "the $1,506.71 needed to make up your deficiency on account of the building project."

Miss Giles replied (April 2, 1906) with more than usual warmth in the following words: "I wish to express to you my hearty appreciation of your interest and constant kindness – you are like a brother to me, and the burden of responsibility that is upon me presses far less heavily because of your ready and timely assistance and encouragement. Please accept my thanks for this cheque which removes the deficit from our books and the anxiety from my heart. You were quick to find 'the psychological moment. . . .' "

Funds for operating also were short, however, and on June 6, 1906, Miss Giles wrote Dr. Buttrick: "You told me we must not get in debt this year; we have though, and I am sorry, but we couldn't help it, and I don't know what will become of us if you do not help us out."

He explained that neither he nor the Board could assume

financial responsibility for any institution; that all estimates for general repairs as well as for the special improvements should be submitted to Dr. Morehouse as Chairman of the Board of Trustees; that such items should come to the General Education Board through the trustees of the Seminary and in connection with its general budget; but he assured her that the Board "so long as I have anything to do with it, will not be found lacking in interest in the Seminary."

Miss Giles returned from New England in early September and was on the campus at the time of the Atlanta Riot, which began on September 22, 1906. The following days were anxious ones. No harm came to the students or teachers of the Seminary. As was stated later to the Trustees, doubts and fears were in the hearts of those who gathered for the opening chapel service "but as the weeks went quietly by, apprehension of danger gradually vanished."

Dr. Mordecai Johnson, president of Howard University, recently told Spelman girls about his acquaintance with Spelman when he attended Morehouse College, from 1907-11. He described the early teachers as "the stern, lovable, unrelenting high-idealists of New England who constituted a blessing to the life of our people." He said: "We boys used to come over to chapel, and we would listen to the preacher with our ears and look at the girls with our eyes, and go away inspired in body, mind, and soul."

He recalled not only the beautiful girls (he married one of them after his and her graduation) but "an atmosphere of cleanliness about the very floors." He added, "I used to say to the boys, 'Why, you can just sit down anywhere, and it would be all right. You can get up without any dust.' All of the occasions were conducted with order and with charm."

A day at Spelman – called the "Mount Holyoke of the South" by Mabel H. Parsons in an article from the *Home Mission Monthly* reprinted in the *Messenger* for November, 1908, is here summarized.

Each student gave an hour's work every day, under supervision, to the institution, in addition to the care of her own room, including her laundry of clothes and bedding. One day a week at the college laundry was assigned to each dormitory. On the day assigned, the girls had to get up at 4:00 a.m. to go in file to the laundry, and wash their personal laundry before breakfast. The rising bell called all students at 5:45 a.m.; at 6:45 a.m. they proceeded to the dining-room in Morgan Hall; at tap of the bell, all were seated and sang a blessing. Ten girls sat at a table; each in turn served as waitress. Over the service and with an eye and ear to low voices and table manners was the dining-room matron. After breakfast, sweeping, dusting, dish-washing and bed-making had to be performed before the ringing of the bell for classes at 8:15 a.m. Luncheon at twelve noon was brief. Classes were held from 12:45 p.m. to 3:00 p.m. The girls who had washed their clothes would go, 50 at a time, once a week to iron them. Advanced classes in dress-making, printing, millinery and cooking met after three o'clock. For many students the time was free for games, fancy work, reading, visiting or basketball.

Dinner was at 5:00 o'clock. A short service in the chapel came at 6:15 p.m. The evenings were spent in the study halls – except for Friday evenings when a lecture or concert offered diversion and when the young men of Atlanta Baptist College came for the event and the social time following it. A nine o'clock bell told 'twas time for the good-night song, and departure to one's room and retirement. On Sundays an extra 15 minutes of sleep was allowed, and breakfast was at seven.

A rigorous schedule? – Yes. It should be considered in comparison with New England seminaries of the period – not with the easy life of present-day academy and college. Compare it with Vassar – at Vassar, breakfast was at 6:45 a.m. or Mount Holyoke, or Oberlin, of the same period. Breakfast at Oberlin was at 6:00 a.m.; the rising bell rang at 5:00 a.m.

The work was strengthened and upgraded from year to year, with little change in the total enrollment. The number in attendance had remained almost constant since 1902, between 650 and 675, but with a gradually increasing number of boarders.

The student body in 1908-09 came from 127 different schools; 19 states were represented besides the District of Columbia and Africa. The college department remained small; only five students were enrolled. Higher qualifications for admission to high school were required; there were 115 students. The teachers' professional department remained about the same in number. The practice school had an enrollment of 419, two-thirds of whom were boarders.

More than half of the 335 boarders were wholly or partly earning their way. The cost for board and tuition was $9.50 per four weeks. Thirty-four of the boarders were over 25 years old; 226 were under 16. The presence of the older students, those over 25 years of age and those between 16 and 25, is what made it possible to take care of young boarding students.

The Seminary at this period had a dairy of 11 cows, 1 bull, 3 yearlings, and 1 calf. There was also a garden in which the younger pupils did a share of the weeding and cultivating.

From a study made of 519 students who were present on a given day, it was found that 53% had fathers who were skilled laborers or professional men and that 35% were the children of widows. The percentage of families of Spelman students that owned their own homes was gratifying; among the boarders 70.5% owned their homes and 10.5% more were in process of buying them. For the day pupils, it was about half and half.

Counting the president and officers, the faculty was 50 in number. There were besides, 13 physicians on the MacVicar Hospital staff, the first closed hospital staff in the region.

Beginning in 1907, the GEB contributed toward the operating budget $12,000 annually – equivalent to the interest on an endowment of $300,000; the Slater Board was giving $5,000 for the normal and industrial departments; the WABHMS – toward salaries of teachers – about $8,000 annually.

Loyal friends made bequests as their means permitted. One was received from Dr. William Howe whose annual visits had been a benediction and had given him a unique place of honor and affection in the Seminary family. He died on November 28, 1906, after passing his 100th birthday. He had celebrated his 93rd birthday with his friends on the campus; that was his last visit.

A Massachusetts lady gave $1,000 for MacVicar Hospital, a fund to be named in honor of Jane Anna Granderson, one of the two college graduates of the first class in 1901, who died in 1905. A young woman of great promise, she had spoken in Northern churches for the WABHMS and made warm friends among them.

Dr. J. H. Hanaford, who for many years contributed a section on "Health Habits" to the Spelman *Messenger*, from time to time had been a benefactor. On the death of Mrs. Hanaford in 1909, the amount he had left for Student Aid was increased by the terms of his will to $1,425.28.

Other bequests included three for prizes as follows: from Dr. J. B. Simmons of New York, as a memorial to his wife, Mary E. Simmons (the founders of Simmons College) – $500; from Seymour Finney of Detroit, – $600; from Willard D. Chamberlin of Dayton, Ohio, – $1000.

Money had always to be raised outside the budget for equipment and repairs. Even the students recognized this. The Packard Hall girls raised the money to pay for papering their study hall; the Morgan Hall students bought themselves a sewing machine.

A Special Appeal was prepared head-lining a $25,000 *Improvement Fund*. It urged the necessity of raising $13,000 within a year ($2,000 plus had been received) to obtain $10,000 from the General Education Board for extraordinary repairs, replacements and improvements. In late May, 1909, Miss Giles was able to report to Dr. Buttrick that the sum of $15,-591.77 had been raised, to qualify for the GEB grant. The date for raising the amount had been extended to May 30, 1909. The ABHMS gave $5,000; the WABHMS also $5,000. The Spelman Alumnae Association surprised and delighted Miss Giles' heart by a gift of $150. A summary shows that there was raised from and through present and former teachers $864; from and through present and former students $554; from Negro churches, schools and friends $372. The Seminary residents celebrated the accomplishment by gathering on the campus, burning a red light, cheering and singing school songs.

CHAPTER X

THE DEATH OF MISS GILES

MISS GILES had been *"very tired"* after the Commencement exercises in 1909; no wonder, since they lasted from mid-morning to 1:45 p.m. There is no record, however, of weakness or ill health during that summer in New England. She was back in Atlanta and carrying her load on September 22, looking stronger and better than usual; school opened October 5 with every indication of a good year to follow. The Improvement Fund had made possible new walks and gutters; thorough renovation of Packard and Rockefeller Halls, which after all were over 20 years old; and new single iron beds for the renovated halls. A plea went out at once to the Northern church women to put sheets in their barrels. Said the *Messenger*, "340 boarders and all need sheets . . . – a thousand sheets, three for each bed – to revolve them properly."

A month passed swiftly. The spirit of teachers and students, the full attendance, the prospering of plans – everything was favorable. Then suddenly their peace was shattered.

Miss Giles had a cold; it developed into pneumonia. The illness lasted only a week; was regarded as serious only two days. On November 12, just as the day was fading, her spirit passed. "Her end was peace. She passed as passes the day."

The girls remarked that Miss Giles had been in every building on the campus to see that everything in every room was in perfect order, even examining the window shades. She also examined the trees and shrubs on the campus and noted where pruning and new planting was needed. Afterwards everyone said that she had done too much.

Camilla Weems, a graduate who performed heroic work for most of her life-time as Director of Home Demonstration Work among Negroes in Georgia was then a freshman college student. She has written a touching account.

She recalls vividly the first Thursday evening in November, 1909, the last time she talked with Miss Giles. Miss Giles had arrived early in Howe Memorial Hall and sat watching the girls come in for the weekly prayer-meeting. Camilla sat with the freshman group. Miss Giles heard them admiring the painting and new furnishings. She turned around and said to Camilla who sat directly behind her, "The lights are beautiful, aren't they? I am so glad we have them. We shall be able to see much better with the new electric lights. . . ."

The last time Camilla saw Miss Giles alive was perhaps a week later when she looked out of her first floor room window in Packard Hall. Miss Giles had been inspecting Giles Hall and was then coming down the front steps on the west side of the building. Camilla and other Packard girls watched her walk down the path in front of Giles, past Packard Hall towards Reynolds Cottage. "The dinner bell had just rung and we said, 'Miss Giles is through for the day and is going home to dinner.'

"The November afternoon was very chilly and Miss Giles was dressed in a heavy dark blue dress made with a basque and a long, wide skirt with brush braid at the bottom. She had a red woolen scarf over her head coming down and tied under her chin. She looked just like a picture and I shall never forget this picture of her.

"A day or two later the news went around the campus that Miss Giles was sick with a terrible cold . . . and after several days . . . she passed away and left a campus full of broken-hearted teachers and students."

The girls, Miss Weems recalls, were sad and quiet and orderly that night because the teachers begged them not to cry out loud. . . . The next day a funeral service was held in Howe Memorial Hall. It was indeed sad and impressive. . . . After the services, the girls were lined up on both sides of the walk from Rockefeller Hall to the front gate and "slowly the black hearse passed on through the two lines of girls and bore Miss Giles' body away to a place unknown to us at that time and seemed to have been in another world." The *Messenger* records that the students sang softly "Swing low, sweet chariot." "Even to this day," writes Camilla Weems in 1956, "Miss Giles' funeral seemed to be the saddest funeral I ever witnessed."

After the hearse had passed out of sight, the girls let out their pent-up feelings. They wondered, as they cried, what would become of them "now that Miss Giles has gone away from us forever." It is fitting to quote from Miss Weems' last paragraph – for it shows the spirit instilled in the students by the Founders:

"God is a great and merciful God. He has given many consecrated people to help us. Miss Packard, whom I did not know, Miss Giles . . . and many consecrated teachers, and He will continue to send good people to help us in our struggle to become first class citizens and good Christians."

Nor was the grief and sense of loss confined to the Spelman campus. President John Hope was in New England at Miss Giles' death. He telegraphed that the football game with Fisk University should not be played although the team was already there. Accompanied by Dr. George Sale, the body was carried to Athol, Massachusetts for burial, to lie beside that of Miss Packard in Silver Lake Cemetery. One long low stone marks the burial place, on Joseph Packard's lot. One side bears their names; the other, the words "Founders of Spelman Seminary."

The leading article in the May 1910 *Messenger* was an exceptionally fine sketch of, and tribute to, the "Founders of Spelman Seminary" by Lucy Houghton Upton, the person preeminently fitted to write it. At the Class Day exercises on May 17, a bronze tablet in memory of Miss Giles was unveiled. Flora Zeto, the girl from the Congo, spoke in behalf of the students; Mrs. Selena Sloan Butler '88, in behalf of the alumnae; and Miss Evelina O. Werden, an associate of Miss Giles since 1886, in behalf of the teachers.

Harriet E. Giles

"She was a queenly character," wrote Dr. Morehouse, "modest, meek, yet majestic; deeply religious, absolutely surrendered joyfully to her divinely appointed task; adored by her associates and by the thousands of students who have come under her influence during these more than twenty-seven years of her Christian ministry. . . ."

Perhaps no better summing up of her character and personality can be made than in those words of Dr. Morehouse. They were preceded by a reference to the beginning of the enterprise: "With true Christian heroism and sublime self-effacement," he said, "Miss Sophia B. Packard and Miss Harriet E. Giles left their attachments and privileges in New England in 1881 to engage in the lowly work of establishing a school for Negro girls in Atlanta; beginning the enterprise in the most humble way in the dingy basement of the Friendship Baptist Church in April, 1881. God honored their faith and led them on to larger undertakings, until Spelman Seminary has become the foremost school in the world for colored young women. . . ."

"After the death of Miss Packard, June 21, 1891, Miss Giles became the president of the institution, and during these 18 years has most wisely administered its affairs and won the admiration and love of all who knew her. The largest development of the institution, in the extension and improvement of its campus, the erection of buildings and the broadening of its work, has taken place during this period.

"In the midst of heavy responsibilities and frequent perplexities, she maintained remarkable equanimity and developed a degree of ability and sagacity that was a surprise both to her friends and herself."

How did she do it? With her gentle spirit and tender heart, and her diffidence and dislike of publicity, she had leaned on Sophia Packard's leadership for nearly 40 years – alert and steadfast, but quiet in the background. When Miss Packard was ill and left her in charge for the closing two months of school in 1890, she confided to her diary, "I know not what will befall me. . . . If only my dear Sophia can be restored to health, I am willing to bear the burdens . . . a trying day . . . but I will trust in the Lord and ask for wisdom to carry on this great work."

When she attended the Board meeting 10 days after Miss

Packard's death, the times she had sat there with her friend Sophia came so vividly to mind that she "thought she could not stay at first." But stay she did; and was appointed Principal. "How I shrink from such *responsibility* – but trust in the Lord for strength."

In those last words lies the secret – her faith in God was deep and ever present. She believed in his promises; in the rightness of her cause; and in prayer. She had the love of Jesus in her heart, and strove to share it.

"Only a stern sense of duty nerved her retiring spirit" to the performance of her public duties, Claudia White, then a Spelman teacher, observed; she also pointed out that Miss Giles had an added strand in the garment her soul wore – "the graciousness and sweetness that love alone can bestow." This was expressed in her thoughtfulness of her teachers and concern for their welfare, as well as in the never-ceasing care and affection she accorded to the needs of the students.

She always used to call the students "My dear Girls." It was with tender accents that she admonished and advised them. She coveted for them the best things in life. One day she wrote in her diary: "I can truly say 'The mistakes of my life have been many.' I have made a great mistake today in not sending one of our girls directly home instead of allowing her to have her freedom and poison the minds of others." She had her misgivings and embarrassments, but as one graduate said at the 1909 Commencement, "love of the cause and reliance upon God steeled her for the task." The same graduate, TPC '94, characterized her in these words: "Ripe experience, a Christian character, and genuine consecration were her great assets. *To these the Lord has delightfully added every needed grace.*"

The young Yale graduate, Edward Twichell Ware, son of the founder of Atlanta University, himself President of Atlanta University at the time of Miss Giles' death, was one of the speakers at the alumnae memorial service. His remarks showed keen insight into the quality of Miss Giles' character. He said: ". . . her personality made a very marked impression on me.

In her character seemed to predominate two elements which may seem antagonistic, but which in her were perfectly harmonized – dignity and simplicity. Her very presence in a company seemed to lend a tone to it. . . . If you were with Miss Giles you were satisfied that you were in the best company. She had a certain poise which marked her as a leader.

He mentioned "the keen joy" he and his sister had felt in the companionship with Miss Giles and Miss Upton one morning at breakfast in Aiken, South Carolina. It was "this dignity and poise" which made Miss Giles to him "always seem the best possible company."

"And then her simplicity; it was always a surprise to me, when Miss Giles spoke, to note the almost childlike simplicity of her utterance. She spoke from the heart directly to the heart of her listeners . . . to a company of educators . . . to a group of students . . . her words were the simplest possible and the most direct. . . . I am convinced that both of these characteristics . . . can be nothing less than the expression of a very close communion with God. . . . To be in her presence was a benediction, for near her one always felt near God. . . . Her dignity of bearing . . . and in the same way, the simplicity of her utterance was an expression of her fellowship with God. . . ."

Lines from Wordsworth's *Sonnet on Milton*, he said, came to his mind, as he thought of Miss Giles, suggesting "the union of dignity and simplicity" characteristic of her.

> Thy soul was like a Star and dwelt apart;
> Thou hadst a voice whose sound was like the sea,
> Pure as the naked heaven, majestic, free;
> So didst thou travel on life's common way
> In cheerful godliness, and yet thy heart
> The lowliest duties on herself did lay.

CHAPTER XI
SPELMAN UNDER MISS UPTON
1909-1910

MISS LUCY HOUGHTON UPTON was appointed Acting President in November, 1909, by the Executive Committee of the Board of Trustees. Because they acted promptly, the work of the Seminary went on steadily and smoothly in its customary routine with the hearty support of teachers and students. The Trustees had urged Miss Upton to accept the presidency of Spelman College after Miss Giles' death. According to Mrs. Reynolds of the WABHMS and a member of the Spelman Board, Miss Upton's reply was: "You cannot change the fact that I am sixty-three years old."

The students had anticipated her appointment as president. One of the early graduates of the Seminary and College, who served as matron from 1909-11, wrote in her memories of this period: "Miss Upton – most likely to be President . . . however, Miss Tapley was pulled up from the ranks to become President."

When the Trustees passed resolutions regarding Miss Giles, they included formal record of their appreciation of Miss Upton and of Miss Mary J. Packard, and referred to "the judgment of those most conversant with the affairs of the Seminary, and especially of the late president [that] the success of the school has been in large measure due to their ability and devotion. . . ."

Even casual study of the first 30-odd years of Spelman's history reveals the great influence that Miss Upton quietly wielded in its development. Surely she stands next to the Founders – and alongside them. She possessed quality of mind and of character, deep understanding and rare breadth of experience; and with complete devotion, she offered them all to Spelman students.

Lucy Houghton Upton, born in 1846, came from a well-known family of shipmasters and importing merchants of Salem, Massachusetts. Her father, James Upton, was the Upton mentioned by Hawthorne in the famous introduction to the *Scarlet Letter* as one of those who came into the old custom house to do business with him as the surveyor of the port. A gentleman of the old school, Mr. Upton possessed intellectual power, ample means, and withal, was a devoted Christian. The daughter profited from his interest in scientific and philosophical subjects. Her mother also was a person of superior mind and broad interests.

There is clear evidence that Lucy from childhood had an unusual mind. She possessed an observant eye, a retentive memory, and a critical faculty. When she was nine years old, she wrote a description of a store she had visited. She named 48 items, and said there were "many more things which it would take too long to write." An essay on "Freedom" written at 10 years of age quoted the Declaration of Independence, the freedom given to slaves in Canada, and the views of George Washington.

Lucy Upton was graduated from the Salem High School when few colleges, only Oberlin and Elmira, were open to women; and she had an appetite for learning that could not be denied.

A picture of her in high school comes from a younger schoolmate, Albert S. Flint,[1] friend of her brother Winslow, and later, like Winslow, a noted astronomer. He recalled Lucy as "a bright-looking black-eyed young lady who came regularly through the boys' study hall to join the class in Greek in the little recitation room beyond." The study of Greek was the distinctive mark of boys destined to go to college, and Lucy Upton too expected to go to college and take the full classical course offered to men. The death of her mother in 1865 prevented this. With four younger children at home, Lucy stepped into her mother's role, and even after the brothers and sisters

---

[1] Albert S. Flint, Harvard 1875, Phi Beta Kappa, Sigma Xi, astronomer of Washburn Observatory, University of Wisconsin. Born in Salem, Mass., exactly one month earlier than Winslow Upton.

were grown, she was her father's comfort and stay until he died in 1879. But even so Lucy could not give up her intellectual pursuits. When her brother Winslow became a student at Brown University in 1874, she wrote him about a course in history he was taking under Professor Diman: "What is Prof. Diman's definition of civilization, and take the world through, is its progress ever onward, or does it retrograde at times? Do you think I might profitably study some of the history you do, perhaps two weeks behind you. . . ." And that she proceeded to do.

Many years later (on August 3, 1915), Lucy Upton wrote Winslow's daughter soon to be graduated from Smith College: "While I love botany which, after dabbling in for years, I studied according to the methods of that day exactly forty years ago in a summer school,[1] it must be fascinating to take up zoology in the way you are doing. Whatever was the science in the high school course for the time being, that was my favorite study. Mathematics came next."

Her study of history was persistently pursued. She read Maitland's *Dark Ages,* "which I enjoyed very much"; La Croix on the *Customs of the Middle Ages;* 16 chapters of Bryce "and liked it more and more"; more chapters of Guizot; Lecky and Stanley's *Eastern Church.* She discussed in her letters to Winslow some of the questions that came to her as she studied alone.

Lucy's correspondence with brother Winslow during his college days was not entirely taken up with academic studies. She played chess with him by postcard. Also Lucy and Winslow had a private contest to see which one could make the most words from the letters in "importunately." Who won is not revealed, but Winslow's daughter Eleanor says they got up to 1,212 words.

There was another family interest also. Winslow had musical talents, as had his father before him. At different times he served as glee-club and choir leader and as organist. And it was

[1] In the Harvard College Summer School, a six weeks' course in 1875, consisting of 25 lectures, with several hours of investigation at the Botanical Laboratory. Fee $25.

Lucy Upton who first started the idea of a regular course in Music at Spelman College.

Winslow Upton after graduation from Brown University and two years of graduate study, accepted a position at the Harvard Observatory. For three years he was connected with the U.S. Naval Observatory and with the U.S. Signal Corps; and after 1883, was professor of astronomy at Brown University. The six expeditions to study eclipses of the sun, of which he was a member, took him to Colorado, Virginia, and California as well as to the South Pacific and to Russia. After her father's death, Lucy and her youngest sister lived for a few years with Winslow in Washington, D.C. "Their house," writes Albert S. Flint, "was always a haven of hospitality and good cheer, especially grateful to one like myself far from home." Lucy was a lively part of the household. Moreover, she had physical as well as mental vigor. Winslow, as his daughters Eleanor and Margaret recall, used to characterize her as "our iron sister." There is reason to suppose that Lucy would have made a record as publicly distinguished as her brother had it not been that her mother's death occurred just as she was about to enter college. As a matter of fact, Albert S. Flint expressed his conviction that "her physical strength, her mental power, her lively interest in all objects about her and her readiness to serve her fellow beings" would have led her "to a distinguished career amongst the noted women of this country."

While in Washington, D.C., Lucy Upton held positions in the U.S. Census Office, and in the Pension Bureau. They were not sufficiently challenging however, and she resigned in 1887, to go to Germany with her brother Winslow and his family while he was there on study. After the months in Europe, she returned to Boston and became active in church and community life.

What was called an "accidental meeting" with Miss Packard in Washington turned her attention to Spelman. Here was a cause she believed in. After correspondence with Miss Packard and to the joy of Miss Packard and Miss Giles, she came to

Atlanta, in the fall of 1888, to help wherever needed, although there was then no money available to pay her a salary. She served for a number of years without pay beyond her travel and maintenance.

Her students have spoken of the exacting standards of scholarship and of manners and conduct she expected and achieved from the students; of her "great power of discernment"; of "her exquisiteness of dress," "her well-modulated voice that went straight to the hearts of the hearers"; her great love of flowers and plants and birds; and her close knowledge of individual students.

She drew on all her resources of mind and heart to help them – to make them at home in the world; and as graduates gratefully recall, she drew on her purse as well. Many a student was able to remain at Spelman, only because of her unobtrusive help.

Under Miss Upton, the work of the year 1909-10 went forward without interruption. After all, she had come to Spelman Seminary in 1888, and had been since 1891 except for one year, Associate Principal or Dean. She had taught classes in botany, astronomy (with the aid of a telescope), geometry, and psychology.

Miss Upton and Miss Packard, as a matter of fact, had many tastes in common. Both had eager and inquiring minds; and both believed that intellectual growth must go hand in hand with the development of sturdy character and Christian zeal. Both loved the out-of-doors, including mountain climbing and horseback riding. In 1890 when the trip to Europe and the Holy Land was arranged for Miss Packard, it was Miss Upton who planned the trip, and "with rare executive ability" bore the brunt of "the entire pilgrimage from beginning to end." So strenuous it was physically, with its days of horseback riding over rough roads that it seems an amazing feat of endurance for both Miss Packard and Miss Upton. Yet they thrived on it.

At the Fifteenth Anniversary (1896) as already quoted, Miss Upton projected with force and eloquence the Spelman of

the Future as a college of first rank, with expanding and un-
limited horizons. When Dr. Wallace Buttrick, wise in his judgment of people, declined to have the Science Building named
for him, he wrote Miss Tapley (April 7, 1923) "... If you had
asked me, I think I would have suggested that you name the
building for Miss Upton. Her services to the School for many
years were of a very high character, and I have often thought
that one of the buildings should be named for her."

Such were the qualities of the Acting-President of the Seminary after the death of Miss Giles.

At the meeting of the Board of Trustees, on March 3, 1910,
Miss Upton presented the annual report of the President. She
noted that no student had been withdrawn through loss of confidence; that the enrollment showed an increase of boarding
students as was desired; and that the year's work had gone forward smoothly. She urged the importance of more thorough
preparation for admission. The raising of the $25,000 Improve-
ment Fund two days before the time limit expired, and the
spontaneous "praise demonstration" held afterward on the
campus, were reported as events which had brought happiness
to Miss Giles. With the Fund in hand, the debt on the boilers
had been paid; Rockefeller and Packard Halls had been renovated; walks laid; and ground had been broken for the superintendent's home. Miss Upton spoke gratefully of the response of
Spelman graduates and Negro friends in helping to raise the
Fund, and their continuing efforts to raise money for greatly
needed current expenses. She spoke also with deep thankfulness
of the many individuals and agencies whose interest and efforts
through the years had made the work so fruitful in results.

Two bequests were recorded: one of $200 under the will of
Mrs. Harriet A. Copp of Los Angeles; and one of $2,000 un-
der the will of Miss Celia L. Brett of Hamilton, New York, a
friend from the early days.

Miss Upton told the Trustees that the death of Miss Giles
was "the sorest grief" the Seminary had ever been called upon
to bear. The daughters of Spelman, she said, had never known
or thought of Spelman without her. The removal of Miss Pack-

ard 18 years earlier had caused them great sorrow, but they still had Miss Giles. Now the school was indeed bereft. "Yet Spelman has strong, deep roots, and will live for the blessing of generations to come."

Miss Mary Jane Packard, Sophia's half-sister, became ill in March, 1910; and when school closed, she was unable to travel to Massachusetts. She remained in Atlanta through June and July; she died on August sixth.

Before coming on a visit to Spelman in 1885, Miss Mary had been a successful teacher in Worcester, and her position there was held open for her for a considerable period. But she decided to stay at Spelman. She helped with teaching as well as office work for a few years – the catalogues show that she had classes in geography, rhetoric and bookkeeping. Soon the office work claimed all her time. She was closely associated with the Founders in all their trials and hardships. Quiet and energetic, cheerful and calm, she too was a power in the development of the Seminary. Miss Giles always used to refer to her as "Sister." She served as secretary in the Seminary office for 25 years, and was in charge of correspondence, records, and bookkeeping. The books of the school hold a memorial to her; and so do the hearts of students and of teachers.

Mary J. Packard, states a *Messenger* editorial, was "efficient, pains-taking, self-effacing, loving, radiating the spirit of her Master. With infinite patience she responded to every call, no matter at what cost to herself, and to her all went, for she was sure to have the needed information or word of cheer. How we miss her none can tell."

At the funeral service at her summer home in Wollaston, Massachusetts, appreciative words were spoken by President John Hope of Atlanta Baptist College and by the Rev. Lucian Drury. The brick pillars which frame the opening to the Spelman campus are dedicated in her honor.

Miss Upton remained at her post on the campus all that summer of 1910 and in fact, until November when she went North.

Her presence was a steadying power while the new regime was being established under the leadership of Miss Tapley. After a few weeks with her New England family, Miss Upton returned to the campus and served as "General Secretary." She had founded the Granddaughters Club in 1909-10. Now she continued to work with the students whenever needed, and with the alumnae.

Miss Upton had aided in securing a landscape gardener some years before. In 1915, she named and located every tree and shrub on the campus. Miss Upton's knowledge of plants, flowers, and trees was phenomenal, considering her limited formal training. She studied botany as a scientist would; made careful and accurate observations; owned and consulted the best reference books whenever she found a new specimen. Her botanical encyclopedias are tomes still cherished and used by her nieces. In the judgment of her friends, if Miss Upton had chosen a career in this field, she might have become one of the leading botanists of the country.

The articles Miss Upton wrote for the *Spelman Messenger*, before and after 1910, about matters of history and art, of travel and of people, illuminated by the personal touch she gave them, are of interest to old and new students alike, even to a reader of today.

In the later years of her service, when she visited the graduates in their homes and on their jobs, encouraged them in difficulties and rejoiced with them in accomplishment, she was gratified to observe comfort and refinement in their homes; order and earnestness in their schools. After one visit to Florida, she wrote: "We were proud of every Spelman girl we met." In every way possible, she helped as long as her life lasted. She died at her sister's home in Providence, Rhode Island, on January 12, 1919.

Lucy Houghton Upton

"The possessor of a rare culture" is the way Mrs. Hattie Rutherford Watson, student, staff member and alumna trustee, characterizes Miss Upton. She was refined in manners, always dressed becomingly, never raised her voice high in speaking, whether in conversation or from the chapel platform, was exacting but with a great power of discernment. She compared her to Solomon "when it came to wisdom about things of the earth . . . ." but noted most of all "the spiritual richness of her life." Her very presence made the students do and be their best.

The Bible lessons frequently reported in the *Messenger* can be described as intriguing. They were as full of homely wisdom for daily life as was Benjamin Franklin in his *Poor Richard*; but the wise counsel was hung on pegs of Scripture – on Bible illustrations that made them stick. "To miss one of these talks," Mrs. Watson reported, "was to miss a rare treat."

Another early student, Mrs. Sallie Walker Wilder, recalls today 'her quick step and lively sparkling eyes,' and writes: "She could say so much in one minute that one would always feel exhilarated after hearing her speak."

"Under her instruction," wrote Mrs. Mary Reynolds of the WABHMS, who lived for fifteen weeks in 1904 on Spelman campus, "her pupils were never satisfied simply to learn lessons. The high standard she held made each one discontented with mediocrity."

The tribute written by Claudia White Harreld, C '01, and printed in the *Spelman Messenger* after Miss Upton's death includes these paragraphs:

Her mind was eager, keen, and richly endowed. We listened in awe when on one of her rare occasions of personal reference she told of the *Aeneid* translated into blank verse while a young girl, of continuing her study in Latin and other difficult subjects when forced to give up formal study. The child of an intellectual heritage, she had acquired not only the usual love of books, but also knew the ways of the woods-folk, could call the birds by their names, could count the stars in their courses, and was the possessor of many of Nature's secrets.

And, with all this endowment of mind, Miss Upton came south to teach us to spell, to guide our stumbling feet over the donkey's bridge, to whisper into our ears the hidden knowledge that would lift our heads and brighten our eyes. . . .

Miss Packard, Miss Giles and Miss Upton did not leave behind them their civilized surroundings, their interests and their friends to go to a barren field. They took their interests, their civilization, their well-stored minds, even their friends, with them, along with their faith and determination of spirit; and shared them with their students.

The visitors too who came to the campus at their behest — some came repeatedly, some stayed three days or three weeks or three months at a stretch, were a vital part of the educative process. Only so can one account for the growth in intellectual grasp, in personality and in character of the earliest graduates who so soon accomplished so much.

CHAPTER XII

THE ROCKEFELLER FAMILY
AND SPELMAN

Five Generations

THE reality that is Spelman College could not have been born without Miss Packard and Miss Giles. In the formative years, Miss Upton and the New England women were indispensable. But the school could not have grown to its status as a College without the interest and aid of the Spelman-Rockefeller family. The philanthropies of Mr. Rockefeller would no doubt have had other stimuli, and the well-being of mankind would have been promoted regardless of these women, but the fact remains, and has its significance, that the catalyzing agent of his interest in Negro education was his acquaintance with Miss Packard and Miss Giles and the students they were teaching in the school they founded.

Before his meeting with Miss Packard and Miss Giles in the Cleveland church in 1882, the pattern was being woven in the Spelman family. The friends of Spelman College surely ought to become better acquainted with their institutional god-parents, as well as get a more comprehensive understanding of the historical importance of the coming together of the Basement School and its Founders with the Spelman-Rockefeller family.

Among the New Englanders who moved from eastern Massachusetts to Ohio were the Samuel Buel Spelmans who traveled west in a two-horse wagon over the Allegheny Mountains. Their son, Harvey Buel Spelman, married Lucy Henry, also of New England parentage, November 16, 1835. Three children were born to them: Lucy Maria in 1837; Laura Celestia in 1839; and a son, Henry Jennings, in 1842, who died in 1857. The family moved to Akron around 1840, and to Cleveland in 1851. Mr. Spelman was a public-spirited citizen; of this there is evidence in each town in which he lived. He helped to organize churches in Kent, Akron, and Cleveland. He was elected to the State Legislature of Ohio in 1849. He was deeply interested in the cause of education and strongly anti-slavery.

He helped to create the public school system of Akron, the first city in Ohio to adopt the principle of free graded schools, supported by general taxation. The "Akron plan" as it came to be known, provided the pattern which gave order to the schools all over the state. Mr. Spelman was elected to the first Board of Education in 1847, and was made its Secretary.

The home of Mr. and Mrs. Spelman was a station on the Underground Railroad and they helped many slaves get to Canada and freedom. Mrs. Spelman, at the Seminary on April 11, 1884, told the assembly that the only dinners she ever cooked on the Sabbath were for the slaves on their journey northward.

Such was the atmosphere of the home in which Lucy and Laura Spelman grew up. They attended The Oread Collegiate Institute, of which Miss Packard later was principal, from April 1858 to June 1859 – an institution founded to provide college education for young women by that remarkable Eli Thayer, also an abolitionist. John Brown had come to Worcester in 1857 at the invitation of Mr. Thayer, gave a public address, and was a guest at the Oread. It was in Mr. Thayer's study in Worcester that the plan was developed to colonize Kansas through an Emigrant Aid Society and thus insure the admission of Kansas to the Union as a free state. Laura wrote a former music teacher of the lectures she heard by Emerson, Henry Ward Beecher, and Wendell Phillips.

Lucy and Laura were serious-minded. Laura's high school graduation essay bore the title, "I can paddle my own canoe." She taught in the public schools of Cleveland about five years. In 1864 she married John D. Rockefeller, then 25 years old and an able young businessman. Both were active in church and Sunday School; and both were concerned about the state of the Negroes.

Mr. Rockefeller throughout his life was happy in his family relationships, genial, understanding, with a lively interest in the activities of his growing children; stern and upright but not

PLATE XI

Harvey Buel Spelman

Lucy Henry Spelman

John D. Rockefeller

Laura Spelman Rockefeller

PLATE XII

Lucy on the right

Laura on the right

THE SPELMAN SISTERS

John D. Rockefeller, Jr.

Abby Aldrich Rockefeller

"hard." Even the most recent biographies fail to do justice to his admirable traits of unselfishness, good humor, loyalty to friends and causes, devotion to human welfare. Far from "narrow" were his interests: they included love of Nature and love of travel, care for horses and road-building, interest in people of all levels. One of his first recorded gifts was to a colored minister; and as early as 1861 he contributed to a Negro church. The large part he and his family had in Spelman's history was by no means confined to gifts of money.

Miss Packard and Miss Giles had many interests in common with the women of the Rockefeller household. All were strong church women; strong believers in education; strong supporters of temperance; strong believers in freedom for all, and the urgent need to educate and Christianize "the freed people." But the association went deeper than an interest in social welfare. There was congeniality of spirit and outlook that grew into friendship. The letters from Mrs. Spelman in her own hand and from daughter Lucy, who was often the scribe for her mother and sometimes for her sister, give ample evidence.

Mrs. Spelman's portrait shows keen blue eyes, wrinkles of good humor around them, a purposeful chin and mouth, and in an undefinable way, an invincibility of spirit. She was a devout and active Christian. She left her mark on her daughters and her grandchildren. After her death in 1897, it was said: "The gentle mother was the strong woman, with vertebrate conscience, uncompromising principles, and convictions settled by rich and long experience"; and again "she was a warm, energetic woman with a lively interest in books." She believed as she wrote her grandson on his twenty-first birthday that "a life enriched by thoughtful study must be a more useful, and a happier life." Her heart was full of love and good cheer for her own family, and for the stranger within or outside of the gate.

Willard S. Richardson, an associate of Mr. Rockefeller, Jr. at Brown University and frequently a member of the Rockefeller family circle, told the writer that Negroes owe a deal of gratitude to the women of the Spelman-Rockefeller family. He was concerned that, at the time of his visit to Spelman College in 1934 as Founders Day speaker, he saw no picture of Miss Lucy Spelman. Thanks to his interest which resulted in a gift from her nephew, John D. Rockefeller, Jr., one now hangs in a place of honor in Rockefeller Hall. It is to Miss Lucy Spelman, "Aunt Lute," as her nephew called her, that we are most indebted for the frequent letters to Miss Packard and Miss Giles, expressing her own and her mother's interest in Spelman Seminary. Aunt Lute "was bright, intelligent, and a good hostess, as well as a good conversationalist." She was interested in music and books and in church activities; and in her mother and her sister's family.

That the friendship of Mrs. Spelman and both daughters, and, indeed, of Mr. Rockefeller himself with the Founders was not superficial nor "routine" can be known best through the letters. Space permits quotations from only a few of them:

To *Miss Packard & Miss Giles*

From Miss Lucy M. Spelman   June 17, 1889

Mother desires me to express to you her thanks for the fine photographs just received from Spelman Seminary. . . . The note from 'The Mutual Aid Band' gave Mother much pleasure; she can now associate the names with the faces and will treasure them in memory, with the prayer that their influence may be wide-spread and abiding for good. . . .

From Mrs. Spelman   April, 1895

I read the *Spelman Messenger* with increasing interest. The brief history of Sojourner Truth recalled the time she spent a few days at our home in Ohio, during the anti-slavery conflict. . . .

From Mrs. Spelman to Miss Giles & Miss Upton   December 2, 1895

With this note I also mail one number of a magazine, called the 'College Number.' If you have not seen it, I am sure you will enjoy looking it over, as I know you are interested in all that pertains to the education, and elevation, of women. . . .

I see by the *Messenger* . . . I always watch for its coming. . . .

Mrs. Lucy Henry Spelman died in Cleveland, Ohio, on September 7, 1897. A memorial service in her honor was held in Howe Memorial Chapel on October 17. The report of the service published in the *Messenger* brought a long letter from Miss Lucy Spelman. She wrote, referring to her mother, "I think she had kept on file every letter she ever received from Spelman teachers and pupils, and the photographs she considered her personal opportunity for interesting young and old in the good work among the colored people. . . ." A new flag was dedicated on the 1901 Founders Day which celebrated the 20th anniversary, presented by Miss Spelman in memory of her mother's 95th birthday.

Mr. John D. Rockefeller was an astute judge of personal character; he believed in Miss Packard and Miss Giles and in their work. It was his influence, as we have seen, that enabled the women to keep the enterprise "a girls' school." It was his financial help that made possible, the erection of the first brick building, and the second, and the third; and the next four, by an outright gift. He wisely commented, when a laundry was desperately needed and a "temporary building," a cheap wooden structure, was under consideration, that "temporary" buildings had a way of becoming permanent and that it would be better to build at the beginning one that would fully answer the purpose. So, with aid from him, Spelman had a brick laundry; it is still in use.

It was Mr. Rockefeller's policy to give and to give generously; but not to give to institutions and causes until convinced of their worth. He wanted his gifts to stimulate others to give (hence the practice of "matching" or conditional gifts); and he wished to assist organizations that had vitality, not to bolster dying causes. He therefore looked to see whether the women at Spelman had "stickative qualities," and found them not wanting.

He was interested in their cause; he also was a friend to them personally. As early as April 3, 1889, he sent to Miss Packard for her personal use his "check for $100 from Mrs. Rockefeller and myself, with warmest regards from all our family, including Mrs. Spelman and Miss Spelman." It seems likely that personal gifts to Miss Packard and to Miss Giles became an annual practice. On the 25th anniversary, Mr. Rockefeller sent Miss Giles $500, "for her own personal use, in appreciation of her long, faithful, and unselfish labors. . . ."

The minute attention Mr. Rockefeller gave to the matter of land purchases adjoining the first nine acres is beyond belief except for the records in the ABHMS files. There was a law in Georgia passed in the sixties, that no foreign citizen could own land in the state. Since there had been investment in real estate by English people and others, it was impossible in many cases in the early eighties to obtain a clear title.

This Mr. Rockefeller insisted on having before the purchase of more land. He employed local lawyers to look into the matter. Conflicting recommendations were made. It did not appear desirable for Spelman Seminary to originate action to abrogate the obstructing law, as the attitude of Southern politicians was not friendly to the education of Negroes. The law, of course, was making trouble for other would-be purchasers of real estate and for other institutions. Finally, based on action taken by a school for white girls, the law was rescinded by the Georgia legislature. And purchases of lots for Spelman began to be made. Miss Packard and Miss Giles gave or raised money to buy a few lots, but in the main Mr. Rockefeller provided the funds. In April, 1897, Dr. Morehouse wrote Miss Giles: "Let me say that Mr. Rockefeller has now bought all of the land fronting on Ella Street, and all of the land fronting on Leonard Street. . . . He also bought three small pieces of land known as lots 21-22 and 23 on the other side of Lizzie Street, a street which has never been opened, so you will see that this does complete the square with the exception of the corner on Greensferry Avenue and Culver Street. . . ."

In the midst of his busy, business life, Mr. Rockefeller gave attention and made decisions and wrote letters in his own hand about these matters. After the disappointment over Mrs. Slack's action in re "Howard" Hall, Mr. Rockefeller wrote Miss Packard and Miss Giles increasing his pledge toward the new building, and added: "Keep up good cheer, and kindly let me know what response you get to this. I hope other friends will come forward with the balance required, and we all believe that the greater the number of contributors, the better the enterprise." He sent a letter of sympathy when Miss Packard was ill in December, 1889, and added: "We greatly rejoice to hear the favorable reports of the Seminary. . . ."

At the turn of the century, Mr. Rockefeller began to refer letters and questions about Spelman to his son, John D. Rockefeller, Jr. It was Mr. John D. Rockefeller, Jr. who transmitted the authorization of his father in June 1900 for four new buildings, and with whom the correspondence was conducted with regard to the names for them. It was Mr. John D. Rockefeller, Jr. who requested that quadruple plated silverware, in place of triple plate, be purchased for the new dining hall. Miss Giles first met the younger Mr. Rockefeller in New York during the Christmas vacation in 1900. His first visit to Spelman Seminary was on April 20-21, 1901. The *Messenger* reported the enthusiasm with which the students greeted his talk. 'Twas not noisy enthusiasm, apparently, as the record states that on this occasion he was greeted by the Chautauqua salute!

Miss Giles immediately wrote General Morgan about the visit: "We are charmed with him, and he expressed himself as delighted with Spelman, and more interested in us than ever, and likely to come again, now that he has made personal acquaintance. . . ."

Mr. Rockefeller, Junior, wrote to Miss Giles in equally glowing terms. He said:

Of all the places of interest which I visited during my Southern trip none were so pleasing and so satisfactory to me as Spelman, and of the various courtesies that were extended to me by the friends in the different cities, none were so highly appreciated and so thoroughly enjoyed as those shown me in your house during the two days spent with you.

Spelman in its grounds, its buildings, its courses of study, its methods, and above all its spirit, far surpasses my highest expectations. I was delighted with everything I saw and am very happy to have had even a small part in helping to build up this splendid work. . . . I count it a benediction on my life to have spent two days in your home . . . and I appreciate most fully the kind hospitality which you, Miss Upton and Miss Packard showed me and the cordial welcome given me by all the other teachers and scholars. . . .

With reference to the added improvements in the grounds and buildings of which I spoke to you, I will write. . . .

In May after his visit, he wrote Miss Giles enclosing his father's check for $1,000 "to constitute a little fund . . . on which you shall be at liberty to draw for such objects in connection with the Seminary which you think specially needed and for which you do not know where else to turn for the money."

A touch of humor appears in a letter from Mr. John D. Rockefeller, Jr. to General Morgan in June, 1901. He said that, when he was in Atlanta, there were certain things that it seemed to him desirable to have done, so he asked the superintendent to figure on them and send him an estimate of the cost. He adds: "This estimate he has presented, making it somewhat fuller, however, than I had suggested." (!) He eliminated certain items but approved a list of improvements to cost $7,300, which, he wrote, "my father will pay for."

In October, 1901, Mr. John D. Rockefeller, Jr. provided $500 for a scholarship at Teachers College, New York. Miss Giles selected for it Mrs. Hannah Howell Reddick, a student at Spelman for ten years, then a teacher. After her marriage, she and her husband, Major Reddick, were in charge of Americus Institute in South Georgia. Still later, she served as the first alumna trustee, 1921-1927; and as hall mother in the freshman dormitory, 1927-1946, in which position she was a blessing to generations of students.

Mr. John D. Rockefeller, Jr. brought his bride to Spelman in February, 1903. Miss Giles wrote that they spent the day and that it was "a most delightful visit."

Due to the development of the General Education Board

program, there were fewer letters after 1903 to and from the members of the Rockefeller family. In May, 1912, however, correspondence between John D. Rockefeller and Miss Upton resulted in a gift to Spelman of a fine victrola and $50 more for the purchase of records. Mr. Rockefeller wrote: "The victrola which we use in our houses cost $200; is known as the Victor-Victrola XVI; made in golden oak or mahogany. I incline to think you would want one as large. . . ." The letter offering the gift arrived on Commencement Day. The victrola was played on the opening day in the fall and victrola concerts were given in the chapel throughout the year.

Miss Upton continued to be a personal tie between the Seminary and the family as long as she remained on the campus. After she went North in 1913, Miss Spelman grieved at her loss; and the personal flavor of the letters ceased. When Mrs. Laura Spelman Rockefeller died early in 1915, her son acknowledged the messages of sympathy in his own hand in a letter to "the teachers and students of Spelman Seminary." The letter concluded with the following paragraph:

"Mother's interest in Spelman Seminary has always been very deep. I know that she will continue to follow with affectionate concern the work of each teacher and student, as she looks down from her heavenly home, and that she will rejoice at your successes and sympathize with you in your difficulties. May her beautiful Christian life ever be an inspiration to us all!"

How the students of the day felt about the Spelmans and Rockefellers comes frequently to light. For example, in a letter to the President of Spelman College written in 1929, Mrs. Carrie *Walls* Gassaway, one of the 1888 graduates, reported a talk she had recently made "at a dinner with some of Cleveland's real good intelligent women. . . ."

"Since I have been in Cleveland (ten years with the exception of two . . .), on Memorial Day my husband or one of my sons has driven me out to Lakeview Cemetery. I went there to see only one grave — that was the grave of the sainted Mrs.

Laura Spelman Rockefeller." Mrs. Gassaway then described with vivid detail the occasion on April 11, 1884, when Mr. Rockefeller visited the Seminary, with his family, and observed that Spelman College has all along received help from Mr. Rockefeller and the foundations he established – and had it not been for these friends and others, Negro women would have had no chance to be educated.

She concluded: "Now you understand why on Memorial Day in Cleveland, Ohio, I visit this sainted woman's grave. To make it plainer, this is the only way I have of showing my appreciation of what Mr. John D. Rockefeller, and his sainted wife, have done for the girls of the Southland, me included, for I am one of them."

The year 1939 marked the 100th Anniversary of the birth of Mrs. Laura Spelman Rockefeller. The Spelman College Granddaughters Club chose Christmas Sunday, December 24, as the date to pay tribute to her memory by placing a wreath on her grave in the Lakeview Cemetery. A group of Spelman alumnae, eight Morehouse alumni and a few others gathered at the grave. Dr. D. R. Sharpe, executive secretary of the Cleveland Baptist Association and a friend of Spelman College, spoke of Mrs. Rockefeller's part in the growth of Spelman; Mrs. Ruth Berry McKinney, '21, gave a brief history; Mrs. Frances Hood Thomas, '22, read a set of resolutions pledging remembrance and loyalty, prepared by the Granddaughters Club and carried to Cleveland by two Spelman freshmen. The wreath of evergreen was then placed on the grave in gratitude for Mrs. Rockefeller's life and her friendship.

Mr. Rockefeller sent regrets that he could not attend the Fiftieth Anniversary in 1931. His telegram was concluded with these words: "Of all the things that we have done as a family, Spelman stands among the best."

To complete the story of the support given by Five Generations of the Spelman-Rockefeller family would involve completing the college history. Consequently, only a few bare facts will be mentioned in this chapter regarding the fourth and fifth generations. Some history-to-be has not yet happened.

John D. Rockefeller, III, represented the family on the occasion of the Fiftieth Anniversary in 1931 and has visited the College on several other occasions. Winthrop Rockefeller, in his uniform as a lieutenant colonel, spoke to Spelman students in Sisters Chapel at a morning chapel service while he was on an army mission to Atlanta to inquire into the needs of Negro war veterans. His great-grandmother Spelman would have been proud of him, as indeed were we all. His short talk was sincere and inspiring.

Mrs. Mary French Rockefeller is a member of the Spelman College Board of Trustees. Her husband, Laurance Spelman Rockefeller, is the middle son of Mr. and Mrs. John D. Rockefeller, Jr., and was named in honor of his grandmother, Laura Spelman. Mary French Rockefeller is the daughter of Mr. and Mrs. John French; the latter was a close friend of Mrs. Abby Aldrich Rockefeller and an associate of hers on the National Board of the YWCA. Able, sympathetic, possessing sound judgment, Mrs. Laurance Spelman Rockefeller takes an interest in individual students as well as in college policy and procedure. She was especially helpful when the College was raising funds to build the Gymnasium. Individual gifts were received from herself, and others of the Rockefeller family. All five of the sons of Mr. Rockefeller, Junior have at one time or another visited Spelman College.

The newest building on the Spelman College campus is Abby Aldrich Rockefeller Hall, a gift of Mr. John D. Rockefeller, Jr., who was represented at the exercises of dedication by his son Laurance. Before going to Sisters Chapel for the exercises, he handed to the President of the College a check from his oldest daughter Laura, drawn on her personal bank account; the first gift to be received by Spelman College from a member of the Fifth Generation of the Spelman-Rockefeller family.

The Fifth Generation is growing fast in numbers and influence – Mr. John D. Rockefeller, Jr.[1] has over 20 grandchildren. That the interest of their generation in Spelman College has just begun is the institution's hope and trust. It is eminently fitting and deeply touching to have the first gift from the Fifth Generation from Laura Spelman Rockefeller, a great-great-granddaughter of Mr. and Mrs. Harvey Buel Spelman and a great-granddaughter of Mrs. Laura Spelman Rockefeller. It marked the seventy-first year since Mr. John D. Rockefeller's first gift to Miss Packard and Miss Giles, the gift which was his first gift to Negro education.

[1] This was written before the death of John D. Rockefeller, Jr., on May 11, 1960.

CHAPTER XIII

SPELMAN UNDER MISS TAPLEY

1910-1927

MISS LUCY HALE TAPLEY was elected president of Spelman Seminary, by vote of the Board of Trustees in March, 1910. Miss Tapley, on the faculty for 20 years, had been for the previous six years the head of the Teachers Professional Department; and for eight months Dean of the Seminary. She succeeded as Dean, Mrs. Florence Cordo who resigned in July, 1909, after serving a year and a half.

Miss Tapley was born in a farm house overlooking the harbor of West Brooksville, Maine, on May 28, 1857; the daughter of Captain Thomas Tapley, one of 11 brothers, all of whom followed the sea, and Lucy Wasson Tapley who came from a family of famous seamen. She attended Miss Lucy Henry's private school in Brooksville and then Bucksport Seminary. She came to Spelman in 1890 as teacher of English and arithmetic. She served as teacher, hall matron, and as principal of the practice school before taking charge in 1903 of the teacher training department, as successor to Miss Elizabeth V. Griffin, who had organized the professional teachers' course after Giles Hall was built.

Miss Tapley was a woman of strong character. She was tall and broad-shouldered and walked with briskness and assurance. She had penetrating blue eyes, a sense of humor, and a hearty, infectious laugh. A member of her faculty once remarked that Miss Tapley had a brother who was a sea-captain but looked like a school teacher, while Miss Tapley was a school teacher but looked like a sea-captain.

She had "the quality that is associated with high command. She had forcefulness, thoroughness, power of organization, confidence in her own judgment, a superb sense of order — " (Claudia White Harreld). She was "exacting with herself and all

187

for whom she felt responsible; indefatigable as a worker; and
... a strong executive with high ideals and ambitions – " (Edith
V. Brill).

Mrs. Cora Hardy Adams relates an incident of Miss Tapley's thoroughness and care of detail even in her youth. Her
father offered to give her one dollar if, for a month at a stretch,
she would set the table for meals without omitting anything –
a salt-cellar or a spoon or any needed item; it was not an easy
assignment but she persisted until she won the reward.

"Miss Tapley was very different from Miss Giles," one
alumna said. She was positive, brisk, and "could give you a
dressing up."

Miss Tapley's insistence on order sometimes led to extreme
measures. Rules became more obvious, even arbitrary. There
was one that now causes merriment among loyal graduates of
the period. At a given date, regardless of the weather, the students were required to don long-sleeved woollen underwear;
at another set date in the spring, they were allowed to stop
wearing it. Three or four graduates recently related gleefully:
"Don't you recall Miss Tapley's coming into the dining-room
early on a spring morning and saying cheerfully: 'Good morning, girls. I have good news for you. Tomorrow you may leave
off your woollies!' " These graduates also remembered that
some of the girls, at a date earlier than the official announcement, had left off their "woollies" on warm days but, in order
not to be caught if the President gently pinched their sleeves,
had worn a wide armlet or half-sleeve under the dress or blouse.

In all matters of discipline, Miss Tapley required strict obedience to the rules; nor apparently were the rules adjusted
much as the times changed. Yet personally Miss Tapley was
said by Dr. Hope to have been "more gentle than the rule."
Moreover, her hearty sense of humor often helped to gain an
end that might otherwise have been difficult. Her loyalty to
her own convictions and her sincerity of purpose commanded
admiration from students, parents and teachers.

The year 1910-11 opened in October with a full quota of

students. Miss Tapley described the prevailing atmosphere as one of peace, earnestness and hearty cooperation. Over 300 boarders registered the first day. The price of board was advanced from $9.50 to $10.00 for each four weeks.

Spelman on its Thirtieth Anniversary

The 30th Anniversary was celebrated on April 11th. The students' rally in the morning was followed by an afternoon of speeches. Miss Grover, the only one left of the four who had taught in the basement school, told of those early days; Mrs. Mary Reynolds of the WABHMS spoke on "Ebenezers"; Dr.. George Sale, Superintendent of Education of the ABHMS, on "The Stamp of Personality," emphasizing the impress that the personality of the Founders had made on all Spelman students. As he had been President of Atlanta Baptist College from 1890 to 1906, he had been a colleague of both Miss Packard and Miss Giles.

At the evening session, Dr. E. P. Johnson's subject was "Over the bridge – the new President"; he compared the change to one conductor stepping off a train and another coming on, taking the train forward on the same track.

In her first annual report to the trustees, Miss Tapley stated that the purpose of the new administration was to carry on in the spirit of the Founders, giving emphasis to moral and religious training. "Surely real education consists in 'the harmonious development of the whole being' and its object may well be said to be 'to render the individual as far as possible an instrument of happiness to himself and to others.' "

She informed the Trustees that Miss Edith V. Brill, her successor as superintendent of the normal department, had been made Dean; and that Miss Edna E. Lamson had been made Superintendent of the Normal Department. Miss Brill had been on the faculty more than a dozen years; Miss Lamson for five years. The statistics prepared for the 30th Anniversary showed that 15 of the 33 members of the faculty had served at Spelman for 10 years or more; 10 had fewer than five years of service.

There were 16 students in the College Department, 136 in the High School; 21 in the TPC; 383 in the Normal Practice School; 22 in Nurse Training and 67 taking Dressmaking, Missionary Training, night school courses and music.

She reported progress in greater average attendance though a slightly smaller enrollment; increased efficiency in teaching agriculture and the handicrafts; extra practice provided in chaircaning, rug weaving and basket-making.

Changes Made by Miss Tapley

From the beginning of Miss Tapley's administration, her annual reports to the trustees stressed industrial training, and teacher training with special emphasis on teachers for the rural schools. The aim of providing higher intellectual training for the ablest students who might become leaders was out of favor. The 1914 report, to take one example, compressed into one sentence of five lines "the work of all the literary departments." Whereas, three long paragraphs dealt with the industrial departments, and a new course in "chicken culture" was described. Teacher training was promoted even for the high school students. Miss Tapley stated that 99 students out of 113 students enrolled in the first-year high school class elected the English normal course in which the first year was devoted to preparation for teaching. Thus, it was thought that many who would not complete even a high school course might "do efficient work in the rural public schools."

Miss Tapley stated in another annual report that the city and county supervisors of schools, in response to inquiry, had borne testimony to the efficiency and excellent character of teachers trained at Spelman "and also voice the growing sentiment of educators everywhere, the need of industrial and vocational training along with literary . . . this idea is growing among our students also."

Spelman's excellence in producing good teachers was shown

from the very first, when the earliest pupils taught in country places during the summer months, teaching as they had been taught and had observed in the Model School. With the professional resources available after Giles Hall was built in 1891, the work was strengthened and expanded, first under Miss Elizabeth V. Griffin and later under Miss Tapley, each in the position of Superintendent of the Normal Department. Dr. George Sale in 1911 had said in a report on the Home Mission schools: "Spelman leads this group of colleges in the extent and quality of its teacher training, and its graduates in this department are in great demand and are found all over the South. . . ."

The February 1914 *Messenger* was enlarged by a two-page Supplement in order to permit a statement about each department and area of life at Spelman. The articles were about Our Campus, Our College Department, Our Teachers Professional Department, Our High School, Our Vocal Music, Our Instrumental Music, Our Family Life, Our Motto, Our Societies, Our S.S. Teacher Training Class, Our Graduates, Our Hospital, Our Nurses Home, Our Bench Work, Our Dressmaking Department, Our Cooking School, Our Millinery, Our Laundry, Our Poultry, Our Finances, Our Storeroom, Our Influence, Our County Work, Our Library, Our Men Folk (building and grounds' staff), Our Leisure Hours, Our Cats, Our Mocking Bird. Signed by the initials of the member of the faculty in charge of each department or category, these statements describe in considerable detail the work and the present aims of the institution.

The shift of emphasis to vocational training is obvious. Following a mention of the privilege that was accorded to Spelman to confer the Bachelor of Arts degree, and the cooperation with Morehouse College in offering the requisite courses, comes the following significant paragraph.

"Any course of study which fails to cultivate a taste and fitness for practical and efficient work in some part of the field of the world's needs is unpopular at Spelman and finds no place in our curriculum. Every course of study which makes young women more womanly, more purposeful, more resourceful and more efficient is earnestly coveted."

Whether by happenstance or by design, the March 1914 *Messenger* carried on its front page a very large cut, 7″ x 9″, of Leonardo da Vinci's *Mona Lisa*; and on the second page pictures of two Madonnas (one by Raphael); with one article entitled "Mona Lisa, a Mystery" and another entitled "Raphael Madonnas Coming to America." Could the prominent display of "Mona Lisa" in this issue have been a nudge from the editor, a teacher and staff member since 1877, to remind readers that efficiency is not all?

Efficiency is a word that begins to appear frequently in reports and discussions. In Miss Tapley's report to the Board of Trustees in 1915, for example, she wrote: "In all the work of the Seminary, the basic purpose is Christian training for efficiency in all forms of service." And the next year: "The dominant aim . . . is the development of Christian womanhood, and all the school activities are planned to give instruction in housewifely arts. Spelman proceeds upon the principle that all work well done is cultural. . . ."

It may be doubtful if the Trustees recognized fully what a shift in emphasis was taking place. Repeatedly Miss Tapley in her annual reports said that "there has been no change in the courses of study or in the policy of the school," and quoted Miss Packard's early statement naming the following five aims:

> to train the intellect
> to store the mind with useful knowledge
> to induce habits of industry and a desire for general information
> to inspire a love for the true and the beautiful
> to prepare the pupils for the practical duties of life

The record shows that there was more implementation of the fifth aim, "to prepare the pupils for the practical duties of life" than of the first, "to train the intellect" or of the fourth, "to inspire a love for the true and the beautiful."

Miss Tapley and her chief co-workers, however, had strong convictions that they were in the right in not placing in the curriculum "any course of study which fails to cultivate a taste and fitness for practical and efficient work in some part of the field of the world's needs." Thoroughness, industry and character were most of all stressed in the courses that were offered.

The lack of good schools in rural areas was distressing, to be sure, and fundamentally important. More and more, the dominant aim became that of sending trained teachers to the rural schools and communities. Preferably, Miss Tapley desired that a Spelman student from a rural community go back to her home community to teach and lift the people's standard of living. That a little leaven in many small communities would surely though gradually raise to higher levels the life of all the Negroes in those communities and so extend the effects of Christian education was her firm conviction. It was the wider spread of education and Christian teaching that she diligently sought. The consequence of this policy was that more average or even below average students were admitted to the Spelman courses, since those in her judgment with the highest intellectual ability and interests were less likely to go back to their small home towns or rural areas. Yet the level of preparation for high school or normal courses was a matter of concern, and the need for greater thoroughness Miss Tapley constantly stressed. Getting better trained teachers in the rural and small town schools would in her opinion, gradually bring to Spelman an increasing number of well-prepared students.

Two new buildings added to the equipment for vocational education. When Miss Tapley became president of Spelman Seminary, the plant consisted of 20 acres of campus, 10 brick buildings in addition to one of the wooden barracks which was used as barn and workshop. Soon the need arose for (1) better accommodations for the students in nurse training; and (2) a building in which the home economics and household arts work could be concentrated. Through appeals to the General Education Board, funds totaling $85,000 were provided for two new buildings: a Nurses' Home to be located next to the hospital; and a building opposite Rockefeller Hall to be known as the Laura Spelman Rockefeller Building for Home Economics.

The nurses' home was to be named in honor of Bessie Rockefeller Strong, the oldest of the children of John D. Rockefeller; a Vassar graduate who married Charles A. Strong, teacher of philosophy at Bryn Mawr College and son of Dr. Augustus H. Strong, president of the Rochester Theological Seminary. Bessie Strong Nurses Home, as it was called, was occupied in October 1917. The building which had housed the student nurses became a teachers' dormitory, and was later known as Upton Home.[1] The courses in nurse training were strengthened; more recognition professionally was given to Negro nurses; and by 1920, the graduate nurses gained the privilege of examination for state certificates.

The Laura Spelman Rockefeller Memorial Building, met with numerous delays, caused mainly by the first World War, and was completed in the fall of 1918. In Miss Tapley's annual report presented in April 1919, is the following statement: "There have been no important changes in any of the school departments but each year there is an effort to improve upon previous work. The only additions to the departments are the two new home economics courses outlined in last year's report. . . . The new building is meeting every need and its usefulness has but begun. . . ." The following year, 1920, Miss Tapley reported: "All the academic and industrial courses have been maintained. . . . When colleges open freely to graduates other than the traditional, classical, or circumscribed scientific ones, more high school graduates will enter for better preparation [to teach]."

In the summer of 1921, Spelman cooperated with Morehouse College in its Summer School to the extent of allowing the Laura Spelman Rockefeller Home Economics Build-

---

[1] Built in 1905, for a nurses' home and isolation ward; one end continued to be used as an isolation ward until the fall of 1927. The name of Miss Upton seems to have been informally assigned to the building in 1918. The President's annual report contains this reference: "Upton Home, formerly the Nurses' Home. . . ."

ing to be used for offering courses in the home economics field.

The year 1921 marked the Fortieth anniversary. The Anniversary Exercises, held on April 6, 7 and 8, included a program of papers by Spelman graduates on the general subject of "The Reach of Spelman's Influence": and one afternoon session with an address by Hon. M. L. Brittain, Superintendent of Education of Georgia; a talk by Dr. James Hardy Dillard, president of the Jeanes and Slater Funds, in which he emphasized that teachers need to be trained to value *accuracy*; speeches by Jackson Davis of the General Education Board, W. T. B. Williams of the Jeanes and Slater Funds, and Walter Hill, Rural School Superintendent of Georgia. One evening session featured an address by Mrs. Alice B. Coleman, President of the WABHMS. On another evening, a pageant depicting the History of Spelman written by Claudia White Harreld C '01, and stage-directed by Mrs. Harreld and Mrs. Hattie Rutherford Watson, C'07, was presented to a crowded house by the Atlanta Spelman Graduates Club.

The report of the President in 1921 again stated: "No change has been made in the departments of study, industrial or academic. . . ." "Some new equipment" had been added in science; and "some new books placed in the library." "A good assortment of the leading standard periodicals is in the reading room, and some good departmental reference books have been supplied."

On March 2, 1922, the President reported: "a period of quiet growth. . . . There has been no change in the number or character of the departments of instruction. The faculty of each department has been working for increased efficiency. . . . The demand for trained teachers grows yet more insistent and the strongest emphasis is placed upon professional training."

Meantime, Miss Edna E. Lamson who had left in 1916 to study at Teachers College, Columbia University, returned to the Spelman faculty in 1921, as Superintendent of its Normal Training Department. Miss Edith V. Brill who had served as Dean since 1910 resigned at the end of 1921-22. Miss Lamson succeeded her in this position, and sat at the right of Miss Tapley at the opening exercises on October third, 1922.

Miss Lamson came back full of new ideas, and enthusiasm for them. Intelligence tests were instituted. Binet-Simon Tests; the Stanford Revision of Binet-Simon; Otis Group Intelligence Scale; Thorndike-McCall Reading Scale; Ayres Spelling Scale; Thorndike Visual Vocabulary; and many others became familiar terms. Tests, battery after battery of them, were given to Spelman applicants and Spelman students. It was discovered that a rather small number of students had IQs showing superior ability. In fact, in 1922-23, there were discovered 26 students in all departments including the practice school, who could be classified according to the Terman tests as "superior" or "very superior." These data were taken very seriously; and assisted in making a new system of grades and promotions.

In 1926-27, 22 students were enrolled who had an IQ of 110 or more, – four out of 77 college students; eight out of 297 students in the senior and junior high schools; and 10 in the elementary grades one through six.

On the whole, the campus upkeep had by 1922 been brought up to pre-war conditions. During World War I, Spelman students not only followed the course of events in their history and geography classes, but they participated in the Wheatless Days, the Heatless Days, the work in the War Gardens on Spelman campus, and in sacrifices to buy War Bonds and to make gifts to the American Red Cross.

The Change in Name to College

Exciting news for Spelman Seminary not yet released for publication but confided by Miss Tapley to Mrs. Reynolds of the WABHMS in January 1923, was that funds for the building of a chapel had been assured by Dr. Buttrick and Dr. Wickliffe Rose, who succeeded Dr. Buttrick as President of the General Education Board on March first, 1923, when Dr. Buttrick became chairman of the GEB. Furthermore, there was good prospect that money might be granted also for a Science building. In that case Spelman could offer on the Spelman campus all the work required for a college degree, and the Spelman students need no longer take a large share of their college work at Morehouse College. This meant that steps were to be taken to change Spelman Seminary to Spelman College by charter alterations, based on the new arrangements and additional facilities and equipment. The stated intention of the administration was to have a college "which will devote its time to the training of teachers."

At the annual meeting of the Board of Trustees of Spelman Seminary in 1923, the gift of money for the construction of a chapel and a science building was accepted. Dr. Wallace Buttrick fortunately for Spelman, consented in 1923 to serve as a member of the Spelman Board of Trustees. His influence worked behind the scenes to promote the development of Spelman Seminary into a college. Miss Tapley quoted him in support of such a plan in letters to Mrs. Reynolds of the WABHMS, and to D. G. Garabrant, who had become president of the Board of Trustees of Spelman Seminary after the death of Dr. Morehouse.

After all, here was Spelman Seminary with a phenomenal record of accomplishment for more than 40 years, with an excellent plant and better than ordinary financial support. Negroes too had made phenomenal progress, as they became trained and had opportunity to assume responsibility in schools, churches, YM and YWCAs, and to a limited extent in business and professions. Why should there not be a college devoted to the higher training of Negro women? Spelman already had prestige because of the record of its graduates. The material equipment ranked high among colleges for Negroes. All the others, except two for men only, were co-educational. As the May 1923 *Messenger* stated, departing somewhat from the tradition of boasting only of its product: "If we are not lacking in information, Spelman College will be the first Negro Women's College in the world."

In the same issue, an article was published over the signature

197

of Miss Lucy Hale Tapley, President, addressed "To School Principals, Prospective Students, and Patrons of Spelman Seminary." The opening paragraphs read:

When Spelman opens school in the fall of 1924, it will open as a Teachers College, offering curricula in secondary education, elementary education, and home economics education. Students may make a choice among the three curricula mentioned. . . . [Details followed concerning the degrees and diplomas and courses.]

Students expecting to pursue college work must have thorough elementary and secondary education. Students who have done only passing work in the high schools cannot expect to do standard college work. . . . All students who included physics and chemistry as part of the 15 units required for entrance were required to present their notebooks to the Dean.

The call was for "young women of character, health and ability," and "a serious purpose in life."

"Internal growth and expansion" characterized Spelman Seminary in 1923-24, according to Miss Tapley's report to the Trustees. The year was marked by a crystallization of ideas, reclassification of students, reorganization of the practice school, and much planning for the future. There were 82 students classified as college students, only 25 of whom were pursuing the liberal arts curriculum; 35 were majoring in elementary education, and 22 in home economics education. The latter two groups would, as formerly, receive diplomas, not degrees. The members of the freshman college class, for the first time had all their classes on the Spelman campus. The 25 students enrolled for the bachelor's degree, Miss Tapley reported, were pursuing a total of 110 courses, of which 70 were offered on Spelman campus. Upperclass college students went to Morehouse College for the remaining 40 courses. This was actually well for them, as the Morehouse faculty included excellent teachers in basic subjects.

The report stated that good results had been obtained in reading achievement throughout the 12 grades in the practice school, and that the objective tests had provided new incentive to the pupils.

The annual meeting of the Board of Trustees held on March 13, 1924, was attended by Mrs. George W. Coleman, president of the WABHMS, Miss Mary Howard of Hartford, also representing Baptist women of the North, Trevor Arnett, vice-president of the University of Chicago, and by invitation, Mr. H. J. Thorkelson of the General Education Board. Atlanta trustees were Robert J. Guinn, Harvey Hatcher and Hugh M. Willet, and two Negro trustees, the Rev. E. P. Johnson and Willis Murphy. D. G. Garabrant of Bloomfield, New Jersey, member of the Board since 1914 and its president since 1918, had died on February 19. Trevor Arnett was elected president of the Board of Trustees and member of the finance committee. This election of Mr. Arnett, and Mr. Arnett's acceptance of the responsibility, were fruits of Dr. Buttrick's foresight and his interest in Spelman. Dr. Buttrick's fellow trustees on the various Rockefeller Boards were aware of what was called his "cat's whiskers" in many matters that proved his insight and sound judgment. Miss Tapley wrote Mrs. Reynolds of this "wonderfully good fortune for Spelman College."

The above-named Trustees passed the resolution that Spelman Seminary should become Spelman College on June 1, 1924. It voted also that present student activities participated in by both schools cease so far as Spelman College is concerned and be replaced by similar activities under the auspices of Spelman College. This action unfortunately marked the end of a joint Morehouse-Spelman literary society, and a joint college paper, the *Athenaeum*.

Legal change, of course, had to be made in the charter through the courts. Harvey Hatcher, lawyer of Atlanta and Spelman trustee since 1912, informed Miss Tapley that the Court signed the decree on Monday, June 2, whereby the Spelman Seminary became Spelman College. Two days later, Miss Tapley was writing Dr. Buttrick on a Spelman College letterhead to report the *fait accompli*. She wrote to Mrs. Reynolds on the same day as follows:

"... The General Education Board gave us all we asked for

and we feel that we can start the first year of Spelman College with fair prospects of success. We have our part to do, both as to work and also the raising of funds, but our appropriations are sufficient to give us strong backing. . . ."

The change in name to Spelman College was fully heralded in all the Spelman publications. As Miss Tapley wrote Major Guinn, vice-president of the Spelman Board, they were "terribly busy getting Spelman changed into a college." The collegiate group of students was divided as follows: Elementary Education 26; Household Arts Education 20; Liberal Arts and Secondary Education 31. The senior high school enrollment was 163, and the total registration was 591.

The faculty increasingly included teachers with college training. During the summer of 1924, 12 members of the Spelman faculty attended summer schools at universities in the North; seven at Columbia, one at Harvard, three at Chicago, one at the University of Wisconsin. The faculty in 1924-25 included, as Miss Tapley stated, "21 degree women." During the year, extension courses were organized.

Ground had been broken on February 15, 1924, for the new science building. It was named Tapley Hall in honor of President Tapley. Construction was begun promptly. The delays encountered were at times discouraging. Miss Tapley wrote Mrs. Reynolds on February 3, 1925:

. . . College is just fine. The new buildings are going so slowly we have ceased to take much heart or interest in them. The Tapley Hall may be done sometime. We will be in bad shape if we cannot have it for use in the fall. We simply must have it, but will we? Chapel plans have been help up until we hardly know what to expect. The foundation is in. . . .

We have been having financial problems. . . . The Woman's Board cut $500 in July and the Slater Fund $1,000 in December. . . .

Worrying problems were arising in connection with MacVicar Hospital because of the closed hospital staff composed only of white physicians and surgeons. Negro physicians were permitted no participation, and their patients could enter only through a white physician and subsequent treatment in the hospital had to be confined to the regular staff.

The annual Board meeting held on March 19, 1925, brought some items of cheer. A legacy of $2,000 was reported from the estate of Oliver M. Wentworth; and the fact that the bequest of $5,000 from Col. Haskell's estate would be paid at the end of five years, with interest at 5% until settlement. The meeting brought a large attendance of the trustees, including six trustees from the North, five from Atlanta, and one recently elected Spelman graduate, Mrs. Hannah Howell Reddick. To strengthen business representation on the Board, William Travers Jerome, Jr. of New York was elected to fill a vacancy. The action that was most far-reaching, however, came from a suggestion made by Dr. Buttrick that the General Education Board be requested to make a survey of the work, organization, and resources of Spelman College. A resolution in favor of the suggestion met "with hearty approval." Results followed promptly. Dr. Frank E. Bachman of the GEB staff came early in May, to begin the survey. Miss Tapley wrote Dr. Buttrick that month of the profitable discussions. She said: "It is a long while since we have had an educator who came in here and gave us so much as four full days, considering some of these vital things that concern the Institution. I appreciate so much your sending him. . . ." Dr. Bachman's typed report concerned present and future plans of development for Spelman College, and was a valuable reference for several years to follow.

In June, Miss Tapley had a cataract removed from her right eye at the Emory Hospital. The operation was successful and by July 7, Miss Tapley wrote that "she was seeing just splendid" with that eye and her new glasses.

The occupancy of Tapley Hall, the new science and recitation building, in 1925 was a significant development. The three-story brick building included separate college and high school laboratories for physics, biology, and chemistry, with a lecture room adjoining each; together with good-sized classrooms and a number of offices. With the scientific equipment it provided,

Spelman College could claim superior facilities for academic courses.

The faculty for the first time was classified into Instructional Staff in College, Instructional Staff in High School, Training School, Piano, Other Officers. The minutiae and number of education courses offered were bewildering. Forty-five semester courses in Education are listed in the Bulletin for 1925-26.

Among the chapel and assembly speakers were noted: Rev. S. P. Smith of England who had previously visited Spelman in 1887; Miss Mabel Shaw of Northern Rhodesia; Franklin W. Johnson of Columbia University; Francis Miller, Jr., of the National YMCA; Mordecai Johnson of Charleston, West Virginia; Plato Durham of Emory University.

Spelman College and Spelman High School were charter members of the Association of Georgia Negro Colleges and Secondary Schools organized on January 21, 1927, for the purpose of closer relationships between the colleges and the high schools, and the raising of their standards.

The Georgia State Department of Education recognized Spelman as an "A" College; and the high school was rated in Class I by the state accrediting commission. The North Carolina State Department, more strict than Georgia's, allowed three years of credit for the degree course, and two years' credit for the two-year course, toward its certificates to teach.

At Spelman, 38% of the freshman class of 1926-27, and over 39% of the whole college group were graduates of the Spelman High School. For that year, there were 18 women listed on the Instructional Staff in College, 15 of whom held Bachelor's degrees and 7 of the 15 the Master's degree; in addition to the Dean and President. Eleven out of 14 high school teachers held the Bachelor's degree; the teacher of Latin had both Bachelor's and Master's degrees. Surprisingly, since less than half of the number had earned the Master's degree, fifteen of the eighteen college teachers were given rank as professors; only three as instructors. The College faculty included Margaret Nabrit, A.B.,

Spelman, 1924; the high school faculty, another able Negro college woman, Marjorie E. Parsons, A.B., Smith College.

Spelman alumnae were proud of the change in name from Seminary to College. They were equally loyal to the early teachers to whom they owed so much. The names of four of these were commemorated in Packard Hall, Giles Hall, Upton Home, and the Mary J. Packard Gateway Pillars. The graduates cherished the memory of two other associates of the Founders, Caroline M. Grover, and Evelina O. Werden.

Miss Grover had left a position as a school teacher near Boston to join Miss Packard and Miss Giles in December, 1882. She lived with them in the five-room cottage at 231 Mitchell Street not far from Friendship Church and the Basement School. She helped them move to the Army Barracks in 1883, had charge of the Model School and also of the first boarding students. As Miss Clara Howard said: – "She understood girls. She knew just how to reprove, and soundly, too, when it was necessary, as well as to encourage and inspire to better things. . . . Miss Grover in her later years served as a most successful hall mother, and the girls in her hall were "among the best trained and disciplined on the campus." She died at Spelman in 1919. As was stated, she always had a "heart at leisure from itself to soothe and sympathize."

Miss Werden, born in Canada and a graduate of Hamilton Ladies College, also had been a successful school teacher in the province of Ontario. When, on a visit to friends in Cincinnati, she heard of the work of Spelman Seminary, she was moved to have a part in it. She came to Spelman in the fall of 1887. In 1888, she became publisher of the *Spelman Messenger*, and teacher of printing. Beginning with January 1896, she served as both Editor and Publisher. As a teacher, she was exacting and thorough. She had broad interests and read extensively, and she sometimes wrote articles under the name, *The Woman in Grey*. One of the College graduates who was her right-hand helper in the printing office for nine years testifies to her warmth and friendliness as well as to her competence and scholarship. She cared for "literary excellence," and for subject matter worthy of it. These qualities made the *Messenger* a superior paper, but did not deter Miss Werden from entering fully into the need and activities of the students. Her skills other than printing contributed in numerous ways to their social and religious life.

The alumnae desired to have the names and service of these women remembered by future Spelman students. The matter therefore became one for action by the Alumnae Association.

The Spelman Alumnae Association was organized in May, 1892, with Miss Clara Howard as President. Miss Howard was succeeded by Mrs. Claudia White Harreld. At the 1925 meeting, the alumnae discussed plans for giving the College some memorial to Miss Grover and Miss Werden. The suggestion made by Mrs. Gertrude Fisher Anderson that the memorial be a fountain was adopted; and Mrs. Hattie Rutherford Watson asked for the honor of pledging the first $25. Others quickly followed her lead, and made gifts of varying amounts. A lovely spot on the campus between Packard and Morehouse Halls, south of Giles Hall, was selected as the site.

The Grover-Werden Memorial Fountain was dedicated on May 31, 1927, Mrs. Harreld presiding; the program does not carry her name, but it bears evidence of her good planning. Addresses were made by Miss Clara Howard; Mrs. Lillian Decatur Suttles, whose mother had been a student in the basement days; Mrs. Watson; and Mrs. Gertrude Fisher Anderson who later was president of the Alumnae Association. They recalled vividly by anecdote and tribute the lives on the campus of these two beloved teachers, Miss Grover and Miss Werden. The presentation to President Tapley was made by Mrs. Anderson. The fountain, beautiful in line and setting and built so as to provide ice-cold water, had been chosen both for practical usefulness, since cold water was not available elsewhere on hot summer days; and for its symbolism – a fountain of waters, a fountain of knowledge, a fountain of Life Eternal.

Sisters Chapel

The crowning glory of the year 1927, and the crowning glory of Miss Tapley's administration was the dedication of Sisters Chapel. A beautiful building dedicated to the worship of God would help to keep central in the life of the campus the ultimate purpose of Christian education; this Miss Tapley earnestly thought and felt.

The gift of funds for a chapel had been made in 1923. An Atlanta architect, Hal F. Hentz, made admirable plans. But there were many delays in the work of construction and the building was not completed until 1927. The dedication took place on the evening of May 19, in the presence of trustees, alumnae, students, faculty and other friends. There were many distinguished guests, among whom were Mr. and Mrs. John D. Rockefeller, Jr., and Trevor Arnett, President of the Board of Trustees.

President Tapley was master of the ceremony. As Miss Neptune wrote in the *Messenger*: "In girl language she 'looked grand' and all agree that she was queen of the occasion. Her brief, significant explanations as she presented each number of the program, and her own response in the formal ceremony told how deeply she felt the significance of this prayed-for blessing which she has lived to see. . . ."

After the invocation, Scripture reading and three addresses, interspersed with music, the building was formally presented by Mr. John D. Rockefeller, Jr., to Mr. Arnett and the trustees of Spelman, in words remarkable for their fitness and grace. The prayer of dedication was offered by the Rev. Dr. Carter Helm Jones, whose father had been Chief Chaplain for General Robert E. Lee.

Mr. Rockefeller began his remarks by saying: "Simplicity was one of the dominant characteristics of Laura Spelman Rockefeller, my mother, and Lucy Maria Spelman, my aunt, the sisters from whose estates came the money which has made possible the erection of this building. It is fitting, therefore, that only a few simple words should be spoken at this time."

He described briefly the lives of these sisters, whose interests centered in the school, the home, and the church; and gave witness to their influence on his own life. Then he added: "And so, girls of Spelman, the mantle of these sisters falls upon you, their younger sisters. . . . May you justify their high hopes for you, follow loyally the ideals they have set up, and develop in your own lives that beauty of spirit, that simple nobility of womanhood which they so beautifully exemplified. . . .

And as he presented the building to Mr. Arnett, "to be used for the spiritual, intellectual and social well-being of the College and of the people of this community," he said: "Neither the beauty of the building, its suitability to its uses nor yet the cunning and skill with which it has been fashioned, is the measure of the value of the gift. Its value lies rather in the rich heritage of love, of faith, of hope, of confidence in the womanhood of the Negro race with which it is so richly endowed. In token of this gift I hand you these keys. May the spirit of these sisters and the lofty ideals that they typify ever pervade this building and rest in benediction and inspiration upon all who enter its doors!"

Sisters Chapel provides a beautiful auditorium for religious services and for many dignified occasions. When Mrs. Mary McLeod Bethune saw it for the first time, she was deeply moved. She paused, and then she said, "To think that this is for *my people*!" The chapel has the largest seating capacity available in the Atlanta University Center. It is used for the joint Baccalaureate Service of Spelman, Morehouse and Atlanta University, for the All-University Center Annual Convocation, for regular and special University Convocations.

One of the first of the special occasions was a service in 1930, when the Harmon Award for Distinguished Achievement in the field of education was presented to Dr. John Hope, President of Morehouse College and Atlanta University, and a trustee of Spelman College. The service was sponsored by an interracial committee of prominent citizens. The main address was made by Dr. Theodore Collier, head of the department of History and International Relations of Brown University, Dr. Hope's Alma Mater. The award was presented by Dr. Plato Durham of Emory University whose memorable tribute to his friend, Dr. Hope, was his last public utterance.

Twenty years later, another distinguished event filled Sisters Chapel to overflowing, with hundreds of people outside listening through the loud speaker to Dr. Ralph J. Bunche as he gave the fifth John Hope lecture. Then as now Director of the Department of Trusteeship of the United Nations, Dr. Bunche spoke out of his own experience about what he called "the international facts of life." His illustrations from his part in the negotiations as a mediator in Palestine between Israeli and seven Arab states, before and after the death of Count Bernadotte, were graphic and enlightening. After citing the significance of the human factor in international affairs, he spoke briefly of the importance to American leadership of race relations in the United States, and stated that the only way Negro citizens can pull their weight in society is to have the rights, privileges and opportunities to which all American citizens are entitled—no more and no less. In conclusion, he said:

"Far be it from me, one among 15 million Negroes, to assume the right to speak for anyone but myself. But I do know what I as an individual Negro want. It is simple. That the American Negro be allowed to run the race of life not over an obstacle course but on the flat, like other Americans. Not that American society should offer a special opportunity to Negroes, while others compete on an even basis, but that American society should lift the ban of race from our shoulders; lift segregation so that we may find our own level in a democratic society, and walk with dignity, and with full self-respect and whatever respect we deserve from our fellow citizens. I want what every good American must wish in these times – that our country may be strong in every way, in moral fiber as well as in material acts;

strong in world leadership and world prestige; strong in the hearts and minds of every citizen."

Another kind of event was the Atlanta Student-Faculty Conference on Civil Rights held in February 1948. Group sessions and two general sessions at the several colleges were followed by a forum in Sisters Chapel sponsored jointly by the Southern Regional Council and Atlanta University. The speakers at the forum were: Ralph McGill, Editor of the *Atlanta Constitution*; Mrs. M. E. Tilly, member of the President's Committee on Civil Rights, and of the Southern Regional Council; W. Abbot Rosen, Chief of the Civil Rights Section of the Department of Justice; Boris Shishkin, Research Director of the A. F. of L.; P. L. Prattis, Executive Editor of the *Pittsburgh Courier*; and Austen T. Walden, Atlanta lawyer, member of the Legal Committee of the NAACP. Dr. Ira De A. Reid presided over the lively discussion.

At occasions such as these, and as, for example, the annual Christmas Carol Concerts, the recital by Marian Anderson and some other events, – recitals, concerts and lectures – when Sisters Chapel has been filled, the non-segregated seating – unobtrusive but a matter of course – has silently promoted a friendly and helpful relationship between the races.

Miss Tapley was 70 years old minus nine days when Sisters Chapel was dedicated. Commencement Day was June 2, 1927, two weeks later. Miss Tapley's resignation dated May 1, 1925, was in the hands of the Trustees. Sisters Chapel was looked upon as a happy culmination of a long and honorable career for a woman who had spent more than half her life at Spelman and had rendered devoted service. In the earlier years, she taught Arithmetic, English, Psychology, Pedagogy, History and Education. She served as Matron of the dining hall; as Principal of the Grammar School; as Superintendent of the Normal Department; and for a few months as Dean. She, as President, had held the top responsibility for 17 years.

PLATE XIII

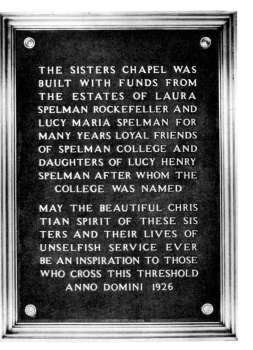

Lucy Hale Tapley

Sisters Chapel

PLATE XIV

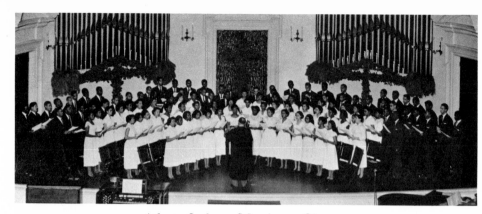

Atlanta-Spelman-Morehouse Chorus

Harreld String Quartet

Spelman College Glee Club

With grateful appreciation of her efforts and her services, her resignation was accepted at a meeting of the trustees held on the campus on June 15, 1927. At the same meeting, the trustees elected as her successor Florence Matilda Read, a graduate of Mount Holyoke College, at the time Executive Secretary of the International Health Division of the Rockefeller Foundation. As Secretary to the President and Secretary of the Faculty, and for one semester member of the Administrative Committee of Reed College, Portland, Oregon, she had gained a degree of experience in college administration, which was especially valuable since she had worked at Reed with its remarkably able first president, Dr. William Trufant Foster.

Miss Tapley was made President emeritus. She died at her brother's home in McKinley, Maine, on June 6, 1932. A Thanksgiving Memorial Service to honor her memory was held in Sisters Chapel on November 30, 1933. The tributes from her students and her colleagues were expressive of her strength, her friendship, her forcefulness or as one alumna put it "her calmness undivorced from vigor." Her letters to students now in their files reveal her sympathy for them and her understanding of their problems.

Camilla Weems, C '12, who was a student of Miss Tapley in the teachers' professional course, summed up well Miss Tapley's aim by expressing her own thankfulness for Miss Tapley's frequently emphasized conviction "that a teacher of clean habits, good character, high ideals, and having a noble aim in view, is one of the greatest assets for good that a community can have."

Another alumna wrote:

"When I think of Miss Tapley, I think of a huge oak tree, stalwart, steady, big-hearted, deep-rooted, towering above the ordinary, ever reaching outward and upward, protecting, strengthening, radiating beauty, with her face always toward the sun."

CHAPTER XIV

SPELMAN'S GROWTH AS A COLLEGE

1927-1953

Florence M. Read Becomes President

MISS READ's term of service began on the first of September, 1927. Most of the arrangements for the year ahead had been made by President Tapley. A few vacancies on the faculty, however, were filled during the summer by the incoming president, notably in the position of dean, and in the departments of Biology, English, French and Physical Education. The opening exercises were held in Sisters Chapel at eight a.m. on September 28, and classes began immediately thereafter.

The task laid upon Miss Read by Mr. Arnett and the trustees was to develop a strong liberal arts college. This involved a shift from the main emphasis on a normal school, and the centering of all the resources, human and material, on the development of a small, liberal arts college of high quality. Spelman had had the chartered right to grant degrees since 1901, but in the 27 years beginning in 1901, only 62 bachelor's degrees had been granted.

Spelman included in 1927-28 work on five levels, each with its administrative problems:

A college of	125 students
A senior high school of	170 students
A junior high school of	137 students
An elementary school of	138 students
A nurse training department of	17 students

The work as a whole clearly could not have gone forward smoothly, as it did, under its new direction, without much help and full cooperation from teachers, students, and administrative staff.

Some problems had to be met before the students arrived — problems having to do with student housing, space for offices and classrooms, a college bookstore, and a cafeteria for city students. The former reception room for callers in Rockefeller Hall was abolished. Instead, the students were to have open house for two hours each Saturday afternoon, when they might receive their friends in the various dormitory reception rooms, formerly study-halls, the students with the matron in each hall acting as hostesses for the occasion.

In previous years, a Morehouse College man could call on a particular Spelman student for only 20 minutes once a month — unless he was a brother. Brothers might call on their sisters once each week. The relationships were sometimes swapped! The callers all came through a designated entrance to the reception room in Rockefeller Hall, and each asked for the girl he wished to see; a messenger was sent for the girl and the length of the call was clocked. Many Morehouse College graduates through the years had courted and later married Spelman's daughters under these strict regulations. Perhaps the very difficulty served as a spur! Occasionally, a Morehouse man looked elsewhere, and now states that he could not work fast enough to succeed on the 20-minute allowance.

The use of the new Sisters Chapel for morning devotions was initiated. With the advice of members of the faculty, the whole program of religious exercises was reviewed, reduced, and revised to increase participation and responsibility on the part of the students themselves.

Miss Read's qualifications for the position as president of Spelman College were somewhat anomalous. Her experience, however, at Mount Holyoke College, one of the oldest women's institutions of college rank, and at co-educational Reed College in its first decade of existence, was an invaluable asset. It was also in her favor that Dr. Wallace Buttrick pointed his finger at her for the place about a year before he died; that Wickliffe Rose, then President of the General Education Board, under whom she had worked as Executive Secretary of the International Health Board of the Rockefeller Foundation, recommended her to Mr. Arnett; and that Mr. Arnett himself brushed off all the reservations and reasons-against-consideration posed by Miss Read. Furthermore, Dr. Buttrick on one occasion had called her to his office on some plausible pretext, and introduced her to Mrs. Alice B. Coleman, President of the WABHMS, who thereafter favored her appointment. Dr. Abraham Flexner assured Miss Read that for special qualifications all she needed was "a mind that functions."

Before her decision was reached, Mr. Arnett arranged for Miss Read to visit several institutions under the guidance of Dr. Eben S. Sage, recently retired Assistant Secretary of the General Education Board. He had for twenty-odd years been actively concerned with the schools and colleges of the South. The itinerary included visits to Hampton Institute, Virginia State College, Shaw University, Penn School on St. Helena Island, Tuskegee Institute, and lastly Spelman College.

To a reluctant candidate devoted to her present position, all these doors opened up a vision of the opportunity confronting her which could not be denied. Dr. Eben Sage noting her growing interest quoted to Miss Read the title of a famous sermon by Dr. Thomas Chalmers of Glasgow, "The Expulsive Power of a New Affection." She returned to New York ready to talk with Mr. Arnett; she was not, however, yet ready off-hand to accept the position. The opportunity was overwhelming. But what about the resources to meet it? Spelman College had been receiving an annual grant toward its current expenses from the GEB. In early years, Miss Packard, Miss Giles and Miss Upton had felt that such support was hazardous and had wanted the security of endowment. Miss Read had seen Foundations change in personnel and in policy, and knew that dependence on the annual action of a Board was too great a risk. In her oral report to the chairman, she admitted the lure and the need of the work to be done; but declined to accept the position unless approximately the annual grant was capitalized. Mr. Arnett, who himself desired to have Spelman's future protected by endowment, proceeded to use the condition imposed as leverage. In an informal conference soon thereafter, Mr. Rose and Mr. John D. Rockefeller, Jr. agreed with Mr. Arnett that the endowment they discussed for Spelman College was desirable. Their follow-up action was, of course, assured; and Miss Read accepted the proffered position.

The informal agreement was formally implemented during the academic year, 1928-29. In that year, the General Education Board offered, in response to the Spelman College request for endowment, to give one and one-half million dollars on condition that the College raise an equal amount. At the same time, on the initiative of Mr. Rockefeller, Jr., a gift of one million dollars was received from the Laura Spelman Rockefeller Memorial to establish a fund to be known as the Laura Spelman Rockefeller Memorial Fund: for the purpose of promoting the well-being, physical, mental, social and spiritual, of the young women and girls of the Negro race in the United States. The latter gift was applicable to the matching sum to be raised. Spelman College had then to raise $500,000 in addition in order to profit by the GEB offer. It was understood that at least two million of the anticipated three million dollars must be counted for endowment.

Mr. Julius Rosenwald became the next large donor. He pledged $100,000 personally; and arranged for a gift of another $100,000 from the Julius Rosenwald Fund. The WAB-HMS gave $25,000. The depression came, and delayed payment in full of some pledges. The required sum was completed, however, in 1935. The endowment fund totaled as of:

> June 15, 1928 – $ 57,501.98
> June 15, 1929 – $1,063,519.96
> June 30, 1937 – $3,163,057.13
> June 30, 1953 – $3,612,740.73

As income from endowment became available, the annual grants from the GEB ceased. All churches and mission societies were, of course, faced with a sharp decline in money raised during the depression of the nineteen-thirties. Consequently, the financial support from the WABHMS declined gradually and soon ceased. So likewise annual grants from the ABHMS declined from $5,000 to $3,000, to $1,000, and then stopped altogether.

Obviously, with its available resources, the institution could not grow as a college, and also maintain excellence in the four other departments then under the aegis of Spelman College.

The trustees had voted in May 1927 to discontinue the Elementary School in June 1928; and this was done — to the grief of many parents and particularly of Miss Amy Chadwick, the director of the Leonard Street Orphans Home. Her children had always had free tuition and the protection of the private school.

In regard to Nurse Training, it had become apparent that first-class training could not be offered with the facilities provided by MacVicar Hospital. The hospital contained too small a number of beds; the variety of cases was too limited; and the equipment was insufficient for modern techniques. A trustees' committee had been studying the matter, and on May 20, 1927, the trustees had voted that no new nurses should be admitted to training. During the fall the question was further discussed. Finally, on December 15, 1927, definite official action was taken to close the hospital to outside patients and to end the Nurse Training Course. This action involved not simply the campus, inasmuch as the sizable staff of white doctors had used MacVicar Hospital for their patients when desired ever since the building was opened in 1901.

Letters were written to all the doctors on the staff and visiting staff informing them that no patients from outside the College would be admitted after February 1, 1928. Provision was made for the student nurses to complete their training and receive diplomas from the Spelman hospital or from the Hubbard Hospital in Nashville, or be transferred to other hospitals.

MacVicar Hospital was retained as a college hospital and infirmary. The following year, a joint arrangement was made with Morehouse College, by the terms of which Mrs. Ludie

Andrews, R.N., a graduate of the Nurse Training Course at Spelman, and at the time in charge of the Morehouse College Infirmary, was engaged as Superintendent of the Hospital; and service was to be provided for both Spelman and Morehouse students. Two Negro doctors were appointed to make the medical examinations and to have, with Mrs. Andrews, general responsibility for the health of the students. A consulting staff of white physicians and surgeons included leading medical men of Atlanta. The joint hospital arrangement served the colleges well, and with minor changes from time to time was in effect until federal aid to army veterans enabled Morehouse College in the late forties to build a hospital on the Morehouse campus.

Four factors at least made it desirable to retain the high school. First, few public high schools for Negroes were then in existence. In 1926, the whole state of Georgia maintained but two accredited high schools for 376,217 Negro children. In 1927, there were only six four-year accredited public high schools for Negroes in Georgia; Alabama and South Carolina had neither public nor private Negro high schools.

Second, students trained in the Spelman High School and other academies of church-related colleges offered better preparation for college.

Third, about 60% of the Spelman High School students lived on the campus and thus benefited by training in and outside of the classroom.

Fourth, the number of college students, while steadily increasing, was small. There was a dearth of young Negro women with adequate preparation for college. Most of them had no opportunity even to complete high school.

Out of a total of 327 students registered as of March 1, 1929, 102 college students and 130 high school students were boarders on campus. Beginning in 1927-28, students were not counted in the enrollment unless they had completed one semester of work. The Spelman high school was discontinued in 1930.

From 1928 onward, the declared aim of Spelman College was to provide, within a limited scope and with a relatively small number of students, as good educational facilities as were available in any college of liberal arts. The emphasis was to be on quality. With "loyal scorn of second-best," the goal was diligently pursued. Accordingly, more college courses were provided in the humanities, in science and mathematics, in history and social sciences, philosophy and fine arts; and the college faculty was increased and strengthened.

As Wendell Willkie said in an address at Duke University in 1943, "Freedom is of the mind. Freedom is in that library of yours, around which this campus is built. . . ." Miss Packard, too, held that conviction, and early in the life of the Seminary, she solicited books from friends and publishers, and purchased them as funds permitted. The reading-room with substantial shelves on the first floor of Packard Hall, named the Quarles Memorial Library, was attractive but both the space and the book collection were inadequate for college work.

Pending a new library building, the south end of the ground floor of the Laura Spelman Rockefeller Memorial Building, was made into reading room and stacks. By the purchase of steel library shelves and of cork covering for the concrete floor, the place was transformed. To transport the books without interrupting academic work and library use posed a problem. The answer, dictated by urgency and economy, was to walk the books across the campus!

So on Monday afternoon at 3:30, March 26, 1928, after announcement of the procedure in chapel that morning, the big bell rang. The students and teachers assembled at the front entrance of Packard Hall, formed in line, moved to and through the old library room. Books were taken from the shelves in order; placed in arms held out to receive them. Then out by the south door under the guidance of a few student captains, the procession in single file, led by president and dean, walked across the campus (by the curving sidewalk, of course!) to the more commodious quarters which had previously been made suitable for a library. There the books were placed on their proper shelves, which had already been numbered and classified to receive them. The process was then repeated until in two hours, approximately 8,000 books had been transferred onto the shelves in the new quarters; and the library was used by students that very evening.

The new reading room had accommodations for seating 50 students; and contained the reference books, newspaper and magazine racks, and the card catalog. The adjoining stack room held steel shelves with a capacity of 12,000 volumes. Over 1,000 books were added during the first year. Sums of $2,500 and $2,900 were spent for books in the following two years.

A needed provision for the comfort of the teachers came from the renovation of the Bessie Strong Nurses' Home as a teachers' residence, with a large, attractive lounge. Among the excellent teachers already on the Spelman College faculty were Laura A. Dickinson in Chemistry (1913-33), and her sister Louise Dickinson in Latin (1920-33), both graduates of Mount Holyoke College, with Master's degrees respectively from the University of Michigan and Smith College; in History (1924-to date), Margaret Nabrit, Spelman A.B. 1924, the only Negro on the college faculty; in English, 1926-42, M. Mae Neptune, A.B., Ohio Wesleyan, A.M. Columbia; and Viola Jenson, A.B. and A.M. University of Wisconsin, in Mathematics, 1926-29, Registrar, 1929-50. Every Spelman student of those years owes a debt to Miss Jenson for her accuracy and for her zeal for superior achievement.

Added to Music in September 1927 was Kemper Harreld, who was jointly employed with Morehouse College. Trained in the Chicago Musical College, Frederick Fredericksen Violin School, and Stern Conservatory in Berlin, Germany, where he studied under Siegfried Eberhardt; gifted, versatile, and competent in music theory as well as in teaching and conducting; for 27 years, he was chairman of the Music Departments of Spelman College and Morehouse College and made a truly great contribution to music on the campuses, and through his students throughout the South.

Added to Zoology in 1928 was Louise Baird Wallace, B.A.,

Mount Holyoke, M.A. and Ph.D. University of Pennsylvania. Miss Wallace had taught on the Mount Holyoke College faculty for 14 years, and for 13 years at Constantinople College in Turkey. At the latter, she had served also as Dean and in the dangerous years of World War I, as Acting President. Added to Education was Elizabeth Perry (Cannon), graduate of Atlanta University and Columbia University, whose versatility and skill made her noteworthy for 13 years until her health compelled her retirement in April, 1941. She died seven months later. The appointment of Anne M. Cooke, a graduate of Oberlin College who had made drama her first interest, to the high school in 1928 as teacher of English, later to the college faculty, signalized the beginning of extraordinary developments in college dramatics. All of those mentioned above except Miss Wallace had long terms of service. Space forbids mention of scores of others who made fine contribution to the life of scholarship in the decades beginning in 1927.

Honor must be given here, however, to Miriam Feronia Carpenter, who came to Spelman in 1927 as Dean on a year's leave of absence from her position of Registrar and Adviser of Women Students of the Harvard Graduate School of Education. Not only did she handle with distinction, sympathy and zeal, the usual work of the dean's office; but her wide experience had its influence in the total life of the campus. Her counsel was invaluable in connection with the work of the Alumnae Association and alumnae clubs; and with the various student organizations. As editor of the *Spelman Messenger*, she gave form and substance – and wit – to the reorganized bulletin which became a quarterly magazine rather than one issued monthly from October to June. She came to the campus in June 1929 as the Commencement speaker. She had resumed in 1928 her position at Harvard University. In 1929, she became Dean of Wheaton College, Norton, Massachusetts, and served in that position until her retirement.

Notable progress was made in the development of cooperation with Morehouse College. In 1928-29, three members of the faculty were employed jointly by the two colleges. There were additional exchanges of teachers. Courses at Spelman College opened to election by Morehouse juniors and seniors and courses at Morehouse College opened to election by Spelman juniors and seniors enriched the offerings of both colleges. Thoroughness in academic work was emphasized throughout. The Summer School was operated jointly by Morehouse and Spelman, with Atlanta University affiliated. These beginnings were prophetic of the greater things to come. And come they did with surprising rapidity.

Three graduates of the class of 1929 and one of the class of 1928 were awarded fellowships for graduate study in Northern institutions; and were the forerunners of many others in the years to come, the grants in aid coming chiefly from the General Education Board or the Julius Rosenwald Fund.

These first fellowships for graduate study were granted to: Julia Pate, '29, to study English at University of Chicago; Alma Ferguson, '29, for Mathematics at the University of Wisconsin; Camilla Howard, '28, for French at Middlebury College. These three were awards from the Julius Rosenwald Fund. Gaston Bradford, '29, was awarded the Mary Walker Fellowship for graduate study at the New York School of Social Work.

Now that they must study harder, the students found life less arduous because of the changed arrangement regarding laundry. An additional charge of $2 per month added to the board enabled the college to do the necessary laundry work for all students – bedding, table linen, and a limited number of personal articles. They still must demonstrate at the end of the year that they knew *how* to wash and iron properly and with some degree of skill. But they no longer had to get up at 4:45 one morning each week to do their washing!

The higher standard achieved in academic work was commented on in an article in *Opportunity* magazine by W. A. Robinson of the State Department of Education of North Carolina. He listed the colleges which were given *A* rating in North Carolina; and pointed "to the remarkable progress of one school, Spelman College, which was still rated as a high school by North Carolina as late as 1925."

Besides the academic program, Spelman students enjoyed significant offerings in music and fine arts. One such event preceded the opening day in September 1927. Jan and Cora Gordon, writers, artists, musicians, whose "Two Vagabonds in Albania" and other books about remote countries had made a name for them, were guests of the President. They told of their adventures; and reproduced on the guitar and Spanish lute primitive music which they had picked up in their wanderings, music never written out but handed down from one generation to the next.

Another musical event of the first four months was the concert by the Russian Cossack Chorus in Sisters Chapel on the afternoon of December 14, to which all the Negro colleges of Atlanta were invited. The quality of the highly trained Russian voices and the precision with which they sang delighted their listeners. At the request of the Russian chorus leader, the audience sang Negro melodies which enchanted the Russians. It is not often that two groups of different nationality have an opportunity to sing their folk songs to each other; and their mutual appreciation was strong and sincere.

Progress in dramatics was accelerated by the appointment to the faculty of Miss Anne Cooke, as already mentioned; after graduation from Oberlin College, she had studied at the Chicago Art Theater with Ivan Lazareff. "The Passing of the Third Floor Back" by Jerome K. Jerome; "The Chinese Lantern" by Laurence Housman; and "The Piper" by Josephine Preston Peabody were noteworthy productions, showing imagination, skill, and acting ability.

These plays were the beginning of outstanding work in dramatics. The quality has continued under the sponsorship of Spelman College which furnished the direction and usually the stage, Morehouse College, and Atlanta University. Morehouse College for many years presented a Shakespeare play under the direction of Dr. Nathaniel P. Tillman, who was a superior teacher of Shakespeare at Morehouse College, on the Spelman campus, and later in the University system. This, and he, deserve inclusion in this history.

An area in which the students had been deprived of all exposure except through the printed page was in painting and sculpture.

By a fortunate acquaintance with the artist, it was possible to have an exhibition of water color portraits of West African natives by Erick Berry shown at Spelman for 10 days in December, 1928. More than 700 students and teachers of the Booker Washington High School came to see it by invitation, as did many students from Morehouse, Clark and Atlanta University.

Erick Berry, a New Englander who married Herbert Best of the British government service in Northern Nigeria, had studied art in Boston under Eric Pape and at the Pennsylvania Academy of Fine Arts. On her second trip up the Niger Valley, she was commissioned by Harper and Brothers to edit and illustrate five volumes of a new edition of the works of Paul du Chaillu concerning Nigeria. She herself is the author of *Black Folk Tales, Girls in Africa*, and *Human as We Are*. Erick Berry is her pen name.

A second exhibition of her water color portraits and scenes painted during her third trip to Nigeria was shown at Spelman College the following year. The paintings were exhibited at the Bernheim Jeune Gallery in Paris in September 1929; then at the Milch galleries in New York; and they came to Spelman directly from the Milch galleries.

Dr. Joseph M. Artman of Chicago, General Secretary of the Religious Education Association, a chapel speaker at Spelman who visited the exhibition purchased "The White Cap" and presented it to the College toward the nucleus of an art collection. The Class of 1929 presented the College with another delightful portrait from the collection entitled, "Abuya, the Friendly One."

The exhibit of Fine Arts by American Negro artists sponsored by the Harmon Foundation and the Committee on the Church and Race Relations of the Federal Council of Churches, was shown at Spelman College for a week, April 28-May 5, 1929. It was shown at the Central YWCA of Atlanta the following week. More than a thousand visitors attended in one day at Spelman; there was a total registration in Atlanta of more than 3,300 individuals. The exhibit comprised 63 paintings, including the "Octoroon Girl" by Archibald J. Motley, Jr. which received the Harmon Gold Award. Its purpose was to encourage the Negro in creative expression of a high order and to acquaint the public more generally with accomplishment in fine arts by Negroes.

A second Harmon Foundation Exhibit was shown at Spelman College for 10 days the following year. It comprised 68 paintings and pieces of sculpture, by 41 Negro artists, and attracted much attention not only from the students but from the citizens of Atlanta. Spelman students acted as hostesses. The Director of the High Museum of Art on one afternoon gave a lecture on the exhibit. The High Art Museum, although a city museum, was not open to Negro citizens. At the time of the second exhibition, the College was honored by a visit from Miss Helen Harmon, trustee of the Harmon Foundation, and Miss Mary Beattie Brady, its director.

The Erick Berry and Harmon Foundation Exhibits yielded an exhilarating experience to the students. Such progress has been made since 1928 and 1929 that present-day interested persons can scarcely imagine the dearth of cultural opportunities open to Negroes in the South as late as the nineteen-twenties. The Harmon Foundation deserves acclaim for the work it accomplished in bridging a wide gulf. It not only through its circulating exhibits enlightened many communities concerning the artistic gifts of Negroes; but it also provided at a critical time for them encouragement for young Negro artists, including Hale Woodruff, Aaron Douglas, Palmer Hayden, Archibald Motley, Jr.

In April 1934, Erick Berry came in person to the Spelman

campus. She and her husband, Herbert Best, engaged in a series of conferences with groups of students of Atlanta University, Morehouse College and Spelman College. Mrs. Best spoke at the Spelman morning chapel service on "Nigerian Women." Mr. Best had served for 12 years in the British government service as chief civil officer in northern Nigeria. Mr. and Mrs. Best were accustomed to make long trips by motorcycle throughout the province. They admired and liked the people, and through their friendliness Mrs. Best was able to have access to many homes and to paint studies of the men, women, and children. In Nigeria, they reported, the natives had been allowed to retain their land, to maintain their original religion and civilization, and so far as possible to govern themselves. Thus, the process of self-government was making progress 25 years and more before the country gained its independence in 1960. From May 13-20, 1934, water color and pen-and-ink sketches of the colorful market places and streets of Katsina, Nigeria, were shown in the Exhibition Gallery of the Atlanta University Library.

Lectures, addresses and chapel talks brought to Spelman students and teachers mental stimulus and made connections with the world at large.

Among the speakers in 1927-28 were:

Rabbi Stephen Wise, of the Free Synagogue of New York City

Dr. Roy Akagi, National Secretary of the Japanese Student Movement

Miss Mary McDowell, Director of the University Settlement of Chicago

Dr. Mordecai W. Johnson, President of Howard University

Right Reverend Robert E. Jones, Bishop of the Methodist Episcopal Church

Mr. Julius Rosenwald of Chicago

Dr. Mary McLeod Bethune, President of the National Council of Negro Women; and of Bethune-Cookman College.

Mrs. Bethune gave the Founders Day Address. She is an orator; and she made her hearers feel with her the significance of the occasion and the stimulus of the avenues that now stretched out before all young people.

For the first time, the friends of Spelman saw the pageantry of an academic procession from Rockefeller Hall to Sisters Chapel, with the organ providing music for the march down the aisle. Among the guests on the platform were President-emeritus Tapley, and the presidents of Atlanta University, Emory University, Clark College, Morris Brown College and the Dean of Morehouse College.

Baccalaureate Sunday, June 3, 1928, was observed by joint service of Morehouse College and Spelman College in Sisters Chapel. Dr. Robert Russa Moton, Principal of Tuskegee Institute, preached the sermon on the subject: "Who Is My Neighbor?" The chapel was crowded; in spite of additional chairs, many listened from outside at the windows. No public address system was yet in use. Members of the graduating classes and faculties of both colleges, in academic regalia, marched in the procession.

Dr. William Trufant Foster, first president of Reed College, Portland, Oregon, later Director of the Pollak Foundation for Economic Research, gave the Commencement address on June 6, 1928. His subject was: "Should Students Study?" The academic procession of graduating classes, faculty and guests formed at Rockefeller Hall and marched to Sisters Chapel proceeding to their seats to the music of Mendelssohn's "War March of the Priests" played by Kemper Harreld.

The academic procession was again impressive. Partly due to the distinguished speaker, along with the presidents of Morehouse College, Clark College and Morris Brown College, three deans from Emory University were on the platform, namely: Dr. Goodrich C. White, Dean of the College of Liberal Arts, later to be President of Emory; Dr. Edgar H. Johnson, Dean of the School of Business Administration; Dr. Theodore H. Jack, Dean of the Graduate School, later President of

Randolph Macon Woman's College. It was for the Emory deans an eye-opening experience about which they commented later. One of them said he thought how his father, a Confederate Army Captain, would have marvelled to see that platform assemblage and him a member of it.

This visit of these three men from Emory University was the forerunner of a closer acquaintance with Emory on the part of Spelman College and other Atlanta colleges for Negroes.

If any readers of this story have available the July 1928 issue of the *Spelman Messenger*, it would be well worth their while to read the reports it contains of the addresses by Dr. Moton and Dr. Foster; and the reprint from the *World's Work* of an article by Dr. James Hardy Dillard, a Virginian, a member of the General Education Board, and President of the Slater Fund and the Jeanes Fund. The article bears the title "The Negro Goes to College."

At the joint Baccalaureate Service of Spelman College and Morehouse College, in 1929, everyone who came was inspired and entertained by the pithy and witty address of Dr. George Edgar Vincent, president of the Rockefeller Foundation; formerly dean of the University of Chicago and president of the University of Minnesota.

Chapel and assembly speakers in 1928-29 included: Dr. James Hardy Dillard, president of the Jeanes Fund and the Slater Fund; Dr. W. E. B. Dubois, editor of *Crisis*; Mrs. John H. Finley, chairman of the foreign division of the National Board of the YWCA; Ivy Lee, public relations adviser of New York; Bishop Francis J. McConnell, president of the Federal Council of Churches of Christ in America; Dr. Charles S. Johnson, Fisk University; Dr. James Weldon Johnson, Secretary of the N.A.A.C.P., author of *God's Trombones*; Dr. Howard W. Odum, Professor of Sociology, University of North Carolina, author of *Rainbow Round My Shoulder*; Dr. Beardsley Ruml, Executive of the Spelman Fund; Mr. William Allen White, editor of the *Emporia Gazette*.

A factor of importance in developing a genuinely liberal atmosphere on the campus through these years, one not new in the life of Spelman but now receiving renewed emphasis, was the bringing to the campus, for longer or shorter periods, of men and women of top achievement from many different countries. This has special value in a section where students do not have free access to the cultural resources of the community. International relationships were thus stimulated in 1928-29 by the speakers noted below:

Dr. T. Ninan Jacob, principal of the State Teachers' College, Travancore, India, who spoke on several occasions, including the International Dinner sponsored by the college YWCA; Miss Georgina Gollock of London, author of *Sons of Africa*; Dr. Louise Baird Wallace, who had served as professor and dean of the Girls College in Constantinople for 13 years and had experience with students of 17 nationalities.

From Africa came Monsieur Chazeaud, Principal of the Normal School, West African Mission of the Presbyterian Church; Madame Jezouin of the French Camerouns; Miss Ruth Morris from Liberia; Miss Margaret E. Walbridge from Inanda Seminary, Natal; Mr. and Mrs. Charles Crabtree and Miss Amelia Njongwana of Cape Colony, South Africa.

Noteworthy addresses were made in assembly by Will Irwin, author and journalist, who accompanied President-elect Hoover on his Good-Will Tour of South America and who spoke on South America; and by James G. McDonald, chairman of the Foreign Policy Association, and authority on foreign affairs. He and Mr. John D. Rockefeller, III, had recently traveled together across Russia to Japan.

Two events in lighter vein also stimulated interest in other countries: a Japanese entertainment by Mr. and Mrs. Michitaro Ongawa, with scenery and in costume; and a program of songs and sketches from countries in Central and Eastern Europe, also in costume, by Miss Ellenor Cook.

The Christmas Carol Concerts

The first Spelman-Morehouse Christmas Carol Concert was sung in 1928, in holly-bedecked Sisters Chapel, while the brave deodar cedar shining with blue and white lights welcomed the incomers and suggested to them the stars and sky of the Holy Night. This was the first of such concerts which later became an anticipated Christmas event for all Atlanta. For 27 years, the concert master was Professor Kemper Harreld, who was head of the music departments of both Morehouse College and Spelman College from 1927 to 1954. From 1933, he was assisted at Spelman by Willis Laurence James, who had charge of the Spelman College Glee Club and developed it to a high point of near-perfection. On Mr. Harreld's retirement, Mr. James succeeded Mr. Harreld on the Spelman faculty.

Seven years passed before the auditorium was filled to overflowing. Then, as hundreds of people, white and Negro, for several successive years had been turned away, it was arranged beginning in 1940 to present the Concert on two nights, Friday and Saturday. After 10 years or so, that plan too was inadequate. Beginning with 1952, three evening performances have been necessary to accommodate the audiences. Scores of persons who came in the early years had never before attended any concert in the South where the seating was not segregated by race.

The Christmas Carol Concerts through the years have brought hundreds of persons to the campus who would not otherwise have seen the College or its students. Sometimes an "unreconstructed rebel" would attend. One such who came with her liberal daughter but became separated from her in seating was so impressed by the occasion that she went up front after the concert to compliment the director — and later said to her daughter: "I went up to tell the Director how beautiful the concert was; and I shook hands with him!"

Christmas Is For Everyone was the title of the column by Celestine Sibley which was printed in *The Atlanta Constitution* of December 16, 1952. Six of her eight paragraphs are quoted below:

"The carol concert, which has been given in the Sisters chapel for the last 26 years, is one of the loveliest things that happens in Atlanta. So many people go to hear it that this year they gave three performances and still had crowds lining the walls, filling the vestibule and overflowing into the cold, windy out-of-doors.

"The voices of the Negro students are, of course, magnificent but I think more than anything it is the choice of carols on the program that fills your heart with a sudden warming awareness of the Christmas miracle.

"You realize suddenly in the middle of the program that Christmas belongs to all people, that people of all lands have felt the wonder of it and put it in their folk songs. There were French, English, German, Swedish, Silesian, Spanish, Italian, Galician and Haitian songs on the program and finally, to bring tears of remembrance to your eyes, the most haunting of all American folksongs, some Negro spirituals.

"Of course, the most familiar Christmas songs were there — 'Silent Night,' sung with the chorus seated and only the golden flames of candles to light the auditorium, the joyous, booming Hallelujah Chorus and 'Hark the Herald Angels Sing' — but the tenderest songs were the ones which were the personal out-pourings of the people who composed them. A John Jacob Niles arrangement of a North Carolina mountain carol, 'The Seven Joys of Mary,' made you think of the people who sat around their cabin fires lovingly recounting blessings of the little moth-er, who was herself a simple country girl.

> 'The very first blessing that Mary had,
> Hit was the blessing of one:
> To think her little Jesus
> Was God's only Son.'

"The 'blessing of two' was to think that her little Jesus 'could read the Bible through,' and so on through his crucifixion and ascension into Heaven, ending with the spine-tingling chorus:

> 'Come all ye out of the wilderness
> And glory be,
> Father, Son, and the Holy Ghost,
> Through all eternity.'

"A South Carolina fisherman's carol, 'The New-born Baby,' was touching but when the entire audience got to its feet and joined the singers in 'Go Tell it On the Mountain' you felt the stirring of the Christmas spirit beyond all the weariness that we let ourselves in for these days. Christmas is wonderful and miraculous and I thank the Spelman-Morehouse chorus for reminding me."

The Affiliation of
Spelman College, Morehouse College,
and Atlanta University

A monumental event took place in the second half of the year 1928-29. It had been dreamed of by Dr. Buttrick years before – not in the same form, but in its general outlines. Dr. Buttrick had looked upon Atlanta as strategically located for a great center of higher education for Negroes. Here were situated five undergraduate colleges, namely, Spelman College for women and Morehouse College for men, both fostered by Baptists of the North; Atlanta University – an undergraduate coeducational college, undenominational by its charter but historically under the aegis of the Congregationalists; Clark University, a coeducational college owned by the Methodists of the North; Morris Brown University, also a coeducational college, owned and operated by the African Methodist Episcopal Church. All five maintained schools of high school rank; and at this time the high school students outnumbered the college students. All five had to struggle to raise money for operation. Could they be brought to work together for the sake of the benefit to the students? And how?

Atlanta University, with its campus of 55 acres; Morehouse College with 12 acres; Spelman College with 20 acres; these three were located in the same vicinity.

In June 1928, the Board of Trustees of Atlanta University had named a committee authorized to confer with Morehouse College and Spelman College with a view to some measure of cooperation which would result in economy of operation for all three. At the moment, Atlanta University was in dire straits financially and had been forced to use unrestricted legacies to

meet the annual budget. There are relatively few Congregationalists in the Southern States, white or colored; thus virtually the only clientele in the South to be cultivated for funds
was the alumni. Spelman College had the best financial prospects and the best buildings, but a smaller and younger college
department. Morehouse College had a strong administration
headed by Dr. John Hope and the most vigorous faculty. Atlanta University had an honorable history, a loyal alumni body,
but had few younger college teachers because of its budget
stresses and strains. The president of Atlanta University, Dr.
Myron W. Adams, was just completing 40 years in the service
of the University, first as a teacher, then for 33 years as dean
and president; and his resignation was pending on the election
of a new president.

In order to attract a qualified man, the Atlanta University
Board of Trustees recognized the urgency of finding a field of
service, wholly or in part unique; and both a program and a
president were prerequisite to raising funds. There seemed to
be no defensible program for Atlanta University on the college
level, which would appeal to boards or individuals in the light
of the fact that there were four other undergraduate colleges
for Negroes in Atlanta, each with a larger potential clientele.

In December 1928, there was held in the city of Washington,
D. C., a National Interracial Conference of representatives of
all the organizations and agencies concerned with the education
and welfare of American Negroes. The aim was to take stock
of the existing status on all levels of life; to survey the gains
and to consider the lacks in progress.

The agencies included colleges and universities for Negroes,
the General Education Board, the Julius Rosenwald Fund, the
Russell Sage Foundation, the Phelps-Stokes Fund, the Federal Council of Churches, the Social Science Research Council,
the Commission on Interracial Cooperation, the National Association for the Advancement of Colored People, the National
Urban League, the United States Bureau of Education, and
others. An important by-product of this Conference, of course,

was the opportunity it afforded for the men and women most concerned with policies and programs to confer informally. Thus it happened that the situation of Negro education in Atlanta was talked about. How could the various colleges there be brought into a united effort? The General Education Board, recognizing the need of library facilities, had already suggested that the president of Spelman College invite the presidents of the other four institutions to consider together possible ways of using the resources of a library; two meetings of the presidents had already been held in the president's office at Spelman College.

What, then, could bring about greater cooperation among the three institutions located so near each other? (Dr. Myron W. Adams had stated that it required 12 minutes for him to walk from the Main Building of Atlanta University to Rockefeller Hall.) The suggestion made some 20 years earlier by Atlanta University to Spelman and Morehouse that the latter two be developed as preparatory academies with Atlanta University as the college department, had been firmly declined. Did any ground exist for supposing that association of the three on a higher level would in 1929 be regarded with favor?

Here was Morehouse College, forging ahead academically under Dr. Hope's leadership, with the prospect of increasing its endowment by $600,000 on the strength of a conditional offer of $300,000 made in June 1928 by the General Education Board. Here was Spelman with the Laura Spelman Rockefeller Memorial Fund gift of one million dollars, now concentrating on the development of a strong college of Liberal Arts and Sciences. Atlanta University had a proud heritage: its name; its honorable history; many distinguished alumni; and by far the largest amount of land. But Atlanta University needed a program; a president, to succeed the present incumbent at his behest; and both of these before financial support could be secured.

Then, out of one of the pro- and con-discussions, an idea was born. Clark Foreman, nephew of Clark Howell, editor of the

Atlanta Constitution, on the staff of the Phelps-Stokes Fund since leaving his position with the Commission on Interracial Cooperation, maintained a lively interest in matters affecting Atlanta. Clark Foreman, in a flash of insight, said "I'll tell you how a plan of cooperation could be made to work. Make John Hope president of Atlanta University!" Dr. Hope had just made one of the addresses at the Conference.

For the first time, the dream of Dr. Buttrick began to take shape. Apparently Dr. Hope was apprised of the suggestion by Dr. Will W. Alexander only after his return to Atlanta. The prospect of a university in Atlanta for Negro young men and women made a strong appeal to Dr. Hope. He had already advocated the idea, and his life work was to promote educational opportunities for Negro youth.

As a matter of fact, Dr. Hope had shown remarkable prophetic insight many years before in an article he wrote for the first issue of *The Voice of the Negro* published in January, 1904, discussing the six institutions of learning for colored people in Atlanta and their individual contributions to "the thought, and life of the age."[1] This was two years and more before he became president of Morehouse College.

"When the time comes," wrote Dr. Hope, "the Atlanta schools, so close together and aiming at the same thing . . . will probably come to some agreement." And he thought it not "Utopian" even then to forecast certain divisions of labor. "Gammon Theological Seminary," he thought, might "enlarge its sphere" denominationally. "Let Atlanta University become a graduate school. . . ." And so on, ascribing a special field of work to each and ending "Such is an opinion of the present work and future possibilities of our Atlanta schools, than which there is no greater lifting power in this country."

But in 1929 Dr. Hope had a special responsibility to Morehouse College. Plans had to be made and followed up to raise the amount required to meet the endowment offer from the General Education Board. Furthermore, the suggestion was

[1] Ridgely Torrence, *The Story of John Hope*, pp. 145 ff.

yet only in a nebulous state. There was no certainty that he would ever be called upon to make a decision.

The Atlanta University trustees, however, through their committee above mentioned, became active immediately. They invited consultation with representatives of Spelman College and Morehouse College. The chairman of the Spelman Board of Trustees designated the President of the College to represent the institution at the conference. The Morehouse Board similarly authorized President Hope to serve in its behalf. Two meetings of the group were held in the conference room in Rockefeller Hall. Representing Atlanta University were three of its trustees, namely, Will W. Alexander, James Weldon Johnson, and W. D. Weatherford.

A plan was agreed upon by the conference held on February 25 and 26 whereby the three institutions might become affiliated in a university plan; with the graduate and professional work to be carried on by Atlanta University; the college work to be done by Morehouse College and Spelman College.

The proposed agreement provided:

1. That Spelman College and Morehouse College should retain their own boards of trustees and officers and management.

2. That the board of trustees of Atlanta University should be reorganized to include three members nominated by Spelman College, three members nominated by Morehouse College, and three members of the existing board of Atlanta University, to be selected by that board; these nine having power to elect five additional members. (By-laws adopted in April 1932 increased the total number of members permitted to 21.) There were 10 other items of agreement in addition to those having to do with the transition period while the undergraduate work of Atlanta University was in the process of being discontinued and the graduate work being developed. It was agreed that no freshmen would be admitted to Atlanta University in September, 1929.

The plan proposed by the conference left the door open for the admission later of other colleges or schools, under prescribed conditions.

Discussions took place by each president with his trustees. The whole matter was one of first importance. Each institution would have to yield certain sovereign rights. Furthermore, there was absolutely no promise in advance of financial support from any foundation or individual. One long conference that ran into the small hours was held on the porch at Reynolds Cottage at which this financial factor was faced by several trustees and members of the finance committees, including the chairmen of the Morehouse and Spelman Boards, and members of the finance committee of Spelman. It was obvious that any recommendation from the two presidents to their respective boards for the adoption of the plan had to be an act of faith. The decision finally arrived at, with the support of all the trustees present, was to take the step.

The matter was presented to the Spelman Board of Trustees at its meeting on March 26, 1929; and the participation of Spelman College in the plan was heartily approved. Similar action was taken by the Morehouse Board of Trustees. The proposal was fully discussed with Mr. Dean Sage, chairman of the University's finance committee. He gave his approval, and worked out the necessary procedures to be taken by the Atlanta University Board of Trustees.

At a meeting in New York on April first, 1929, the arrangements were completed in behalf of Atlanta University; Dean Sage was elected chairman of the Board of Trustees; and John Hope was unanimously invited to become President of Atlanta University as of July 1, 1929, with the understanding that he might, in response to the insistence of the Morehouse Board of Trustees, remain as President of Morehouse College in order to continue the endowment campaign and the plans which would grow out of the campaign for strengthening Morehouse College. A few days later, Dr. Hope accepted the position, with its great opportunity, fully aware of its equally great responsibility.

On the eleventh of April, 1929, the Agreement of Affiliation, then in legal form, was signed in triplicate, by the three
presidents: Myron W. Adams in behalf of Atlanta University;
John Hope in behalf of Morehouse College; Florence M.
Read, in behalf of Spelman College. The signing took place in
the office of the president of Spelman College, and after the
signing, they celebrated the occasion by having breakfast together in Reynolds Cottage. The day celebrated also Spelman's
48th Founder's Day.

In view of all the rivalries, all the traditions and activities
of three colleges; in view of matters involving property and
financial support; in view of everything, it is a wonder that such
a plan could come to fruition in even less than three months.
Again a miracle, many would call it. Again "the fulness of
time" had come, as Dr. Morehouse described the coming to
Atlanta of Miss Packard and her acquaintance with Mr. Rockefeller just as he was becoming able to make great benefactions
to education. Dr. Hope had sensed the fulness of time in that
February 1929 meeting when the 'blueprint' was drafted.
Drawing a picture of a great university center starting with a
graduate school of liberal arts, later to include professional
schools, he said that the idea had come to fruit at a "fateful
hour" in the history of Negro education in Atlanta with circumstances favoring co-operation that might not occur again for a
hundred years.

The Atlanta University affiliation was a trail-blazer for cooperative arrangements among American colleges. The only
place in the United States that had put into operation a similar
idea was in Claremont, California. There President James A.
Blaisdell, holding the conviction that several small colleges
were preferable to one large one, and that graduate work and
common services might well operate cooperatively, had brought
into being the "Claremont Colleges."

Thus it was that a new era in education began in Atlanta in
July, 1929. Thereafter it is impossible fully to relate the history
of Spelman College without frequent reference to its develop-

ment as a member of the Atlanta University System. Later as Clark College and Morris Brown College entered increasingly into a cooperative relationship, the whole group came to be called the Atlanta University Center. The pioneer stage in the development of the Atlanta University System and the Atlanta University Center parallels the development of Spelman College as a college of liberal arts and sciences.

As an outgrowth of the University affiliation, and in line with the logical development of both Spelman College and Atlanta University, it was agreed in 1930 that: 1) Atlanta University should conduct, as part of the work of the Department of Education, a coeducational Laboratory School which would include kindergarten and elementary grades to be taught in the Oglethorpe School on the old University campus, and high school grades; 2) Spelman College would discontinue the operation of a high school although continuing for the time being to care for the high school boarding students, and cooperate with Atlanta University in conducting the laboratory high school; 3) Spelman College would lend the use of Giles Hall for the high school grades, thus making a considerable contribution to the developing University. The cost of the renovation and equipment for a coeducational school was about $40,000.

This Laboratory School was to serve to give graduate students in the Department of Education more than training in teaching methods. One purpose, as stated by President Hope, was "to provide them with the opportunity to observe good teaching and its results."

For the first three years, Spelman College contributed to Atlanta University a total of $60,000 for the expenses of the High School.[1]

The students best prepared to do work of college grade in these years came from the high school department of Spelman College and other private church-related colleges. Over half the members of the last class to be graduated from the Spelman High School entered Spelman College. In later years, most of

[1] Trevor Arnett: Report of the Development in Cooperation, 1941, page 9.

the girls in the upper half of the graduating classes of the Atlanta University Laboratory High School entered Spelman College.

Dr. Charles S. Johnson reports[1] that in 18 Southern states in 1926-27 there were only 167 accredited public high schools for Negroes, and 53 of the 167 were located in North Carolina and Texas.

The registrars of the University System each year made up a combined report, which showed by departments all the courses offered by the three institutions in the University System, with an identifying initial, the name of the teacher and the enrollment for each course. The freshman and sophomore courses were offered separately by each college. Exchanges of students began in the junior year. In some courses, there were students from Spelman, Morehouse, and Atlanta University; sometimes also from Clark and Morris Brown.

Study of these tables annually by the presidents showed the teacher load; the places where classes were too large or too small; imbalance by departments or divisions. The latter might indicate where an additional teacher was needed in the University System, or where an exchange-teacher arrangement would help. These reports made it possible for each president to know thoroughly his or her own institution; and they revealed plainly the advantages of co-operation. With small undergraduate colleges, it was extremely important to eliminate overlapping and duplication of courses and so be enabled to provide for each student a fuller academic diet.

Yet steady progress was made. Dozens of conferences, formal and informal, were held by President Hope with the presidents and church officials responsible for these colleges. Each had to obtain the approval of its Board of Education. Clark, in addition, had to get money for new buildings and endowment. When Mrs. Henry Pfeiffer accompanied by her nephew, Garfield Merner of San Francisco, now a trustee of Atlanta University, and Presi-

[1] *The Negro in American Civilization*, C. S. Johnson, page 257; a table is quoted from article by N. C. Newbold of North Carolina published in Annals of the American Academy.

dent Davage of Clark College, visited the new Atlanta University campus, Mrs. Pfeiffer was so well impressed by the development that she added $100,000 to the gifts she had already made to make it possible for Clark to move from south Atlanta to the vicinity of the University.

After Morris Brown moved to the old Atlanta campus in 1932, and after Clark College moved to its new site opposite Harkness Hall in 1941, the exchange of students and teachers was extended further. There were almost from the beginning a few Morris Brown students and a few Clark students registered in courses offered by Spelman and Morehouse. But the pattern had to become established first, and that was easier to do with the two colleges located close together, one for men and one for women. The two colleges furnished classrooms and laboratories for the graduate courses of the University for the first 25 years of the affiliation.

The academic program held its central place. The opportunity to undertake graduate work in liberal arts and sciences now opened to the students was added stimulus to excellence.

As a transition from undergraduate work to graduate work, the University in cooperation with Morehouse College and Spelman College offered in 1929-30 fifteen undergraduate-graduate courses in biology, economics, English, French, Latin, mathematics. They were conducted by members of the faculties of Morehouse College, Spelman College, and Atlanta University; and were open to specially qualified juniors and seniors and to graduate students. Such courses were continued in 1930-31. History was then added, and the number was increased to 28. In addition the University offered graduate courses in Economics and Business Administration, Education, English, and History. These four were selected first because they were departments that would minister in peculiar ways to the needs and lacks of the total Negro community.

The first professor to be appointed to the graduate faculty was in History, Clarence A. Bacote, who joined the group in

September, 1930. Fortunately for hundreds of Spelman students he early began to teach also the required sophomore course in American History through an exchange arrangement with Atlanta University; the arrangement was operative for most of the next 25 years; and generations of Spelman students have regarded him as a member of the Spelman faculty, as did also his associates and the administration.

The first Master's degree earned at Atlanta University was awarded in 1931, in a special Commencement convocation at the University's Stone Hall, to Joseph Alexander Bailey, A.B. Morehouse, for work in the department of History. The subject of his thesis was "The Attitude of Georgia Toward Secession, 1845-1860." The Commencement speaker was Channing H. Tobias. Fuller description of this significant occasion is given by Ridgely Torrence in *The Story of John Hope.*

Undergraduate college work at Atlanta University was soon eliminated; no freshmen were admitted in 1929 and the following year all undergraduate courses were discontinued. In fairness to students already registered for college work in Atlanta University, an agreement was made whereby the juniors and seniors might complete their work in Spelman College and Morehouse College and receive a bachelor of arts degree from Atlanta University. With a fine spirit of co-operation, the wrinkles were ironed out; Atlanta University college women were received into the Spelman student body.

At the Commencement exercises in June 1931 and again in June 1932, immediately following the awarding of Spelman College degrees by President Read, she as Secretary of Atlanta University presented to President John Hope of the University 16 young women in 1931, and 12 young women in 1932, as eligible for the Atlanta University bachelor of arts degree. (Some undergraduate men in similar fashion received the University's A.B. degree at the Morehouse College Commencement exercises.) These were the last bachelor's degrees awarded by Atlanta University. Other than this differentiation on the final day, the young women from Atlanta University were completely a part of the Spelman College campus life.

Official witness to the quality of the academic work came from the Southern Association of Colleges and Secondary Schools first in December 1930. For a number of years, effort had been made to persuade the Southern Association to rate the colleges for Negroes. They persistently declined to do so, in spite of the fact that outside funds were ready to provide the cost of the necessary surveys. The officers of the Southern Association took the position that the Negro colleges were not members; the Association rated only its member institutions; *ergo* the only answer to the appeals was "no." Period. At one meeting, in 1928, of a small group which included Dean Theodore H. Jack of Emory University, a woman officer representing secondary schools, a representative of the General Education Board, Dr. Will Alexander of the Interracial Commission and the presidents of Atlanta University, Morehouse College and Spelman College, the question was raised again. The customary answer was given.

Then Mr. Hope rose to speak. He said in essence: "Let us look at the matter further. Here are these colleges for Negroes. We want to be good colleges; and we want to be good colleges by the recognized standards of universities. We want to know how we stand by those standards, not by separate Negro listings. We need to know what our weaknesses, our limitations, are, in order to improve and become better colleges; in order that our graduates may have training according to the best accepted standards."

The atmosphere changed perceptibly. One could even feel it change. The discussion took a new direction: that of a willingness to explore the possibilities. That meeting led to a workable arrangement and resulted in the appointment of a standing committee of the Southern Association of Colleges and Secondary Schools, consisting of Dean Theodore H. Jack of Emory University; H. M. Ivey of Meridian, Mississippi; H. H. Highsmith of Raleigh, North Carolina, to make a study of

PLATE XV

The Painting Studio

Sculpture on Exhibit

PLATE XVI

The Silver Whistle

The Barretts of Wimpole Street

Mary Tudor

"Ariel" in *The Tempest*

Modern Dance

Rhythmic Dance: "The Mowers" in The Boy With the Cart

Kemper Harreld at the Organ

Medea

PLATE XVIII

Marian Anderson on one of her campus visits

Mattiwilda Dobbs as
The Queen of Shemakhan
in *Le Coq d'Or*

*From the London Daily Ex-
press, May 26, 1961.*—Mozart's
"Seraglio" is a perfect Glyndebourne opera — enhanced last
night by Oliver Messel's en-
chanting designs and a well-
chosen cast. The only survivor
from Peter Ebert's original production five years ago is Mattiwilda Dobbs, the American Negro soprano, who is practically
irreplaceable as the heroine
Constanze. She moves through
this farcical comedy of captives
in a Turkish harem with the
dignity of a goddess and the
voice of an angel. The florid
music she has to sing reveals
her clarity and accuracy of technique, a marvellous sweetness of
tone, and eloquent dramatic expression when required.

institutions for Negroes. The committee was assisted by Professor Arthur D. Wright of the Department of Education of Dartmouth College who was granted a year's leave of absence to undertake the inspection of Negro colleges. This marked a milestone in the relationship to each other of the Southern colleges and universities, white and colored. Dean Jack stated publicly in an address to the Association of Colleges and Secondary Schools for Negroes (which superseded the Association of Colleges for Negro Youth) that the person who converted him to the need and values of this action was John Hope.

At their annual meeting in December, 1930, seven institutions for Negroes were added to the approved list of the Southern Association which meant that the credits and degrees conferred by them would be accepted by institutions to which their students might go for further study. Only Fisk University of the seven received "A" rating in 1930, which signified meeting all the standards including salaries. Spelman and Morehouse Colleges received "Class B" rating, along with Johnson C. Smith, Talladega, Virginia State College and Virginia Union University. In December 1932, the Southern Association of Colleges and Secondary Schools in annual meeting voted to give "Class A" rating to Atlanta University with its affiliated colleges, Spelman College and Morehouse College. This gave the highest rating of the Southern Association to the bachelor of arts degrees conferred by Spelman College and Morehouse College, and to the master's degrees conferred by Atlanta University.

Spelman College was elected to membership in the Association of American Colleges in 1930. The only six institutions for Negroes then among the 400 members of the Association were Howard, Lincoln, Fisk and Wilberforce Universities, Morehouse College and Spelman College.

Atlanta University, meanwhile, progressed with commendable speed as a strictly graduate institution. President Hope applied his fine mind to the situation. The result appeared first in a memorandum.

Recognizing that an unselfish interest in the welfare of others had been inbred in Negro students by their dedicated teachers from the North, noting that Negroes were more and more taking the places as teachers and leaders, John Hope wrote that to him it seemed "absolutely necessary at the outset in planning for the building up of a university for Negroes" to seek for means that would produce the kind of educated man and woman who would have a "constant, quiet, inexorable influence for better things. . . ." He brought together his idealism, his high academic standards, and the practical conditions that were facing Negroes in 1930, and based on them a program that would apply in 1930-1931, and also 50 years hence. He projected as early as January, 1930, a graduate school of liberal arts; a graduate department of education; a school of business administration; a library school; through affiliation, a school of social work, and a theological school; and as the mainspring of the plan, the general affiliation with the University, of Clark and Morris Brown, the other colleges for Negroes in Atlanta. Professional schools of law, medicine, dentistry were for the longer view.

By the first of April, most of these ideas were embodied in a definite proposal called "The Six Year Plan," (see Appendix) which took into account practical considerations of students, faculty, cost of operation; and the financial implications of the program. The Plan took into account the increase in teachers and courses from year to year; participation by Morehouse and Spelman faculties; and the new University faculty appointments required. The sum needed by the end of six years for endowment on a modest basis, and for four new buildings in addition to the library was $6,400,000. This for those times was an astounding sum to be raised for the education of Negroes. The program, with a request for help, was presented to the General Education Board and to other friends of the Atlanta group of colleges. The urgent need for both graduate and undergraduate work was a library; and this was the first need to be met.

The New Library

In June, 1930, a gift was announced from the General Education Board of $450,000 for the cost of a site and for the erection of a library for Atlanta University and the affiliated colleges. The grant was made to Atlanta University. Spelman College and Morehouse College were mentioned by name in the contract, which stated also that the Library would aim to serve as far as possible the other institutions for Negroes in Atlanta. The site, already purchased, was on Chestnut Street between Spelman College and Morehouse College.

When the affiliation agreement was approved on April 1, 1929, the Atlanta board of trustees had proceeded with its reorganization; and Mr. Dean Sage of New York was at once elected chairman of the Board. The three persons nominated by the Spelman Board and elected to the University Board were Mrs. Alice B. Coleman, who had been since 1892 president of the WABHMS, William Travers Jerome, Jr., and Florence M. Read. Nominated by the Morehouse Board and elected were John Hope, James Madison Nabrit, President of the General Missionary Baptist Convention of Georgia, and Kendall Weisiger, Assistant to the President of the Southern Bell Telephone Company. Continued from the old University board were Will W. Alexander, Executive Director of the Commission on Interracial Cooperation, James Weldon Johnson, Atlanta University A.B. '94, and Dean Sage. These nine soon elected to the University Board five others: James Hardy Dillard, president of the Jeanes Fund and the Slater Fund; Willette R. Banks, Atlanta University A.B. '09, president of Prairie View College, Texas; Mrs. Hattie Rutherford Watson, Spelman College A.B. '07; John Jacob Coss, professor of Columbia University; Charles C. Huitt, president of the Dunbar Bank, New York City. The trustees elected did not 'represent' the institutions which had nominated them. From the start, they gave wholehearted attention to the needs of the whole center.

At the conclusion of the annual meeting on March 29, 1930, Mr. Sage had stated: "What we are interested in is not the promotion of Atlanta University, Morehouse College, or Spelman College, or any individual institution. What we are interested in is *the promotion of Negro education*, and what we look forward to is a great center of such education in Atlanta. To that great end we must subordinate every other consideration."

That policy, to which all the trustees subscribed and which was a tenet of John Hope's philosophy translated into action throughout his life, is perhaps the basis of the remarkable progress in educational co-operation developed in Atlanta. The objective was always what is best to bring out the best in Negro youth.

Mr. Sage named as a Building Committee for the Library and later buildings: Kendall Weisiger, chairman, John Hope, and Florence M. Read. James Gamble Rogers of New York, architect for Yale, Northwestern, Cornell and other universities, was chosen as architect. The plans were carefully studied, and advice was obtained from the librarians of Princeton University, the University of Chicago, and others. Space was provided in four tiers of stacks for 118,400 volumes, and seating space for 400 students. The general reading room was two stories in height and extended the full length of the building. Beautiful in design and virtually perfect in functional use, the building caught the imagination of all who beheld it.

The day of official dedication was set for April 30, 1932. Previously, the books from the Spelman College library, the books from the Morehouse College library, and the books from the Carnegie Library of Atlanta University had been moved to the new main library. The librarian had been appointed and was at work. Miss Charlotte Templeton, a graduate of the University of Nebraska, President of the Southeastern Library Association, and one of the well-known librarians of the country, had in 1930 directed a library institute for Negro librarians held in conjunction with the Morehouse-Spelman Summer School. In 1931 she was called upon to administer the University Library and to have oversight of the affiliated college libraries as well. The re-cataloging and reorganization of the separate libraries into one system was indeed a laborious task. The week before the dedication, the new building was opened to the students and faculties of the three institutions. They were overjoyed with the resources it provided.

There had been a rather informal ceremony of Breaking of Ground on June 1, 1931, and a more formal ceremony of Laying the Cornerstone on November 1, 1931. At the latter, the audience had to stand through the service and the Masonic ceremony at the corner of the Library. When Kemper Harreld suggested musical numbers for the program to Mr. Hope, and included the spiritual "Lord, I can't sit down," Mr. Hope speedily ruled it out!

It was the aim and purpose of Atlanta University, in accordance with the terms of the gift, to make the library serve not only Atlanta University and affiliated colleges, Spelman and Morehouse, but the other institutions of higher learning as well, namely, Clark, Morris Brown and the Gammon Theological Seminary. Catalogues of all these institutions were placed in the corner-stone along with a score of other items.

These two ceremonies, especially the latter one, had been impressive. But the building then was only in chrysalis. By the time of the exercises of dedication, the doors were hospitably open to reveal the wonders within. The dedication of the building was truly a great event.

A special convocation was called on the night of April 29. Will W. Alexander, Director of the Commission on Interracial Cooperation presided at the meeting. Kendall Weisiger, chairman of the Library Building Committee, made the address of welcome; representatives of the Rosenwald Fund, the Jeanes Fund and Slater Fund, and of three religious societies related to these institutions – the WABHMS, the Northern Methodist Church, and the African Methodist Episcopal Church – brought greetings; and an address on the problem of leisure was made by Dr. George Barton Cutten, President of Colgate University.

The Spelman-Morehouse Chorus sang Randegger's "Praise Ye the Lord"; and the Spelman and Morehouse quartets sang. The Negro jubilee "Go Tell It On The Mountain" sung by the large audience brought the service of joy to a fitting benediction pronounced by President Matthew S. Davage of Clark College.

Friday evening, however, was merely preliminary to the Big Event. The dedication exercises proper were held on Saturday afternoon, April 30. The academic procession from Rockefeller Hall into Sisters Chapel included the presidents and faculties of the six Negro institutions of higher learning in Atlanta — the first and so far the only time this has taken place; members of the governing boards of these institutions, special delegates and guests, and the nationally-known speakers for the occasion.

Introduced by President John Hope who presided, addresses were made by United States Senator Frederic Collin Walcott of Connecticut; James Weldon Johnson, Professor of Creative Literature at Fisk University; and Dean Sage, chairman of the Board of Trustees of Atlanta University, who accepted the keys of the new building and gave formal thanks to the General Education Board, donor of the library. All were fine, unstilted addresses. We quote here only the words of Mr. Sage. "The keys," he said, "will be held symbolic of an open door to this stately building, this repository of accumulated learning — a wide way, beckoning to entrance and a welcome to all who *through knowledge seek wisdom.*' . . . Only through the storied knowledge of the Past can the Present hope to understand the great adventure of life, and so understanding, to solidify those foundations which the wisdom of experience has slowly fashioned and upon which the Future must build.

"I envision this library as the heart of a great center of cultural learning — an abiding home for that freedom of thought which denies prejudice, prompts the search for wisdom, and fights an eternal battle against the disorganization of ignorance and the deadness of materialism; an institution which shall give to America leadership measured in terms of men and women

246

of the Negro race, a leadership fully competent, because of the advantages here gained, to match with the best leadership of the white race for the solution of those problems which the oneness of our country makes common to both.

"Mr. Arnett, to you and to the great foundation which you represent (the General Education Board) I tender the deepest and sincerest thanks of Atlanta University. Your magnificent gift is the keystone of our entire university structure, present and future. Permit me to say to you in words that are not my own, to express to you a thought that is within my heart:

> 'Help thou thy brother's boat across,
> And, lo! Thine own has reached the shore.' "

If one reads those words of Mr. Sage thoughtfully, one can understand something of the quality of this man, who with Mr. Arnett and Mr. Hope, made the Atlanta University Affiliation possible.

The prayer of dedication was offered by Rev. Howard Thurman, Religious Adviser of Morehouse and Spelman Colleges. The Scriptures were read by President Harvey Warren Cox of Emory University and the benediction was spoken by President James Ross McCain of Agnes Scott College.

President Hope's announcement of a gift from the author of the works of Joel E. Spingarn, and the purchase through gift of the papers of Thomas Clarkson, noted English abolitionist, brought much applause; as also did his introduction of the architect. We quote the *Spelman Messenger*:

"The applause which greeted the presentation to the audience of James Gamble Rogers, the architect of the library, however, was like thunder in its volume; and eclipsed itself when that architect — whose fame as a designer of great academic buildings has been enhanced in recent years by his work as architect of the new Yale University Library and the Columbia-Presbyterian Hospital Medical Center in New York City — told the audience in a choice, clipped sentence that 'Whatever inspiration was manifest in the planning of the building' was received a year ago from the students of the affiliation themselves!

"The memorable occasion closed with the singing of the Negro anthem 'Lift Every Voice and Sing' and the stirring strength of James Weldon Johnson's last lines: —

> 'Shadowed beneath thy hand
> May we forever stand;
> True to our God,
> True to our native land,'

pulsed through the brief calm of the benediction, and seemed carried out in the minds of the great assembly which left Sisters Chapel to find . . . the lovely winding curve through Spelman Campus to the stately new edifice just across the way."

There were five Yale men who took part in the Library Dedication: Dean Sage, '97; James Gamble Rogers, '89; United States Senator Frederic C. Walcott, '91; George B. Cutten, '97; and Albert B. Kerr, '97. Mr. Sage, Mr. Cutten and Mr. Kerr were classmates of Edward Twichell Ware, the late president of Atlanta University, and of Edward Stephen Harkness, of whom more will soon be said.

The University Library was, by vote of the Board of Trustees in 1949, named the Trevor Arnett Library. A library for the Atlanta colleges for Negroes had been one of Mr. Arnett's primary interests, first, as Secretary, and later as President of the General Education Board.

"The New Negro"

Only half a century after the first students came in numbers to Miss Packard and Miss Giles, the ambition for college animated many high school girls, and their parents in their behalf. Again as Dr. Morehouse had said of the first decade, "the fulness of time had come," and the students responded eagerly to the opportunities. Under the guidance of college teachers possessed by contagious enthusiasm, they not only tackled their courses energetically but they entered with spirit into other activities. They listened to a lecture on "the seven wonders of modern medicine" by Dr. Bowman C. Crowell, Director of Clinical Research of the American College of Surgeons, which began with the development of a cell from the ovum of a rabbit shown by microphotography. They saw E. H. Sothern portray on the stage at Spelman the Shakespearean parts which had made him world famous. They themselves took part, with Morehouse students, in Ibsen's "The Wild Duck" on the new stage in Howe Memorial Hall.

The renovation of the old chapel in the summer of 1929 had far-reaching effects. One gallery was removed; a stage built in its space on the west end of the room; stage curtains, footlights and dressing-rooms were added. The auditorium with rearranged seating accommodated about 600. Thus was provided an assembly-room for student-body meetings, prayer meetings, Sunday School exercises, lectures, entertainments, movies, in addition to its becoming for the college and university community a "little theater." It so remains to this day.

Life on the Spelman campus was a wonderful experience in those days—the adjective is used advisedly. As students in the first years were fired with the desire to learn; as later they welcomed the emergence of college from seminary; so now they responded to the stimulus of the stiffer college program, expanded as it was in scope and delving deeper into subject matter. The foundations had been well laid. Now new curiosity was awakened. *The New Negro* described by Alain Locke and others stirred Negro students into more awareness of their lacks and their opportunities; and at the same time created a greater enthusiasm to enlarge their capacities, greater self-confidence, and a greater sense of responsibility to develop their latent abilities. They enjoyed the intellectual and cultural side of life opened up by enthusiastic teachers; and they valued the added facilities provided in the way of library and laboratory, music and other fine arts.

The spectator attitude had no place in their day's routine. The students participated by listening, to be sure, but also by doing. The extra-curricular life encouraged getting together on the basis of common interests, not at all on the snobbishness of sororities which were non-existent. Instead, the English Club; the Biology Club; the Music groups; the Pan Americana for students of Spanish and Latin-American History; the French Club; the Dramatics organization which included University, Morehouse and Spelman students and took as its name the University Players: all these and other activities, including tennis, basketball and track, demanded the best the students had to give outside the classroom. There was zest — and at times fatigue — but always growth.

One sign of the students' alertness was the interest they took in competition with other students, and sometimes they won awards. For example: The American Chemical Society conducted a series of national prize essay contests made possible by funds contributed by Mr. and Mrs. Francis P. Garvan: one contest was open to all students enrolled in high schools, white and colored. The Georgia Committee selected the essay of Lottie Margaret Lyons as the best in the State, and on that basis she was awarded a suitably inscribed certificate for winning in the National Contest, and a $20 gold piece.

John Murray, Principal of University College of the Southwest, Exeter, England, speaker at Spelman in 1929, offered a prize to Spelman students for the best essays on "The Essentials of Internationalism," the essays to be submitted to him. The prize-winners, selected by him, were announced at a special assembly. Three books were received as prizes: To Mabel Dockett, '31, was given *An Anthology of Franciscan Poetry and Prose*, gathered by Vincent; Cassandra Maxwell received *Valour and Vision: Poems of the War* collected and edited by Trotter; and Mary Griggs H.S. '30, received *The Old English Gardening Books*, by Rohde.

Professor E. Franklin Frazier of Fisk University, in connection with a survey of which he was director, offered prizes for the "most acceptable" family history papers. Nineteen students of Atlanta Negro colleges competed, and many others. The first prize was won by Elnora James, and the second prize by Magnolia Dixon, both Spelman students of the class of 1931.

Carrie Louise Adams, Spelman College freshman, and graduate of Spelman High School, won one of the 1930 prizes in an essay contest open to young people, 14 to 19 years of age, in 36 states of the U.S.A. and in ten Latin American countries. This contest was administered by the Committee on World Friendship among Young People of the Federal Council of Churches of Christ in America.

Ida Louise Miller, Spelman College sophomore, received for her junior year the Racial Minority Scholarship of $1,000, offered by Mount Holyoke College to a Negro girl on the basis of scholarship and personality. The scholarship was continued in her senior year; and she was graduated from Mount Holyoke College in 1933.

So far as the civic and cultural life of the South is concerned, Negroes live in a separate world. They are permitted, and often encouraged by relatively good treatment, to patronize the stores which sell furniture, clothing and food. Self-service in grocery chain stores has been a boon. Until recently, the city parks in Atlanta were segregated. The Atlanta Art Museum was open even to art students only through special arrangement with a Director who was friendly. When Hale Woodruff was not invited to hear Grant Wood's lecture at the Art Museum, this Director brought Grant Wood to the Spelman campus, and all three were entertained at lunch by Spelman's President. The Atlanta public libraries were closed to Negroes; the so-called branch Carnegie library for Negroes was not a true 'branch' as there was no circulation of books from the main library. Negroes could not buy tickets to concerts or lectures, except to those given in the Municipal auditorium, where a few seats in the top gallery might be reserved for them.

It is difficult, not to say impossible, for mind and spirit to operate freely under such a pattern of discrimination. Only on the campuses of the colleges for Negroes was free association of Negro and white citizens possible. And on those campuses, the separateness of the two streams of life made communication infrequent. For Southern white people who were friendly and interested, – and the number of them steadily increased – were busy in *their* own world, and did not find the time or convenience to leave it in order to come to events at the Negro institutions. That is why the artists and speakers from the world outside were so important. They provided the live connection with the rest of mankind.

In order that graduate students might have fuller opportunity to feel that they were part of the whole institution, as well as have the privilege of hearing the speakers of distinction, President Hope, with cooperation from Morehouse and Spelman, instituted a plan of holding University Convocations in Sisters Chapel approximately once each month, usually on Thursday. Morehouse College and Spelman College and Atlanta University altered their schedules of classes to provide a free period on that day for all the students and teachers in the University System. Separate chapel exercises were not held, but instead all the students, graduate and undergraduate, joined in a single service. Always there was an opening hymn. Usually all the presidents participated in the service. Frequently the Atlanta-Spelman-Morehouse chorus sang.

Chapel, assemblies, university convocations – all added richness and challenge to the mind and spirit. The students, before and after graduation, felt grateful for the communication with the life of the world through these opportunities. It was a senior who wrote in a formal document ". . . we rub elbows with Marian Anderson and T. Z. Koo, make snapshots of President [Henry Sloan] Coffin and President [Donald J.] Cowling. . . ." It was a graduate of 1929 who said "International speakers have graced our platform, sharing with us the richness of their experience, travel, and contacts." And a graduate eight years later emphasized in a speech "the broadening and enriching cultural program of the College."

The "New Negro" had intellectual curiosity about what was

going on in the world. Consequently, he listened avidly to the addresses given by such men as:

Dr. Andre Siegfried, economic expert of the French Foreign Office, who interpreted French life and people and contrasted the French people and Americans;

Dr. Friedrich Schoenemann, the first professor of American literature and culture at the University of Berlin;

Mr. Charles F. Andrews, of the Tagore School, India;

Dr. John Murray, Principal of University College of the Southwest, Exeter, England, who discussed Political Tendencies in England;

T. Z. Koo, Vice-president of the World Student Federation and Secretary of the National Council of the YMCA in China;

Toyohiko Kagawa, noted Christian leader of Japan.

A stirring call to World Citizenship had been brought by Fletcher Brockman, an early Baccalaureate speaker. When he, with his family, had gone from Georgia to China a quarter century earlier, he had to travel four weeks to get to Nanking; that is, four weeks in time. But the distance was 3,000 years in civilization, from modern America to the same life there had been in Ur of the Chaldees in the days of Abraham. Times have changed, however, he said, and the world has shrunk. Time may run out before brotherhood comes, if young people do not wake up to the call. Living next to people does not make us love or understand them. To be a world citizen requires a plowing up, and often a plowing under, of one's ideas and prejudices; and opening of the eyes to see the values in other civilizations. It requires doing away with national, racial, and class prejudices. Those were the ideas he drove home to us. Ample opportunity was open, fortunately, for exposure to the "values in other civilizations" through visits and talks, formal and informal, given by men and women, from Europe, Asia and Africa. The students heard citizens of Latvia and Estonia, Austria, Germany, Hungary, Italy, France, Great Britain; also of Hawaii, India, Java, China, Japan. Many came from Africa, both Europeans who lived there and natives of Nigeria, Liberia, Uganda, Sierra Leone, Congo Free State, and South Africa.

A unique experience was a special University Assembly on May 31, 1930, called in honor of a group of European journalists who visited Atlanta during a tour of the United States which was sponsored by the Carnegie Endowment for World Peace. Each visitor was introduced with the name of the country he represented. There were three men from Germany, and one each from Austria, Bulgaria, Czechoslovakia, Denmark, Estonia, Finland, Holland, Hungary, Norway, Sweden, Switzerland. Felix Salten of Austria, author of *Bambi*, had made a trip to the Spelman campus by himself on the previous day, and happily chanced to talk with students who had read *Bambi*. The assembly met in Sisters Chapel; and after a brief program there adjourned to the campus. Sitting under the shadow of the spreading water-oak between Sisters Chapel and Reynolds Cottage, the visitors listened to and asked questions of President John Hope; Superintendent of Atlanta Schools, Willis Sutton; Lorimer D. Milton, Negro banker; Jesse D. Blayton, Negro professor and the first Negro certified public accountant of the state of Georgia; Austin J. Walden, Negro lawyer.

As writers and newspaper men, the visitors were keenly interested to learn at first hand of Negro progress. This experience was a revelation to them. When the Atlanta committee's schedule required them to depart to view the Atlanta Federal penitentiary, they left reluctantly.

Through the courses they studied, the teachers who taught them, and the men and women from all corners of the globe whom they listened to and often had the chance to talk with, the students of these days were brought to feel – (1) that the work of the world was something in which they earnestly desired to play a part, and (2) that in order to take as varied and responsible places as their character and competence deserved, they must have more and better preparation through education.

CHAPTER XV

THE GROWTH IN FINE ARTS

N
O ONE can spend a casual hour on the Spelman campus . . . without being conscious of a great deal of activity in the creative arts," reads the opening sentence of an article published in the *Spelman Messenger* for February, 1937. Students in one building model in clay; in another set of studios, students paint from still life, cut linoleum blocks, or work at pencil or charcoal studies; others gather in the "Blue Room" listening to recordings of great orchestras or singers. In the little theater, a cast rehearses for the next University Players production; or a crew constructs a stage set. The rhythmic beat as of a drum announces that a class in the dance is at work. Over and above all floats the sound of women's voices from the music studio, or perhaps the strains of a lonely violin. At other times the College orchestra is rehearsing. And in the early evening once a week in Sisters Chapel the full volume of the mixed chorus, accompanied perhaps by the organ, bursts forth on the evening calm.

To quote again: — "At first these diverse activities may seem unrelated. But a definite pattern is being followed. First of all, the fine arts have been given their proper place in the curricula of Spelman College and Morehouse College." Courses are offered for credit in painting, sculpture, music, and dramatics; and at Spelman training in the art of the dance is available. "A staff of nine men and women, all of whom have had advanced training in their fields, teach these courses which seek to lay a groundwork for professional training or to advance the students' appreciation of the arts. It is now possible for a student at Spelman College to elect music or art as her major or minor course of study leading to her degree.

"Then, too, the arts offer students a variety of opportunities to engage in campus activities that are broadening." In the field of music, membership is open in the glee club, the quartet, the mixed chorus, and the orchestra. In dramatics, students in their second year may enter the University Players, an organization of Spelman, Morehouse, and University students which produces in the course of every academic year three or four plays of major importance under direction of the drama department staff.

The faculty in Music, Painting, Sculpture and Dramatics was early augmented. Kemper Harreld in Music and Anne M. Cooke in English and Drama were joined by Willis Laurence James and Naomah Williams Maise in Music, John M. Ross in Drama and Speech, Elizabeth Prophet in Sculpture, and Hale Woodruff in Painting.

An unusual course in *Introduction to Fine Arts* was added to the curriculum. The aim was "to give the student an acquaintance with various fields of art, including music, dramatics, the dance, painting, sculpture; to relate these arts; and to develop interest in creative activities that will be of profit to the student and possibly a pleasure to others; and to quicken the powers of observation and perception and so add to the student's enjoyment of life."

The course was conducted by all the faculty members in the fields mentioned, by means of lectures, discussions, demonstrations of technique, exhibitions, musical programs, and even actual participation in creative effort. To help in coordination, all the teachers attended every session of the class the first time the course was given. That was rather overwhelming, and too costly to be continued. But the dearth of any previous exposure to the arts, except to music, for all the students but a few from Northern states was its justification until the arts found its place in the setting, and the students became at home with the arts.

At the first meeting of the Fine Arts staff, Dr. Hope quoted to its members Cicero's saying, "All the arts are held together as it were links in a chain." The truth of this statement was demonstrated both to students and staff by means of this course; and the course also enlarged their sense of appreciation so that

256

they could better understand and enjoy the offerings of the College in drama, concert, and art exhibits.

Of all the arts, music ranked first in the general interest and had the greatest student participation. Courses for credit were offered in music history and appreciation, harmony, counterpoint, sight singing, and analysis of music composition. Lessons were available in piano, voice, violin and cello. About two-thirds of the students enrolled participated in some way in the musical life of the campus.

Resources in music were multiplied when the Carnegie Corporation presented to Atlanta University in 1937 one of its Music Sets. The Carnegie Corporation, independently and through the Arts Commission of the Association of American Colleges, put money and skill into assembling a collection of nearly 1,000 records; 100 volumes of reference works, musical history, biographies of musicians, books on folk music and other phases of musical arts; and 151 bound music scores.

The records include complete recordings of the outstanding symphonies, operas in their entirety; and a selection of the world's greatest liturgical music. The composers range from Palestrina of the sixteenth century to the present-day Stravinsky. The Bach B Minor Mass completely recorded is a part of the collection. Native music of India, China, and other Oriental countries is included.

A special room easy of access on the ground floor of Laura Spelman Memorial Building was suitably furnished for the use of this equipment; with its more comfortable seats and powder-blue walls, it came to be called the "Blue Room." A feature was made of the opening of the new Music Library to the college community on a Sunday afternoon in January, 1937, following the vesper service.

The collection was a wonderful asset for the formal courses in music; provision also was made for others than music students who would find relaxation and enjoyment in listening to music.

Another potent stimulus toward creative activity was and is the Jerome Award for Creative Achievement, established in

1930 by William Travers Jerome, Jr., a trustee of Spelman College and Mrs. Jerome, for an original achievement in any field, – in art, dramatics, writing, music, or research. The prize of $50 was awarded the first year (1930) to Bessie H. Mayle, '31, for an original one-act play entitled "Clogged Springs." The play was published in the *Spelman Messenger*. The Jerome award has, during the years, been given for musical compositions, sculpture, painting, and acting.

The coming of Hale Woodruff to the Atlanta University system in 1931, and the gift in 1933 from the Carnegie Corporation of a fine set of reproductions of paintings in color or in black and white carefully mounted and labelled front and back for easy classroom use, gave impetus to student interest in painting. Courses in Drawing and Painting were offered as early as 1932. In 1934, a sculptor, Elizabeth Prophet, joined the staff of the Art Department; and courses were offered in Sculpture and in History of Art and Architecture.

The Trevor Arnett Library provides an exhibition gallery, and after 1932 the art exhibits were held in the university library. There have been many of them through the years. Some were traveling loan exhibits assembled especially for showing in colleges; some were loans from art museums, for example, one in 1934 from the Whitney Museum of Modern Art of New York City; one was of paintings by two Negro artists of nationally recognized merit, Henry O. Tanner and Edward M. Bannister; one was of illuminated manuscripts; one was of fifteenth century prints; another of African Negro Art. The walls of the exhibition gallery were used also to exhibit the work of the students.

A new plan to provide a series of loan exhibits illustrative of various art forms and containing rare and valuable objects usually available only to students who have access to great art collections came into being in 1937. The idea was conceived by John Henry Hatch, Jr., an art museum director engaged in surveying their traveling exhibits for the Carnegie Corporation, who assembled a pioneer exhibit "The Negro Artist Comes of

Age." His proposal to provide loan exhibits received such enthusiastic response from the Negro colleges that Mr. Hatch worked out the practical arrangements for what was called the Circuit Case Extension Service. The Carnegie Corporation generously donated exhibition cases to each of the 12 colleges which became charter members.

The first exhibit under the new venture, shown at Atlanta University in October 1937, was a collection of 14 original Japanese color prints by the leading Japanese print makers from the twelfth century to the present time. The second exhibit was a display of African Negro Carving. Other exhibits included the work of Allan Crite, young Negro artist of Boston; a display of illuminated manuscripts dating between the eleventh and the seventeenth century; examples of Greek art from about 1,000 B.C. through the Golden Age of Art to the decline in the third century B.C. The Case Extension Cooperative included in their series several displays of special interest to students of Negro history.

Exhibitions were not so frequent during the war years. But the Annual Exhibition of Works by Negro Artists which President Clement and the Art Department faculty initiated in 1941 continued to draw the attendance of more and more people.

H. S. Ede, for 15 years Curator of the Tate Gallery in London, spent a month on the Spelman campus and gave a series of six lectures, illustrated by lantern slides.

Hale Woodruff of the Spelman faculty was commissioned by Talladega College to paint three murals for their new college library showing features of the famous *Amistad* case. The murals, painted in Mr. Woodruff's studio in Laura Spelman Hall, were done with extreme care as to the historical details and are themselves an exciting portrayal of the incident involving slaves who mutinied on the way to the New World, their imprisonment, and subsequent trial first in New Haven, later in the United States Supreme Court. The case in the Supreme Court was the last case argued there by ex-President John Quincy Adams; he won the decision. The Africans were liberated and permitted to return to Africa. The *Amistad* case inspired the organization of the American Missionary Association. Mr. Woodruff exhibited the murals in Sisters Chapel and explained the *Amistad* incident, a few days before they were taken to Talladega.

Drama

The work in dramatics was at all times closely associated with the classroom work of the College. Courses were offered in Elizabethan Drama, Shakespeare, Development of the Drama, and Play Production. The plays chosen for production were representative of the best in modern and classical drama, and included major plays of such playwrights as Sophocles, Shakespeare, Tolstoi, Galsworthy, Barrie, Chekhov, Sierra, Milne, Victor Hugo, Shaw, Sidney Howard and Channing Pollock. Miss Anne M. Cooke, director of dramatics, had enthusiasm and skill, and was uncanny in selecting the cast for any play. John McLin Ross, graduate of Yale University School of the Drama became assistant director; he gave special attention to stage design and production, and speech. Later directors of note were Owen Dodson, also a graduate of the Yale School; and Baldwin W. Burroughs, who studied both at Yale and at Western Reserve University.

The University Players, organized in 1931, presented annually full length plays or series of one-act plays before audiences of the college community and townspeople. Mention can be given only to a few of them.

Antigone, the Greek tragedy by Sophocles, called for much originality in adapting the plan of the Greek theater to the Spelman stage; and carrying out essential characteristics. The stage set was designed by Wilmer Jennings, a gifted Morehouse student. The triple interpretation of speech, choreography and music followed the Greek style; and the music for the choruses, composed by Evelyn Pittman and Josephine Harreld, two Spelman students, was written on the Greek music scale. Six other Spelman students, under the direction of Miss Lisle Arduser of

the Spelman faculty, made the Grecian costumes. Florence Warwick, '35, made the masks for the *Dance of Death* in which she
herself was the chief dancer; and composed several of the choreographic units.

The production of *Antigone* in 1933 was one of the most
elaborate and most perfectly executed of any that have been
seen. Beginning in 1934, all plays were presented on two succeeding nights.

An informal talk in 1932 by Lennox Robinson, Irish playwright and manager of the Abbey Theater Players, had special
significance for his hearers. In speaking of the determination
of the early members of the Irish Players to raise the level of
Irish culture and get away from the stereotyped "Irish" on
stage, he related some of their difficulties and ideals, and the
later success they achieved. Their concentration on their particular racial aptitudes, he thought, might have a suggestion for
those interested and active as Negro players and playwrights.
"Use the sticks and stones around your own doorstep" was
his advice.

One unusual program of the University Players was an ex-
periment in audience education called "An Evening of Theater
Arts." For the first part, John M. Ross of the faculty, assisted
by members of the play production classes, gave an explanation
of stage-lighting, describing the kinds of equipment and the
function of lighting in creating mood and atmosphere. He illustrated his points by actual demonstration of the apparatus and
its use with a stage-set and costumed actors.

As the next part of the program, the Verse Speaking Choir
under the direction of Miss Cooke made its first public appearance. The rich tonal qualities and the variations in solo and an-
tiphonal effects possible with the speaking voice came as a revelation to most of the audience.

Then, to demonstrate the different styles in acting which
various periods and types of drama require, the University Players, under the direction of Miss Cooke, gave a scene from Mo-

lière's *Le Bourgeois Gentilhomme* as typical of a period costume play and of the formal style of acting proper to Molière's comic satire. To illustrate the drama of realism and the straightforward natural type of acting that it requires, the Players performed a scene from Paul Green's *No 'Count Boy*, a play of contemporary Negro life. Expressionism was demonstrated by a scene from Ernst Toller's *Man and the Masses*, in which the characters are abstractions and the senses of the audience are assaulted by artificial group patterns, unrealistic lighting, and varied sound effects designed to drive home the author's emotions and ideas.

An attempt to select from many memorable plays some for special mention is difficult. Following are a few entitled to notice because of their excellence, but especially because of what they tell about the students who took part in acting or production.

Berkeley Square, a delightful play itself, charmingly presented under the direction of Mr. Ross. The stage setting was designed by Gladys Forde, a junior, who followed her interest in drama by graduate study and earned a Ph.D. in this field. The lead part, Peter Standish, was taken by Walter Westmoreland, who joined the U.S. Air Corps after graduation from Morehouse and never came back from the Italian front.

The *Medea* of Euripides, in the Countee Cullen version, was given under the direction of Owen Dodson. The part of Medea was played by Dorothy Ateca, then a Spelman junior. She brought to the difficult role a maturity of understanding and a sense of timing and of dramatic effects which were unusual and thrilling. She later studied Dramatic Art in New York under a Rosenwald Fund grant, and had one leading part in a Broadway play, but found that the theater did not offer for her a career. She is now a teacher.

In *Outward Bound* by Sutton Vane, the students next succeeded in producing another mood and atmosphere. Each character was vividly portrayed. Raphael McIver, as the preacher, lifted the play above the amateur level; and Dorothy Ateca's performance in the last scene as the mother of the staggering intemperate youth, was outstanding.

The Cherry Orchard by Chekhov was produced with distinction in several respects. The stage set planned by Miss Cooke was elaborate and unusual. The acting was supremely good. Marion Douglas (incidentally more to the theater born than most students since her grandfather was Will Marion Cook) as the Countess who owned the cherry orchard, Eleanor Bell as the coldly practical adopted daughter, and Richard Wells as Firs, the old valet, deserve special mention.

Pride and Prejudice was given an enjoyable performance, in war days when only a play with mainly a female cast could be presented. The Victorian melodrama, *Angel Street*, by Patrick Hamilton, directed by Miss Frances Perkins, was an ambitious and polished performance. The set was designed by a student, Mary Jeanne Parks; even the wallpaper color and pattern suggested subtly the confused mind and distorted hearts within the house. Marian Davis as Mrs. Manningham and Solomon Johnson as her husband gave one a feeling they were the parts they played.

One of the most interesting productions of any year by the University Players was *Family Portrait*, by Leonore Coffin and William Joyce Cowen. The play, as all readers will recall, centered on the family of Jesus. Dorothy Ateca gave a superb performance as Mary, the mother of Jesus, the part played on Broadway by Judith Anderson. Noteworthy performances were given also by Jennie Strickland as Mary Cleophas, the sister-in-law of Mary; Bessie Joyce Sampson as Mary of Magdala; Owen Dodson as Judas and Charles Lain as James, the brother of Judas. Miss Cooke directed the production; the set was designed by Owen Dodson.

In the years between 1940 and 1950 there were four different directors of the University Players, each of whom did creditable work, some of it excellent. Yet the field of dramatics did not and could not have priority of attention in colleges during the war period; and there was a dearth of available men. The enrollment at Morehouse was as low as 272 in 1943-44; but came back fast after 1945.

Baldwin B. Burroughs returned in 1950 as Director of Dramatics and teacher of courses in play production and speech. There was in the fall an outstanding production of *The Velvet Glove*. A real renascence with a Shakespeare play came in the spring.

In March, 1951, in addition to the usual two evening performances, for the first time three matinee performances of *The Tempest* by William Shakespeare were given especially for Negro high school students. The Atlanta city schools cooperated generously. The Little Theater was filled on Thursday afternoon with Booker T. Washington High School students; on Friday afternoon with David T. Howard High School students; on Saturday afternoon, Carver High School students had their chance; the Saturday matinee was open also to college students.

The play itself was exceptionally well-directed and well-acted. Dr. Anne M. Cooke came from Howard University, and made a convocation address on *The Tempest* which contributed greatly to the interest and understanding of the play by the students and others. After she witnessed the production, she remarked that the Spelman sophomore, Wilma White, who played the part, was "the first Ariel I have seen who caught the essential spirit." Wilma White after graduation studied at the Yale University School of the Drama. Raphael McIver, Morehouse '31, who played the lead in many University Players productions and in the Summer Theater, played the part of the banished Duke in his reliably distinguished manner. The play also was a financial success, and the net proceeds of $750 were contributed to the Spelman Gymnasium Fund.

The next year, another Shakespeare play, *Romeo and Juliet*, was presented in three matinee performances for the students in the three Atlanta Negro high schools, in addition to the regular two evening performances.

The presentation in 1953 of *Medea,* the play of Euripides in the Robinson Jeffers version, won additional laurels for the Director, the University Players, and notably for Jarcelyn Fields, Spelman senior for her extraordinary acting of the part of Medea.

The 1952-53 season opened with one of the most remarkable plays undertaken by the University Players. It was *The Boy with the Cart* by Christopher Fry. A telling criticism written by Dr. Coragreene Johnstone, professor of English, for the *Spelman Messenger* ended with these words:

"Original music, three-part in madrigal style, for violin, cello, and recorder, was composed by Willis Laurence James for the production, and the playing of the recorder by Mrs. Florence Boynton of the original scores and of traditional folk music gave the production the right lyrical tone. The choreography by Harriet Anderson, Spelman senior, for the Mowers' scene expressed in movement the joy of reaping. In all, the production fused the arts of painting, music, costume design, and drama to create that 'suspension of disbelief' which a modern playgoer rarely finds. Mr. Burroughs, the cast, and production staff turned in the most brilliant performance which this college generation has witnessed. Cg.J."

The Atlanta University Summer Theater was an idea born in the hilltop home in Atlanta of President John Hope as he and Anne Cooke sat talking in May 1934. They talked about the limited opportunity of the Negro in the South to see the great plays being performed throughout the country by great artists. To widen that opportunity, they discussed a plan for a Summer Theater to be conducted in connection with the Summer School. Not giving it time to cool, they went immediately to Reynolds Cottage and sought President Read's cooperation.

The plan as contemplated provided for training in dramatic art for talented young Negroes; for the building up of confidence through repeated performances; for education in drama and theater arts through a wide diversity of plays; for bringing together the community and the college students through their enjoyment of the productions. A part of the plan was to seek out Negro artists, Negro play-writers, and plays about Negroes.

Wheels were set in motion. The faculty and student bodies of the Atlanta University System were combed for talent, and ten were selected who had some professional or amateur experience. With Anne Cooke as director, the members of the company in its first season were: from the Spelman faculty, – Miss William B. Geter and Miss Ernestine Erskine; from students and recent alumnae of Spelman; Florence Warwick, Naomah Williams Maise, Eldra Monsanto; and from Morehouse Raphael McIver, Frank B. Adair, Frederick Maise, Wilmer A. Jennings. John M. Ross served as assistant director. A few guest actors took part in one or more productions.

A schedule of plays for the six weeks was soon agreed upon. It was as follows: *Sun Up*, a play of North Carolina mountain life by Lulu Vollmer; *Mr. Pim Passes By* by A. A. Milne; three plays of Negro life (*Mimi La Croix* by Erostine Coles, A.B. Atlanta University '32, *The Broken Banjo* by Willis Richardson, and *The Seer* by J. W. Butcher, Jr.); *Candida* by Bernard Shaw; *Lady Windermere's Fan* by Oscar Wilde. The next summer schedule, equally ambitious, included plays by Sheridan, Sierra, Belasco (*The Return of Peter Grimm*) and Drinkwater, plus three plays of Negro life.

Observe the variety of dramatic fare. Each six weeks' season included five plays, with at least one "period" piece; one or more plays of Negro life; and one comedy or mystery. Each play was presented three times. The average daily rehearsal was eight hours, before or after which lines were learned, scenery and costumes made. A new play was in rehearsal every week; and lines for the current show also were rehearsed daily. The enthusiasm and interest of the company carried them through – supplemented by enthusiastic response from the audiences.

The work in Dramatics, one of the cooperative experiences of the University System, was supported budget-wise by Spelman College. Spelman provided the theater, employed the directors, and paid for the maintenance costs. The acting was done in the main by Morehouse and Spelman undergraduate students supplemented by University graduate students. The carry-over organization was the University Players.

The Summer Theater program was carried out on Spelman's campus, but its budget was supplied by the Atlanta University Summer School. Undergraduate students made up part of the casts, but faculty members, alumnae members of University Players, and summer-school graduate students were happily available for acting and help in management. The Summer Theater, in fact, provided the laboratory for the School of the Theater.

The Dance

Instruction in the Dance has been offered to Spelman students since the early thirties. Frequently a dance group was an integral part of the dramatic productions, as it was in *Antigone*, in 1933, in *The Boy with the Cart* in 1952 and many plays in between. A Dance Recital by Spelman students became a looked-for annual event.

Delegates to a national convention of the American Association for Health and Physical Education meeting in Atlanta came to Spelman College one afternoon to see a dance demonstration given by Spelman students under the direction of Miss Florence Warwick, '35, the dance instructor. First, the students demonstrated the elementary movements used in the modern dance. This was followed by the more abstract techniques. Then five students performed a dance which Miss Warwick and they had created — "A Southern Landscape," depicting by shifting accents and varying movements the emotional history of the American Negro and his progress through hopeful dreams, dark despair and frustration, ever sustained by his innate feeling for the joys and goodness of life. The accompanying music composed by Willis Laurence James of the Spelman faculty, formed an integral part of the dance.

The convention delegates had been eager to see Spelman's dance demonstration, and they journeyed to the Spelman campus to see it. The public school auditorium where the Convention met was not open for any performance by Negro students.

Music

It is even more difficult to select samples for mention in Music than in Dramatics. As one person said, in giving up the attempt, "That we have had always; it is our own and a part of daily living. Organ preludes and singing in Sisters Chapel are a daily experience. Student recitals and the concerts by glee clubs, chorus, and orchestra are a part of Spelman's life. Artists' recitals are not infrequent. The benefits from music on the campus are almost as constant and imperceptible as the benefits from our daily bread."

Special musical events were frequent. The first of the annual spring concerts by Spelman and Morehouse students under the direction of Kemper Harreld was given in 1928. Later they became Atlanta-Morehouse-Spelman Chorus and Orchestra Concerts. The Christmas Carol Concert has been described. These two annual events were especially appreciated by the people of the Atlanta community as well as by those on the campuses.

The Harreld String Quartet made up of Kemper Harreld and Willis Laurence James, violins, Richard Durant, Morehouse student, viola, and Geraldine Ward, violoncello, Spelman student, was organized in 1936. The Spelman College Glee Club, directed by Willis Laurence James became known as an exceptionally fine singing group. There was a Spelman College Quartet, a Morehouse College Quartet, and sometimes a mixed Spelman Morehouse Quartet — all of which sang frequently. There were individual student recitals — piano, organ, violin, and voice.

All of these were heard and enjoyed, but perhaps the highest value in music was the congregational singing, whether of hymns or spirituals or secular music. That was superb. Virgil Fox, the organist at the Riverside Church in New York, who played in Sisters Chapel whenever he came to Atlanta, was accustomed to close his program after the encores by inviting the audience, made up of Morehouse as well as Spelman students, to join him in a stirring hymn. They did—and the result was astounding. He told the students on one occasion that he had talked about the singing at Spelman all the way across the United States!

Organ Recitals

The organists who played their programs in Sisters Chapel must have come because of the music-wise intelligence and warm responsiveness of the audience. Fortunately, for Spelman College, the Georgia chapter of the American Guild of Organists brought distinguished organists to Atlanta, and was friendly about sharing them.

Carl Weinrich, now organist at Princeton University, was a guest on the campus for two days, which enabled students to become acquainted with him in an informal lecture-recital the day before he played superbly in Sisters Chapel a program of Bach, Buxtehude, Handel, Mozart, Hindemith and Lamb. The audience of 800 was captivated by his brilliant technique and colorful interpretations.

Edwin Arthur Kraft, organist and choirmaster of Trinity Cathedral, Cleveland, Ohio, is noted for his transcriptions for the organ of operatic and orchestral works. He plays the organ like an orchestra conductor. One of his numbers was a minuet written by Beethoven for string quartet but arranged by Kraft for organ. Other numbers were by Bach, Walond, Bonnet, Stamitz, Bossi, and Wagner. Mr. Kraft came again a year later, and gave a varied program, from Marcello, Bach, Dallier, d'Antalffy, Mulet, Vierne, and was enthusiastically applauded for his amazing fluency in technique.

Thomas Richner, organist of the Fifth Church of Christ Scientist, New York City, gave a piano and organ recital. The programs of Orrin Suthern of the Dillard College faculty, and of Claire Coci, the first outstanding woman organist the students had heard, aroused special interest. So did the recital by Alexander Schreiner, organist of the Salt Lake City Tabernacle.

E. Power Biggs, internationally known artist on the organ, who came to Atlanta to give a recital at Agnes Scott College for the Georgia chapter of the American Guild of Organists, was gracious in coming to Spelman the next morning and giving an informal program at an eleven o'clock assembly. He played a concerto in D major by Handel; a suite in three movements by William Selby (1750); Pièce Heroïque by Cesar Franck; a chorale prelude by Brahms; three Noels with Variations by Louis Claude Duparc (c. 1750); "Sheep may safely graze," and Toccata and Fugue in D minor by Bach. At his request, the Atlanta-Morehouse-Spelman chorus sang Mozart's "Alleluia" and the spiritual, "There are angels hovering round." Seeing him and hearing him play on the Hook and Hastings organ in Sisters Chapel (which he found to be "a fine instrument") added immensely to the pleasure of his remarkable playing over the radio.

Virgil Fox, organist of the Riverside Church of New York City, has played the organ in Sisters Chapel six times or more. His brilliant playing interspersed with informal comments is received by the students with beaming faces and thunderous applause. His program varies. One of them included Purcell, Bach, Franck, Karg-Elert, Guilmant, Vierne, and Mulet. Bach's "Come, Sweet Death" is a favorite of the students; so is Elgar's "Pomp and Circumstance." When he asked the students to sing "The Church's One Foundation" with all the fervor and variations natural to such an audience, to his improvised accompaniment, with an "Amen" that should lift the roof, the response was tremendous. He exclaimed "I have been looking forward to this for a long, long time!"

Voice, Strings, Piano

Marian Anderson and Dorothy Maynor were heard by all Spelman students. Mattiwilda Dobbs gave her first recital after her successes in Europe in Sisters Chapel. Luther King, tenor, and Edward Mathews, baritone, sang in recitals. Roland Hayes sang at a vesper service. There were concerts by the Westminster *a capella* Choir and by The English Folk Singers. Recitals were given by Ellabelle Davis, soprano; and Camilla Williams, soprano, who had sung in 1946 the title role in "Madame Butterfly" at New York's City Center.

Max Rosen and Frederic Balazs, concert violinists, each was heard in recital. Likewise, Luigi Silva, master player of the 'cello. The Danish String Quartet gave a concert; and so did the Curtis String Quartet; and the Mannes-Gimpel-Silva trio consisting of piano, violin, and 'cello. The DeVolt Sisters gave a program on harp and violin. The Otto Luenings of Bennington College gave a recital with flute and piano. Charles D. Stratton of Amherst College brought his clavichord, and provided a new musical experience for the students. As did also John Jacob Niles, folk singer, with his original stringed instruments.

Edwin Gerchefski, Leroy Anspach, Erno Daniel of the Budapest Royal Conservatory, Saulima Stravinski, Hazel Harrison, and Natalie Hinderas may have special mention among a score of concert pianists. Carol Blanton, Spelman '33, who was awarded the first Master's degree given by the Juilliard School of Music won acclaim by her recital at Spelman College. The article by the *Atlanta Constitution's* music critic the next morning, placed conspicuously at the top of the page (a non-segregated location!), was headlined *Blanton Piano Concert Spellbinds Throng of 2,000*. Many of the artists, and always those who came under the Concert Project of the Association of American Colleges, did more than appear for a concert or recital. They were campus guests for two or three or four days, and the students had the privilege of a brief acquaintance with them. Harold Bauer, famous pianist, is an illustration. His visit commenced with chapel on Wednesday morning of Thanksgiving week. The Spelman and Morehouse Glee Clubs sang special numbers at the service, and the entire student body joined in the singing of spirituals. During the day, Mr. Bauer visited several classes and entered into the discussions.

His formal recital, which took place Wednesday evening, was heard by a large audience assembled in Sisters Chapel. Harold Bauer was called "perhaps the supreme interpreter of Bach and Beethoven among contemporary pianists." His program at Spelman included Handel, Beethoven, Schumann, Debussy and Chopin, and was enthusiastically received.

Thursday morning, after the Thanksgiving service, the music organizations of the University system gathered in an informal meeting for the purpose of giving Mr. Bauer an idea of the musical program of the colleges, academic and otherwise. He entered into the spirit of the occasion, talking with the students and playing for them.

Other entertainment was offered in less serious vein: such as Franz Polgar in his "Fun with the Mind"; Charles Gorst in imitation of birds' songs; the Edwin Strawbridge Players in "Pinocchio"; the Jitney Players in a hilarious entertainment called "Footlight Americana" – a group which included Ethel Barrymore Colt; the General Motors Parade of Progress; a program by the members of the *Information Please* radio show, Clifton Fadiman, John Kieran, Franklin P. Adams, and Dan Golenpaul. The traveling groups of players were always enjoyed, whether they produced Shakespeare, as did the Chekhov Theater Company and the Avon Players; or whether they presented comedy as did the American Repertory Theater in "The Queen's Husband," or the Hedgerow Players.

Concerts and plays were scheduled on Friday or Saturday evenings, as were the various dances, movies, class entertainments and other student activities.

PLATE XIX

A Service of Commemoration at the Barn,
formerly Barrack Number One, before its demolition

PLATE XX

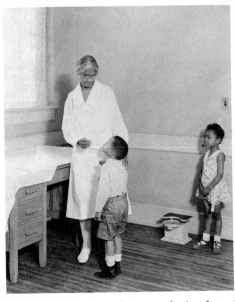

The Nurse and the Director look after the health of Nursery School children

Play Time at the Nursery School

CHAPTER XVI

THE NURSERY SCHOOL

A NURSERY SCHOOL was added to the resources of Spelman College in 1930. A grant from the Spelman Fund of New York made it possible to provide the physical facilities, a trained director, two full-time assistants, and several student assistants. Miss Pearlie E. Reed, graduate of Fisk University with a Master of Arts degree from the University of Cincinnati and further graduate work at the University of Minnesota and Columbia University, was made director. She had previously had experience as supervisor of elementary schools at the Fort Valley Normal and Industrial School in Georgia and as director of Negro work in child care and parent education at the University of Cincinnati.

The school was opened on November 6, 1930, in rooms on the ground floor of the Laura Spelman Rockefeller Memorial Building. In addition to the work of caring for and teaching the children, courses which included a study of the mental and physical growth of the pre-school child, nursery school procedure, and behavior problems in young children were offered to college students for credit. A senior-graduate course was added for graduate students, especially those in education or sociology.

Under Miss Reed's leadership, not only did the children get a proper start, but the school served also as a training center for parents; a practice field for college students interested in professions dealing with young children; a fertile field for graduate students doing research in home economics, education, and psychology; and an observation center for all interested in the care and training of young children.

Financed in its early years by the Spelman Fund, the Nursery School continued to be operated by Spelman College after the five-year grant expired. It was the first such school to be organized in a Negro college, and probably the first among the eastern colleges for women. As long as it was housed in the

Laura Spelman Rockefeller Memorial Building, only about 20 or 30 children could be accommodated, but fortunately larger quarters became available.

The work of the Leonard Street Orphans Home located on land adjoining the Spelman campus was discontinued in 1935. In accordance with a provision in the deed given by Spelman College when the land was sold to the Orphanage, the property was offered for sale to Spelman College. Application for funds to purchase the property was made to the General Education Board. The Board, having in mind the relation of the Nursery School to the department of education of Atlanta University, gave the University $50,000 to purchase the property and remodel the building. The Nursery School thus opened in the fall of 1936 in new quarters, but it was conducted and maintained by Spelman College. In 1945, Atlanta University deeded the building and land west of Leonard Street to Spelman College; one small building and land east of Leonard Street the University had already sold for about five thousand dollars.

The Leonard Street Orphans' Home began its work in 1890; for 36 years it was housed in three army barracks which had been purchased from Spelman College. The founder of the Home, Miss L. M. Lawson, was forced by ill health to give up her work in 1903. Miss Amy C. Chadwick, an English woman who had been educated at the Northfield Training School in Massachusetts, succeeded Miss Lawson; and for 33 years until her retirement in 1936, Miss Chadwick made the orphanage truly a home for the Negro girls admitted to her care, – a home to which they returned for visits and advice and encouragement long after they had jobs or homes of their own. The children in the Home attended the Spelman elementary school and the high school as long as they were operated by Spelman College; and some of them received scholarships for the college course. Spelman College named the building Chadwick Hall in honor of Miss Amy Chadwick.

The new quarters were ideally suited for the Nursery School, as the building which replaced the barracks in 1926 was built expressly for the use of children, and was well-planned, well-built, attractively light and sunny. The yard provided ample space for playground activities. The larger quarters made it possible to admit more pupils.

One hundred children, ranging in age from 18 months to five years were enrolled in 1936. In 1938-39, 110 children were enrolled, divided into five groups.

There is no need here to discuss the daily program and procedures. The school was fully up to high standards. Miss Reed, in addition to conducting the Nursery School itself, had supervision of the undergraduate and graduate students working with pre-school children. For example, in 1938-39, 21 students were enrolled in the senior-graduate course on child development, including ten graduate students, nine Spelman seniors, two Morris Brown seniors. Each year also, some graduate students of Atlanta University, under the direction of Miss Reed, used as thesis material the results of their observations at the Nursery School.

Many graduate students enrolled in the summer school courses. In 1938, for example, there were 68 in Child Development, 72 in Behavior Problems, and 14 were enrolled in Research Problems in Child Development. High School principals in increasing numbers enrolled for these courses for the background it gave them for understanding the needs of children.

One advantage of the Nursery School for Spelman College might be overlooked if not mentioned. The presence of the nursery school at the entrance to the campus provides a counterbalance for what is sometimes regarded as the artificial atmosphere and "academic" tendency of a college campus. The school is a constant object lesson, even for the students not taking the specific courses, for it calls attention to home and family life, and helps to keep book-learning in proper perspective. Of all the parts of the Atlanta University Center, there is probably none more frequented by visitors and none remembered with keener interest than the Nursery School.

Miss Reed served as Director of the Nursery School and

teacher of the college and university courses offered in connection with it, from its beginning in 1930 until her untimely death in December, 1945. She had laid the groundwork well, and she had trained Spelman College graduates in this field. Several taught in the Spelman Nursery School under her direction and later became directors of Nursery Schools; for example, at Hampton Institute (Ida Jones Curry, '32); Bennett College (Mary Menafee Garvin, '34).

The Nursery School was operated by able teachers, most of them trained by Miss Reed, with teachers in the Department of Education giving the college and university courses, after the death of Miss Reed until the appointment in 1948 of Miss Florence E. Thorp. Miss Thorp had served nearly 20 years as Assistant Director and Supervisor of the University of Pennsylvania's Illman Training School, and was a valued addition to the University Center.

The training of nursery school directors and teachers offered one field in which Spelman had superior resources for aiding the war effort. The Lanham Act passed by Congress in October 1940 set aside funds to provide nursery school care for children of defense workers. In other areas, too, the war greatly increased the need for trained and competent nursery school teachers; and obviously the necessity for such services for children of veterans and their working wives has not ceased since the war was over. Visits, arranged by governmental and private social agencies, brought scores of prospective nursery school workers, white and colored, to Chadwick Hall to observe the Spelman Nursery School program in action.

CHAPTER XVII

THE FIFTIETH ANNIVERSARY

THE Fiftieth Anniversary of Spelman College celebrated on April 10, 11, and 12, 1931 "was unique" says the *Messenger*, "in that although tribute was paid to the fifty years past, it was more to a future worthy of such a past that all thoughts were turned. Truly Miss Packard and Miss Giles built for the days to come. . . ."

At the Friday morning chapel on April 10, on the platform were John D. Rockefeller III, representing the Spelman-Rockefeller family; William Travers Jerome, Jr., trustee of Spelman College and Atlanta University; Mrs. Mary C. Reynolds, for 23 years corresponding secretary of the WABHMS, who had first visited Spelman in 1888; President John Hope of Morehouse College and Atlanta University, and President Florence M. Read. All took part in the service. An athletic meet was held in the Morehouse College gymnasium on Friday afternoon.

For Friday evening, the Alumnae, with Mrs. Claudia White Harreld, president of the Alumnae Association in charge, had arranged a series of living pictures posed by present Spelman students. There followed reminiscences, some formally, others informally presented. The latter included one by Mrs. Sarah Lay Knight, the only child in the group of eleven on that first morning, April 11, 1881, when Miss Packard and Miss Giles, armed only with their Bibles, notebooks and pencils, plus an invincible faith, opened their school in the dark damp basement of Friendship Church, and now the only living survivor.

The concluding address of the evening on "Spelman's Contribution to the World Civilization," was given by Miss Cora Bell Finley, Seminary '94, College '31, who hung her account of alumnae achievements on a quotation from Miss Packard. She first recalled the "unusual culture" Miss Packard and Miss Giles had brought to Atlanta and sought to instill into the lives of Spelman students; and then their success in building an institution. Miss Finley knew at first hand because she had been a student in the first decade, while Miss Packard was living.

"Girls," she quotes Miss Packard as saying, "I am building for a hundred years hence, not only for today."

So reviewing the scene for half a century and giving specific evidence by names, places, types of work, and accomplishments, Miss Finley presented a proud record for all to see and hear.

Repeating Miss Packard's saying, "Girls, I am building for a hundred years hence," she talked of the program of Spelman a half century — nay, a century — hence. With the new Nursery School begun, the first in a college for women; the more highly trained college faculty which included Negro men and women; with the increased resources, the University affiliation, the new library: — through these achievements and more in process of becoming, the future promise kept faith with the honored past.

The graduates and former students have carried Spelman ideals into all parts of the United States, into Europe, into Africa. As Claudia White Harreld stated, "Before the phrase 'social work' was created, the Spelman girl taught and worked for health, sanitation, and community improvement, and introduced higher standards in home and church life." Spelman girls have worked in public and private schools, in all manner of positions. "They are doctors, private and public health nurses, pharmacists, journalists, social workers. Many have engaged in business, some as secretaries and clerks, some as heads of departments, some as founders and proprietors." An exhibit of the work of the alumnae and of the present Spelman College through all its departments interested hundreds of visitors and reinforced the spoken word.

The Saturday morning session, planned and executed by the students, was a special feature, and reflected great credit on them. A sister college greeting, given in person by a student of Agnes Scott College, was part of their program — the first time such a thing had happened.

The formal Founders Day Exercises were held on Saturday afternoon in Sisters Chapel. The long and colorful academic procession from Rockefeller Hall; singing by the Spelman Glee Club and by the congregation; and Scripture reading by President Harvey W. Cox of Emory University preceded the first address by Dr. Julian Lewis, Assistant Professor of Pathology of the University of Chicago Medical School, and one of two Negroes then holding regular appointment in a Northern Medical College. His subject was "The Basic Elements of an Education." He used illustrative incidents with imagination and skill, as he emphasized the values inherent in all true education.

After another hymn; a prayer fittingly offered by the Rev. Dr. Edward R. Carter, pastor for 49 years of Friendship Baptist Church in which Spelman began; and the spiritual, *O Seek and Ye Shall Find*, Dr. Jackson Davis, Assistant Director of Education of the General Education Board (later its Director) gave a stimulating report of "The Negro Woman in the Classroom."

Greetings were brought from many organizations, schools and colleges. Among the delegates presenting them were:

Mrs. George Caleb Moor, President of the WABHMS

Dr. James M. Nabrit, President of the General Missionary Baptist Convention of Georgia, in behalf of Negro Baptists

The Rev. Louie D. Newton, pastor of the Druid Hills Baptist Church, in behalf of the white Baptists of Georgia

The Rev. Dr. Everett Carleton Herrick, President of Newton Theological Seminary, Newton, Massachusetts, in behalf of Northern Baptists

President James Ross McCain, of Agnes Scott College and

President John Hope, President of Morehouse College and Atlanta University, in behalf of Spelman's sister institutions.

The Spelman-Morehouse chorus sang Keller's *Magnificat*; the students and congregation sang the spiritual, *I'm Going Down to the River of Jordan* and the Negro anthem, *Lift Every Voice*; the benediction was pronounced by President Franklin Halsted Clapp of Gammon Theological Seminary.

The reader might think these two programs were enough for one day and one small college. 'Twas emphatically not so. There had even been an important special meeting of the Board of Trustees of Atlanta University beginning early Saturday morning in which were considered many important and urgent matters including the location for the new Library. The minutes of this meeting cover 21 typed pages, single-spaced. This schedule required fast movement as well as concentrated attention on the part of the trustees concerned also with the Spelman Anniversary. Furthermore, the Saturday evening event in Sisters Chapel was a high point in the whole program and not a thing to be missed.

The History of Spelman as told in Pageant was presented that evening to a large and appreciative audience. By means of choreographic groups, music, short dialogues, and tableaux, the story was unfolded. The simplicity of setting and of action; and the accuracy of historical detail in costuming and dialogue gave a confident strength to the production. The pageant portrayed vividly incidents of trouble, anxiety, hope, and ultimate attainment which make up the story of the first fifty years. The parts were taken by present students of Spelman and Morehouse Colleges with the exception of Miss Clara Howard, the 1887 graduate, who took her own part. There were four episodes: 1) the arrival of Miss Packard and Miss Giles in Atlanta and the school's beginning; 2) the period of the early days and Spelman's struggle for existence, to the time when Mr. Rockefeller came to its aid; 3) Miss Tapley's period; 4) the immediate past from 1927.

The pageant closed with a choreographic interpretation of the Negro anthem, *Lift Every Voice and Sing* by James Weldon Johnson and Rosamond Johnson. Miss Anne M. Cooke was the composer and director; and the performance was of highest quality. The pageant was repeated during Commencement week, and again held the audience spellbound. It remains a memorable event of Spelman history.

Ida Louise Miller, Spelman sophomore, wrote in the *Campus Mirror*: "The pageant seemed to renew the deep knowledge that our dreams and hopes are with us always and that because of them we will always go on. And each generation will have a cup full to overflowing, drink deeply, and pass the cup — still filled — to those who are coming after in the eagerness for truth."

A quiet service of worship, arranged and led by the Rev. Howard Thurman was held in Sisters Chapel at nine o'clock on Sunday morning. The ritual and music represented life as adventure, life as labor, and life as worship. Mr. Thurman, now Dean of the Chapel, Boston University, was at the time a member of the Spelman faculty, employed jointly with Morehouse College.

The anniversary sermon was preached by President Rush Rhees of the University of Rochester on Sunday afternoon. Assisting in this service were Presidents Davage of Clark, Fountain of Morris Brown, Hope of Morehouse and Atlanta University, and Dr. Will W. Alexander, Executive Director of the Commission on Interracial Cooperation.

The vesper service on Sunday evening marked the close of the three days' observance. President Everett Carleton Herrick was the speaker. His sincerity of speech and understanding wit brought alive for his hearers some simple but vital truths connected with the story of Mary and Martha. The spirituals sung included *The Rocks and the Mountains, Daniel Saw the Stone, Steal Away, Standing in the Need of Prayer, Swing Low, Sweet Chariot*. The closing prayer and benediction were pronounced by Trustee William Travers Jerome, Jr. So was fittingly closed the celebration of the Fiftieth Anniversary.

A significant message which pleased all friends of Spelman had been received from Mr. John D. Rockefeller. He wrote Miss Read from Ormond Beach on April 8, 1931, as follows:

> I regret exceedingly that it will be impossible
> for me to give myself the pleasure of being present at the celebration of the Founding of Spel-

man College. Be assured of my appreciation of your kind invitation.

I extend heartiest congratulations to Spelman for all that it has accomplished during these fifty years, and am happy to feel that of all the investments which we have made as a family, Spelman stands among the best.

I send cordial best wishes for the future of the College, and for each and every one who has had or will have a part in its administration; also every sincere hope for the continued welfare of the colored people in whom we have always felt the deepest interest and concern. We rejoice in the progress which they have made, and devoutly pray that the good work may continue with ever-increasing success.

Sincerely,

(Signed) John D. Rockefeller

CHAPTER XVIII

GROWTH IN BUILDINGS AND
LANDSCAPING

N
O READER 40 years old as this page is written can
help having a vivid recollection of the "hard times"
of the early nineteen-thirties. The depression placed
a great handicap on the financial campaigns to raise endowment
funds. In one respect, however, it may have made for good
fortune for the greater Atlanta University.

When Mr. Sage presented to Edward S. Harkness the statement of needs and opportunity as outlined in the Six Year Plan,
Mr. Harkness, Yale classmate of both Mr. Sage and Edward
Twichell Ware, took a deep look at the whole situation. He
was aware of the pledge of the General Education Board to give
to Atlanta University $1,500,000 on condition that a like sum
be raised from other sources; and after that to pay dollar for
dollar up to $1,700,000 more. (The total sum of $6,400,000
sought included additional endowment for Morehouse College
of $1,000,000.) He was aware also of the desperate unemploy-
ment in the nation, with thousands of jobless in Atlanta. He
looked at the item in the University's Six Year Plan which indicated the need of $1,000,000 for new buildings with a sum
included for their maintenance. Then he acted.

Mr. Harkness said he would give $1,000,000 for the build-
ings budget provided the University raised $500,000 by April
1, 1931, and thereby ensured payment of the first $1,500,000
conditionally pledged by the General Education Board. That
would bring three results: a big lift to employment in Atlanta;
assured endowment for Atlanta University of $2,000,000; the
new buildings which would make easier the development of the
University's academic work.

To raise $500,000 in 90 days, however, was one of the im-
possible things that *had* to be done. The times were bad for

finding donors. Strenuous efforts brought in a considerable sum but not the total needed to meet the conditions of the offer. Mr. Harkness had requested that his proposed gift be held anonymous. Fortunately, another anonymous friend came to the rescue and was willing to underwrite the half million required; later, and through the help of Trevor Arnett, money was raised to repay in full the underwriter. Both the gift for buildings and the GEB grant were thus secured; and the building program went forward.

The Administration Building, designed by James Gamble Rogers, was erected on the site of Quarles Hall. Quarles Hall, built facing Chestnut Street so that Spelman College students might have ready access from the street without going into the Morehouse campus, was moved west and south, and now houses the Atlanta University School of Social Work. The land was deeded by the ABHMS to Atlanta University, with a condition which prescribed that offices of administration be available in the building for Morehouse College and Spelman College. That was done. There are offices for president, dean, registrar and bursar, and their secretaries – for Spelman as much as for Morehouse. The main entrance faces Graves Hall far down on Morehouse campus; walks lead south to the University Library. Large elm trees, alternating with pink dogwood, were moved to frame the Library quadrangle.

After the death of Mr. Harkness, Mrs. Harkness consented to remove the condition of anonymity, and permitted the University to name the building, Harkness Hall, in honor of Mr. Harkness. It was so dedicated on April 16, 1950.

Two new dormitories for graduate students, one for men, one for women, now called Ware Hall and Bumstead Hall in honor of the University's first two presidents, Edmund Asa Ware and Horace Bumstead, were built on land long owned by Atlanta University bordering Chestnut Street, between Hunter and Beckwith. They were ready for occupancy in 1933.

Harkness Hall, as the Administration Building will henceforth be called, was completed in December, 1932. Morris

Brown College had moved in 1931 from the other side of Atlanta to the old Atlanta University buildings, in order to have readier access to the new Library and other advantages. President Hope established offices temporarily in Rockefeller Hall as once Dr. George Sale had done, until the new offices were ready for occupancy.

The committee first appointed by Mr. Sage as the University Library Building Committee, consisting of Mr. Weisiger, Mr. Hope, and Miss Read was continued during the construction of Harkness Hall and the two student housing units now called Ware and Bumstead. Hundreds of questions were decided by this committee as choices had to be made between this and that; always the opinions and the judgment of the contractors, Otis A. Barge and William B. Thompson who constituted The Barge-Thompson Company, carried weight. Sometimes the answers depended on the cost of alternatives. For example, the architect's first plan for Harkness Hall was a corner building bordering West Fair and Chestnut Streets; Quarles Hall to be left on its original site. Mr. Hope and Miss Read regarded this as undesirable for several valid reasons; Mr. Weisiger concurred; Barge-Thompson had confidence that Quarles Hall could be moved without real damage to the building and at a tolerable cost. Consultation with James Gamble Rogers and Mr. Sage in New York effected the change to the present site, and resulted in new plans which were better functionally and much more pleasing architecturally as regards both building and campus development.

The architect, James Gamble Rogers, with Ainslie M. Ballantyne of his staff, and the builders, Otis A. Barge and William B. Thompson, were a fortunate selection. They worked happily together and with the University. They gave freely of their great experience, the former in design, specifications and supervision; the latter in their high standard of workmanship, their knowledge of materials and costs; and both in their genuine interest in the enterprise. These buildings, and others designed and constructed later, are a worthy monument to architects and builders.

The acquisition of additional land, first of the block between the Spelman and Morehouse campuses on which the Library was located, then of two blocks lying north of the Spelman campus bounded by Greensferry, Chestnut, Fair, and Lawshe Streets, was made possible by the General Education Board. It was cause for rejoicing that the land, bit by bit, could be purchased. The time and attention required was sometimes burdensome. Between 1931 and 1941 approximately 22 acres were purchased at a cost of $483,955. Nine and one-half acres of this property costing $245,436 were deeded by Atlanta University to Clark College for its new campus. The General Education Board was not ready to pay fancy prices; and required reports accurate to the penny. Monthly statements were submitted by Miss Read, Assistant Treasurer, and the money to pay for each piece was obtained by requisition.

On one occasion, Miss Read received a letter from the Comptroller of the GEB stating that there was a discrepancy of one cent in the last two reports; what, please, was the explanation? The bookkeeper on being summoned found that the discrepancy arose from his having counted one half-cent up on one report and down on the other, and the explanation was accepted.

The accounting part was not the difficult end of the many transactions. The heavy end was President Hope's who needed often to encourage the owners to sell at a reasonable price – or perhaps to bring heirs together to a mind to sell when they disagreed. On the whole, the owners responded well to the incentive of "the cause," and in every case, they received a fair price.

Spelman's North Gate

The building of the new University Library on land opposite the northwest corner of the Spelman College property called for attention to the north end of the campus. On February 10, 1932, preceding the April dedication of the library, a new paved road to Greensferry Avenue was built. The engineer was Edward Swain Hope, elder son of President Hope, a graduate of the Massachusetts Institute of Technology, who returned from a position in Brazil just in time to be engaged for this project. The students who participated in the spontaneous ceremony to celebrate the occasion may think it worthy of mention in this history.

A procession of cars and of marchers started from Rockefeller Hall just before noon, moved around the oval past Tapley, Laura Spelman, Morehouse and Giles and out by the old dirt road into Greensferry. It halted at the entrance to the campus while two seniors, Marjorie Stewart and Augusta Johnson, removed the barrier of blue ribbon, thus formally admitting the procession to enter the campus by the new road. A second barrier for the procession to pass was removed by the presidents of the three college dormitories: Curtis Miller, Gleaner Simmons and Margarette Singleton.

In the first car rode the Presidents of Spelman College, Morehouse College, and Atlanta University. The next car held the Dean, the Treasurer, and the Registrar of Spelman. The third car carried the presidents of the four college classes: Oteele Nichols, Frankie Butler, Lottie Lyons and Jessie Wilson. There were more than 20 cars carrying teachers, secretaries, and students, followed by a marching procession. Every car on the campus joined in the spree. And after the marching students, came the campus truck loaded with as many students as could possibly stand in the bed or ride on the fenders. It was a pity that no one foresaw the gleefulness of the occasion in time to arrange for a photographer, especially of the students on the truck at the end of the procession, lustily singing college songs. As the *Campus Mirror* stated: "The students responded to the full significance of the gala occasion with songs led by Evelyn Pittman[1] who despite very cramped quarters, was able to direct with her usual fervor."

[1] Evelyn LaRue Pittman '33 has achieved distinction as a teacher of music, founder of a choir heard over a national radio network, composer of songs for children, and recently as composer of an opera based on the Bible story of Esther which had a presentation in Paris.

It is down this paved road that students travel to and from the Trevor Arnett Library and classes at Atlanta University or the other colleges. For five years, this route was flanked by one of the old barracks, but not after 1937.

Barrack Number One Demolished

Early in October 1937, Dr. Otis W. Caldwell, Visiting Professor for the year at Atlanta University, propounded this question to the morning chapel audience, "Is the purpose of education the goals or the journey?" It was a good question at the beginning of the year for the institution as well as for the students. It called for looking back to the past; and forward to the future. It was likewise a pat circumstance that the first unusual event of the college calendar was a service commemorating the early days of Spelman.

The Old Barn, long used as a workshop and storage area, had previously been Barrack Number One in which Miss Packard and Miss Giles, and other teachers, had lived beginning in 1883. It was the only home on the campus Miss Packard ever had, and Miss Giles had lived there until 1901 when Reynolds Cottage was built. For these reasons, the alumnae felt a sentimental attachment for the building in spite of the eyesore it had become. But the new roadway, with the new north entrance to the campus, and new landscaping plans cried aloud for its demolition.

Accordingly, on the morning of October 18, 1937, when the students met as usual in Sisters Chapel for the eight o'clock morning chapel, they were invited to adjourn to the Old Barn for a commemoration service, inasmuch as this last visible reminder of the early days on the campus was to be torn down at once in line with the demands of progress.

"To the music of *Forward Through the Ages* the procession set out briskly from Sisters Chapel, in a downpour of rain which served as an appropriate prelude to memories of the hardships of pioneer days. Soon the last student had folded her umbrella and crowded inside the shelter of the Barn, facing the narrow stairway now serving as a stage. On it were grouped, Trevor Arnett, President of the Board of Trustees of Spelman College, and Mrs. Arnett, Rufus E. Clement, President of Atlanta University, President Florence M. Read and Dean Jane Hope Lyons of Spelman College, Otis W. Caldwell, visiting Professor of Education at Atlanta University, Miss Johnnie Louise Fowler and Mrs. Kemper Harreld representing Spelman alumnae, and Eloise Usher, '38, representing Spelman undergraduates." (*Spelman Messenger*, vol. 52, no. 9).

After the singing of the college song whose words were written by the author of *America*[1], two speakers took part.

Eloise Usher, Student Chairman of the Community Council, later to be on the Spelman faculty in charge of Dramatics, narrated with terseness the story of the founding, and reminded the assembled students that hereafter, with the disappearance of the last building actually connected with the early days "the link remaining between the Founders and the generations of Spelman students to come must be a purely spiritual one – a continuance of their vision and courage."

Miss Johnnie Louise Fowler, TPC '04, had begun her years at Spelman Seminary living in one of the barracks similar to the Barn "I was assigned to a room occupied by six other girls," Miss Fowler said, "and though living in crowded quarters, we were happy. . . . We were taught the right principles of living, – to be true, upright, and dependable. We were taught cleanliness and sanitation even though we had to go outside of the building to get water for scrubbing and for our baths. The water was heated in a large boiler in the laundry, and the girls had to carry it in pails to their rooms after it had been measured out so that each could have a share." She closed with a challenge to Spelman students of the day to use their comforts and privileges to accomplish even greater things than had their predecessors. Miss Fowler, whose diploma had been given her by Miss Giles, was loved and trusted by students of five decades. She served

---

[1] Rev. Samuel F. Smith, who married Miss Nellie M. Kemp, a music teacher at Spelman for four years, wrote *Fair Spelman* in 1895.

in the Spelman Treasurer's Office for 30 years, and was herself Treasurer of the Loyalty Fund. She died in 1960. The Loyalty Fund Scholarship has since been named in her honor.

University and John Hope Homes

On the morning of September 29, 1934, Secretary of the Interior Harold L. Ickes, Housing Division Director of PWA (the Public Works Administration) Horatio B. Hackett, and architects and engineers of the University Housing Project came to a temporary platform erected between Laura Spelman Rockefeller and Tapley Halls where were gathered President John Hope and other members of the University Homes local committee in order to inaugurate officially the first slum clearance and low-cost housing enterprise in the nation to be undertaken by the Federal Government.

A large number of Atlanta citizens and students of the local colleges assembled in view of the housing site. A short program was carried out. Secretary Ickes, introduced by President Hope, spoke briefly. The singing of *Great Day* and the Negro anthem *Lift Every Voice* was recorded by sound cameras. Then "the detonator which was to release the dynamite under the house selected for demolition was placed on the platform. As movie cameras ground from every possible point of vantage and the audience stood with bated breath, the Secretary pressed the plunger and across the street below the Spelman campus a small red-painted cottage rose in the air and then fell into a mass of distorted timber, bricks, and broken glass. The audience cheered. The Atlanta University Housing Project was officially begun." (*Spelman Messenger*, Nov. 1934).

The pictures taken were widely shown in motion picture theaters, as the house dynamited was the first in the nation to be demolished in the PWA program. The PWA announced that 675 modern dwelling units would replace the houses on the 17½ acres lying between the campuses of Spelman College and Atlanta University.

The environment of Spelman College was vastly improved by

the University Homes project since many of the buildings taken by the government were slums in very fact, without running water, electricity, or sewer connections. The area surrounding the campus was further improved in 1939. Then, thanks to the interest of friends of Spelman College and Atlanta University, an area of 30 acres adjoining the Spelman College campus at Leonard Street and touching University Homes at Greensferry, was selected as one of the first three projects to be built by the Atlanta Housing Authority. When government control of housing was transferred by the Wagner-Steagall Act from the Public Works Administration to the United States Housing Authority in the Department of the Interior, the local Advisory Committee was superseded in May 1938 by the Atlanta Housing Authority.

It was under the direction of this group of white citizens: Charles F. Palmer, chairman; James D. Robinson, Jr., vice-chairman; A. R. Dorsey, treasurer; Frank Etheridge; O. M. Harper; and Philip Weltner – that this area was cleared; and buildings containing 606 apartment units (2,481 rooms) were built at a cost of $1,800,000; including the land, the cost was about $3,000,000. Thus another slum area was supplanted; 78% of the 625 dwellings torn down were sub-standard. This same group of white citizens chose to name the project, the second one for Negroes in Atlanta, John Hope Homes in honor of Dr. Hope, whose vision and untiring efforts did so much to bring the plight of poorly housed Negroes to the attention of Atlanta citizens and made them realize that "a slum never gets better of itself." Dr. Hope also had "found" Alonzo G. Moron who became the first manager of University Homes and later of University and John Hope Homes; and was outstanding among the managers of federal housing projects, colored and white. He later became president of Hampton Institute.

Central Power Plant

The physical plant of the University received an important boost in 1937 when a grant from the General Education Board of $300,000 made it possible to build a new central power plant to serve Spelman College, Morehouse College, the University Library and Administration Building; and later to serve also the new Clark College unit.

The plans were prepared by Lockwood Greene Engineers, Incorporated, of New York, Boston and Spartansburg. The construction of the plant, the steam tunnel and the auxiliary lines was carried on by The Barge-Thompson Company of Atlanta.

The laying of new steam pipe-lines and lines to carry light and power to the 14 Spelman buildings necessitated a great deal of digging on the Spelman campus. A tunnel was constructed from the new Power Plant at the corner of Greensferry Avenue and Lee Street crossing Greensferry underground to the coal pocket of the old Spelman power house, a tunnel large enough to walk through. The work began in March 1937, and was completed the following October.

The students were not fully aware of the tunnel until their Hallowe'en Party on October 30. With Morehouse students as their guests, they were invited to take a walk of exploration from Morgan Hall dining-room, where the party convened, to unknown parts where they would be faced by ghosts, black cats, witches, and flickering lights. After a block-long journey filled with such hazards, it was a surprised procession which emerged into the brightly lighted new Power Plant. The Power Plant, incidentally, became one of the show places of the campuses.

CHAPTER XIX

SPELMAN IN WAR-TIME

1939-41: 1941-47

THE seriousness of the world situation became more and more apparent with the rise of Hitler to power, the German invasion of Poland, and Russia's campaign against Finland, as many visitors who spoke out of personal experience of the holocaust, gave witness. The invasion of China by Japan, too, was brought closer by citizens who came from those countries.

Harrison Brown, British journalist, for example, was a campus guest for three days. After service in the British army in World War I, Mr. Brown had traveled almost constantly in Europe, Asia, and America. He had lived in Germany for four years, preceding and following the Nazi Revolution. In 1936-37, he spent several months in Japan and in China, penetrating even to the borders of French Indo-China. Not his miles of travel, but the intelligence of his observations made his visit memorable.

Thus actual world conditions before Pearl Harbor were made vivid by persons who knew them at first hand: the situation in China and Japan by Dr. Walter H. Judd since 1943 a Member of Congress, but then just returned from service as a medical missionary in three different provinces of China, from northern Shansi to Southeastern Fukien; as well as by T. Z. Koo of China, and Professor Kiichi Miyake of Tokyo University, Japan.

Speakers from European countries included Dr. Michael A. Heilperin of Poland, M. André Maurois and M. Pierre de Lanux of France, Lord Marley of England, also Sir Hubert Wilkins, who had been in Paris when the Nazi invasion began.

Raymond Gram Swing, in the third John Hope Lecture presented by Atlanta University in Sisters Chapel, spoke convincingly on "The Choice of Freedom."

South America also had attention. The Fiftieth Anniversary of the Pan-American Union was celebrated at an assembly in Howe Hall on April 18, 1940, under the auspices of the French Department of Atlanta University. The 21 republics of the Western Hemisphere were each represented by a Spelman student who gave a one-minute original description of the country which she portrayed and whose national colors she wore in the sash over her white dress. The speaker at the assembly was Dr. Dantes Bellegarde of Haiti, a former member of the Governing Board of the Pan-American Union and guest professor of French at Atlanta University. On another occasion, Señor Fernando Romero, anthropologist and sociologist from Peru, spoke on the importance of Pan-American relations and strong Western Hemisphere defense.

Rushton Coulborn, professor of history of Atlanta University, who taught European History at Spelman, spoke at a University Convocation, and later conducted five forums in the exhibition room of the Trevor Arnett Library dealing with the danger spots of Eastern and Central Europe. Dr. Coulborn, British-born, had been assistant in history at University College in London, and teacher in a London school which trained men for service in the diplomatic field.

The annual reports of the President to the Board of Trustees and articles in the *Spelman Messenger* further reveal the underlying concern of the College in the world conflict during the years from 1937 through the period of World War II. One *Messenger* article published in the November 1940 issue was written by Alma W. Stone, an honor graduate in the class of 1940, who, as a graduate assistant the following year, served as editor of the *Messenger*. Entitled "Spelman College and National Defense," the article set forth ways for a woman's college to play an important part in national defense, and told what was being done to that end at Spelman. The article was so pithy that the United States Office of Education requested 50 reprints in order to include a copy in their loan library of educational materials.

Members of the faculty gave book reviews, followed by discussion, in a series of faculty meetings. Among books considered were *The Irresponsibles* by Archibald MacLeish, Thomas Mann's *Essays on Democracy*, and Ralph Barton Perry's *Shall Not Perish from the Earth*.

In recognition of the need of every student to understand the issues at stake, a one-hour course running throughout the year in Political Orientation was introduced, and was made a requirement for graduation for all students who did not take the regular three-hour course. A handicrafts laboratory was opened; and every student was urged to develop one skill with the hands. Instruction was offered in metal and leather work in addition to decorative needle-work, knitting, crocheting, weaving and block printing. These activities carried no college credit. Members of the faculty attended a conference held at Hampton Institute on Negro participation in national defense.

December 7, 1941, fateful day in history, fell on a Sunday. The speaker scheduled for the vesper service was Dr. William J. Hutchins, president emeritus of Berea College, who was a guest of President Mays at Morehouse College. Living in Reynolds Cottage, next door to Sisters Chapel, Miss Read was listening to the radio just before three o'clock. The program was interrupted; and the news came that Japan had attacked United States naval and air forces at Hawaii. She felt impelled to impart this dire information to the two gentlemen as they were donning their academic robes. They said, "This means war. . . . Mention should be made of it at the vesper service." By which one? Dr. Mays turned to the president of Spelman, "You are the one who heard the news. We think you should make the announcement." The three walked onto the platform. Miss Read stepped forward, and before the beginning of the organ prelude, she made a simple statement, that the grave news had just come over the radio that Japan had attacked American ships and planes in Hawaii and the Philippine Islands.

The service then proceeded as usual, except that the prayer offered by Dr. Mays was especially relevant to the occasion and expressed the earnest desire of each one who heard and shared in it.

The President of the College attended the National Conference of University and College Presidents held in Baltimore, January 2-4, 1942, and reported the proposals and some of the discussions to the faculty, staff and students. As a result, a War Council was formed with committees of faculty and students working on: curriculum, safety, health and physical fitness, prevention of waste, defense bonds and stamps.

In accord with the suggestions of the curriculum committee, some new courses were offered, – for example, world geography, war ideologies, and economics of war, for credit; typing, shorthand, first aid, without degree credit. A fourth class hour was added for students in the required sophomore course in American history; this was given to the discussion of world events. Regular courses of timely interest in view of the war, in several departments, were brought especially to the attention of the students to aid them in choosing a well-rounded schedule.

Each committee was active but space does not permit detailed reports of activities similar to those undertaken in colleges and schools throughout the land. Early in the program, class rivalry was stimulated in knitting afghans for Britain by the provision of yarn in the class colors – deep yellow and green for the odd classes, blue and red for the even classes. Again in the drive for the sale of war stamps and war bonds, the "barometer" gauge indicated the progress by classes. But these were merely devices. Always was the emphasis placed on preparation for the responsibilities of citizenship – in our own country and in the world; on acquiring understanding of the common past of humanity and a sense of the common future; on acquiring mastery of the tools and implements of life's activities and above all clarity of perception as to the values that give purpose to living.

Campus morale was high and teachers and students took on extra work willingly. The regular schedule of classes and study, meals, exercise and sleep had to go on without letdown. At least, effort was spent to that end. The aim was to keep the students constantly aware of the tremendous forces in conflict around the globe and at the same time to cultivate such added earnestness and steadiness as would enable them to do their daily work well, face life with cheerfulness, and make themselves as competent and resourceful and spiritually tough as possible. The word "tough" is used deliberately in its meaning of "able to endure great strain." This was no easy task.

Discrimination on the basis of race is particularly difficult to endure with equanimity in time of war. One would hear or read, for example, about the girls in other women's colleges developing their skill in reading or even drafting blue-prints; making maps; becoming effective "spotters" of planes; but no opportunities of this sort were open to Negro women students in the South. Then too controversy over segregation of the blood for the much needed blood-plasma was a discouraging factor which emphasized second-class citizenship.

Until this war, the roles that any woman could play were limited to civilian areas, except in the field of nursing. The organization of the Women's Army Auxiliary Corps in May 1942 changed that situation. (The WAAC soon became WAC.) It was therefore with pride that Spelman College received word that two of its graduates, Sarah Murphy, '37, and Dovey Johnson, '38, were two among 39 Negro women who reported at Fort Des Moines, Iowa, along with 400 white women, to begin training on July 20, 1942, as the first women to become soldiers in the United States Army. On August 29, both Spelman graduates took part in the first WAC graduation exercises and were commissioned. Second lieutenant Sarah Murphy remained stationed at Fort Des Moines for a time. In 1943 she went to Camp Atterbury, Indiana, in command of a detachment of 144 women sent there to fill hospital positions, releasing men for other duties. She was promoted to the grade of captain, and served as WAC recruiting officer in the Cleveland area of Ohio. Dovey

Johnson, promoted to the rank of first lieutenant on December 29, 1942, was appointed as WAC recruiting officer for the 4th Service Command. On April 12, 1943, she became a captain and had become a major by the time the war ended. Lt. Thelma B. Brown, '29, trained a WAC band, as one of her duties. Lt. Gracie Hewell '40, after service as a company officer, was engaged by Army Special Services to establish Service Clubs in Europe. She was a Service Club Director in France and in Germany from 1945 to 1950.

With reluctance, however, it must be stated that as late as February 1944, according to the *Southern Frontier*, Negro women were "still barred from service in the WAVES, SPARS and Marines."

The visits to the campus of Spelman WACs in uniform stimulated a feeling of "belonging" to the war effort. So also did the visit later of Glenna Stewart Hayes, '40, in her trim army-nurse uniform. She was instructor of nursing arts at the School of Nursing of Meharry Medical College after her graduation with honors from the School of Nursing of the University of Toronto, and was pressed into service as a recruiting officer in her field.

In the American Red Cross service, at least eight Spelman College graduates served overseas. Virginia Hannon, '34, Fannie Allen, '35, Mary Elizabeth Adams, '38, Ida B. Wood, '39, Julia Allen, '41, Mary E. Stamper, '41, Myrtle Bowers, '42, served in the European area of operations; Juanita Samuels, '43, and Billie Reed, '35, served in the Philippines.

Gloria Starks, '43, served for three years as program director with the Department of the Army in Okinawa, and two years longer as club director at Fort Lee, Virginia. One graduate of Spelman's Nurse Training Department, Marie August, and one college graduate, Mary Culver, '42, were lieutenants in the Army Nurse Corps. Lt. August served in North Africa. Scores of Spelman women were in government service, some in clerical positions and some in industry. At least four Spelman graduates were camp librarians in the United States.

For six months in 1943, Spelman College gave the United States Army the use of the Laura Spelman Rockefeller Memorial Building for classes in Army Administration, to accommodate a unit of 270 soldiers of the United States Army Administration School, Branch No. 7, housed in the Atlanta University dormitories. The soldiers marched onto the campus four abreast in their olive-drab uniforms, early in the morning and ascended the wide staircase inside the building; returned to the university dormitory mess hall in formation; and marched back again for afternoon classes. They had to work hard, but there were occasions when they were entertained in a body, as it were, by the Spelman student body. During the six months the school was in session, approximately 1500 soldiers received certificates of graduation.

The colleges for women had new conditions to face during the war years. The students increased in number. At Spelman College, many were better able to meet expenses because of allotments from their brothers in military service. The women's colleges shared with others shortages of trained personnel; vacancies on the administrative staff were more difficult to fill than on the teaching faculty.

When the second academic year after Pearl Harbor opened with more students knocking at the door than there was room for, the space in the Laura Spelman Rockefeller Memorial Building, vacated in June by the Army Administration School, offered the best temporary quarters. Double decker beds in two large classrooms on the third floor, new showers, built-in locker-closets and a reception room on the second floor, made reasonably comfortable quarters. The freshmen dubbed their dormitory "the barracks" and settled in. They seemed to enjoy sharing unusual accommodations in war-time.

Courses, convocations and assemblies, plays, concerts, class activities, annual college observances all proceeded on an even keel, yet with an added earnestness. As one member of the faculty wrote in a *Messenger* article:

"Tying together the entire program of the departments at Spelman are the chapel services, convocations and other religious services. They have always been a central feature of the college life – Spelman's 'spiritual classroom' they have been called; but never has their influence seemed so earnestly and soberly received as now. Closely connected in the minds of this generation with the sudden fracture of their normal world is the realization that the winning of the war and the peace to follow will take more than human powers. The comfort of an organ prelude; the encouragement of the old, stalwart hymns; messages of profound value in establishing that inner calm that is beyond the defeat of enemies; prayer – in such unforgettable moments of communication grows that creative dynamo which shall justify all this anguish, the understanding soul."

Academically, the effort, during the war years was to continue the preparation and training of the students in the fundamental courses in the arts and sciences, and at the same time to relate as much as possible the long-range training to what was going on in the world at the time. All colleges suffer from the dilemma presented by striving to give something vital to war efforts, an immediate urgency, and at the same time to emphasize the durable values of life and living.

Colleges for Negroes have an additional compulsion. The lines of separation, visible and invisible, are particularly prickly to the sensibilities in war-time. Love of country and love of home are common to all peoples. Negroes, full of patriotic fervor, were giving sons and brothers to fight for country and for the freedom of the individual as opposed to domination by the state.

Yet the rallies and the English Speaking Union in the South were not for them. To be sure, there were some exceptions. Two men from the State Fire Force talked to the assembled students about incendiary and contact bombs, and explained clearly how they must be handled. Friendly white nurses from the all-white local Red Cross chapter were efficient and gentle in the blood donation operations in the campus hospital. Nineteen members of the faculty and staff completed the standard course in First Aid; sixteen completed the advanced course; nine or 10 took the course for instructors of First Aid. The College participated efficiently in the black-out conducted by the city of Atlanta. The purchase of War Stamps and War Bonds was zealously promoted. In these ways, and probably to a degree hitherto unknown, there were no hurdles to hinder.

One remedy for the more subtle forms of discrimination came as a by-product through the many speakers from foreign countries, and from our own, who shared their close experience with war and the war-torn peoples of Europe and Asia. For example:

A young student from Vienna, Verena von Lieben, who had got caught between the Nazi and the Communist lines;

A university student from France, Frances Bouillon, who described her experiences as a member of the Maquis. Captured by the Germans and sent to a concentration camp in a cattle car with her hands tied, later aided by the Student Relief Fund, her appeal was poignant.

A delegate from China to the World Youth Congress, Pearl Liu, and the holder of an exchange fellowship from China (Miss) Kung Pu-Sheng, chapel speakers in different years, who told of the conditions and needs of youth in China.

A play about China and the War, called "Everybody Join Hands," written by Owen Dodson, former member of the Spelman faculty, for use at the Great Lakes Naval Training Station, was presented three times by Spelman students. With its mass movement, verse choir, choreographic numbers and Oriental music, it caught the spirit of China's struggles and her glimpses of distant yet ultimate success.

No persons who have not experienced living in the midst of events in which they are vitally concerned but locally can have no active part can understand the frustration and the need of outlet. On the Spelman campus, all the above events had their part in removing the isolation and creating in its place, a world-community feeling. So also notably did association with men and women whose names are known to a larger public, whether they were citizens of a foreign country, or of the United States. Illustrative of such visitors and speakers are the following:

William Hung, visiting lecturer at Harvard University, on leave of absence from Yenching University, China; Max Brauer, for 14 years mayor of Altona, Germany, whose property was confiscated by the Nazis; Dr. Oscar Jaszi, professor emeritus of Oberlin College, member of Count Karolyi's cabinet, who was compelled to leave Hungary in the nineteen-twenties by a coup of the Bolsheviks; Dr. Tibor K. Bebek, Hungarian scholar, member of the resistance movement under the Nazi dictatorship, who also experienced the terrifying "liberation" of Hungary by the Russians in February, 1945; Count Carlo Sforza, formerly Minister of Foreign Affairs for Italy; Mrs. Duksoo Chang of Seoul, Korea, principal of a high school of 2,000 students, accompanied by Mrs. Ki Poong Lee, wife of the mayor of Seoul and college teacher of English in a girls' school; Dr. Sigmund Skard, Norwegian lecturer, now professor of American literature at the University of Oslo; Per Monson, president of the Norway Press Association. Mr. and Mrs. Monson were campus guests over the week-end. All the above-named men except Count Sforza were guests on the campus for from one to three days.

Among many speakers from Great Britain the students were pleased to hear, each for a different reason, were Lady Astor, Muriel Lester, Dr. Winifred C. Cullis of the University of London, Dr. John J. Mallon, warden of Toynbee Hall; also Oliver Duff, editor of *The Listener* of New Zealand, who spoke in glowing terms of the achievements of the original New Zealanders, the Maoris.

Cuba, Burma, Denmark, Estonia, India, Philippine Islands, Pakistan, Sweden, are other countries whose representatives came and talked of their own lands and the world situation. Russia looms large, and space commensurate with the attention given to this country cannot be granted in this history. One who should be mentioned is Louis Fischer, writer and special student of the Soviet Union, who with his wife and children lived several years in Russia in the days of Stalin. Another is Maurice Hindus, whose books and lectures were enlightening especially on many aspects of life in Russia—he made an annual visit for many years and traveled off the beaten track. He spoke at Spelman at least nine times between 1934 and 1948. He had been in Czechoslovakia in 1938, before and after Munich; his lecture in February 1939 left his audience sobered and saddened. He came again the next year after spending the summer of 1939 visiting Danzig, Lithuania, Latvia, Estonia, and Finland, and told of the disastrous conditions the people of these countries were compelled to face. He visited the Middle East in 1948, especially Egypt, Palestine and Iran; and predicted trouble in that area unless land reforms were carried out with vigor and despatch.

During the war and the post-war period, helpful discussions were directed by Dr. Edgar J. Fisher, for approximately 20 years a teacher of history and dean of Robert College in Constantinople, and for 13 years, assistant director of the Institute of International Education; and by Donald Grant, Scottish Highlander, one of the organizers of the International Students Relief, and a serious student at first hand of social and political changes in the countries of Europe, particularly in Poland, Germany, Spain and France. He gave a series of talks, followed by discussion, in five different years. Both men might be called lecturer-teachers. They have clear command of facts and know how to present them to students.

That the cultural offerings of the campus made an impact on the students is illustrated by a letter from a 1943 graduate who worked with the American Red Cross in the Philippines.

Juanita Samuels sent from the Pacific Theater of Operations this letter dated March 10, 1946, enclosing her Founders Day gift. She wrote as follows:

". . . Being a great distance from home does not dull my memory [of Spelman] because on every hand I am reminded of her. Listening to the weekly programs of the Manila symphony in the Rex Theatre in Chinatown, I thought anew of Sisters Chapel and the many concerts I had heard there. The Rex Theatre was partially destroyed by bombings, it is far from being air-conditioned, the seats are not what one could possibly call comfortable, but it had one thing in common with Sisters Chapel – fine music. I can look at the calmness of Manila Bay full of sunken ships and visualize the peace that prevails over the campus. We like to say of our Founders and those who followed them that they were brave, strong, and full of determination, their eyes upon a better tomorrow; this can also be said of the Filipino people in spite of their long suffering. Perhaps it is because all these things are true that I do not feel 'many miles' from home, and why my newly acquired friends do not seem strange and foreign to me. . . ."

Spelman College was host from June 5 to 12, 1944, to a conference on Current Problems and Programs in the Higher Education of Negro Women, conducted by the National Association of Deans of Women in cooperation with The Commission on Higher Education of the Southern Association of Colleges and Secondary Schools and the General Education Board.

The objectives of the conference were:

1. To review pre-war findings on the higher education of Negroes, especially as they pertain to the education of Negro women, and to evaluate these findings in the light of the current problems and programs of colleges in war times.
2. To indicate and propose directions for the post-war education of Negro women, and to present these findings to the responsible authorities in the several colleges and professional associations.

In the general sessions, such topics as The Curriculum of the Negro College, Mental Health on the College Campus, Women's Work and War, and Higher Education in Human Relations were discussed by qualified speakers. The problem clinic hours and the groups meetings brought out practical ways to meet some of the problems. A full report of the conference was

PLATE XXII

Packing Clothes for War Refugees

WAC Lieutenants

War Time Activities

Army Administration School Entering Laura Spelman

PLATE XXIII

Seniors March Through the Alumnae Arch

Advanced Students in Zoology Laboratory

PLATE XXIV

The Alumnae President Awards a Citation

The oldest employee presents
Founders Day Gift

Breaking Ground for the Gymnasium

Campus Mirror Staff

printed in *The Quarterly Review of Higher Education among Negroes.* The conference was beneficial as a working fellowship that restated or reemphasized common problems; and that developed, along with a new sense of the important influence of women, a new vigor to fire the young women with a purpose to get ready to meet their opportunities. As Pasteur once asserted: Chance favors the prepared mind.

CHAPTER XX

GROWTH

ACADEMIC, CULTURAL, FINANCIAL

1931-1953

ACADEMIC progress steadily continued although there were occasional setbacks. As the college students increased in number, so also did the faculty. President Mary Emma Woolley of Mount Holyoke College had told Miss Read, in a friendly conversation before she went to Spelman that, in her (Miss Woolley's) judgment, the most important single duty of a college president was in the selection of the faculty. That advice was never forgotten. Top rank teachers are scarce in any place or age. Constant effort must be made not only to find such teachers of maturity and experience, but also to detect the "germ" and to help the younger teachers to become first-rate.

The courses offered made up what might be called in a later day a "core curriculum" plus enough specialized courses to keep the student striving for excellence in the field of her choice. Knowledge of and zest for the field of study, and enthusiasm to reveal that knowledge to students were primarily considered in appraising a teacher's qualifications for appointment to the faculty. The possession of a Ph.D. was respected, but did not take precedence of the other qualifications.

The courses for the first two years were, for the most part, prescribed – English, History, and Science; certain of them could be deferred from the sophomore to the junior year; there was, in addition, a foreign language requirement for the Bachelor of Arts degree which could be met by two years' study of *French, German,* or *Spanish.* A three-hour course in *Philosophy* was required for the A.B. from 1936 onward. Beginning in 1940, *every* student was required to take before graduation either a three-hour course in *Political Science* or a one-hour course for two semesters called *Political Orientation.* The times made essential an understanding of the democratic or representative system of government as contrasted with other systems. The foreign language requirement was considered important in providing a foundation or base for understanding people of some country besides the United States of America as well as for its language value *per se*.

The junior and senior years were occupied mainly with the major subject and other electives. The curriculum in Home Economics had fewer electives, because of the rigidity of requirements of state boards of education. As many courses in the humanities as could be were included; the foreign language requirement and that in Philosophy were omitted. Home Economics graduates received the Bachelor of Science degree.

With the junior and senior courses of Morehouse College open to Spelman juniors and seniors, and senior-graduate courses of Atlanta University also open to qualified seniors, Spelman College students had no excuse for boredom.

The names and numbers of the courses look much alike, year after year, in the catalog. The descriptions varied somewhat from time to time, but the variety and aliveness came from teachers who were eager constantly to enrich their offerings, through additional study and reading, attendance at professional meetings and conferences, and conversations with their associates.

New courses were added as indicated by need and resources, for example: in the classics, – Greek Civilization; Roman Civilization; Greek itself; Greek Literature in English; or Latin American History, to cite only a few. Additional courses in Philosophy, Music, Psychology, Literary Criticism, and in all departments appeared from time to time. The schedule of courses was not static. But novelty in the curriculum pattern was not sought for the sake of novelty.

Additions to the faculty that should be noted in the years after 1931 were:

Helen Tucker Albro, A.B., A.M., and Ph.D. Brown University who succeeded Dr. Louise Baird Wallace as head of the Department of Biology in 1931. She had previously taught at

Mount Holyoke College, Brown University, and Hood College.

Also appointed in biology in 1931 was Anna Grace Newell, A.B. and A.M., Smith College, Ph.D. University of Illinois, who had taught at Smith College and at Huguenot University-College in South Africa; had studied one year at the University of Leipzig and at Naples Laboratory.

Georgia Caldwell (Smith), A.B. and A.M., University of Kansas; member of Phi Beta Kappa and Phi Mu Epsilon, the honorary mathematical society. The chairman of the Mathematics department of the University wrote that she completed a major of 35 hours in mathematics with A grade; was elected to a fellowship in mathematics and was "doing her graduate work with a number of unusually bright men and is the equal of any of them"; and that she excelled in her understanding of mathematical theory.

In English, Luella F. Norwood, A.B. and A.M., Carleton College, Ph.D., Yale University, with experience in teaching at Carleton and at Beloit was in 1931 jointly employed with Atlanta University.

Kurt Volz, Ph.D. University of Heidelberg, was jointly employed by Spelman and Morehouse in the Department of German.

Billie Geter (Thomas) A.B. Boston University, A.M. Radcliffe College, came to the Spelman faculty in French in 1933, holding diplomas from the Université de Nancy and the Université de Paris. Mercer Cook, A.B. Amherst College, Ph.D. Brown University, who joined the Atlanta University faculty in 1936, always taught at least one undergraduate course at Spelman College in addition to senior-graduate and graduate courses at the University.

As a matter of fact, the French department illustrated well the advantages of the cooperative program. The French professors, one or more from each institution, all of whom had studied in France, made the program to be followed by French majors, with the advanced courses assigned to the particular professor most competent in each field or century to be covered. Few small colleges could support such a staff.

Mary Kibbe Allen, Ph.D. Clark University, Worcester, Massachusetts, who came to Spelman in 1930, and Mary Eloise Bradshaw, Ph.D. University of Wisconsin, added to the resources in History for both Spelman College and Atlanta University, as did Cornelia M. Paustian, Ph.D. University of Missouri, from 1946 on. Rayford W. Logan, A.B. Williams College, Ph.D. Harvard University, was from 1933 an exchange teacher in History from Atlanta University.

In Psychology, Spelman was fortunate in having as professor from 1936 on, well-trained and well-balanced Oran Wendle Eagleson, A.B., A.M., and Ph.D. Indiana University. In Sociology, Spelman students registered for courses taught by W. E. Burghardt Dubois, Ph.D. Harvard, and Ira deA. Reid, Ph.D. Columbia; and in Economics for courses taught by Lorimer Douglas Milton, A.M. Brown, and William Henry Dean, Jr., A.M. (later Ph.D.) Harvard. Of the sixteen just named, nine are Negroes.

Visiting professors, too, made a valuable contribution: notably Dr. Norman F. Coleman, retired Professor of English at Reed College; Dr. Benjamin R. Andrews, retired Professor of Household Economics at Teachers College, Columbia University; Dr. Richard H. Edwards, a teacher for short periods in three Divinity Schools, viz., University of Chicago, Union, and Colgate-Rochester, who, with his wife, took over a required course in Religion for the whole sophomore class; and a Chinese scholar, Dr. John Wong-Quincy who taught English courses and a course in Chinese Classical Culture. Also Dr. Otis W. Caldwell who was Visiting Professor of Education at Atlanta University. All these men and their wives were in residence for one year or longer.

Early in the affiliation, it appeared that the few Spelman students who chose to major in Chemistry and Economics, could more advantageously take most of their advanced courses at

Morehouse College and/or Atlanta University. On the other hand, Morehouse College offered fewer advanced courses in English and History, and none in Fine Arts except in Music.

For excellence of teaching, and this must be emphasized, *many other members of the faculty*, on the staff for shorter or longer periods, deserve mention if space did not forbid. From year to year, more Negro college graduates prepared for teaching on the college level. Gradually the Spelman College faculty became more evenly balanced interracially, and as between men and women.

In 1926-1927, there were no men on the faculty although there had been two in the early Seminary years, one from 1881 to 1887 and another from 1887 to 1897. In 1927-1928 there were two men on the Spelman College faculty plus one on part-time; ten years later there were 12 male members on the Spelman faculty; and 19 men as exchange teachers either taught courses on the Spelman campus or had Spelman students enrolled in their University or Morehouse classes.

It was college policy to have an interracial faculty; the number of Negroes on faculty and staff by 1937 was at least twice the number of others, and in the year 1952-53, there were three times as many Negroes. The number of Negroes who earned the Doctor of Philosophy degree increased markedly in this period, but although intellectually as competent, fewer Negro women than men had the opportunity to pursue graduate work to that end. The wives often worked to support the family through the time required.

Stronger academic programs could be offered at Spelman, Morehouse, and Atlanta University in the years following the Affiliation because of the forthright collaboration of the Presidents. Dr. Hope held the presidency of both Atlanta University and Morehouse College until July 1, 1931. He always was interested in having better educational opportunities open to all Negro students, and he cared for the welfare of the girls as well as that of the boys. This made it easy to arrange for exchange teachers, and for the exchanges of students in the junior and senior years. Dr. Hope, like Miss Packard, had the magic quality of making people want to *do* and *be* their best. His wisdom and his wide acquaintance with Negroes were assets to the total academic community. Moreover, when he was considering a man or a woman for appointment to a position, he arranged a personal interview on the candidate's home ground, and thus gained far more insight into character and qualifications than would have been possible otherwise. His counsel in matters of personnel was invaluable.

Trained in the classics at Worcester Academy and Brown University, he had in addition been a lover of good theater and good music. He had met Marian Anderson in New York when she first returned to the U.S. from her triumphs in Europe. It was on his initiative and with his encouragement that Spelman College arranged to present her in one of the few concerts for which she was available in 1936. The support of the local alumni of Morehouse and Atlanta University as well as those of Spelman made it financially feasible. Scores of music lovers in Atlanta came to hear her. Her concert given in Sisters Chapel on Friday, February 14, was brilliant and heart-warming. Proud and happy – and inspired – was every member of the college and university community.

A week later, sorrow enveloped the campus because of John Hope's death. He had helped throughout with the arrangements for the Marian Anderson Concert, and had returned to Atlanta on Wednesday, February 12, Lincoln's Birthday, from a speaking engagement with the Oklahoma State Teachers Association in Oklahoma City. In spite of a bad cold, he went to the Negro History Week assembly at the Oglethorpe elementary school on Thursday and "painstakingly wrote statistics on the blackboard to impress the children with the growth in numbers and importance of the Negro race in the United States." On Friday morning he was taken to MacVicar Hospital, sick with pneumonia. On Saturday morning, the largest basket of roses Marian Anderson had received the evening before was taken up to the

hospital; and his nurse reported to him the success of the concert he had missed.

In spite of all the good wishes sent in his direction and the
prayers from hundreds of his friends for his recovery, it was
not to be. He died on February 20, 1936.

There were hundreds, from far and near, more than the
Morehouse chapel could hold, who gathered on the campus —
between Harkness Hall, the Morehouse buildings and Trevor
Arnett Library, three days later. The desire of his friends including especially Will W. Alexander and other University
trustees that he be buried on the campus, was concurred in by
his family. Carried by his students after the service in the chapel
to a simple grave below what had been his office, he was laid
to rest as the students sang in translation the words of the Roman
poet Horace:

> He who is upright, kind and free from error
> Needs not the aid of arms or men to guard him;
> Safely he moves, a child to guilty terrors,
> Strong in his virtues.

His friends lingered, hundreds of them. They conversed
quietly as if reluctant to leave him; as if they felt his friendly
presence among them. One sentence from a message sent by
Dean Sage, chairman of the Atlanta University Board of Trustees, is perhaps what was in the mind and heart of each one
who knew John Hope: "I will not again meet his equal."

His spirit spoke to his friends and associates also later on
when they learned of the request he made of his secretary, Mrs.
Constance Crocker Nabrit, a few years before. After he had attended Harold Grimshaw's simple funeral in Geneva, Switzerland, he wrote: "If you are about when they are planning for
me, do not let them do expensive things and lying things, but
make it brief and honest; make it simple. Do not let the halting
be too long. People should do their work. . . ."[1]

As soon as the first shock of Mr. Hope's death was over,

---

[1] Ridgely Torrence: *The Story of John Hope*, page 311.

people turned to their work as he had wanted. They did not forget. Rather they tried to continue in his spirit and purpose. Faculty and students and administrative staff responded with a will to prevent a lowering of standards or a lessening of growth. Many things had been arranged by him: and the plans were carried out as far as was possible without him. That it could be so is a witness to the fine spirit of cooperation he had created on the three campuses of the University system.

The University Trustees elected Miss Read Acting-President of Atlanta University. With unusually competent secretaries in the office of the president in both the University and Spelman College, with registrars and deans and professors and students full of determination to carry on, the work went smoothly. Never does a college or university exist without problems; and problems there were of many kinds, but there was no friction. On the contrary, good-will and the will-to-do were noticeably present.

Highly respected and greatly beloved, Mr. Hope – he usually was called Mr. Hope – was constantly missed; yet some of the spirit he put into people continued to be felt. For example, there was a Morehouse graduate, one of three brothers, all of whom had to work for their college expenses, who dropped in just to say how much he missed Mr. Hope. "Every time I talked with Mr. Hope," he said, "I felt better for it, and better able to tackle my problems."

Or again, there was the Atlanta citizen, wise though unschooled, who remarked: "He was always friendly with the common people. You never had to get on stilts to talk to Mr. Hope."

Dr. Mordecai Johnson spoke of "his rise to a position as the trusted leader of interracial action, not alone in the United States but throughout the world, and trusted both by the white leaders of the South and by his own people."

Dr. Will W. Alexander, white Southerner, wrote, "I have given few men the unreserved confidence which I had in Dr. Hope." And in informal conversation, he had in an earlier day

313

remarked, "I always like to talk things over with John Hope. I think if I knew I was going to hell, I'd want to talk it over with Hope before I started."

Dr. Trevor Arnett, President of the General Education Board, as well as the Spelman Board of Trustees, spoke out of a friendship of many years and after paying tribute to Mr. Hope's personal traits said:

"The extraordinary development which Atlanta University has had under Dr. Hope's guidance and direction has astonished and gratified his friends and has far surpassed their highest expectations. He has laid secure foundations of an institution in the South, on which can be built an edifice at which the Negro can obtain higher education comparable to that obtainable in any other part of the country. His accomplishments entitle him to a foremost place among educational statesmen. . . ."

Dr. Frederick P. Keppel, president of the Carnegie Corporation, spoke of his long friendship with Mr. Hope and his high regard for him as an educator and a man, and then said "From the nature of my business, I think I can claim some right to an opinion about college presidents, and when I put John Hope, as I do, at the top rank, I think I know what I am talking about."

At the colleges and the university, the routine of classes, faculty meetings, committee meetings, convocations, examinations, calendar events went on as usual. The Baccalaureate speaker, Dr. John Haynes Holmes, had accepted an invitation from Dr. Hope about a year earlier. He made a special trip all the way from Kennebunkport, Maine, to Atlanta to fill the engagement. His account of his experience at the Joint Service of Spelman, Morehouse, and Atlanta University and of this visit to Atlanta, published in *Unity* (printed in Chicago) under the title "An Excursion into the Southland," bears re-reading for its insight and atmosphere.

In July 1936, the National Association of Teachers in Colored Schools and the National Congress of Colored Parents and

Teachers met on the campuses of the affiliated schools. On the opening evening in Sisters Chapel, Miss Read, as acting-president of Atlanta University presided; and presented the gavel to the President of the National Association, Dr. Rufus E. Clement, who then delivered the annual address. Dr. Hope had been president of the Association in 1916; and had invited the body to hold their 1936 meeting at Atlanta University.

In the year, 1936-37, there was a slight increase in the university enrollment from the Atlanta colleges, and in the total enrollment. The number of colleges represented in the enrollment continued to increase.

The faculty was strengthened by the coming as Professor of French of Mercer Cook, A.B. Amherst, Ph.D. Brown University; and as Professor of Sociology, of Ira deA. Reid, A.B. Morehouse, Ph.D. Columbia University, appointments which had been made by President Hope.

In December 1936, the university community profited by a week's visit of Dr. Charles Henry Rieber, Professor emeritus of Philosophy of the University of California and for 15 years dean of its College of Arts and Letters.

In January 1937, Dr. Walter Bartky, Associate Professor of Astronomy at the University of Chicago, brought three amazingly effective motion picture films, prepared under his direction and released only two days before. The showing in Howe Hall was the third public exhibition of the films. "The World in Motion" gave a vivid representation of the movement of the earth in its great orbit around the sun; the second film "The Moon" showed "close-up" pictures of the face of the moon during periods of waxing and waning; the third film, "The Solar Family" showed intricate movements of the planets in their courses; and also pictures of a total eclipse of the sun as viewed at Fryeburg, Maine.

The number of Master's degrees conferred in June 1936 was 23 (to 16 women and 7 men) in nine departments; the number conferred in June 1937 was 48 in nine departments (to 28 women and 20 men). Four of the 16 women who received the Master's degree in 1936, and 10 of the 28 women in 1937 were Spelman College graduates. Master's degrees had been conferred on 141 students in the period 1931-37; 69 were men, 72 were women. Of the 72 women, 20 were graduates of Spelman College.

The Six Year Program (q.v. in Appendix) projected in 1930 had been fulfilled to a much greater degree than could have been anticipated by the most optimistic. The estimated number of teachers needed for the University faculty in addition to professors on the faculties of Morehouse College and Spelman College had been realized.

Cooperative relationships among Atlanta institutions of higher learning had been increasingly developed from year to year. Frequent meetings of the presidents and discussions on matters of common concern had brought about a mutual confidence that augured well for the future. Cooperation with Morris Brown College in the way of exchanges of teachers and students had increased. Arrangements for bringing Clark College into closer relationship, even to the point of their moving to a site adjacent to Atlanta University and Spelman College had made progress. The material development of the University as to buildings and endowment had taken place to an extent that seems a miracle to those who in 1929 took the step of affiliating.

The Summer School

The Summer School, which had been started by Morehouse College in 1921, was reorganized in 1928 as the Morehouse-Spelman Summer School and conducted jointly by the two institutions. Atlanta University became affiliated in 1928, and the Atlanta School of Social Work in 1929. With increasing cooperation among the Atlanta institutions, centering in Atlanta University, the Summer School since 1933 has been conducted by Atlanta University, with Morehouse College, Spelman College, Clark College, Morris Brown College, and Gammon Theological Seminary affiliated. In 1932, for the first time graduate courses were offered. In that year, 14 men and 22 women registered for graduate courses.

The last day President Hope was in his office, February 13, 1936, he was working on plans for the 1936 Summer School. It was, therefore, particularly gratifying to have an unusually successful Summer School that year. The total enrollment was 630, the largest to date. Of that number, 327 (51.9%) already were college graduates; and 225 registered for graduate courses, 104 men and 121 women. They came from 85 institutions.

There were in attendance at the 1936 summer school 107 principals of schools and 30 school supervisors. Five young Negro physicians (men) were sent by the state of North Carolina to take the course in Child Development and Behavior Problems offered in connection with the Nursery School, by its director, Miss Pearlie Reed.

Special features were: the French Institute; the Library Institute; the Summer Theater; the Rural Institute; an Interdenominational Ministers Institute; a Progressive Education Demonstration School; and a One-Teacher Rural School.

The 1937 Summer School ran from June 14 to July 23. During the six weeks' session, 758 men and women carried on college and graduate work; 265 were registered as graduate students and 493 in courses which earned college credit. They came from 22 states, the District of Columbia and the Virgin Islands; and represented 96 schools and colleges.

Again featured were a school for teacher-librarians; the institute for teachers of French; the curriculum laboratory; the rural institute. Offered for the first time for credit in summer were courses in acting, directing, speech and in the allied arts of the theater. These courses were of wide-spread interest to teachers who might be called on to direct the dramatics in their school or college. A new extra-curricular feature was a weekly open forum over which Professor Ira DeA. Reid presided.

The able and devoted director of the Summer School through these years was John P. Whittaker, registrar of Atlanta University and Morehouse College. From 1928 through 1940, Spelman College conducted the boarding department for the Summer Session. Most of the classrooms were on the Spelman campus during that period, and until Dean Sage Hall was built by the University in 1952. Giles Hall has continued to be in demand – and is especially favored because its rooms are cooler. The laboratory courses were, and are still, mostly held in the Morehouse College science buildings.

New University President

Dr. Rufus Early Clement, dean of the Louisville Municipal College for Negroes, was unanimously elected the second president of the Atlanta University system by the Board of Trustees of Atlanta University, at the annual meeting held on April 24, 1937. Dr. Clement is a graduate of Livingstone College, holds the degrees of Bachelor of Divinity from Garrett Biblical Institute, Master of Arts and Doctor of Philosophy from Northwestern University. He had served as professor of history and as dean at Livingstone College, before becoming Dean of the Municipal College in Louisville. He took over the active duties of the Atlanta University presidency on July 1, 1937.

Atlanta University continues to grow under his leadership. Not only have plans initiated or proposed by his predecessor come to fruition, but progress in the development of the University has constantly been pursued with persistence and wisdom. It is pertinent also to report here, as a striking comment on progress in race relations, that Dr. Clement was in 1953 elected a member of the Board of Education of the city of Atlanta, in a city-wide election; and he was re-elected in 1957 for a second four-year term.

By the terms of the Affiliation Agreement, the president of Atlanta University is *ex officio* a member of the Spelman College Board of Trustees. Dr. Clement has, through the years, been a most helpful member of the Board of Trustees, and most helpful as a colleague.

The pattern of cooperation between the colleges and the University was set in the first years of the affiliation, and has been continued, with changes in details. There may be fewer words given to the University hereafter in this history, but the fact remains that the life of Spelman College and the life of Atlanta University are closely interwoven. While this is especially apparent with reference to exchanges of students and teachers, use of the library, enjoyment of speakers, plays and musical events, the fundamental relationship goes deeper than these more or less superficial expressions.

During and after World War II, the high schools from which the students came had been afflicted with many changes of teachers, and the preparation of the students was poorer. In fact, the reading level, even of some students who had been valedictorians and salutatorians in their high school classes, was incredibly low. The weakness in reading ability which still prevails in pupils across the nation showed up earliest in institutions whose students came mainly from the Southern States. The standard of public education in the South was considerably lower than the national standard in virtually every category: length of the school year; average attendance; preparation of teachers; salaries of teachers; size of classes; equipment. This was true of schools for white children; and the support of Negro schools was far behind the support of white schools. Studies of nine Southern States in 1940 showed that more than three times as many dollars were spent per white child in public schools as per Negro child.[1]

Spelman College was a pioneer in providing specially trained personnel to help students who were weak in ability to read. Miss Georgia Cowen (now Mrs. Poole) was appointed to the Spelman faculty in 1937. She had done graduate work related to the teaching of reading at the University of Chicago and, what is more important, was a singularly gifted and effective

[1] *Brown Americans* (1943) by Edwin R. Embree: "Average annual expenditure of $58.69 per capita for whites and only $18.82 for Negroes." The average expenditure per pupil throughout the United States as a whole in 1940 was $88.09.

teacher. She inspired several undergraduate students at Spelman to specialize in this field; two of them, Lynette Saine, Spelman '41, and Geraldine Clark, Spelman '43, later earned degrees of Doctor of Philosophy from the University of Chicago.

Constant effort brought some good results, but the problem of adequate preparation for college work will remain a problem for years to come.

After new admission procedures were worked out by Spelman College, Morehouse College and Fisk University and proved helpful, a more comprehensive plan was initiated and put into operation in 1952. In that year, Spelman College joined with 12 other members of the United Negro College Fund group in conducting examinations in 81 centers in all the eastern states and as far west as San Antonio, Texas, to determine entrance to these various colleges, and eligibility for scholarship awards. The American Council on Education Psychological Test and a Cooperative Test for reading ability were administered. These tests came from and were scored by the Educational Testing Service, Princeton, New Jersey. In all the centers, a total of 236 named Spelman as the college of first choice in making application for the examination; and of 263 students (girls *and* boys) who took the Cooperative Intercollegiate Examination in Atlanta, 98 girls selected Spelman College as their first choice.

In her annual report to the Board of Trustees made after 20 years of service, the President reasserted the aims of the College and reviewed the values which must be constantly emphasized. After a preliminary statement, the report reads:

"We believe in the liberal arts college. We believe that the liberal arts studies tend to give students 'a deeper, broader, better-ventilated and better lighted inner life.' We agree with President J. Edgar Park of Wheaton College, who said on his retirement from that Massachusetts woman's college that a person who has some knowledge and appreciation of art, music, literature, languages, theoretical science, philosophy, history, is more likely – say, in a 10-year period – to grow, deepen, and

PLATE XXV

President Dwight D. Eisenhower, Frederick Douglass Patterson and
John D. Rockefeller III at United Negro College Fund Tenth Anniversary Luncheon

The six presidents of the Atlanta University Center

Aerial View of the Campus

PLATE XXVIII

Some Spelman College Trustees

Mrs. Jane Hope Lyons regards the bust of her brother, John Hope

become more valuable in any position in life. . . . He asserted also that students should have the opportunity to try out their theoretical knowledge in practice.

"As the Spelman catalogue states it: – 'Knowledge must be lighted with imagination if the student is to relate her learning to the facts and realities of life. Added knowledge should go hand in hand with practical application of knowledge; straight courageous thinking with honesty, clean living, thorough-going mastery of the task in hand, kindness and helpfulness to one's neighbors. . . .' "

There followed a quotation from the book, *Liberal Education Re-examined*, written mainly by Dr. Theodore M. Greene, then professor at Princeton University: "The essential difference between education and training is simple and basic. *Education* is designed to prepare men to do what they have never done before. Its emphasis is upon power to adapt oneself and go on alone. *Training* seeks to supply the skills and techniques to do again and again what has once been learned."

"Notwithstanding that there is today," the Spelman President pointed out, "less willing obedience to authority, – parental, academic, civic or military; less awareness of the need of competence, thoroughness and effort; less recognition of the role of toil and sweat in human progress; more of wanting something for nothing, the task of the college remains to create a longing for *excellence* as over against mediocrity; to develop maturity; to encourage self-discipline; to waken a sense of responsibility and an eagerness to do and be their best. . . ." Happily it could be reported that Spelman students for the most part were responsive to *the first rate*, to use an expression given them by Sir Richard Livingstone of Oxford University.

Evidence that the aims of the College sometimes "worked," like vaccination, would occasionally appear unexpectedly as in the following incident.

"Why do you wish to come to Spelman College?" is one of the questions on the application blank filled by every student who applies for admission. Frequently the answer gives a clue to the student's interests, even to her "readiness" for college. One high-school senior wrote in reply to the question, under the date of March 22, 1948:

"My interest in your school was first aroused when I as a little girl noticed the change that came over my sister while she was a student there. She assumed a quiet dignity along with a rugged determination. Ever since that time, having come in contact with other alumnae of your college, I have sensed that there was some inner quality that characterized them and set them apart from others. This characteristic coupled with a desire to master subject matter because of your splendid faculty and curriculum offered are the determining factors which point Spelman out to me. . . ."

A constant and compelling influence in the lives of Spelman students for much of this period was Dean Jane Hope Lyons. Quiet and observant, possessed of high intelligence, a fine sense of humor, and an unselfish attitude to life, she was quick to detect the signs when any student, because of personal, family or other difficulties, was uneasy or not at her best. With sympathy and firmness, wisdom and common sense, she met the need for counsel or incited new impetus and encouragement.

A significant evidence of achievement came from the academic rating given by the Association of American Universities. At its annual meeting in December, 1947, the Association of American Universities voted to place the names of Spelman College, Morehouse College and Atlanta University on the list of approved institutions whose qualified graduates are admitted to graduate schools of the Association. This was the highest accreditation possible for an educational institution to receive in this country.

The Association of American Universities is an organization of graduate schools. Before including a college or university on its approved list, a committee of the Association examines the character and quality of the student body; the faculty and the conditions under which it works; the administration of the institution; its library, laboratories and educational facilities; its curriculum and its character as an institution, and the scholarly achievements of its graduates. There are seven institutions for the higher education of Negroes on the approved list of the Association of American Universities. Besides Spelman College, Morehouse College, and Atlanta University, there are Howard, Fisk, Talladega, and North Carolina College for Negroes.

While the rating is gratifying, it could bring no complacency. New England college sophomores had higher standing on the tests applied. The examining committee said Spelman and Morehouse students at entrance were less well-qualified but that the teachers accomplish better results, really, considering the low admission quality, surprisingly good results, from the four years of college work.

———

Speakers at the University convocations, the morning chapel services, the annual anniversary exercises of Founders Day, Baccalaureate and Commencement, are a line of communication between the campuses and the life of action and life of thought in the world today. Students and teachers alike are stimulated and even educated by them. Gratitude is given to Ralph McGill, editor of *The Atlanta Constitution,* for sharing with the College many guests from abroad who were sent to him after World War II by the U.S. Department of State. It was mainly the speakers, although occasionally also visitors who did not talk in public, who remained for a week or a day, or even for a meal, who made possible the atmosphere of a liberal arts college.

Among men concerned with the public weal, who could rightly be called Christian statesmen, it was inspiring to hear:

Ralph Bunche, Director of the Department of Trusteeship, later Under-Secretary of the United Nations

William B. Hartsfield, Mayor of Atlanta since 1937, re-elected in 1957 for an unprecedented fifth term

E. Stanley Jones, Missionary-statesman in India, and in the church ecumenical movement

Frank C. Laubach of "each-one-teach-one" fame; co-author of

more than 200 primers for illiterate adults in over 165 languages in 51 countries

Robert J. McCracken, Minister of the Riverside Church

Pastor Martin Niemoeller of Germany

Among distinguished philosophers and scientists were:

Arthur H. Compton, professor of physics and Nobel Prize win-
ner

Theodore M. Greene, professor of philosophy, Princeton University, later Yale University

William Ernest Hocking, professor of philosophy, Harvard
University

Doublas V. Steere, professor of philosophy, Haverford College

T. V. Smith, professor of political science, University of Chicago

Elton Trueblood, professor of philosophy, Earlham College

Among well-known authors who gave talks in these years,
should be mentioned:

Sterling Brown, of *Negro Caravan* fame

Mary Ellen Chase, novelist, educator, author of *Abby Aldrich
Rockefeller*

Douglas S. Freeman, author, editor, *The News Leader*, Richmond, Va.

Ralph McGill, editor of *The Atlanta Constitution*, and author

Vladimir Nabokov, poet and novelist (an inspiring visitor for
six days)

Kurt Singer, editor of underground weekly, author of *3000
Years of Espionage*

Ridgely Torrence, playwright, poet, and author of *The Story
of John Hope*

Walter White, secretary of the NAACP, author of *Rope and
Faggot; A Man Called White.*

And poets: Langston Hughes, Wilbert Snow, Stephen Spender,
and Louis Untermeyer.

Other speakers, difficult to classify, several of whom came more than once, are:

Ely Culbertson, who pleaded for his peace plan which included a United Nations police force made up of nationals not from the Big Four or Big Five. He advocated much the same sort of force as was created in the Suez crisis.

Grace Sloan Overton, whose talks on marriage and human relations reached all the students from '30 through '51.

Anauta, whose description of life in Baffinland was an excellent introduction to the study of sociology

Sherwood Eddy, ex-secretary for Asia of the YMCA

Sir Hubert Wilkins, who, on five occasions in different years, inducted the community into the life of the Arctic, the Antarctic, and Australia.

The interest of ministers in the outgrowth of the home mission schools can be taken for granted. The full list of preachers who have spoken at Spelman in Sisters Chapel from 1927-53, is extensive and impressive. Approximately half of the Sunday afternoon vesper service preachers were white ministers, mainly from Atlanta. They were men who believed in the brotherhood of man as well as the fatherhood of God. They came from Emory University, Columbia Theological Seminary, and churches of various denominations, – Baptist, Methodist, Presbyterian, Congregational, Episcopalian, Lutheran, Unitarian. Many other ministers of both races, mainly outside of Atlanta, spoke at morning chapel services or at university convocations. Some of the most inspiring talks came from men not nationally known. A few among many clergymen of distinction who were heard are listed in the Appendix.

The Atlanta colleges and universities for white students in the main showed a friendly attitude to the administrative officers and to the idea of the colleges for Negroes. But there was little communication between the members of the faculties. The teachers without regard to race – Spelman had always an interracial faculty from 1887 – were professionally isolated. That a Negro teacher could draw a book from the Atlanta main library only through a white member of the faculty, indicates one measure of isolation.[1]

Even the Atlanta branch of the *Alliance française* did not admit Negro teachers of French, so our white teachers of French refrained from attending the meetings. The situation varied with different professional groups. On the whole, the groups made up in the main of men were more liberal, *e.g.*, the teachers of science. The social scientists, too, and they occasionally invited a Negro professor to speak. Because of the pattern of segregation, visitors from the academic world were important. A distinguished list of college and university presidents and deans who blessed us by their visits will be found in the Appendix.

Geographical Distribution of Students

The geographical distribution of students has been compiled from year to year almost from the beginning. As college work developed, it was accepted as desirable that Spelman become a regional institution, and not a local college in its composition.

In the last 20 years, the relative number of students from other states has increased, but the enrollment has not yet reached the optimum proportion. In 1934, 66% of the students came from Georgia; in 1943 – 49%; in 1952 – 57%, which is the highest with one exception for the 10 previous years. For seven years of this period for which data are available, more than half the students have come from other states.

Study of the University Center

A study of cooperation in the Atlanta University Center was made in 1946 by a Survey Committee made up of Donald J. Cowling, president of Carleton College from 1909-45; J. Curtis

---

[1] A new dispensation has been in effect since May 20, 1959. The Atlanta public library system is no longer segregated. Henceforth Negro patrons are to be served in the downtown library and in 14 white branches, as well as in the three Negro branches.

Dixon, vice-president of the Southern Education Foundation;[1] Charles H. Thompson, Dean of the Graduate School of Howard University; and Malcolm W. Wallace, Principal from 1928-44 of University College, University of Toronto. The survey was made possible by a grant of funds from the General Education Board; and the persons above-named were invited to make the study by President Clement, acting in behalf of the seven private institutions for the education of Negroes in Atlanta. A fifth member was invited to be a member of the Survey Committee but was unable to serve.

The report of the Survey, entitled *A Study of Cooperation in the Atlanta University Center*, first submitted under date of December 1, 1946, and revised December 27, 1947, is available in bound mimeographed form, 150 pages long. No adequate summary can be presented here; but a few items especially significant to Spelman College are noted.

The Committee first stated "that considerable distance in cooperation has already been travelled. . . . There are few if any groups of higher educational institutions in the country which have gone as far as these institutions in voluntary co-operation." It conceived its primary task to be to study further the effectiveness of the present cooperative endeavors; to suggest how they might be made more effective; and to recommend new areas and ways by which further cooperation may be achieved.

The Committee, from the start, acted on the basic assumption that the University Center exists for the purpose of providing the highest possible training for Negro youth selected on the basis of good minds, excellent preparation, and high promise; and that the success of the institutions in the Center would be determined by the *quality* rather than the quantity of their output.

The Committee found "that the library resources of the affiliation are *very good* in comparison with white Southern *college*

[1] Previously when vice-chancellor of the University System of Georgia, he had been fired by Gov. Eugene Talmadge; he then became vice-president of Mercer University, and later the chief administrative officer of the Southern Education Foundation.

libraries, but they are considerably below the holdings of the best *college* libraries in the East."

The Committee recommended "that the several undergraduate colleges should rigidly limit their enrollments to 500 students each." This is the number of students for whom Spelman College has aimed to provide adequate resources in buildings, equipment and teaching staff.

The Committee noted that in 1934, 62% of Spelman students came from Georgia; in 1944, 46% came from Georgia (28% of these from Atlanta): and advised Spelman to increase the percentage of students from outside the region.

Regarding physical needs, the Committee recommended "that a Fine Arts Building, to be owned and administered by Spelman, should be constructed for the use of all of the institutions. . . ." There was mention also of the gymnasium and additional dormitory needed by Spelman: these have already been provided.

The above items have special pertinence to Spelman. Many recommendations were applicable to all four undergraduate colleges. For example, those regarding standards of admission requirements and their administration, exchanges of students, departmental cooperation between colleges. Additional income for faculty salaries was emphasized as the most pressing need.

One of the most fruitful gains from the Survey came from the necessity it imposed on each president to look up from immediately pressing problems of administration and give concentrated attention to values in length and depth.

A survey of organization and administrative operations of the Atlanta University Center, made in 1952 by Cresap, McCormick and Paget, Management Consultants, was more in the nature of an efficiency study, with recommendations for individual improvement of the colleges and of Atlanta University. The cost of the Survey was provided by the [Ford] Fund for the Advancement of Education. In addition to formalizing certain of the cooperative relationships among the several institutions, and promoting more uniformity, the recommendations were mainly concerned with questions of fiscal and business activities, use of buildings, plant resources and plant needs, and overall business management.

This report again showed clearly the importance of the whole educational venture in Atlanta, and indicated belief in its growing potential and usefulness.

Financial Support

Financial support for the strengthened program of Spelman College was made possible in large part by another development, which again blazed a new trail, this time in college financing. Most private colleges were pinched for funds during and after World War II. The colleges for Negroes were specially hard hit. They had during the years of their history received donations from friends in the North, but the list of annual givers had, with time, been steadily diminishing. The new generation had not the same acquaintance with, or interest in, the cause of Negro education. The income from tuition and fees was necessarily small. Something had to be done. In January, 1943, Dr. Frederick D. Patterson, President of Tuskegee Institute, proposed a possible plan for a united drive for operating funds for some of the Negro colleges. At first, it was regarded skeptically by many persons concerned as it required that each institution give up its separate annual campaign and agree to pool the names of annual donors.

Spelman College was among the first to endorse the proposed plan, and was represented by its president at the meetings for discussion, planning, and organization. It was early decided that all the colleges for Negroes on the accredited list of the Southern Association of Colleges (or the North Central Association) should be invited to join in the plan. After a meeting in Atlanta on September 27, 1943, 27 colleges agreed to ally themselves formally in a chartered corporation and to begin the first annual campaign in May, 1944.

A certificate of incorporation for the *United Negro College Fund* was obtained from New York State in April 1944; the organization meeting was held on May 18, 1944. The Board

329

of Directors held its first meeting in Atlanta on June 27, 1944. The institutions themselves were the members of the corporation; the presidents of the institutions plus five directors-at-large comprised the Board of Directors. Dr. Frederick D. Patterson was elected President of the Board of Directors; and also Chairman of the Executive Committee of 13 members.

Plans for the first campaign went steadily forward. The goal was $1,500,000; the budget not to exceed $100,000, half of which the member colleges agreed to pay. The other half was assured by the General Education Board and the Julius Rosenwald Fund. A formula for the distribution of the money raised was adopted by the member colleges. The John Price Jones Corporation, which had had experience in raising endowment funds for three of the member institutions, was employed. Paul Franklin, vice-president of the John Price Jones Corporation, organized the first campaign. William J. Trent, Jr., a graduate of Livingstone College, was employed as Executive Secretary and soon became the Executive Director of the Fund, which post he still holds.

The formula for the distribution of the money raised in the annual campaigns since 1948 has been: 45% divided equally; 45% based on the previous five-year average income from endowment, gifts and grants; and 10% based on the five-year enrollment. Enrollment was not considered in the first two distributions. Each president agreed to spend 30 days in campaign work. The city assigned to Spelman College in 1944, and for the nine succeeding campaigns, with one exception, was Cleveland. In the 1944 campaign, Cleveland ranked fifth in the amount raised, following New York, Chicago, Philadelphia, and Pittsburgh; but it did not always hold so high a place.

The National Campaign Fund Chairman for the first campaign was Walter Hoving; the National Treasurer, Winthrop W. Aldrich; and the Chairman of the National Campaign Advisory Committee was John D. Rockefeller, Jr. The total fund raised in the 1944 campaign was $765,562.63. Spelman's share was $35,350.74. The total amount received by Spelman College in the ten annual campaigns from 1944 through 1953, was $365,037.72.

Mr. Rockefeller's support, moral and practical, was the *sine qua non* of the success of the first and succeeding campaigns. He stated publicly on March 8, 1944: "All my life and during the lifetime of my father before me, our family has had a profound interest in Negro education . . ." and on May 26, 1944 in a network radio broadcast, he said: "I want to express my appreciation for the opportunity and honor of being related to this enterprise. When it comes to a question of interest in the twenty-seven institutions that are here represented and all they stand for, I take second place to no man."

The enlistment of many men and women of prominence as sponsors was possible only because of Mr. Rockefeller's endorsement. He knew whereof he spoke; others who followed his lead have become enthusiastic and active supporters of the campaigns. But "none of these can parallel the contribution made by Mr. John D. Rockefeller, Jr.," states the unpublished "History of the United Negro College Fund."

The annual UNCF campaign provides approximately 10% of the minimum budget requirement of the member institutions. But the colleges had other imperative needs, – for new buildings, major repairs to old ones, and plant improvements, in general. Some feared that a proposed Capital Funds Campaign might interfere with the annual campaigns for operating expenses. After long study and discussion, however, a campaign plan was approved in 1951 for the National Mobilization of Resources of the United Negro Colleges. The goal set was $25,000,000.

In November, 1952, Spelman College was one of seven member colleges in the UNCF, six of them in Atlanta, to be visited by a very distinguished party of men concerned with the Capital Funds campaign. The trip to Atlanta was made by private planes scheduled to start simultaneously from New York, Chicago, Pittsburgh, and Akron. The hosts for the air were respectively Winthrop W. Aldrich, Chairman of the Chase National Bank; Robert E. Wilson, Chairman of the Standard Oil Company of

Indiana; Richard K. Mellon, Chairman of the Mellon National Bank; Harvey S. Firestone, Chairman of the Firestone Tire and Rubber Company. On leaving Atlanta, Robert W. Woodruff, Chairman of the Executive Committee of the Coca Cola Company, was host at a dinner served aboard a private train en route to Tuskegee Institute.

The New York group included Devereux C. Josephs, President of the New York Life Insurance Company; John D. Rockefeller III, President of the Rockefeller Brothers Fund; Samuel D. Leidesdorf, Partner, S. D. Leidesdorf and Company; Charles Dollard, President of the Carnegie Corporation. With Dr. Wilson from Chicago were Harold H. Swift, Chairman of Swift and Company; Charles Bryan, Jr., President of the Pullman Standard Car Company. Mr. Mellon's Pittsburgh party included A. W. Robertson, Chairman of the Finance Committee, Westinghouse Electric Corporation; A. V. Murray, President of the Scaife Company; B. Homer Hall, Director of the Sarah Mellon Scaife Foundation. And with Harvey Firestone was his brother, Raymond C. Firestone, vice-president of the Firestone Tire and Rubber Company. A complete list was published in the *Spelman Messenger*, November, 1952.

The guests were met at the Atlanta airport by the presidents and trustees of the Atlanta group and by President Patterson. They were taken to Atlanta University for a brief introduction and then to luncheon before starting on a trip to each college in the Atlanta group. The president of each college acted as host during the visit to his institution.

At a convocation held in Sisters Chapel at Spelman College each member of the party was presented to the audience by President Rufus E. Clement of Atlanta University. Harvey Firestone, Jr., responded in behalf of the visitors.

Sisters Chapel was filled to overflowing, – students, members of the faculties, trustees, and citizens from Atlanta, with as many persons standing as the chapel would hold. The whole congregation sang *Gaudeamus Igitur*; a Negro jubilee, *Ride*

On, King Jesus, and for a closing number, *Lift Every Voice and Sing*. Interspersed in the program were other musical numbers which included a duet from Clark College, a sextette from Morris Brown College, and two numbers, one a Christmas spiritual, from the 100-voice Atlanta-Morehouse-Spelman Chorus.

The visitors were impressed with what they saw and heard. They spoke especially of the singing of the students, and of the general atmosphere which was a mixture of good-will and earnestness and lively interest. Such a first-hand acquaintance with colleges for Negroes undoubtedly helped forward the Capital Funds campaign. The visit aroused interest on the part of Atlanta, as was shown by the front-page headlines, interviews, and pictures printed in the *Atlanta Constitution* and the *Atlanta Journal*, with editorials in both papers. The trip was, of course, well covered in the *Atlanta Daily World*, a Negro newspaper, but the unprecedented space given by the other newspapers was enlightening to thousands of Atlanta citizens previously unaware of the importance or even existence of the Atlanta University Center.

The goal of $25,000,000 was not fully reached, but the amount raised was inspiring. When the campaign was concluded, the total in cash and pledges was $17,903,817. By June 30, 1953, Spelman College had received $328,520, in capital funds, a sum which was held untouched at the end of that fiscal year with the expectation that it would be used toward the item for which the trustees had previously voted priority in building needs, – namely, a Fine Arts Building. As of January 31, 1955, the amount received by Spelman College was $453,440; and by 1958 the total sum received was $479,948.

To celebrate the tenth anniversary of the founding of the United Negro College Fund, a luncheon was held in Washington, D.C. on May 19, 1953.

The President of the United States, the Honorable Dwight D. Eisenhower, addressed the luncheon guests on the subject

"A Case of Private Initiative." Also on this occasion, Dr. Patterson, in behalf of the Fund, presented a citation of appreciation to the General Education Board for its service to Negro education. The award was accepted by John D. Rockefeller III, Chairman of the General Education Board. The statement by President Eisenhower, together with the remarks of Dr. Patterson and Mr. Rockefeller III, may be read in a booklet later published by the Fund. This event was attended by "a formidable array of great and famous people" including most of the members of the President's Cabinet and other leaders of business and the professions.

The United Negro College Fund has significance in the history of colleges in America, as well as in the history of Spelman College, because of its *firsts*. It was (1) a pioneer in cooperative solicitation and the idea has since been copied by groups of colleges in the North; and (2) it was a pioneer in seeking operating funds from business and corporations. The gifts of corporations to colleges is now commonplace. In 1944, it was virtually a new idea to which stockholders and officers alike had in most cases to be converted.

The appeal for national support of the Negro colleges was based on their financial needs; what the money given does for them; what the colleges do for their students and for the country.

A study made by Charles S. Johnson in 1937 of *The Negro College Graduate* cites the following:

Number of Negroes who received the bachelor's degree between 1914 and 1936:

from Negro colleges	21,000	
from Northern colleges	3,500	24,500

85% of Negro college teachers	were products of the private Negro colleges
95% of Negro ministers	
83% of Negro physicians and dentists	
86% of Negro lawyers	

In 1940, according to the U.S. Office of Education, 5,700 Negroes, and in 1950, 13,100 Negroes received the bachelor's degree. Facts like these gave weight to the appeal.

In an address at the opening of the 1950 UNCF campaign, Dr. Ira DeA. Reid said, "Thanks to the Negro college, we have in the United States, the most highly literate mass of colored peoples in the world...."

CHAPTER XXI

THE SEVENTIETH ANNIVERSARY YEAR

FOUNDERS DAY 1951 was a memorable occasion. The seventieth anniversary compelled a thoughtful appraisal of the miracles of the past, – Miss Packard, Miss Giles, Miss Upton, the debt owed to them; the teachers who joined them; their convictions and their moral stamina; the pattern they set; the friends they made: to all of these was tribute paid. It had been just 67 years since Mr. John D. Rockefeller and his wife, Laura Spelman Rockefeller, her mother, Mrs. Spelman, and her sister, Miss Lucy Spelman, and two children of the Rockefeller family had made a visit to Union Hall and the barracks; a visit to a campus without proper drives or walks, and without a single brick building, with only a few board walks on land that was mostly mud.

By contrast, on April 11, 1951, the campus and ivy-covered buildings were most inviting. The sun was shining, the grass was green, the trees bore their new spring foliage, the azaleas were in bloom. Not only did the dozen brick buildings known and loved by the students who had entered in the past quarter century look scrubbed and in good order, but the walls of the new gymnasium were rising fast. For every one of these, the College was indebted, in part or in whole, to the Rockefeller-Spelman family directly, or through the General Education Board. Several of the gifts to the Gymnasium Fund came from the fourth generation of the family, though the major cost of that building came from other sources.

The dearth of opportunities for recreation for Negro girls and boys in the South can be comprehended only by persons, north and south, who know and think about the parks and playgrounds, beaches and swimming pools, eating places and recreation centers closed to Negroes. On one occasion, the President of Spelman spoke with utter disparagement of a cafe which a few students were disciplined for patronizing; she said finally

PLATE XXIX

Africa

The New Jerusalem Temple, Nyasaland

Convention of women meets at Temple in 1959

Flora Zeto Malekebu

Dr. Daniel Malekebu

PLATE XXX

Nora Gordon   Clara Howard   Emma Delany

Mrs. Horton's School in Monrovia

Spelman Reading Room,
Brewerville, Liberia

Spelman Hall, Chiradzulu, Nyasaland

that any student should have known better than to enter it from the look of it outside. A young member of the faculty who was a Spelman graduate stopped by the office the next day, and said: "You mustn't be too hard on the girls, Miss Read, for not being discriminating. The only places in most towns or cities where colored people can go look as bad as that."

The need of wholesome recreation made it imperative that Spelman students have better provision for physical exercise, games and sports, – that they learn to play, and have a chance to learn to swim. At the urgent request of the President, the Board of Trustees voted in November, 1949, to go ahead with plans to build a gymnasium. The alumnae and the students, the faculty and their friends, continued with renewed enthusiasm the campaign they had begun in 1946 to raise as much money as they could to build one. The action of the trustees created new impetus. The rally on the following Founders Day was the best ever. The students themselves turned in over $2,000. If only you could have seen and heard them, you would have formed a new definition of hilarious giving. The faculty and staff gave that day over $1,200. The project seemed sure to succeed now that the trustees officially were behind it.

Miss Pauline Kline, who was secretary to President Read for several years and who earlier served in the office of President Hope of Atlanta University – nearly eight years in the two offices – died in Belmont, Massachusetts, on November 12, 1949. In a talk with her sister during the last week of her life, she suggested that she would be pleased if any of her friends who wished to do something for her made a gift instead to the Spelman College Gymnasium Fund. In response to her wishes, the College soon received over $600 from Miss Kline's friends around Boston. The President of the Spelman board designated his gift of $1,000 to the memorial for Miss Kline, as did many other friends. The lounge was furnished and later dedicated in her honor.

On the morning of Founders Day, 1950, a letter came from Cincinnati from the Spelman mother of a student who should have completed her work in June, 1949, enclosing a gift to purchase a drinking fountain in the new gymnasium as a memorial to her daughter, Harriette *Brown* Frazier, who had died in April, 1949. The letter enclosed a $100 bill.

The first gift of $1,000 to Spelman from an alumna was made to the Gymnasium Fund in 1950 by Mrs. Blanche Perdue Mitchell of Birmingham. The second alumnae gift of $1,000 came from Mrs. Sadye Harris Powell. In addition to gifts from many individual alumnae, the Spelman College Alumnae Association contributed from its Loyalty Fund the sum of $5,000.

Several memorial gifts were made to the Gymnasium Fund in honor of Mrs. Trevor Arnett who died on July 18, 1950; Spelman College was a beneficiary under her will. For 25 years she was a welcome visitor to the campus and always took a lively interest in the activities of Spelman students. The attractive room on the northeast corner of the second floor equipped for table games, was designated in her honor as the Bertha Stetson Arnett room. A bronze plaque bears her name.

After their class day exercises on June 3, 1950, the seniors extended their march to the site selected for the building. Surrounded by alumnae, faculty and other guests, ground was broken for the long-looked-for gymnasium. The cornerstone was laid on November 5, 1950, with appropriate ceremony by the Prince Hall Lodge, Free and Accepted Masons, jurisdiction of Georgia, John Wesley Dobbs, Grand Master. The program was participated in also by Dr. John Curtis Dixon, Spelman trustee, Executive Director of the Southern Education Foundation, and Mrs. Julia Pate Borders, President of the Spelman Alumnae Association. Gratitude was expressed to all who had shared in bringing the project to its present fulfilment, including John D. Rockefeller, Jr. whose gift purchased the land; Colonel Mose Cox who had charge of the Highway Development bordering the college property on the south; the Mayor and the City Council who acceded to Spelman's request for the closing of Ella Street; the architect, the contractors, and the workers – all.

Mr. John D. Rockefeller, Jr., had in the thirties made possible the purchase of the land south of Ella Street. Long-range efforts begun in 1930 looking to eventual closing of Ella Street where it bordered the Spelman campus had been brought to a successful conclusion, with the new throughway made the southern boundary of the campus. The Gymnasium was located south of Sisters Chapel and at a reasonable distance which did not prevent the chapel windows from being glorified by sunlight during the morning chapel services.

The dedication of the Gymnasium took place on December 6, 1951. A panel discussion in Howe Memorial Hall in the morning on the theme "Today's Challenge for Fitness" was followed in the afternoon by exercises in the building itself when the keys of the building were turned over by Otis A. Barge, representing the architect and builders, including the workmen, to Trevor Arnett, chairman of the Board of Trustees. The students, by classes, read in unison a specially prepared litany which concluded the ceremony.

The building is complete and completely functional in operation. It also has beauty in its interior arrangements which makes the use of it pleasing to the eye as well as inviting to muscle and skill. It serves admirably as a center of health, recreation, and community life.

The students took an opportunity on the first-Founders-Day-after-Occupation-of-the-Gymnasium to demonstrate in appropriate costume Spelman's physical exercises by periods from 1881 to 1952. The students who first had use of the gymnasium's modern facilities were thus enlightened by the contrast with their present privileges. Swimming early became the ambition of many. Miss Gloria Starks, '43, became instructor of swimming in 1952. Over 341 Spelman students were enrolled that year in swimming classes; 297 were beginners. Many of them had never been in water before except in a bathtub or when baptized. It is only in recent years that Negroes have been permitted the use for swimming of any of the beaches along the ocean and gulf front from Virginia to New Orleans. A small frontage at Waveland, Mississippi, where for 25 years or more, Bishop Robert E. Jones of the Methodist Church had been developing an assembly ground and camp, modeled somewhat on Chautauqua, contained until the forties the only section where Negroes were free to swim. The Second World War opened to Negro soldiers some of the Florida beaches.

In the physical development of the University system, Spelman, Morehouse and Atlanta University had decided, through their boards of trustees, that they would work cooperatively rather than competitively. Each institution named its first, second, third and fourth priority of need. For the first priority, Atlanta University named a classroom building; Morehouse College a chemistry building; Spelman College, a gymnasium. The gymnasium had become a reality. Spelman's second priority was a dormitory, and her third priority a fine arts building.

Mr. John D. Rockefeller, Jr., as a ten-year old boy could not have been greatly impressed by the physical plant on his first visit in 1884. He came again 17 years later; again with his bride in February, 1903; and still again in 1927. At the *Seventieth Anniversary* Exercises, although absent in the flesh, he was felt to be very much present through a letter from him which the President of Spelman College presented after the excellent and specially appropriate Founders Day address by Dr. Wilbour Eddy Saunders, president of the Colgate-Rochester Divinity School, had been received with applause. Except for Mr. Arnett who was present on the platform, the letter came as a surprise to all hearers.

"Because Spelman was named after my grandmother," wrote Mr. Rockefeller, "because my parents took a deep interest in the college, because my wife and I have continued that interest, which is now being shared by our children, I am happy to contribute the securities [thereafter listed] to be applied to the cost of constructing and furnishing the proposed dormitory. . . . This gift I am making in memory of my wife whose life was primarily dedicated to home building." The amount of this gift was half a million dollars.

The students were eager to express their feelings to Mr. Rockefeller in their own behalf, and they sent him a telegram. A few days later their faces were beaming as they received a letter from Mr. Rockefeller in reply. Both are quoted in the *Messenger* for May, 1951.

Abby Aldrich Rockefeller Hall

Due to the foresight of the architect, James Gamble Rogers, preliminary plans for a dormitory to house 100 students had been prepared before World War II ended. To be sure, the money for it was not in sight, but Mr. Rogers knew that when building materials were released after the close of the war, the persons who had their plans ready and knew what orders should be placed would have a great advantage. Fortunate it was for Spelman College that this advice had been given and accepted. In the first place, the readiness of the preliminary plans had made it possible to present a specific request to Mr. Rockefeller. Further than that, they expedited the contract for the building, and the procurement of building materials.

Ground was broken in a ceremony participated in by alumnae, faculty and students, following the class-day exercises in June, 1951. Following a brief statement by the President, and a prayer of thanksgiving by Mrs. Ruth Berry McKinney '21, the first earth was turned by Claudia White Harreld '01, one of the first two college graduates, who was proud to be able thus to celebrate her fiftieth anniversary. Another spadeful was happily turned by Mrs. Victoria Maddox Simmons, class of 1888; as a student she had experienced the building of Rockefeller Hall, completed in 1886, Spelman's first building after "the barracks."

The corner-stone was laid on December 2, 1951. The service began in Sisters Chapel and was continued at the dormitory. After remarks by Mr. Arnett, the service was turned over to John Wesley Dobbs, Grand Master of the Masons of Georgia. As the father of six Spelman College graduates, Mr. Dobbs himself paid an unscheduled tribute to the College. The reverent and dignified service of the Masonic order was then carried out; two spirituals were sung by the Masonic Glee Club; and the closing prayer was made by the Grand Chaplain. The building was furnished and open to students in September, 1952.

The formal dedication took place on Founders Day, 1953. All the students marched in the procession as they do on each Founders Day. The seniors came first, wearing cap and gown for the first time, followed by all the students in white dresses, then the faculty, and last the speakers and other members of the platform party. It was as always an impressive sight. The speakers for this occasion were Dr. Rosemary Park, President of Connecticut College, and Laurance Spelman Rockefeller. The service was concluded with an original Litany of Dedication by the students, and the Prayer of Dedication. Dr. Park's address was timely and especially challenging to women students. In his address, Laurance Rockefeller pointed out the interest of five generations of the Spelman-Rockefeller family in the equality of Negroes and the equality of women. He paid a beautiful tribute to his mother, Abby Aldrich Rockefeller, who, he said, "always believed in, looked for, and almost invariably found and brought out the best in other people." He quoted from a letter she had addressed to three of her sons which urged them as a matter of personal and of national policy, "never to say or to do anything which would wound the feelings or the self-respect of any human being. . . ."

At the conclusion of his address, he presented to the College in behalf of his father and his brothers, a lovely portrait of his mother to be hung in the Abby Aldrich Rockefeller Hall. He expressed the hope that those who see it would always think of her primarily as a person who cared for people. "She was a specialist in friendship."

The portrait was unveiled by two seniors, Ruth and Mary McKinney, twin daughters of Mrs. Ruth Berry McKinney '21, who had made the opening prayer at the ground-breaking ceremony on June 2, 1951. They were also the highest ranking students in the class of 1953.

The Campus in 1953

A new main campus entrance was officially opened amid the blowing of horns and the waving of balloons and pennants on September 30, 1951. Made necessary by the addition to the campus of Ella Street and the section south of it, it fortunately was possible to make the driveway lead from Leonard Street, between Tapley and Chadwick Halls, directly to Sisters Chapel. The old entrance pillars, moved to mark the new entrance to the campus, bear the original stone markers to the memory of Miss Mary J. Packard. The ribbons were cut by the president and vice-president of the Spelman Students Association, Shirley Statom '52, of Haines City, Florida, and Mary McKinney '53, of Cleveland, Ohio, to permit the passing through of the students marching four abreast behind the large Spelman College banner. The banner was borne aloft by the presidents and vice-presidents of the upper three classes, namely; Charlye Mae Thompson and Marion Townsend, seniors; Bettye Blasingame and Jean Foster, juniors; Dorothy Gulley and Gwendolyn Walker, sophomores. The freshmen had not yet elected officers. The faculty and others in cars formed part of the cavalcade.

The existing roadway was extended southward beyond Sisters Chapel in a large oval which runs to the Gymnasium and then northward crossing the new driveway. A handsome stone wall was built from the Chadwick corner around the whole south end of the present campus.

Spelman College, bounded on the north by Atlanta University and Clark College along Greensferry Avenue; on the east by University and John Hope Homes; on the north by the express highway (called Northside Drive Southwest!); is hemmed in and can expand only to the west. Considering the number of its buildings, 17 on approximately 24 acres, it is more crowded than any other of the institutions of the Atlanta University Center, as was pointed out in the survey made by Cresap, McCormick and Paget in 1952. It may be said, nevertheless, that Spelman College, with the homogeneous architecture and well-landscaped campus offers a charmful setting for an undergraduate college for women.

343

CHAPTER XXII

THE *SPELMAN MESSENGER*

" . . . far more than a school paper; . . . a journal of intelligence."

THE first issue of the *Spelman Messenger*, Volume I, Number 1, was published in March, 1885. Beginning in the fall of 1885, eight issues were published annually, one each month from November through June, or from October through May.

Miss Packard and Miss Giles felt the need, long before the development of "public relations" as a profession, of a means of communication to inform their friends of the progress of the Seminary; to make new friends for the cause; to inform the students, the graduates, and the Negro community of its work and develop and broaden their interests.

The opportunity to read papers and magazines, even the ability to read them, was relatively a new thing to most Negroes. One can imagine the excitement that the arrival of the *Spelman Messenger* eight times a year would mean in many of their homes and churches. A subscription cost 25 cents per year, and in lots of ten copies to one address, $2.00. A Children's Exchange was added in November, 1886, with a recent graduate, Carrie P. Walls, in charge.

The printing office itself was made possible by a gift from the John F. Slater Fund of the equipment, including type. This in turn made it possible for Spelman Seminary to print not only the *Messenger* but also its own catalogues, announcements, folders and booklets of an educational or promotional nature. The annual catalogue and the *Messenger* were printed by the Spelman printing office for more than 35 years.

In addition to the other benefits mentioned, the composition, type-setting and printing provided training for students in English, accuracy, and skills. There were jobs in the early years for girls who had had experience in the Spelman printing office, and jobs for Negroes were scarce.

The breadth and variety of the articles in the *Messenger* and their quality right from the beginning are remarkable. This applies to the short items quoted from many sources as well as to those originating on the campus. While the objective of keeping the supporters of the Seminary informed was never lost sight of, yet other interests touching on the world outside as well as the current history of the United States and of Georgia and of Negroes were not neglected.

The *Messenger* of the early years thus supplied to a group of people who had few books and no access to libraries, public or private, the printed word on many human activities. It brought, in interesting form, some knowledge of the literature of the past and the authors of it; of the religions of the world including Buddhism, Mohammedanism, and Confucianism; of Art, Nature, Current Events.

At the same time, it reported activities and happenings on the campus, and the work of the graduates. Frequently, students and alumnae wrote articles for the paper, about general subjects as well as about their own experiences. Observe, for example, two illustrations of the latter: 1. An article published in June, 1900, written by a graduate of the TPC, Maggie E. Walker, which begins:

Go with me to a school in Putnam County, not eight miles from Atlanta. . . .

There on a cleared spot in the woods is a small cabin. It has only one room, built of rough boards, standing lengthwise. As we enter the unkept yard, we can see through the building, on account of the large spaces between the boards. We enter by means of a plank, which does duty as step when required and serves as bat during playtime. Within is not a bench with a back, no desk, board, chart, map, or picture. All the light comes from two windows shaded by rough undressed boards.

Go there today. You will see near this cabin a large frame building painted white, with six windows shaded by green shutters, a large heater, benches, desks, blackboards, and pictures on the wall. All this has been done under the inspiration of two students, one from Atlanta Baptist College and one from Spelman Seminary.

The first money for this building came from an opossum supper planned months beforehand. First . . . a meeting of the patrons, gifts from them—pigs, chickens, and lambs set aside in anticipation of the great supper when pigs, chickens, lambs and an opossum would make the community's mouth water.

Pictures . . . a necessity to every school. The Perry Publishing Company offers pictures at one cent each, with 1,400 from which to choose. Pictures teach us unselfishness, love of labor, and beauty in simple life. A pupil who had been given a copy of *The Woman Churning* by Millet wrote in her essay about it that the picture taught her 'that work is beautiful and honorable.'

A school library was needed. The pupils collected money to buy *Aesop's Fables*, *Grimm's Fairy Tales*, *Evangeline*, *Hiawatha*, *Story of George Washington*, Eggleston's *Great Americans for Little Americans*. . . . Some of the patrons asked the privilege of coming to school after work. . . .

2. A letter from Johnnie Sulue Price of Laurel, Mississippi, who could not finish with her class in 1930 and taught in Cairo, Georgia, the following two years. Many teachers in Negro schools had to cope with similar conditions. She wrote:

Last year I had a heavy schedule. I taught seventh grade geography, health and reading; and home economics for the seventh through the tenth grades. Also I opened a cafeteria. They had never had anything of the sort before and everybody was carried away by it.

I started the cafeteria with seventy-five cents of my own, to make money for materials with which to cook and sew. The very first day I made three dollars, and business has been good continually since. Children who had been bringing things from home now buy their lunches from the cafeteria. I stress vegetables, milk, and fruit. The school board has been pleased with my work and has already given me screens for my windows and an ice-box holding seventy-five pounds of ice. . . .

My health classes are doing well. I make them come clean every day—if they don't, I send them back and give them zero. For myself I wear a fresh white nurse uniform every day, white shoes, and a white sweater when it is cool. I try to go just like Miss Smith [her Spelman teacher], white and clean! . . . .

I have a class in Sunday School and B.Y.P.U., and helped with the Christmas exercises and Easter program. . . . I am also to start evening classes soon for the older people. You see I am doing all I can to live up to what Spelman has taught me. . . .

Not until 1936 was Johnnie Price able to complete the work for her bachelor's degree, and she has not to this day ceased to give her best to her pupils and to the communities in which she has taught.

The *Messenger* lived up to its purpose to make the students on campus, their parents, and the graduates who were on their own jobs, mainly then teaching and home-making, conversant both with the life and work of Spelman Seminary, and also with what was going on in the world. Articles appeared about Africa, yes – that might be expected; but also about Labrador, Burma, India, Egypt, Korea, Japan, the Holy Land, Russia, Australia, Alaska, Cuba, Tibet, Mexico.

The students and graduates might be 'fenced in' as all Negroes were restricted in privilege, but they became acquainted with great men and women of all ages, past and present. A succession of "Little Journeys" of which Elbert Hubbard would have approved, provided interesting facts in the lives of writers such as Dickens, Scott, Longfellow, Thoreau, Oliver Wendell Holmes, Paul Lawrence Dunbar, Walt Whitman; and men and women in other walks of life, Agassiz – the scientist, Mendelssohn, Florence Nightingale, Sojourner Truth, Sun Yat Sen, Henry Tanner – the Negro painter, Col. Charles Young, even Bert Williams, and René Maran, French author of *Batouala* which won the *Prix Goncourt*. The frequent citations from the *Messenger* in this History give ample evidence of the wealth of information contained in its pages.

The first editors of the *Messenger* were members of the teaching staff, Miss Hattie Phinney and Miss Grover, Miss Mary J. Packard and Miss M. E. Barnes. Miss Upton succeeded Miss Barnes. Then, in 1887, Miss Werden came to Spelman. She was the teacher of printing in charge of the printing office, and in 1888 became publisher of the *Messenger*, and began writing articles for it. Beginning in January, 1896, she served as both editor and publisher.

The remarkable quality of the publication for the next 28 years was chiefly due to Miss Evelina O. Werden. Under her editorship, the *Spelman Messenger* became one of the important cultural influences of Seminary and College. She was versatile, and her interests were broad. She had great energy and capacity for work. She was exacting in her standards of workmanship. Her distinctive qualities were "intellectual ability" and "literary excellence." The May 1924 issue was the first one since 1896 for which she was not responsible.

After Miss Werden's death in 1924, Miss Edna E. Lamson became editor. In 1927-28, the editor was Miss Miriam Feronia Carpenter. Then in succession, the editorial work was in charge of Miss Edith Glode, Mrs. Marion Wilson Starling, Miss Alma Stone, and Miss Clara D. Craig, all members of faculty or staff. Miss Craig's term was the longest 1947-52; she too had the quality of literary excellence.

In its first 40 years, the *Messenger* was published monthly through the academic year. Beginning with volume 43, in 1927-28, the publication became a quarterly. It continues to serve as an indispensable record and source of information about Spelman College. It can truly be said that in the Seminary's first four decades, the *Spelman Messenger* was unique among college publications. Even now, when there is no dearth of college printed matter, it still retains a high place among college papers for its interest and its quality.

CHAPTER XXIII

SPELMAN AND AFRICA

THERE is material for a worth-while book about Spelman and Africa. Here can be only very brief mention of the work carried on there by Spelman alumnae. Nora Gordon, Clara Howard and Emma DeLany are striking illustrations of the enduring impact of the Founders. The far-reaching influence of the latter two is still alive in Nyasaland through the work of their adopted African children, Flora Zeto and Daniel Malekebu, educated respectively at Spelman and Meharry Medical College, married in the Spelman chapel, and working in Africa ever since.

The Congo

Nora Gordon '88 was the first Spelman student to go to Africa. Nora was born in Columbus, Georgia, August 25, 1866. Her parents were former slaves belonging to General Gordon. Her departure from Spelman in 1889 for Palabala, on the Congo River, has been recounted. She went under the auspices of the Woman's Baptist Foreign Mission Society of the West. She was transferred in 1891 to the mission station at Lukungu which was a center for 24 schools. There she had charge of the afternoon school and also of the printing office. She set up type for printing the first arithmetic to be written in the native language. She returned to America for rest in 1893. In 1895 she married Rev. S. C. Gordon of Jamaica, B.W.I., and they sailed for Africa under appointment by English Baptists. They labored at Stanley Pool on the Congo in a well-established mission which had brick buildings, fine fruit orchards, and a student body of high intelligence. But the period was one of strife between the natives and the Belgian government, and the natives suffered cruelly. Two children were born to the Gordons. Both died and are buried at the mission. In 1900, Nora returned to America, broken in health. She died at Spelman in 1901, only

349

34 years old. Her father, James Gordon, had shown his heroic spirit in 1890 when he said, "I'm glad my daughter is working in Africa for her people — let her work on."

Clara Howard, with Miss Packard's words of farewell to help sustain her, had sailed in 1890 for Lukungu, under the auspices of the Woman's American Baptist Foreign Mission Society. She was in charge of the primary school, and also had sole care of 30 little boys — waifs and stragglers. The primary department soon grew to 100 pupils.

Nora Gordon and Clara Howard graded and organized the school and visited outposts, besides caring for the children at the station. In 1895, Clara's health required her to come to America, and she was never able to return to Africa. She brought with her a young native girl, Flora Zeto, who had been rescued from the jungle, brought first to Stanley Pool and then taken to the Lukungu mission and given to Miss Howard. Flora was graduated from the Spelman High School in 1915, and later took special courses to fit her for mission work in Africa.

Ada Jackson, a teacher in Spelman's elementary school, who had completed the TPC in 1897, became in 1902 the second wife of Rev. S. C. Gordon; and returned with him to Stanley Pool in 1902, and to the lower Congo in 1904. Hostilities between the Belgian officials and the natives had not ceased; the strain on the missionaries was terrific. In 1909, Mr. and Mrs. Gordon took their two small daughters to Jamaica to be educated. On their return to Matadi, Ada was too ill to continue the journey up the Congo. It was thought best for her to return to England. She died on the way and was buried at sea. Her children were sent to her mother in Virginia. Mr. Gordon returned courageously to the Congo.

Dr. Joseph Clarke, a revered missionary from Scotland, was located at Palabala in the Congo when Nora Gordon arrived. He approved of Spelman from his acquaintance with Nora, and in 1891 sent two girls to Spelman to be educated. One was Lena, known as Vunga, who had been sent by a Dutch trader to the mission station at Palabala. Dr. Joseph Clarke adopted her and gave her his name. She was 18 years old and had been in schools in Scotland for two years before she entered the Missionary Training Course at Spelman. She completed the course in 1895 and returned to the Congo with the Rev. S. C. and Nora Gordon. She was stationed at Ikoko on the Congo, working under the supervision of her adopted father. Lena Clarke was especially gifted as a linguist. She learned rapidly the different dialects, and made herself invaluable as an interpreter. She studied in Scotland again from 1900 to 1903. On her return to the Congo, she married Rev. C. L. Whitman, a missionary from Scotland.

Maggie Rattray, a Congolese child of 12, came to Atlanta with Lena Clarke in 1891, sent by Dr. Joseph Clarke. She spent nine years at Spelman. She returned to Palabala in 1900, and was assigned to Ikoko on Lake Ntomba. A letter from Ikoko, signed Margaret C. Rattray, dated Nov. 2, 1902, told of the fine arrangement of the mission station, with its palm trees and lemon groves, its beautiful birds and butterflies "and everything that could make one say, What a lovely place! But there is a great blank over all, and that is the people. Eight or nine years ago they were cannibals, and when they saw the boat bringing Mr. and Mrs. Clarke coming toward the shore, they planned how they would kill and eat the white people, but God took care of them. They do not eat people here now, but we have no doubt that the men from the villages near us still go to the cannibal feast a day's journey away." A description of the school and the work of the boys and girls which followed indicated remarkable progress. Forty-two girls at the station were Margaret's special charge. For 16 years, she worked among her own people as teacher and helper, doing whatever came to hand. In 1916, still under Dr. Clarke's supervision, she was assigned to the station at Ntondo to assist in the girls' work. The mission is a large one, with several workers, a hospital and a school. Besides supervising the work of the girls, she took long journeys into surrounding sections to hold services. She was always modest, even humble about her own ability, but her faithfulness and devotion were appreciated and later won unusual recognition. In 1925, King Albert's medal of honor was presented to her, an honor never before accorded a native worker in recognition of outstanding service in the Congo.

Nigeria

A few years after her marriage, Lena Clarke Whitman and her husband, then working in the Congo, were asked by the United Soudan Mission of England to work in Nigeria at Dongo. There again Mrs. Whitman showed her linguistic ability. She reduced the Jukun dialect to writing, and in 1917 her translation of the gospel of Luke was published, and also her translation of a collection of Bible stories. She was a power on the mission field, and her rare spiritual qualities won many friends.

Mrs. Whitman died in England in 1920. In a letter to Spelman, Mr. Whitman wrote of his wife: "She simply radiated the spirit of the Master. The people at Dongo were her willing servants and came to her with all their troubles and their needs, and she listened with utmost sympathy to their stories. Great will be the mourning. . . ." Their three boys were taken to Scotland to be educated, and her husband returned to the Soudan alone.

Nyasaland

Emma DeLany, the fifth Spelmanite to go to Africa, entered Spelman from Florida in 1888. She was the daughter of Daniel S. DeLany of Fernandino, Florida, who for 30 years was a pilot on the Revenue Cutter *Boutwell*, the only colored pilot in the service. She was graduated from Spelman Seminary in 1894, and from the Missionary Training Course in 1896. She had already completed Spelman's Nurse Training Course, and she was determined to work for the people of Africa. She had to wait a few years before she received an appointment from the National Baptist Convention (Negro), but her purpose did not falter. She sailed on Jan. 15, 1902, on assignment to an entirely new field in British East Africa, Chiradzulu, Blantyre, Nyasaland. The nearest mission was one 12 miles away manned by Mr. and Mrs. Dreyer and supported by Baptists in Scotland. The Seventh Day Adventists later in 1902 "bought out a mission" and sent Mr. Branch and his family from the western U.S.A. They lived at a station 60 miles away. Meanwhile, the Dreyers had to return to Scotland because Mr. Dreyer had a bad heart attack. Their departure left Miss DeLany very much isolated, in a strange country, with a strange language, and in a community not yet civilized. She lived in a two-room mud house. She put bricks together to use as a stove. When hard showers came, rain poured through the grass roof. The weather was very cold. The smoke came down the chimney and the heat went up. She was plagued by lice. She had a nasty attack of fever. In fact, she suffered from frequent attacks of "fever" — from malaria and other causes. But she could enjoy a view of snow-topped Chiradzulu mountain by standing in her doorway. Besides, she was learning the native language and had much work to do.

The people were peaceful. There were three distinct tribes — the Angona, the original settlers; the Yao, who conquered the Angonies; and the Angulus — recent comers and the lowest in the scale of intelligence. Their belief in witches led to unnecessary suffering and even death.

Before she could speak the language, Miss DeLany began to teach the people to make a garden, and to make and burn bricks. She made some progress in teaching the girls to sew and the boys to cook. One new boy who came as a helper was told to make a fire in the stove, and put water in the pot and the pot on the stove. Instead he put the water on the bricks which were the stove, and made the fire in the pot! Fortunately the error was discovered in time to save her only pot from destruction. Her best helper was an earnest youth named Daniel Malekebu. The native food was hard to take. Leopards made visits close to her center, and occasionally a lion. Three persons were killed by lions between the mission and the place Daniel had to go to get the mail.

The superstitions that existed are hard to believe. For example: when a person was accused of stealing, a pot of water was put on the fire. When it came to a boil, the accused was made to drop two rocks into the boiling water and take them out with his hands. Sometimes, just enough meal was put in the water to stick to the skin. If the skin peeled off, the person was guilty; if not, he was innocent.

With all the difficulties and hardships, Miss DeLany wrote in 1902: "These things will never discourage a Spelmanite; when I remember what the Founders of that grand institution had to pass through in order for it to stand as it does today . . . I take fresh courage . . ."; and again in 1905: "I know there would have been no Spelman of today if its pioneer workers had grown discouraged because of hardships."

A brick house for Miss DeLany was completed early in 1904, with windows inside, and a veranda outside, whose pillars held up the thatched roof. This was not only a great comfort to her but it inspired the people to keep their own houses in better order. They began to want chairs and a table and even a bed – and flowers growing. A few coffee trees, a few hills of corn, several acres of cotton also made the outlook more hopeful. The medicines Miss DeLany received after long delay enabled her to heal many serious wounds. The people came long distances to have them tended. Some came on their hands and knees, some had to be carried on the backs of husbands or fathers. Many of the wounds were from jiggers; some from bites either from each other or from insects; but the majority were from burns. They slept around a fire in the middle of the hut; many got horrible burns, and some were burned to death. With all the wounds that came to Miss DeLany's care, not one person had to lose a limb or a joint.

Perhaps the most important thing Miss DeLany accomplished – because it left something to build on after the World War and its aftermath – was to organize a school to train native leaders. This was in operation when in 1905, with health impaired, she left to return home. After four years in Nyasaland, she fur-

ther had the satisfaction of seeing considerable improvement in
the homes of the people around the mission; of having regularly
in her school 64 students, about two boys to one girl; of leaving
at the station 25 grown-up women who were trying to be Christians.

Two African children, who became great friends of Miss De-
Lany were Daniel Malekebu and his sister Ruth. Their parents
were opposed to "the foreign woman." When Miss DeLany
got ready to leave for America, she grieved that she did not
have the money to take also her two little girls — Ruth Malekebu and one other. The boy, Daniel, begged to go with her,
but it was impossible for her to become responsible for him —
then a boy of 16. His parents too refused to approve, and they
appointed guards to watch him until his teacher had been gone
three days. Then he ran away. He started on foot to follow Miss
DeLany to the coast but never was able to overtake her. It was
a journey of over 200 miles. He climbed the trees at night to
escape from the lions and leopards. But he reached Beira, East
Africa, before the steamer sailed for England, and persuaded
the captain to allow him to work his passage to England. He
earned his way to America in the same way. He attended Selma
University in Alabama, and then Meharry Medical College.
He and Miss DeLany were guests of Miss Clara Howard at
Spelman for several days. There he met Flora Zeto. After he
completed his medical course, they were married in the chapel
at Spelman on March 22, 1919.

They got an appointment from the Lott Carey Foreign Mission Board (Negro), and in March 1920 started for Nyasaland.
In January they had had passport trouble, but finally convinced
the authorities in Washington that they were natives of Africa
by singing in their African tongue and showing a letter in the
Yao dialect. They got to South Africa but the government refused them permission to go to the Chiradzulu station. They
therefore went to Liberia, and worked for five years at the
Ricks Institute in Brewerville, near Monrovia, teaching, preaching, helping to raise food for 60 boarding students, taking care

of the sick as well as could be done with limited medical supplies and no hospital. In 1925, they returned to the U.S.A. for a year's rest which they spent in raising funds for Nyasaland; it had by then been opened again to missionaries. They were overjoyed to be able at last to take up Miss DeLany's work in Blantyre. They rebuilt her mission, got the farm lands under cultivation, the school in running condition and built a church and small hospital. Following Miss DeLany's plan, they set about training groups of teachers and preachers, and sending them out into the country round about. After a sufficiently large group of native teachers and preachers had been trained, Dr. Malekebu was able to devote more time to medical work. He sometimes walked 60 or 70 miles into the interior to care for the sick or wounded. The people were eager to learn and flocked to the mission. In one month Dr. Malekebu baptized over a hundred persons. When the foundation to the church was laid, over 2,000 members were present. There were over 300 students in the school and a new building was required. On the strength of the really meager sum sent to Mrs. Malekebu by Spelman College, another "Spelman Hall," 60 x 33 feet, was erected in 1926. Before it was finished, it was inadequate; it has now been restored and enlarged.

In 1935, Mrs. Malekebu wrote: "There are only two teachers for the 300 pupils, who vary in age from six to 35 years. Yet they manifest keen interest in their subjects: agriculture, arithmetic, basketry, geography, hygiene, nature study, physical education. Upon graduation, many find employment with the government; more become teachers and exert their efforts towards bettering their own communities. The school was a boarding school, with facilities also for day pupils.

The Malekebus returned to the U.S.A. at intervals, to rest, regain their physical strength, and raise funds for their Mission. After a recent extended furlough in the United States due to serious illness (Mrs. Malekebu had to spend months in the University Hospital in Philadelphia suffering from a 'broken spine' and is still disabled in walking), Dr. and Mrs. Malekebu returned in 1958 to their beloved Providence Industrial Mission in Chiradzulu, Nyasaland.

A letter from Mrs. Malekebu dated November 5, 1959, enclosed five snapshots. One showed perhaps a hundred Christian women and girls in front of the New Jerusalem Baptist Temple taken during the 1959 session of the National Baptist Assembly of Africa. Two showed Spelman Hall, located next to the Temple – (1) with the old grass roof removed in preparation for a corrugated iron roof; (2) with roofing completed. A fourth showed a Memorial Library built by Dr. Malekebu and members of the church. The fifth was of the entrance to Providence Industrial Mission from Blantyre and shows an impressive pillar inscribed with the name of the Mission and bearing the legend "Founded in 1900, and Reopened in 1926 by Dr. and Mrs. D. S. Malekebu." Dr. Malekebu is Principal of the Mission; Mrs. Malekebu, a teacher of the women and girls of all levels. She wrote: "Schools are all open – many students enrolled from everywhere." Dr. Malekebu is also President of the National Baptist Assembly of Africa, Inc., and Mrs. Malekebu is President of its Women's Auxiliary. The program of their fourteenth Annual Session held in August, 1959, contains the names of Africans, many of whom were taught and ordained by Dr. Malekebu. "Europeans and African chiefs both attended the meetings in large numbers."

Liberia

One of Emma DeLany's African friends said of her that she was two women in one. It surely seems that she accomplished the work of two or more women. After she returned home on furlough in 1906, and found that permission would not then be given for a return to Nyasaland, she set herself the task of raising money for establishing a mission in Liberia. In 1912 she went to Monrovia under the National Baptist Convention (Negro). She selected a spot in the jungle not far from Monrovia, cleared the land, built houses, set out trees, and established the Suehn Industrial Mission.

In one of her letters (October, 1919) she wrote: "Liberia is . . . the only open door for Negroes in Africa. President George Sale . . . told me this." It was Miss DeLany's plan to make the center at Suehn a model station from which to start a chain of industrial settlements, all to be under general supervision of a staff who would travel up and down the river on a mission steamer.

There was great difficulty to keep going during the first World War, even to keep alive. The food shortage was extreme. For three months, with the rice harvest not due for three months longer, she was not able to buy a single quart of rice in a radius of three days' walk; not a quart was to be had in Monrovia. Nor could she buy potatoes or cassava. There was also danger from the war. Communication with the outside world was shut off. Miss DeLany was nine months without receiving a letter; then 50 came all at once on August 12, 1918. Miss DeLany remained at the Suehn Industrial Mission for eight years. Then, although in wretched health, she returned to the U.S.A. mainly for the purpose of raising funds for further work. She was at Spelman in June, 1922, full of plans and hope for the Mission. A few months later, in October, she died of blackwater fever at her mother's home in Fernandino, Florida.

But the Mission still goes on. At present, it includes a busy dispensary, besides a school with 200 boarding students. In 1962 the Suehn Mission will celebrate its fiftieth anniversary.

Ora Milner Horton, who attended Spelman, 1913 to 1916, has given good service in Liberia for more than 40 years. She was married in December, 1916, to Rev. D. R. Horton, a graduate of Morehouse College. They were accepted by the Foreign Mission Board of the Negro National Baptist Convention as missionaries for Liberia, and sailed for Africa in January, 1917. They began work with the largest tribe in Liberia, the Bassa tribe. Results were poor until in 1922 they persuaded some of them to buy ten acres of good land and helped them to begin to develop a civilized Christian community. The plan took hold. Much attention was given to agriculture. A school was established. Homes were built, some of thatch and some of concrete blocks or timber. Church membership increased. The place is called Community Heights. Since 1926, Mrs. Horton has served as principal of the Bassa Community School, and performs many community duties, besides helping her husband with three churches and several out-stations with which he is connected, and looking after her home and children.

Witness that Mrs. Horton's school and home are of high standard has come from Dr. Jackson Davis of the General Education Board, and from Miss Hazel F. Shank, Foreign Secretary of the Woman's American Baptist Foreign Mission Society, both of whom, in different years, visited them. Both reported that Spelman may well be proud of Mrs. Horton. Miss Shank wrote of her: "Nowhere in Africa did I see a Christian family or children so well trained. Her home is a model of cleanliness, and I enjoyed the meals that I had with her. . . . In spite of their meager income, she has managed to give the home a refined and Christian atmosphere."

The Hortons are still in Monrovia hard at work, after 43 years of service.

Other workers who went from Spelman to Liberia were:

Mrs. Louise Hudson Pope, a Georgia girl who finished the High School course in 1916, and later taught at Tuskegee Institute. After her marriage, she and her husband sailed to Africa in 1924. For six years, until Mrs. Pope became ill, they worked at the Mt. Coffee Mission in Monrovia, under the A.M.E. Zion Mission Board.

Miss Minnie C. Lyon took courses in nurse training at Spelman Seminary, and was accordingly adopted as one of the Spelman missionaries to receive annual gifts from the students and teachers. She joined the Lott Carey Mission located in Brewerville, about 15 miles from Monrovia. The teachers are mostly African, more of them men than women. The school accommodates between 200 and 300 children, and has primary, elementary, and high school grades. There were more boys than girls, because of the deep-seated tradition that the education of girls was not important. With some of the money received from Spelman, a reading room was built, a cement building with zinc roof. More books are needed at Brewerville, as also at Suehn. Miss Lyon said at Spelman in 1948 that she thought the missionaries had done more to raise the living standards than the government.

Margaret Stewart was graduated from Spelman College in 1935. Her mother was a native of Liberia and her father an Americo-Liberian. She came from the American Lutheran Mission, and the Lutheran women in the U.S.A. took care of her college expenses. She was a delightful student as well as an able one whose excellence in the field of English won for her a Shakespeare prize at her graduation. She returned to teach in the Lutheran girls' school in Harrisburg, Liberia, and was able there to foster a greater understanding between the missionaries and the Liberians. In 1941, in the church at Zorzor she was married to the Rev. Byron Traub, one of the first pastors to be licensed by the Lutheran Mission in Africa. The church in which they were married was purely native, a large building of mud and thatch. After the marriage, they were sent to a small station, Kpayea, but after two months were moved to the main station. There Margaret has taught in the E. V. Day Girls' School. In 1943, they were moved to Sanoyea, where Margaret was put in charge of the school. Margaret and her husband have done effective and heroic work – with so very little to work with. Hers is a gallant spirit. But sometimes one hears her say "How I miss the music at Spelman! The little organ here wheezes pitifully, but I do my best to make harmony to ease the longing a bit. Oh, I'd love to hear the Christmas Carol Concert once more!"

Postscript 1961

The UNCF is engaged in formulating proper plans for the selection of African students to study in the United States, and for scholarship aid to such students. W. J. Trent, the Executive Director of the UNCF, returned in December 1960 from a trip to several countries in East Africa, including Nyasaland. The African Scholarship Program of leading American Universities is getting under way with the objective of increasing the number of Africans approved for study in American colleges and universities, and safeguarding their assignments and their scholarship aid. Along with several other member-colleges of the UNCF, Spelman College has been invited to participate in this Program.

CHAPTER XXIV

THE ALUMNAE

"By their fruits. . . ."

THE aims and purposes of a college are basic to an appraisal of its value. The honesty and earnestness and effectiveness of daily efforts toward the stated goals which provide the meat and sinew, the blood and marrow for growth, next deserve scrutiny. Yet when all that is said, the real test, the fruit of the undertaking, is the alumnae, the women whom it has trained. What of them?

Mention has been made in an earlier chapter of the only three living graduates of the first two classes and their achievements. Here and there others have been mentioned by name as they came logically into the narrative. But there are hundreds whose life stories merit recounting if only space would allow, not only because they have value but because they are rather exciting, too. To work against the odds involves unusual and stimulating experiences.

The graduates of the early years were true pioneers, great in faith and hardy in spirit. It called for daring plus a dedicated spirit for young Negro women who had never been out of the Southern States to embark for Africa alone, sixty and seventy years ago. Work in the rural South also required valor and still does. Any pioneer undertaking in the United States or in Africa or elsewhere is likely to be full of hardships, and inevitably calls for ingenuity and intelligence as well as industry and a willing spirit. Mary Lyon once, when asked what she considered indispensable qualifications for a missionary to foreign fields, named piety, a strong constitution and "a merry heart." Those are also necessary requirements for most Negro women who work in any position outside of the home.

A question frequently asked is — What do Spelman graduates do? And oftentimes the inquirer implies a wonder if there really are suitable opportunities for college-trained Negroes, especially for Negro women, compatible with their training. As a matter of fact, the shortage is in the number of graduates rather than in the number of positions open.

In the case of Spelman College – and it would be even more true of the Seminary graduates, – the profession of teaching has claimed most of them, teaching in a broad sense to include various kinds of educational work.

A list showing occupations of living graduates of Spelman College up to and including the class of 1952 reveals that of 1290 living college graduates, 625 were teaching or otherwise engaged in educational work. There were 480 teachers in public schools, 68 in colleges, 14 in nursery schools. Others were in specialized fields such as teachers of music, art, or of handicapped children. Some were supervisors or principals, or college personnel deans.

There were 56 social workers; and 54 secretaries, stenographers, or clerks. Forty-one graduates were librarians in a school, college, or in Northern public libraries.

Statistics sometimes impart information but rarely bring to mind a vivid human story. So attempt is here made to describe, all too briefly, a few graduates of Spelman College who are doing unusual things:

1. a physician who has passed the American Board of Pediatrics and the National Medical Board, has her own office in St. Louis, and is Clinical Assistant at the Children's Hospital and Visiting Pediatrician at Homer G. Phillips Hospital;

2. a librarian who is Acting Head of the Reference Department in the Library of Eastern Michigan University, with the rank of Assistant Professor;

3. a singer who has sung in Grand Opera in leading soprano parts in London's Covent Garden, New York's Metropolitan, and at La Scala and Glyndebourne; and has given concerts in France, Switzerland, Spain, Holland, Norway, Sweden, and in Berlin, Vienna, Moscow, Leningrad, Kiev, Jerusalem;

4. a missionary in Pakistan who teaches in the Lucie Harrison School in Lahore;

5. a teacher in Meharry Medical College, Nashville, Tennessee, who now holds the rank of Associate Professor of Physiology;

6. a social worker who is a Supervisor for the American Red Cross in Detroit;

7. a business woman with a Master's degree from Columbia University and a certificate from the Indiana College of Mortuary Science, who is General Manager of a long-established Funeral Home in Louisiana; and also wife of the Dean of Students of Southern University. She is a member of the General Board of Social and Economic Relations of the Methodist Church of the U.S.

8. a government official who is Director of Mental Health for the Virgin Islands. She holds degrees from Columbia University and Harvard University, and is a Fellow of the American Scandinavian Foundation.

9. a home demonstration agent who served for 32 years as State Agent for Negro Work during which the 4-H Club work in Georgia reached 28,000 girls and 22,000 boys;

10. a nurse with a Ph.D. degree in Public Health who is now an Assistant Director in Nursing Education of the Lafayette (psychiatric) Clinic in Detroit;

11. a professor of biology and department head in Atlanta University, Radcliffe Ph.D., elected when a graduate student at Radcliffe to both Phi Beta Kappa and Sigma Xi;

12. a minister's wife in Cleveland who was sent to the Far East to inspect their missions by the Woman's American Baptist Foreign Mission Society in 1960; and who was in 1960 elected a vice-president of the American (Northern) Baptist Convention;

13. a public health nurse who is Assistant Supervisor at the Visiting Nurse Service's Central Harlem Office, New York City;

14. a Jeanes Supervisor of Negro Schools of Fulton County, Georgia, for 31 years;

15. a research associate in the Carver Foundation of Tuskegee Institute, who holds a Ph.D. from the University of Chicago, and was elected to Sigma Xi;

16. a music teacher who was one of six teachers in the USA honored by Columbia University in 1954 for distinguished service to American education. Her career started in 1933 with a $72.90 a month salary in Florida, paid half in cash and half in scrip. She is now a teacher in the Booker Washington High School of Atlanta.

17. a writer whose stories have been published in *Redbook* and *The Ladies Home Journal*;

18. a college teacher, Western Reserve University Ph.D., who is an Associate Professor of English in Colby College, Maine;
19. a teacher who is an Ensign in the U.S. Naval Reserve. She is one of nine women from the Southern area who received in 1952 a commission direct from civilian life.

There are, besides, lawyers, laboratory technicians, and physical therapists, government employees and Y.W.C.A. secretaries. There is at least one policewoman, one labor union interviewer, one dental hygienist, one dress designer who has her own Dress Shop in Detroit, one demonstrator for a large gas company, one insurance agent, — to name some of the more unusual vocations. Of the 1290, 721 were married as of March 15, 1953.

There are at least two families from which have come so many Spelman graduates that they are mentioned here by name. The Harris family's first generation at Spelman included four sisters, — Rosa *Harris* Palmer NT '09, Nellie *Harris* Hannon HS '07, Sadye *Harris* Powell HS '07 (a trustee of Spelman College since 1948), and Florence *Harris* HS '17, C '37. They own and operate the Harris Memorial Hospital which has served Atlanta over 30 years, with its 50 beds and an interracial hospital staff of doctors. From the next generation of the sisters were graduated Julia *Palmer* Howard '38; Virginia Hannon '34; and Courtney Wynelle Hannon '38; and two nieces, Sadye *Harris* Williams '50 and Virginia Dare Powell '60.

Next, the family of John Wesley Dobbs, from which have come six daughters, all graduates of Spelman College in the years between 1929 and 1948. We know of no other instance in the history of colleges in America where six daughters have been graduated from one college. All are gifted, and four were graduated with honors. They are:

> Irene *Dobbs* Jackson '29, Willie *Dobbs* Blackburn '31, Millicent *Dobbs* Jordan '33, Josephine *Dobbs* Clement '37, Mattiwilda *Dobbs* Janzon '46, June *Dobbs* Butts '48

Each of the six has earned a Master's degree or equivalent, the equivalent being Irene's French Diplôme de Professeur de Français a l'étranger, now capped by a Doctorate from the University of Toulouse. Already three from the next generation, one daughter each of Irene, Willie Juliet, and Josephine, have been graduated with honors from Spelman College.

Mention must be made again by name in this chapter of the graduate of the first college class, Claudia White Harreld. Because of the active interest of her father, William Jefferson White, she was a part of Spelman almost from birth. She entered Spelman Seminary in 1890, and was present at the tenth anniversary, Miss Packard's last official appearance. Ten years later, she received the Bachelor's degree, and as she said at her fiftieth reunion she and her classmate, Jane Anna Granderson, had "the high honor of heading the line of graduates of what is the oldest, and for 25 years was the only college for Negro women." They joined a group then of only 5,000 Negro college graduates in the United States.

After graduation and some advanced study at Oberlin College she taught first in Augusta and then became a teacher at Spelman and at Morehouse. After her marriage to Kemper Harreld, their home was always open house to all Spelman and Morehouse students. "In almost every college class there are those who think of her with gratitude and love. . . ." Again and again she was called on by the College for some special service and never did she say no. No one person has been over so long a period, from 1890 to her death in 1952, so closely identified with Spelman, and no one had a deeper and more fruitful loyalty.

Mrs. Harreld had an unobtrusive but powerful influence also in many community activities. Mention is made here of one, the Gate City Day Nursery Association. She was a member of its Board of Directors for 20 years, and for the last 15 years of her life was its president. On June 1, 1958, in the Perry Homes

Community Center of Atlanta, the Claudia White Harreld Day Nursery was dedicated in her honor.

The number of graduates who have followed the college course by additional training in graduate and professional schools is impressive.

Over 37% of the graduates of the years from 1928 to 1953 have earned advanced degrees, or professional degrees or certificates, from 47 institutions, according to the data available. Alas! not every graduate keeps her record in the Alumnae Office up-to-date.

The institutions which have awarded six or more advanced degrees to Spelman graduates of record are:

Atlanta University	235
Chicago, University of (4 were Ph.D.'s)	9
Columbia University	37
Howard University includes one M.D. and 3 LL.B.'s	9
Indiana University	6
Meharry Medical College	9
Michigan, University of	9
New York University	12
Pennsylvania, University of	7
Simmons College (Boston)	6
Western Reserve University	9
Wisconsin, University of	9

Among other institutions which have awarded the Master's degree (or the Ph.D.) to Spelman College graduates are: Cornell University, Harvard University, Middlebury College, Mount Holyoke College, Northwestern University, Radcliffe College, Smith College, Stanford University, Syracuse University, University of Arkansas, University of California,

University of Illinois, University of Iowa, University of Minnesota, University of Pittsburgh, University of Toulouse-Docteur de l'Université (Lettres).

In his Commencement address at Spelman College in 1933, a vice-president of the General Education Board, David H. Stevens, said: "A simple definition of the function of any college is that it should make its students at home in their world. . . ."

William James, in his address to college women 50 years ago, said that "The best claim we can make for the higher education . . . is that 'it should enable us to *know a good man when we see him.*'"

Tying in her remarks with the academic standards, the faculty, and "guests who were invited to our campus," Mattiwilda Dobbs, the 1946 graduate who is indisputably the most illustrious alumna of the last half century, wrote in 1953:

"Spelman gave me something invaluable which has helped me in my career as well as my personal life, and this is an assurance which has enabled me to move about the world and feel at home with peoples of all races and cultures."

Such confidence and such ability can be developed in part through study of biography, history, science and literature. But the study in library or laboratory needs to be supplemented by acquaintance with living men and women, who actually exemplify superior achievement in thought and action.

Familiarity with masterpieces in any field of human endeavor develops a person's ability to discriminate between the excellent and the mediocre, between good and bad. There are masterpieces in miniature, as well as in magnitude: quality and skill are what count, not the size of the undertaking.

Through association with persons of worth, through seeing great works of art in replica, through becoming acquainted with great drama and great music, and also, may it be said, through sitting under some first-rate teachers, Spelman students were encouraged to exert their minds; to emulate the best they saw

368

PLATE XXXI

Founders Day Procession

"... all experience
        is an arch
    where thro'
Gleams that untravelled
    world,
        whose margin fades
For ever and for ever
    when I move"

TENNYSON

The Senior Bench

PLATE XXXII

The Class of 1929 in 1939

The Class of 1943 in 1953

PLATE XXXIII

The Freshman Class in September 1952

Six Sisters, all graduates of Spelman College

A Graduate of 1928 and
a Graduate of 1929
greet their President in 1953

Presidents of the Sophomore, Junior,
and Senior Classes in 1953

PLATE XXXIV

A proud family group examines diploma of their third Spelman graduate

Twin sisters from Cleveland
are first and second honor
students in 1953

Seven Spelman Graduates in 1946
who were classmates from
Nursery School through College

PLATE XXXV

The Academic Procession leaves Sisters Chapel after Miss Read's
26th and last Spelman Commencement

At left: Trevor Arnett with
Albert E. Manley on day of
his inauguration as Spelman's
Sixth President

PLATE XXXVI

Striding On

or heard in music, drama, the graphic arts, writing; to strive for achievement, mental and spiritual; and to achieve a spirit of genuine scholarship and a finer character.

Spelman College is proud of its founders, its co-workers, its benefactors; and likewise proud of its alumnae whose record and accomplishments tell a continuing story of grappling with difficulties, of overcoming obstacles, and of marching forward toward the ideal of a better life for all people.

THE foregoing historical account considers the work of Spelman College up to June 30, 1953. The record would not be complete without further reference to Trevor Arnett. In addition to his help in matters of policy and management, his influence was felt in the life of the campus. The students knew him and enjoyed him as their friend. They saw him on the campus, heard him speak in chapel and sing the hymns with them, watched him enjoy the plays in the Little Theater, welcomed him to their dinners in Morgan Hall. From March 13, 1924 to April 23, 1954, he served as President of the Board of Trustees; and nearly a year longer as a member of the Board. After he died on March 31, 1955, the warmth of the relationship with the graduates was felt in their messages of which this one is typical: "Each of us feels a personal loss. . . ."

An inscribed scroll presented to Mr. Arnett in November 1954, by the Trustees, expressed their great respect and deep affection. "Not only has he guided the financial affairs of Spelman College over these thirty years so successfully that it is today in sound condition, but also his interest in and influence on the academic standards of the College are amply evidenced. Continuously over the years to faculty and students and parents alike he has emphasized quality, rather than quantity. . . ." Spelman College in large measure through this period has been "the reflection and the echo of his love and interest and of the teamwork between him and the faculty and officers of the College."

Under date of February 7, 1953, Mr. Arnett sent a letter to the alumnae. The first paragraph ran as follows:

To the Alumnae of Spelman College: "I wish you to learn promptly from the enclosed copy of a news release of this date that Dr. Albert E. Manley has been elected president of Spelman College to succeed Dr. Florence M. Read on July 1, 1953."

The alumnae thus knew of the action before they read about it in the newspapers. The news release included a statement of the qualifications of the President-elect as follows:

"Dr. Albert E. Manley, Dean of the College of Arts and Sciences of North Carolina College, Durham, North Carolina . . . was graduated from Johnson C. Smith University, *cum laude*, in 1930. His fields of concentration in college were Physics and Mathematics. He holds the Master's degree from Teachers College, Columbia University, and a Doctor's degree in Education conferred by Stanford University in 1946. . . . Dr. Manley had been high school teacher and principal in Asheville, N.C.; and later state inspector of Negro high schools under the North Carolina State Department of Public Instruction. Granted a leave of absence in 1943, he worked at Stanford University under a grant from the General Education Board. In 1946 he accepted a position at North Carolina College as Dean of the College of Arts and Sciences and Professor of Education. . . ."

EPILOGUE

AS is true of all the Southern States, the people of Atlanta live in two different worlds. There is little communication between them. An Emory University president turned to me on the platform of Morehouse College as he looked at the fine-looking upstanding Negro men and women in the audience which filled the hall, and inquired, "Miss Read, where are these people in the day-time? I never see people like these."

But there they were in front of us – respectable, well-dressed, intelligent, responsive. Besides the students, they were teachers, ministers, doctors, lawyers, dentists, proprietors of small businesses, officers and patrons of the Negro bank, directors and employees of the largest Negro business in Atlanta, the Atlanta Life Insurance Company, Federal employees, social workers, undertakers, or here and there master carpenters and electricians. The work of those in the trades might, but not necessarily would, cross the line of race. In other employment, except personal service, there was no communication as of one man or woman to another. There was only the giving of orders – to janitors, gardeners, yard-men, cooks and waiters. Had they troubled to learn, some of the masters would have been surprised to discover the character and intelligence of their own servants.

Negroes have their own churches, lodges, as of now in Georgia completely segregated schools, their own cemeteries, playgrounds, and residential areas – from slums to attractively landscaped homes. They have segregated business sections and, except for the recent court decision relating to interstate bus passengers, segregated railroad and bus waiting rooms. The white people have all these also, and, in addition, all the offices of city, county, and state government. Negroes are not segregated in the U.S. post offices, nor usually when standing in line anywhere to pay a bill.

Although the number of enlightened white citizens has increased markedly in the last quarter century, the fact remains that when white Southerners in general think or speak of Negroes, they usually have in mind the dishwashers, street-cleaners, janitors, ditch-diggers that they see – those on the lowest level of employment – or even the loafers. They have had no opportunity ever to converse with the educated Negro men and women, young or old.

As for Negroes, now that since World War II more of them are employed in industry and fewer in personal service, not so many of them are acquainted in a friendly even if subservient way with white folks.

On both sides this is unfortunate. Not many years ago it could be said that however a white man berated "nigras" in general, there was always some Negro whom he knew and trusted; and likewise, although a Negro was suspicious of white people on principle, there was always some white man whom he respected and liked and counted a just person. That has helped keep the South from race violence.

As said before, the campuses of the Negro colleges are virtually the only places in the South where educated Negro and educated white people can meet on an equal basis.

A graduate of Spelman High School, Oberlin College, and the New York School of Social Work who had returned to Spelman in a responsible post from a social work position in the North said to me one day as we left the offices: "It's good to be back at Spelman. You do not know what a difference in feeling it makes to be in a place where you know that *every* white person you meet will be friendly."

Usually Negroes in Atlanta are kindly treated by the white persons they deal with in the stores or the real estate, gas, and power company or other offices where they pay their bills or by the bus-conductors and ticket-sellers. But not always, by any means. And they never know when a blow may come; they have always to be steeled against the possible insult – or studied neglect. They may deliberately be kept waiting to be waited on. Then, too, some salesladies are inclined to call women teachers by their first names if they pay for purchases by check and sign the full name. Consequently, Negro women frequently sign

373

their checks and other papers, using only the initials before the last name.

Incidents could be multiplied, some of them tragic. But even in ordinary circumstances to retain one's integrity and temper when confronted with injustice is difficult. The attitude of educated Negroes in the past to identify themselves completely with the problems of the race as a whole has been a kind of antiseptic. It helped them to sublimate individual resentment in efforts to get better conditions for all Negroes.

Improvement in race relations and in conditions generally has come about since 1930, though a temporary setback may now be noticed. Some important changes have been mentioned in these pages; more are implicit in the growth described. Today the North, the thinking South, and the entire literate world outside are awakened to the need of our providing full opportunity for all to study, to work, and to exercise the responsibilities of citizenship. More and more, that *principle* is accepted. Yet in the South, the traditional constraint that impedes freedom of thought, speech, and action operates to delay putting the principle into *practice*.

One main reason that the whole matter cannot be resolved immediately, at one stroke of the clock, is because only extremely limited educational opportunities have been open to the great majority of Negroes. These limitations do not in any way justify the legal and civic discrimination, or the prevailing etiquette. But they keep Negroes as a total class from equal privileges. Consider that as late as 1916 there were only 67 Negro public high schools in the South, with fewer than 20,000 students. And as late as 1920, according to Ashmore's *The Negro and the Schools*, 85% of all Negro pupils in the South were enrolled in the first four grades. Very few gestures were made before 1950 toward *equal* and separate provision of educational opportunity. The lag and the resulting lack must be tackled expeditiously; the remedy calls for persistent efforts on the part of all concerned.

374

The Negro does not seek special favors not given to other Americans. His capacity for education when given a chance has been proven, but most Negroes have been deprived of equal educational opportunities.

Freedom to vote without fear of reprisal – by which I mean without loss of job and without violence to person or property – is important, and will gradually bring to an end the prevailing inequality of treatment in the courts and other aspects of civic life, including the public schools. Yet the proper exercise of the ballot depends on an educated citizenry.

Fundamental to all progress is *Education*. Better schools and better trained and more dedicated teachers of both races from the first grade up will steadily lessen the long-existing cultural gap between the Negro people and the white people in the mass, from the school children to the men and women of voting age. To that end, the relative number of educated Negroes should be greatly increased. Now, for example, only 5% of Negro high school graduates enter college whereas 25% of white high school graduates do so.

College-trained Negroes and others must grapple with education as a cause worthy of their utmost support and devotion. Many of them must be willing to give themselves to the unrelenting task of raising the level of educational standards by actual teaching and community work and even work in the professions, in the cities, towns and rural areas of the South, and also in over-crowded urban sections in large Northern cities. Some – but too few – are now so doing.

The desired goal — equal treatment without reference to race – cannot be attained through court action or through appropriation of more money, whether local, state, or federal, necessary as are established legal rights and adequate financial support. The zest for education that animated the students in the first eight decades after Emancipation has been declining and must be revived, along with the eagerness to extend and improve educational opportunities. Moreover, education must be valued most, not for its money increment or its purchasing power of material comforts and luxuries, but as an open door to a more abundant life of the mind and spirit. *Only education,* and only the kind of education which embraces individual discipline and concern for one's fellows, can bring to all the experience of liberty and justice.

APPENDIX I

TRUSTEES OF SPELMAN COLLEGE IN 1953

C. Everett Bacon, New York, New York

Mrs. Ethel McGhee Davis, Institute, West Virginia

Mrs. Catherine Hughes Waddell, New York, New York

Solomon W. Walker, Atlanta, Georgia

Mrs. Hattie Rutherford Watson, Pine Bluff, Arkansas

Trevor Arnett, Grand Beach, Michigan

Lawrence John MacGregor, Summit, New Jersey

Mrs. Laurance Spelman Rockefeller, New York, New York

Elbert P. Tuttle, Atlanta, Georgia

Robert Rout West, Washington, D.C.

J. Curtis Dixon, Atlanta, Georgia

Mrs. Sadye Harris Powell, Atlanta, Georgia

Ernest E. Quantrell, New York, New York

Luther Wesley Smith, New York, New York

E. Marvin Underwood, Atlanta, Georgia

Ex-Officio

Florence M. Read, *President, Spelman College*

Rufus Early Clement, *President, Atlanta University*

Albert Edward Manley, *President-elect, Spelman College*

OFFICERS

Trevor Arnett, *President*

Elbert P. Tuttle, *Vice-President*

Florence M. Read, *Secretary*

Ernest E. Quantrell, *Treasurer*

Albert L. Scott of New York served as trustee for fifteen years; and as vice-president of the Board and member of the Finance Committee from 1933 until his death in 1946. Henry L. Minton was elected to membership on the Board and the Finance Committee in November 1953.

Thirteen of the above-named trustees are included in the top picture of Plate XXVIII.

APPENDIX II

Charges for Board, Room
and Tuition

In 1881-82, the catalogue announced a charge of $1 per month in advance. When the move was made to the Barracks buildings, board was furnished at cost, which was $6 to $7 per month. Beginning in 1885, the amount for board and tuition was slated as $7 per month; instrumental music was $2 extra—and continued to be an "extra." Beginning in 1899, the charge was $8 per month in advance and from 1900, the charge was slated as $8 for four weeks; then it was $9.50 from 1905 to 1909; and $10, for six years from 1909 to 1915. The charge was little by little increased until it was $15 in 1919, and according to the catalogue was for "board and instruction."

The first year after the name was changed, by charter amendment, to Spelman College (1924), the charge for tuition was $30, and for board, $18 per month. An entrance fee of $5 also was required. By 1927-28, the annual tuition charge was $45, the next year $60, and the next eight years $75. For six years, 1937-43, tuition was $80; then $100, $130, $150, $200. From 1948 through 1953, the amount was $250. Board correspondingly was increased five times from $20 in 1927-28 to $40 per month in 1952-53. Some increases were likewise made in fees. No laboratory fees were charged, because of a desire to have students choose freely courses in science. (For 1959-60, the charge for tuition was $325 per year; for board $54 per month.)

From the Circular of the Atlanta Baptist Female Seminary, published in May, 1881. The tuition charge was one dollar per month, in advance.

COURSES OF STUDY.

NORMAL DEPARTMENT.

FIRST YEAR.

FIRST TERM.	SECOND TERM.
Reading and Spelling,	Reading and Spelling,
Primary Arithmetic,	Intellectual Arithmetic,
Geography,	Geography,
Writing.	Writing.

SECOND YEAR.

FIRST TERM.	SECOND TERM.
Reading and Definition,	Reading and Definition,
Written Arithmetic,	Practical Arithmetic,
Geography,	Geography,
Writing.	Writing.

THIRD YEAR.

FIRST TERM.	SECOND TERM.
Practical Arithmetic,	Practical Arithmetic,
English Grammar,	English Grammar,
History of the United States,	History of the United States.
Composition and Recitations.	Composition and Recitations.

ACADEMIC DEPARTMENT.

FIRST YEAR.

FIRST TERM.	SECOND TERM.
Higher English Grammar,	Higher English Grammar,
Algebra,	Algebra,
Physiology and Hygiene,	Physical Geography,
Essays.	Essays.

SECOND YEAR.

FIRST TERM.	SECOND TERM.
Latin or English Analysis,	Latin, or Political Economy.
Rhetoric,	Universal History,
Geometry,	Geometry and Trigonometry,
Essays.	Essays.

THIRD YEAR.

FIRST TERM.	SECOND TERM.
Latin, or English Literature,	Latin or Chemistry,
Natural Philosophy,	English History,
Constitution of United States.	Botany,
Essays.	Essays.

FOURTH YEAR.

FIRST TERM.	SECOND TERM.
Astronomy,	Moral Philosophy,
Mental Philosophy,	Evidences of Christianity,
Zoology,	Geology,
Essays.	Essays.

ATLANTA UNIVERSITY

Six-Year Program

1. To offer work leading to the Master's degree in departments which have suitable facilities by pooling resources of Morehouse College, Spelman College, and Atlanta University.

2. To strengthen college work with reference to teachers, standards of scholarship, courses.

3. To make new appointments to University faculty in specially selected fields, such as:

English	Biology	Economics and Business
French	Chemistry	Administration
History	German	Education

4. To develop or strengthen in the colleges the following departments or courses in addition to those mentioned in paragraph 3.

Anthropology	Fine Arts	Italian
Botany	Geology	Music
Classics	German	Spanish

5. The estimated number of teachers needed for the University faculty, in addition to professors on the faculties of Morehouse College and Spelman College, is as follows:

	1930-31	1931-32	1932-33	1933-34	1934-35	1935-36
Education	1	2	2	2	3	3
Economics & Bus. Adm.	1	2	2	3	3	4
History	1	1	2	2	2	2
English	1	1	2	2	2	2
French		1	1	1	1	1
Sciences (Biol. & Chem.)				1	2	2
Social Sciences		1	1	1	1	2
	4	8	10	12	14	16

6. On the basis of these beginnings, to project by 1935-36, the following University scheme:

1. Department of Education
2. Department of Economics and Business Administration
3. Graduate School of Arts and Sciences

380

4. School of Social Work
5. Library School
6. School of Music and Fine Arts

7. During the six-year period to plan, as opportunity arises, for the time when professional schools could be added in:

Law   Medicine   Physical Education
Dentistry   Theology

8. During this period to develop enough *unity and solidarity of both purpose and machinery* to make it feasible to invite the affiliation of other colleges.

APPENDIX V

A few among many
Ministers Heard in Vespers or Morning Chapel, 1927-1953

Charles N. Arbuckle of Cambridge, Massachusetts
Theodore F. Adams of Richmond, Virginia
William Ketcham Anderson of Nashville, Tennessee
W. J. Bell, Bishop of the Colored Methodist Episcopal Church
William H. Boddy of Chicago and Minneapolis
William Adams Brown of New York City
Harold A. Bosley of Urbana, Illinois
Allan Knight Chalmers of New York City
William J. Faulkner, Dean of Chapel, Fisk University
Charles W. Gilkey of Chicago
Georgia V. Harkness of Chicago
Richard Hurst Hill of Howard University
Vernon L. Johns of Charleston, West Virginia
Edgar DeWitt Jones of Detroit, Michigan
Henry J. Mikell, Protestant Episcopal Bishop of Atlanta
Wade Hampton McKinney of Cleveland
Daniel C. Poling, editor of *The Christian Herald*
Wyatt Aiken Smart of Emory University
Luther Wesley Smith of Philadelphia
Frederick K. Stamm of Chicago and Brooklyn

APPENDIX VI

Presidents of Universities and Deans
of Graduate Schools

University of Chicago – Robert M. Hutchins; Ernest C. Colwell
Dillard University – Albert W. Dent
Emory University – Goodrich C. White
Fisk University – Thomas Elsa Jones; Charles S. Johnson
Howard University – Mordecai Johnson
Southern University – Felton G. Clark
Tulane University Graduate School – Roger P. McCutcheon
University of Toronto – Canon Henry John Cody; Malcolm
    Wallace
University of Virginia Graduate School – Lewis Machen Hammond
Yale University – James Roland Angell

Presidents of Colleges for Women

Agnes Scott College – James Ross McCain; Wallace McPherson
    Alston
Bennett College – David D. Jones
Connecticut College – Rosemary Park
Mount Holyoke College – Mary Emma Woolley
Sarah Lawrence College – Constance Warren
Vassar College – Henry Noble MacCracken
Wellesley College – Mildred McAfee Horton
Women's College of North Carolina – Walter Clinton Jackson

APPENDIX VII

Spelman College Graduates Who Have Earned
the Degree of Doctor of Philosophy

Geraldine Lari Clark, C '43, Ph.D. in Education, 1956, University of Chicago

Juanita Collier, C '51, Ph.D. in Psychology, 1956, University of Chicago

Minnie E. Cureton,* C '30, Ph.D. in History, 1949, Stanford University

Elsie Edmondson,* C '30, Ph.D. in English, 1954, University of Michigan

Gladys Inez Forde,* C '40, Ph.D. in Dramatic Arts, 1955, Western Reserve University

Johnnie *Hines* Watts, C '41, Ph.D. in Food Chemistry, 1952, University of Chicago

Elizabeth *Lipford* Kent, C '42, Ph.D. in Public Health, 1955, University of Michigan

Mary Logan Reddick,† C '35, Ph.D. in Biology, 1944, Radcliffe College

Lynette Saine,* C '40, Ph.D. in Education, 1950, University of Chicago

Eleanor Ison, C '48, Ph.D. in Biology, 1957, University of Wisconsin

Beulah *Johnson* Farmer, C '37, Ph.D. in English, 1955, New York University

Mamie Thompson, C '49, Ph.D. in Education, 1957, Indiana University

---

Irene *Dobbs* Jackson, C '29, Docteur de L'Université (Lettres), 1959, L'Université de Toulouse

Doctor of Education

Grace L. Hewell, C '40, Ed.D. 1958 Teachers College, Columbia University

Doctor of Medicine

Helen E. Nash '42   M.D. 1945 Meharry Medical College

*Mother attended Spelman   †Aunts attended Spelman

Gwendolyn *Cooper* Mannings '44

                          M.D. 1948 Meharry Medical College

Dorothy *Forde* Bolden '39   M.D. 1948 Meharry Medical College

Lelabelle *Freeman* Robinson '44 M.D. 1949 Howard University

Blanche *Sellers* Lavizzo '46   M.D. 1950 Meharry Medical College

Clara A. Brawner '49   M.D. 1954 Meharry Medical College

Wilmotine *Jackson* Neyland '51

                          M.D. 1959 Meharry Medical College

Juel *Borders* Benson '54   M.D. 1960 Woman's Medical College
                                   of Pennsylvania

Audrey Forbes '55   M.D. 1959 Meharry Medical College

Three graduates of Spelman Seminary, Georgia Dwelle '00, Suluka Yongebloed '03, and Shelby L. Boynton '04, earned the degree of Doctor of Medicine from Meharry Medical College, the first-named in 1904, the second in 1910, and Dr. Boynton, who became a Medical Examiner for the Atlanta Public Schools, in 1905.

Important Items for the record

The following items are mentioned because of their continuing importance. A *Granddaughters Club* was organized in 1910, under the guidance of Miss Upton, to be made up each year of students whose mothers or aunts had attended Spelman. This club takes part in the Founders Day Exercises each year.

A *College Loan Fund* was established in 1927-28. The only amount previously available for this purpose was the interest on $230 set aside for loans from the Alice Coleman Fund. The record of payment on student loans made between the academic years 1927-28 and 1952-53 is excellent.

In 1930, a *Community Council,* composed of students and faculty, was organized; in 1942 the *Spelman Students Association,* to be made up of all members of the student body, came into being. The Community Council remained as a constituent branch related to the Spelman Students Association.

In 1950, a new *Address List* was published containing the names and addresses, by classes, of all Spelman graduates, an alphabetical index of the graduates, and the names and addresses of all the living non-graduates for whom addresses could be obtained. This is the third address list published. The first one was contained in the early history compiled by Mrs. A. E. Reynolds in 1920. A second one was prepared by Miss Edith Glode in 1930. The material in 1950 was prepared by Miss Clara D. Craig of the college staff and Mrs. Ernestine Erskine Brazeal, '28, alumnae secretary.

The *Spelman College Loyalty Fund.* One of the most significant actions was one taken by alumnae, with the encouragement of the administration. The class of 1929 of which Mrs. Julia Pate Borders is president, at its tenth reunion in June 1939, started an alumnae fund which they designated as the Spelman College Loyalty Fund. Members of the 10-year reunion classes each year are asked to pledge to give a sum annually, and also members of each graduating class.

The Loyalty Fund has been responsible for increased giving on the part of the alumnae.

BIBLIOGRAPHY AND SOURCES

PARTIAL LIST ONLY

Adams, James Truslow, *The Epic of America*, Boston, Little, 1931

Adams, Myron W., *History of Atlanta University, 1865-1929*, Atlanta University Press, 1930

Alvord, J. W., Letters from the South relating to the condition of the freedmen, addressed to Maj. General O. O. Howard, 1870

American Antiquarian Society, Worcester, Massachusetts: catalogues of the Oread Institute; files of *The Massachusetts Spy*; genealogies of the Packard family and the Spelman family

Ashmore, Harry Scott, *The Negro and the Schools*, Univ. of North Carolina Press, 1954

Atlanta Historical Society, vol. V and bulletins 20-23, Atlanta, Georgia

Baptist Home Mission Monthly, issues beginning in 1870

Beecher, Catherine E., *The Duty of American Women to their Country*, Harper & Brothers, 1845

Boogher, Elbert W. G., *Secondary Education in Georgia, 1732-1858*, University of Pennsylvania, 1933

Brawley, Benjamin G., History of Morehouse College, Atlanta, 1917

Brooks, Van Wyck, *The Flowering of New England*, 1815-1865, Random House, 1941

Brown, Ina Corinne, *Story of the American Negro*, New York, Friendship Press, 1936

Carter, Edward Randolph, *The Black Side*, 355 pp., Atlanta, 1894

Charlestown Female Seminary, catalogues, 1849-50, 1855

Chase, Mary Ellen, *Abby Aldrich Rockefeller*, The Macmillan Co., 1950

Cole, Arthur C., *A Hundred Years of Mount Holyoke College*, New Haven, Yale University Press, 1940

Connecticut Literary Institution, catalogues, 1860-64 and later

Dabbs, James McBride, *The Southern Heritage*, Knopf, 1958

Drury, Lucian, Manuscript Autobiography

DuBois, William E. B., *The Souls of Black Folk*, A. C. McClurg & Co., 1903

Embree, Edwin R., *Brown America*, New York, Viking Press, 1931

——, *Brown Americans*, New York, Viking Press, 1943

Flexner, Abraham, *Funds and Foundations*, Harper & Brothers, 1952

Flexner, Eleanor, *Century of Struggle*, Harvard University Press, 1959

Forten, Charlotte, Journal of, New York, Dryden Press, 1953

Fosdick, Raymond B., *A Portrait of John D. Rockefeller, Jr.*, Harper & Brothers, 1956

Franklin County (Mass.) Court House, Registry of Deeds; and Probate of Wills (will of Samuel Giles written in India ink by his own hand)

Franklin, John Hope, *From Slavery to Freedom*, Alfred A. Knopf, 1950

Garrison, William Lloyd, biography written by his children, 2 vols., The Century Co., 1885

General Education Board, annual reports, 1902-   , New York

Haygood, Atticus G. (President of Emory College), *Our Brother in Black*, Oxford, Georgia, 1881

Higher Education Among Negroes, Quarterly Review of

Johnson, Charles S., *The Negro College Graduate* (1937)

———, *The Negro in American Civilization*, Henry Holt, 1930

Lane, Samuel A. (ex-Sheriff), *Fifty Years and Over of Akron and Summit County* (section re Harvey Buel Spelman), Akron, 1892

Massachusetts Weekly Spy, issues of 1867, Worcester, Mass.

Memoirs of Georgia: Historical and Biographical, vol. 1, 1096 pp., data about Southern Historical Association 1895; especially re George Hillyer, William J. Northen, Sidney Root

Minutes and other records of the ABHMS; WABHMS; Spelman Seminary; Spelman College; and Atlanta University

Moton, Robert R., *What the Negro Thinks*

Nevins, Allan, *John D. Rockefeller*, New York, Charles Scribner's Sons, 1940

New Salem, History of, 1753-1953, by Florence Cogswell Cox, Amherst, Mass., 1953

New Salem Academy, History of, by Eugene Bullard, 1913

New Salem Academy catalogues, beginning 1840

New Salem Sesqui-Centennial, 1903, Athol, Mass., 1904

Opportunity (magazine)

Oread Institute, catalogues of, especially 1864-68

Orr, Gustavus J., State School Commissioner, annual reports of, 1874, 1875

Peabody Education Fund, volume 1, *Proceedings*

Phylon (magazine), quarterly published by Atlanta University

Records in the Akron Public Library concerning the early developments in education and the "Akron plan"

Reunion Banner, published annually by New Salem Academy since 1888

Rockefeller, John D., *Random Reminiscences of Men and Events*, Doubleday Page and Co., 1916

Rose, William Ganson, *Cleveland, The Making of a City*, The World Publishing Co., 1950

Sears, Barnas (agent of Peabody Fund) annual reports, 1872, 73, 74

Southern Education Foundation, Inc.
> Biennial Report for 1950-51 and 1951-52, J. C. Dixon, Executive Director, Office 811 Cypress Street NE, Atlanta, Georgia. Contains brief history of its Constituent Funds:
>> Peabody Education Fund est. by George Peabody in 1867;
>> John F. Slater Fund est. by John F. Slater in 1882;
>> Anna T. Jeanes Foundation created in 1907;
>> Virginia Rudolph Fund est. by Jeanes Teachers in 1938 named in honor of the first Jeanes teacher

Spelman College catalogues and other publications

Spelman Messenger, published by Spelman Seminary 1885-1924; by Spelman College, 1924-

Suffield Academy Alumni Quarterly. (Suffield Academy, successor to the Connecticut Literary Institution, is a private school for boys only)

Tidings, issues of 1881 and 1882, published by Women's Baptist Home Mission Society, headquarters Chicago

Torrence, Ridgely, *The Story of John Hope*, Macmillan, 1948

U.S. Commissioner of Education Reports

U.S. Department of the Interior: Census Office Report of Social Statistics of Cities, part II, 1887. (In 1880 population of Atlanta: 37,309—21,079 white, 16,330 colored.)

Washington, Booker T., *The Story of the Negro*

White, Charles L., *A Century of Faith*, Judson Press, 1932

Woman's American Baptist Home Mission Society, Fifth Ave., New York, Minutes and Annual Reports

Wright, Martha Burt, History of the Oread Collegiate Institute

INDEX

395